The New Institutionalism in Sociology

The New Institutionalism in Sociology

Mary C. Brinton and Victor Nee
editors

Stanford University Press
Stanford, California

Stanford University Press
Stanford, California

Originally published in a hardcover edition
by Russell Sage Foundation, 1998
©1998 Russell Sage Foundation

Printed in the United States of America
on acid-free, archival-quality paper

Library of Congress Cataloging-in-Publication Data
The new institutionalism in sociology / Mary C. Brinton
    and Victor Nee, editors.
        p. cm.
    Originally published: New York : Russell Sage
        Foundation, c1998.
    Includes bibliographical references and index.
    ISBN 0-8047-4276-6 (pbk. : alk. paper)
    1. Sociology. 2. Social institutions. 3. Financial
institutions. 4. Economics--Sociological aspects. 5. Social
norms. 6. Social change. I. Brinton, Mary C. II. Nee, Victor
HM581 .N48 2001
301--dc21
                                        2001020025

Original Printing 2001

Last figure below indicates year of this printing:
10   09   08   07   06   05   04   03   02   01

In memory of George C. Homans and of James S. Coleman

Contents

Contributors

MARY C. BRINTON is professor of sociology at Cornell University.

VICTOR NEE is Goldwin Smith Professor of Sociology at Cornell University.

ROBERT C. ELLICKSON is Walter E. Meyer Professor of Property and Urban Law at Yale Law School.

JEAN ENSMINGER is professor of anthropology at the California Institute of Technology.

ROBERT FEENSTRA is professor in the Department of Economics at the University of California, Davis.

ROBERT H. FRANK is Goldwin Smith Professor of Economics, Ethics, and Public Policy at Cornell University.

AVNER GREIF is associate professor in the Economics Department, Stanford University.

GARY G. HAMILTON is professor of sociology at the University of Washington, Seattle.

ROSEMARY L. HOPCROFT is associate professor of sociology at the University of North Carolina at Charlotte.

PAUL INGRAM is David Zalaznick Associate Professor of Business at Columbia University.

TAKEHIKO KARIYA is professor in the Graduate School of Education at the University of Tokyo.

JACK KNIGHT is professor of political science at Washington University.

ERIC KOSTELLO is a postdoctoral associate at the Yale Center for Comparative Research.

DOUGLASS C. NORTH is Spencer T. Olin Professor in Arts and Science at Washington University.

ALEJANDRO PORTES is professor of sociology at Princeton University and faculty associate of the Woodrow Wilson School of Public Affairs.

JULIA SENSENBRENNER, a freelance writer and editor, holds a Ph.D. in sociology from The Johns Hopkins University.

IVÁN SZELÉNYI is professor in the Department of Sociology at Yale University.

BRUCE WESTERN is professor of sociology at Princeton University.

Foreword

Judging from its title, this fine volume on sociological neo-institutionalism finds its far-off origins in the vast œuvre of Émile Durkheim. After all, it was that founder of sociology who, a century ago, proceeded to define the still fledgling discipline as "the science of institutions, of their genesis and of their functioning" (1958 [1895]). For him, it was also a science in which "a social fact can be explained only by another social fact." And lest the organizational as well as the cognitive context of this declaration of sociological independence in the division of intellectual labor not be fully understood, Durkheim concluded his *Rules of Sociological Method* by insisting that "Sociology is, then, not an auxiliary of any other science; it is itself a distinct and autonomous science."

There are the beginnings of a dedicated methodological holism. A powerful holism that was organizationally defensive as well as theoretically argued. The pioneering Durkheim was plainly engaged in seeking a distinctive legitimacy for his relatively new science. Its impenetrable boundaries were to be maintained at all costs, as he countered the attacks being mounted upon sociology by the established "imperialistic" psychology and also by a contending social psychology, which he was quick to dismiss as "scarcely more than a name, without a definite subject matter, and including all sorts of generalities, diverse and inexact" (1958 [1895]).

That sustained and successful counter-attack in the mode of a commitment of sociology to methodological holism had another, not apparently anticipated, consequence. In effect, it placed a taboo on what amounted to the methodological individualism long established in classical economics. The autonomous science of sociology was not to have excessive theoretical truck with that neighboring social science. As theoretical consequences of this self-induced isolation took hold, practitioners in both sociology and economics came to note the absence of needed interactions between the two disciplines. So it was that as late as the mid-1930s, the sterling economic theorist, J. R. Hicks, managed to be both exacting and eclectic when he voiced this telling charge:

> [The economist always seeks to refer the analysis of a problem] back to some "datum," that is to say, to something which is extra-economic. This something may be apparently very remote from the problem which was first taken up, for the chains of economic causation are often very long. But he always wants to hand over the problem in the end to some sociologist or other—*if there is a sociologist waiting for him. Very often, there isn't.* (italics added [1936] 135)

By mid-century, the structural theory that derived in large part from Durkheim had begun to modify his hyper-holistic stance to provide explicitly for the analysis of interaction between institutional context and individual agent along lines that could make for increasing congruence between the social disciplines. In a greatly clarifying reconstruction, Arthur Stinchcombe (1975) codified the early mode of structural analysis I know best in these terms:

> [T]he core process . . . central to social structure is *the choice between socially structured alternatives.* This differs from the choice process of economic theory, in which the alternatives are conceived to have inherent utilities. It differs from the choice process of learning theory, in which the alternatives are conceived to emit reinforcing or extinguishing stimuli. It differs from both of these in that . . . the utility or reinforcement of a particular alternative choice is thought of as socially established, as part of the institutional order. . . Because the alternatives are socially structured, the resulting choice behavior has institutional consequences. (p. 12)

It would be merely redundant to review more of those early and later modes of disciplinary analysis in a brief foreword. The editors, Mary Brinton and Victor Nee, provide an excellent cognitive map of this encompassing volume, and Nee has gone on to provide a knowing overview of both early and recent "sources of the new institutionalism in sociology." Sources that, after Émile Durkheim and Max Weber, reach back to the diverse pair of Talcott Parsons and George Homans and then to the critical and consequential work of Peter Blau, Raymond Boudon, James Coleman, Mark Granovetter, and Ronald Burt, along with many others. As in much of this volume, those developments in sociology are nicely linked to a converging new institutional economics that extends from the founding work of Ronald Coase and Herbert Simon to the more immediate and varied work of a Gary Becker, Oliver Williamson, and Douglass North, as well as many others.

Thus, the sociological neo-institutional analysis formulated and variously exemplified in this volume stands in striking contrast to Durkheim's classical institutionalism. Brinton, Nee, and their collaborators make abundantly clear how the contemporary paradigm of institutional analysis involves an "intellectual trade" that transcends the traditional boundaries of the social sciences. The benefits of such trade can be seen in the exchange and application of such domain-bridging concepts as choice within institutional and organizational contexts, bounded rationality, social embeddedness and social networks, transaction costs, human and social capital, externalities, and enforceable trust. There appears to be a significant disciplined eclecticism in the making.

By Durkheim's time, the French had fastened on the maxim, which holds that "the more things change, the more they remain the same" or, as they understandably prefer to say, "*plus ça change, plus c'est la même chose.*" But in the case of evolving neo-institutional theory in sociology and related disciplines, that worn bon mot does not quite hold. For, as this volume of engrossing papers attests, there have been truly consequential changes in that mode of theorizing, which have begun to link up congruent key ideas in the neighboring social sciences. And so, as in a toast recently emitted by a sage to his reader: bon appétit!

ROBERT K. MERTON

References

Durkheim, Émile. 1958 [1895]. *The Rules of Sociological Method.* 2d ed. New York: Free Press.

Hicks, J. R. 1936. "Economic Theory and the Social Sciences." In *The Social Sciences: Their Relation in Theory and in Teaching.* London: Le Play Press.

Stinchcombe, Arthur L. 1975. In *The Idea of Social Structure,* edited by Lewis A. Coser. New York: Harcourt Brace Jovanovich.

Introduction

Victor Nee and Mary C. Brinton

Our aim is to present a set of essays that together outline the central theoretical and substantive issues of the new institutionalism in sociology. This book grew out of a series of workshops and conferences on the new institutionalism held at Cornell University from 1991 to 1996, and the Workshop on the New Institutionalism in Sociology held at the Russell Sage Foundation in New York City in May 1995. The new institutionalism as developed herein is a product of cross-disciplinary theorizing. The book thus joins other recent publications that have sought to assemble contributions that span disciplinary boundaries to theorize on issues of economic and social organization; for example, *The Handbook of Economic Sociology*, edited by Neil Smelser and Richard Swedberg, *The New Institutionalism in Organizational Analysis*, edited by Walter Powell and Paul DiMaggio, and *The Limits of Rationality*, edited by Karen Cook and Margaret Levi.

The very idea of a new institutionalism in sociology needs to be clarified, especially in light of the already well-established institutional theory in organizational analysis. This is the purpose of chapter 1, "Sources of the New Institutionalism," which provides a short conceptual introduction to the new institutionalist perspective in sociology, and discusses the new institutionalism as a choice-within-constraints framework of analysis that integrates economic and sociological approaches. Such a framework was pioneered by Max Weber and other classical sociological theorists and was anticipated by central figures such as Talcott Parsons, Robert Merton, and George Homans in American sociology in the post–World War II period. The new institutionalist paradigm thus represents a revival—and revitalization—of interest in classical issues in macrosociology dealing with the emergence and maintenance of institutions, and change within them. Far from constituting a new version of the march of economic imperialism into sociological terrain, the new emphasis on institutional analysis in the social sciences holds the potential for reinforcing the contribution of sociology to social science theorizing and research. New institutionalist sociology revisits the idea of context-bound rationality developed in the classical period of sociology and focuses on the social structural context within which individual interests and group norms develop as well as on the reciprocal role of norms and interests in effecting institutional change.

The analysis of classical macrosociological themes requires the recognition, argued eloquently in recent years by Mark Granovetter in his seminal 1985 piece in the *American Journal of Sociology*, that economic action is embedded in interpersonal relations and subject to informal norms. But increased recognition of the role of formal norms is also essential for, we argue, the formal rules and institutions to which economists and political scientists have paid particular attention have not been sufficiently incorporated into the sociological analysis of economic action. We believe that sociology has a strong comparative advantage in providing subtle analyses of the constraints of the interlocking roles of the informal *and* the formal in structuring action.

The chapters in part I of this book examine the production and maintenance of norms, the interplay between formal and informal systems of constraints, and the effect of belief systems on economic action and institutional change. The chapters explore the ways in which institutions as systems of rules constrain or encourage innovative individual action, using empirical cases to examine the resulting group-level outcomes (for example, the development or retardation of a system of interpersonal exchange that can facilitate economic growth). Nee and Ingram's "Embeddedness and Beyond" (chapter 2) directs attention to the interface between institutions and network ties and argues that the theoretical link between the two is properly located in social exchange theory. A series of propositions predicts how social interaction produces informal norms and monitors compliance to them. What then, are the processes leading to the coupling or decoupling of informal norms and formal rules in organizations? Although new institutional economists have increasingly become interested in understanding social norms, they have lacked a theory specifying the mechanisms integrating informal norms and formal organizational rules. Nee and Ingram argue that these mechanisms are by-products of ongoing social relationships. They outline a multilevel conceptual framework that integrates the social network literature in sociology with institutions, and proffer propositions explaining variation in organizational performance.

Ellickson's "Of Coase and Cattle" (chapter 3) is a case study of property disputes and their resolution in Shasta County, California. In this classic piece, combining theoretical sophistication and detailed fieldwork, Ellickson illustrates the conditions under which individuals forgo recourse to formal litigation in favor of informal workaday norms. His findings shed light on the real and nonnegligible transaction costs entailed in becoming educated about the law, engaging in formal negotiations, and litigating disagreements—transaction costs that are too often ignored by law-and-economics scholars.

A synthesis of theory and attention to empirical detail also characterizes chapter 4, "Cultural Beliefs and the Organization of Society," where Greif examines the relationship between cultural beliefs and institutional structures. In a comparative-historical analysis of Genoese and Maghribi traders in the Mediterranean world during the late medieval period, he shows that a common problem faced by both sets of traders was the issue of trust in the merchant-agent relationship. Using game theory and historical materials, Greif analyzes how cultural beliefs influenced the evolution of institutions to regulate long-distance overseas trade. The consequences of whether such institutions developed had long-term implications for the two sets of traders. Greif argues that there are parallels between the individualist and collectivist responses he describes in a particular historical context and the problem of trust in the contemporary world, stimulating readers to think further about the conditions that create the possibility for exchange relations among strangers, a condition necessary for economic development.

The effect of cultural beliefs on the selection of institutions is also explored by

Knight and Ensminger in chapter 5, "Conflict over Changing Social Norms." They employ rational choice–theoretic assumptions to explain emergence and change in social norms. Their theory emphasizes the importance of how resource asymmetries structure the bargaining process between sets of actors. They argue that when norms have a distributional consequence, the selection of norms enforced by the community depends on the interests and preferences of the actors who have a bargaining advantage. In this fashion, Knight and Ensminger go beyond a self-interest view of norm selection to incorporate the ways in which cultural beliefs complicate the enforcement of norms by influencing the preferences of both powerful and subordinate groups.

In chapter 6, "Embeddedness and Immigration," Portes and Sensenbrenner examine the historical roots of the concept "social capital" in classical sociological works that emphasized the mechanisms through which social structures affect economic action, citing Max Weber, Emile Durkheim, Georg Simmel, and Karl Marx. They specify four sources or types of social capital and then turn to the literature on immigrant communities to demonstrate how these sources can be used to understand economic action in such communities. Of particular importance is their illustration that certain types of social capital, such as community solidarity, can have *negative* effects on such economic outcomes as entrepreneurship. In this respect, this chapter parallels Greif's examination of how community belief systems can forestall the development of economic institutions.

The chapters in part II develop the idea of institutional embeddedness in capitalist economies. The idea of institutional embeddedness as a macroscopic approach is theorized by Hamilton and Feenstra in chapter 7, "The Organization of Economies." They argue that the Walrasian conception of the economy as interconnected markets, in general equilibrium theory, provides an alternative to "bottom-up" theories that derive economic institutions from the aggregation of individual actions. It is through such a Walrasian conception that Hamilton and Feenstra envision sociologists and economists engaging in the most productive interchange, rather than at the level of micro-level interaction analyzed through rational choice and game-theoretic approaches. They incorporate Weberian ideas on the organization of production and the ownership of assets into the Walrasian general equilibrium framework and argue that a Weberian perspective provides an invaluable way of addressing how it is that economic organizations can have independent effects on the development of a complex capitalist economy. That is, attention to the historical and *noneconomic* as well as the economic foundations of organizations is a critical sociological component in the explanation of why the structural features of capitalist economies such as the United States, Taiwan, Germany, South Korea, Italy, and Japan vary as widely as they do.

Chapter 8, "Institutional Embeddedness in Japanese Labor Markets," by Brinton and Kariya also shifts the analytic focus away from the microscopic setting of interpersonal ties to examine the embeddedness of labor market behavior in cultural and institutional contexts. Their macroscopic approach to job matching in labor markets examines the mechanisms through which students move from school to work in Japan. Using data for several cohorts of Japanese men in the twentieth century, they document a decline in reliance on atomistic and social network mechanisms of job search and a rise in what they term institutional embeddedness—ties between schools and firms. Their subsequent examination of the history of recruitment practices in Japan explains how the shift to school-employer cooperation occurred and the types of criticism this new form faced, through charges of particularism. Theoretically, Brinton and Kariya argue that sociological research should give more attention to the endogeneity of social and institutional embeddedness in cultural and historical contexts.

In chapter 9, "Winner-Take-All Markets and Wage Discrimination," Frank develops a welcome alternative to the standard economic theory of labor market discrimination by shifting attention away from the human capital stock of individuals and toward changes in the structure of highly paid jobs in advanced capitalist economies. His analysis of "tournaments" in which job-seekers compete for highly leveraged jobs in internal labor markets clarifies how wage inequality between ascriptive groups (for example, men and women) has become institutionally embedded in "winner-take-all" labor markets. Frank is able to explain the mechanisms through which wage differentials based on employer discrimination can persist even in competitive labor market conditions, a puzzle that has for some time troubled sociological researchers in the areas of gender and ethnic stratification.

In chapter 10, "Institutions and the Labor Market," Western argues that institutions have too often been relegated to the sidelines in research on the structure of wages in advanced capitalist economies. He draws particular attention to the way that conflict between owners and workers has historically patterned the institutions through which wage setting takes place. Drawing on cases from Western Europe and North America, Western demonstrates the wide variability in the extent to which wage determination is institutionally centralized or decentralized, and draws out the implications for worker outcomes. Like others in this volume, Western makes a strong case for research that is contextual and comparative.

The chapters in part III of the book turn to the analysis of institutional change and organizational dynamism within institutional environments. In his acceptance speech for the 1994 Nobel Prize in economics (chapter 11, "Economic Performance Through Time") North outlines a theory of institutional change drawing on advances in cognitive science. He argues that classifications embedded in the cultural heritage of a society structure the mental models of actors in organizations. This institutional/cognitive analysis leads North inexorably away from neoclassical assumptions to embrace instead a Lamarckian theory of institutional change emphasizing the interactions between organizations and institutions. His emphasis on cultural beliefs in the form of religion, myths, and dogma leads to a convergence with institutional theory in organizational analysis (see chapter 1).

Ingram (chapter 12, "Changing the Rules") takes up North's ideas on the interaction between organizations and the institutional environment but argues from the organizational ecology literature that organizations face strong inertial forces. New organizational forms—rather than intraorganizational change through learning—are, he argues, the more common source of institutional change. His case study of the hospitality industry in the United States illustrates how a new organizational form in this industry at the beginning of the twentieth century led to a shift in the institutional locus of hotelier training and education from trade schools to universities. While learning was the engine driving institutional change, it was new rather than existing organizations that implemented this learning.

New institutionalists in economics and political science have often emphasized state-centered theories in their explanation of economic development. In chapter 13, "The Importance of the Local," Hopcroft questions this state-centered approach by focusing on the importance of local institutions and arguing that a primary emphasis on the role of the state as a source of institutional innovations promoting economic growth overlooks the role of regional variation in the institutional environment. Her analysis of rural institutions in preindustrial England shows that regional variation in the institutions governing property rights corresponded to important differences in economic performance. Regions with well-established communal property rights had higher transaction costs with respect to land usage, crop selection, animal husbandry, feudal dues, and taxes. In these areas, labor services and other manorial dues were imposed on farmers, and free riding lowered the productivity of communal land managed by village councils. By contrast, the East Anglia region of England benefited from a system of well-defined property rights that encouraged technical innovation and agricultural productivity.

Szelényi and Kostello (chapter 14, "Outline of an Institutionalist Theory of Inequality") examine the importance of institutional change for the distribution of rewards in an economy. They outline a neo-Polanyian conceptual framework that specifies discrete stages in the transitions from state socialism to the development of market institutions, applying this to Eastern Europe. In contrast to Polanyi, they look not to markets as the inevitable source of inequality but rather to what they term the dominant mechanism of integration in an economy, the mechanism regulating how factors of production are allocated. Such a dominant mechanism is the basis of class power and, they argue, will be contested by other classes through compensatory mechanisms. Like the authors in part II, Szelényi and Kostello move beyond the micro-level focus of the social embeddedness approach. They argue for the importance of collective actors, especially classes, as agents of choice driving institutional change.

Running throughout this book is an emphasis on the emergence, persistence, and change of and in institutions, and on the interaction between institutions, informal norms, and economic action. We hope that readers will agree that this collection of essays demonstrates the richness of the theoretical work and empirical research currently underway in the new institutionalist sociology, which is moving beyond a thin account of rationality toward a renewed interest in the idea of context-bound rationality pioneered by classical sociologists. We invite readers to engage these essays in an ongoing discourse on why institutions matter in the analysis of social and economic life, and why institutional origins, maintenance, and change are central to social scientific theorizing and research.

1

Sources of the New Institutionalism

Victor Nee

T he new institutionalism in sociology is part of an emerging paradigm in the social sciences. Interest in the new institutional paradigm is being driven by advances in interdisciplinary research directed at understanding and explaining institutions. In economics, this has involved rejection of the neoclassical assumption of efficiency in transactions that purportedly are costless and based on complete information. In political science, intellectual trade with economics has given rise to the field of positive political economy, which is extending the paradigm to the analysis of political institutions and the politics of markets. There this paradigm has established itself as the most influential, but political science has had a long history of being the "beneficiary as well as the victim of many intellectual currents from other disciplines" (Ordeshook 1990, 9). Although sociology has been less responsive than political science, this is quickly changing. Just as central themes in classical sociology have influenced the new institutionalists in economics (North 1981), this branch of economics has led sociologists to examine economic phenomena anew. The new institutional economics has contributed to stimulating research on social institutions and economic action (Granovetter 1985; Hamilton and Biggart 1988; Friedman and Hechter 1988; Weakliem 1989; Campbell and Lindberg 1990; Cook and Levi 1990; England and Kilbourne 1990; Fligstein 1996; DiMaggio and Powell 1991; Friedland and Alford 1991; Lindenberg 1992; Brinton 1992; Ensminger 1992; Petersen 1993; Hopcroft 1994; Nee and Lian 1994; Smelser and Swedberg 1994; Zelizer 1994; Evans 1995; Adams 1996; Sanders and Nee 1996; Nee and Su 1996). What, then, is the new institutionalism in sociology?[1]

Since its founding, sociology as a discipline has been closely associated with the study of social institutions and the comparative analysis of institutional change. Sociologists have all along argued that institutions have consequences for social and economic action. Unlike the earlier sociological institutionalism pioneered by Talcott Parsons (1937), however, the new institutionalism seeks to explain institutions rather than simply to assume their existence.[2] In this endeavor, new institutionalists in the social sciences generally presume purposive action on the part of individuals, albeit under conditions of incomplete information, inaccurate mental models, and costly transactions. Such conditions are common to everyday social and economic transactions.[3] Although the new institutionalist paradigm rejects the basic assumptions of neoclassical economics, it remains committed to the choice-theoretic tradition of explanation in the social sciences.

The new institutionalist paradigm involves integrating the assumption of purposive action with comparative institutional analysis central to the sociological tradition. Although rational action has long been associated with economics and psychology, the idea of context-bound rationality was also tacitly incorporated into macrosociological theory early in the development of the discipline, through the writings of Max Weber, Alexis de Tocqueville, Karl Marx, and Vilfredo Pareto. It was also assumed by an entire generation of theorists—including Talcott Parsons, George Homans, and Robert Merton—who led American sociology to prominence in the post–World War II era. Far from being threatened by the paradigm shift taking place in economics, sociology has much to gain from the new interest in producing a theory of institutions and institutional change. Sociology also has much to lose by not participating in this cross-disciplinary paradigm.

INSTITUTIONALISM IN ECONOMIC AND POLITICAL THOUGHT

Neoclassical economics argued that social relationships and institutions do not fundamentally matter—that is, do not alter fundamentally the choice-set of actors—since it assumes perfect information and stable preferences, and therefore efficiency. These basic assumptions of the neoclassical paradigm were challenged by Ronald Coase (1960) in his celebrated article "The Problem of Social Cost," which laid the theoretical foundations for bringing institutions back into economics. Coase's discovery that transaction costs matter provided the key insight that spawned a new interest in understanding and explaining institutions. He showed that only in the absence of positive transaction costs does the efficiency assumption in neoclassical economics hold true. Fundamentally, transaction costs pertain to the problem of trust. Informational asymmetry and uncertainty make credible commitment to agreements difficult to secure. In a world in which information is costly, different institutional environments imply differences in the credibility of commitment and hence the cost of transacting (Williamson 1975). Because transaction costs make up a significant part of the cost of production and exchange in modern economies, alternative institutional arrangements can make the difference between economic growth, stagnation, or decline (North 1981).

The new institutionalism in economics and political science has emphasized formal norms and their monitoring by third-party enforcers, the state and the firm. Coase's essay "The Nature of the Firm" (1937) laid the foundation for the law, economics, and organizations approach in economics (Williamson 1975; North 1981). Combined with his essay "The Problem of Social Cost," it identified the focal points for research in the new institutionalist economics. The resulting research agenda has been cross-disciplinary in scope, incorporating a focus on the state and the firm as the key institutions. Ruler and entrepreneur in their respective domains specify and enforce the formal organizational constraints that shape the structure of opportunities.

Coase (1937) argued that the firm represents an alternative governance structure to the market by providing an environment in which the price mechanism is replaced by the power and authority of the entrepreneur. The existence of the firm, Coase reasoned, implies that there are costs to market transactions. It depends on the entrepreneur's ability to economize on costs stemming from uncertainties associated with markets. These uncertainties pertain to the costs of measuring the performance of agents and of enforcing commitment to contractual agreements. Although the same agency problems are found within the firm, entrepreneurs are in a position to use their power and authority to direct employees. In Coase's firm, the employment contract is essentially the same as Hobbes's view of the relationship between citizen and state. By entering into a contract, Coase argues, the employee in exchange for remuneration agrees to comply with the orders of the entrepreneur, within certain limits. The essence of the contract, in Coase's view, is that it states only the limits of the entrepreneur's power. Within these limits, entrepreneurs can direct their employees as they do other factors of production.

The Coasian framework of transaction cost economics was extended by Douglass North to build a theory of the state based on an exchange view of the relationship between ruler and constituent, with the state exchanging protection and justice for revenue. Because the essence of property rights is the right to exclude, the state, which has a comparative advantage in violence, plays a key role in specifying and enforcing property rights. The ruler as a revenue maximizer acts "like a discriminating monopolist, separating each group of constituents and devising property rights for each so as to maximize state revenue." He is constrained, however, by the existence of potential rivals who provide the same services. North (1981) argues that institutional innovations will come from rulers because the free-rider problem limits the ability of constituents to initiate society-wide institutional change. For North, the central task in explaining economic growth is to specify the events and conditions that provide incentives for political actors to establish formal institutional arrangements supporting efficient property rights. These entail the dilution of state control over resources and the emergence of some form of political pluralism. This does not imply a weak state, but a state and society context in which the tension between ruler and constituent allows for the evolution of institutions that limit the capacity of the state to expropriate resources from producers (North and Weingast 1989).

While the new institutionalism in economics has developed theories explaining formal constraints, the subinstitutional social basis of formal institutions has been undertheorized. This is the domain of ongoing social relationships, the social matrix that comprises the basis of informal constraints. The micro-macro linkage is a central issue in the developing new institutionalist paradigm (Alexander et al. 1987). Sociology's role can profitably be to go beyond the insights from game theory to explain the connection between the subinstitutional domain of social action and concrete relationships, and the meso- and macroinstitutional domains of custom, conventions, law, organizations, ideology, and the state. This connection involves social norms that bridge the microworld of individual actors and networks, and the larger institutional framework (see Nee and Ingram in this volume).

DEALING WITH DURKHEIM'S LEGACY

The rediscovery of institutions by economists has elicited mixed responses from sociologists. This is not surprising, for sociology since the time of Auguste Comte has defined itself as an imperial discipline. This self-image was reinforced in the writings of Emile Durkheim, who sought to establish sociology in opposition to psychology and economics. Durkheim proposed a distinct sociological approach, laying the foundations for what today is identified as methodological holism. Although few sociologists now identify themselves as followers of Durkheim, his intellectual legacy persists through the continuing influence of his methodological contribution. In contrast to methodological individualism, which assumes that the social order is a product of the aggregation of individual actions, methodological holism assumes that the social order cannot be reduced to the behavior of individual actors. Its mode of analysis starts with the specification of the "social facts" or structures that, it is posited, constitute the building blocks of the social order.[4] From the vantage point of strict methodological holism, the relationship between individuals and society can be metaphorically compared to that between leaves and the tree. Leaves come and go according to the seasons, but it is the tree's branches and trunk that over the years shape their pattern and distribution. In this view, individual action is likened to the fluttering of leaves in a breeze.

Despite the enduring legacy of Durkheim's methodological influence, his perspective is not synonymous with the sociological approach, as some insist. Many sociologists underestimate the important representation of methodological individualism in macroscopic studies in sociology. From Tocqueville's analysis of the French Revolution and Weber's seminal study of Protestant sects in the rise of capitalism in the West to contemporary studies of development, social movements, and social mobility, the idea of rational action bounded by institutions—cultural beliefs, myths, custom, norms—has been effectively utilized in explaining macrosociological phenomena. As Raymond Boudon (1987, 64) remarks:

> On the whole, if the various theoretical reflections of Weber, Pareto, and others on the theory of social action were systematized and combined with the implicit theory of action incorporated in the many studies using the individualistic paradigm, the main idea that would emerge from such an inventory might be the notion of *context-bound rationality*. In the individualistic sociological tradition individual action is considered rational, but this rationality can take various forms as a function of the context. The actions of the social actors are always in principle *understandable*, provided we are sufficiently informed about their situation.

The reciprocal interactions between purposive action and social structure were addressed at least implicitly in the earlier American sociological institutionalism. Robert Merton ([1949] 1968) maintained that social structure operates both as a constraint on behavior and as a structure of opportunity that facilitates or inhibits social action. Although Merton did not specify the mechanisms through which social structure mediated choice, he nonetheless assumed that choice between socially structured opportunities was central (Stinchcombe 1975). Similarly, in a previously unpublished essay written in 1934, Talcott Parsons (1990) contended that a theory of institutions must incorporate the rational action of individuals. Parsons recognized the importance of positive and negative sanctions, but he subordinated these social mechanisms to what he perceived to be a more fundamental cement of society: its ultimate values. Although neither Merton nor Parsons developed a theory of institutions, they recognized that this was of central importance to sociology as a discipline. Likewise, they saw that a theory of institutions needed to incorporate agency, conceived as the outcome of choices by individual actors.

George Homans (1950) thought of the causal relationship between individual action and social structure as one of mutual dependence. In his view, the problem with Durkheim's "social mold" theory was that it left out individual agency. Socially isolated individuals may be more at risk of committing suicide, but the act of suicide is an individual decision. Not everybody in similar social circumstances commits suicide. Mutual dependence is the underlying assumption of the rapidly growing literature integrating network analysis with social exchange theory (Cook et al. 1983); it is also the insight motivating the concept of structuration (Giddens 1984; Sewell 1992). As Douglas Heckathorn (1997) proposes, rather than argue over the relative merits of methodological individualism or holism, a more constructive approach is to model the reciprocal interactions between purposive action and social structure. Heckathorn demonstrates formally that game theoretic models can be specified both at the individual and group levels, decisively blurring the distinction between methodological individualism and holism.

Although the idea of context-bound rationality has appeared at least tacitly in sociology since the founding of the discipline, models of rationality and rational choice have meanwhile progressed considerably in economics, especially through advances in game theory. Game theory is a standard tool used to analyze multi-person decision problems (Gibbons 1992). In game theory, actors are engaged in strategic interactions with others, as exemplified in the well-known prisoner's dilemma game. This game and variations of it have been employed to dissect the choice-set of actors caught in common social dilemmas (Hardin 1982). Game theory provides deep insights on the dynamics of choices within constraints but does not provide a theory of the constraints, which is where sociology fits in. What sociology has to offer is an integrated framework of the totality of societal relations. The literature of sociology is a rich storehouse of theoretical and empirical findings that pertain to the constraint side of the choice-within-constraint framework of analysis emphasized by Durkheim.

CLASSICAL SOURCES OF THE NEW INSTITUTIONALIST PARADIGM

The tradition of comparative institutional analysis established in the classical and modern periods of sociology provides an appropriate foundation for the new institutionalist approach in sociology. Of the classical theorists, Max Weber's ([1922] 1968) *Economy and Society* perhaps best exemplifies the sociological approach to comparative institutional analysis. This work grew out of *The Outline of Social Economics* series Weber edited, which brought together contributions by prominent social scientists of the time on topics from institutional economics and sociology (Roth 1968). Although Weber was a sociologist, his institutional theory drew liberally from economics. As Randall Collins (1980, 928) observes, Weber's conception of the market was virtually indistinguishable from that of neoclassical economists:

He sees the market as providing the maximal amount of calculability for the individual entrepreneur. Goods, labor, and capital flow continuously to the areas of maximal return; at the same time, competition in all markets reduces costs to their minimum. Thus, prices serve to summarize all the necessary information about the optimal allocation of resources for maximizing profit; on this basis, entrepreneurs can most reliably make calculations for long-term production of large amounts of goods.

In *Economy and Society*, Weber developed concepts, definitions, and typologies that he employed in a comparative historical analysis of law, organizations, and economic action. In effect, he pioneered the context-bound rationality approach in sociology. He maintained that rationality and choice must be understood within the context of the institutional framework of a given society and historical epoch. For Weber, the institutional framework encompassed customs, conventions, social norms, religious and cultural beliefs, households, kinship, ethnic boundaries, organizations, community, class, status groups, markets, law, and the state. His ideal-type and comparative methodology specified historically grounded concepts that identified institutional forms with distinct structures of power and opportunity. As demonstrated by Hamilton and Feenstra (in this volume), Weber offers a rich storehouse of theoretical contributions that can be fruitfully used in the new institutionalist research program.

Like Weber, Karl Marx also borrowed extensively from economists, particularly from Adam Smith and David Ricardo, so much so that the economist Paul Samuelson dismissed Marx as a "minor post-Ricardian" (Elster 1985). This, combined with the sloppiness of Marx's scholarship in *Capital*, led North (1986) to pose the question, "Is it worth making sense of Marx?" In his answer, North credited Marx with foreshadowing the concept of transaction cost in exploring the tension in the relationship between production and the forces of production.[5] What set Marx apart from neoclassical economics, in North's assessment (1981, 61), was an integrated perception of the totality of societal relations:

> The Marxian framework is the most powerful of the existing statements of secular change precisely because it includes all of the elements left out of the neoclassical framework: institutions, property rights, the state, and ideology. Marx's emphasis on the crucial role of property rights in efficient economic organization and on the tension that develops between an existing body of property rights and the productive potential of a new technology is a fundamental contribution. It is technological change that produces the tension in the Marxian system; but it is through class conflict that change is realized.

Marx's influence on the new institutionalist paradigm is manifest not only in economic history but in analyses that focus on societal governance structures in which the state plays a decisive role in establishing the pattern of property rights (Bates 1989; Campbell and Lindberg 1990; Evans 1995).

Karl Polanyi ([1944] 1957) was closely associated with the "substantivist school," which sought to develop an alternative economic analysis to the formalism of the neoclassical paradigm. Polanyi's writings took on a distinct antimarket bias, as reflected in his characterization of the unregulated market as a satanic mill ravaging the social and cultural fabric of society. His ideal-types of non-market and market institutional forms greatly overstated the distinction between social and economic goals. In the same vein, Polanyi overstated the extent to which embeddedness applied to archaic markets and understated the extent of embeddedness in modern markets (Granovetter 1985). Despite these limitations, Polanyi's enduring contributions to the new institutionalist approach are his insight that the state plays a decisive role in the construction of the "unregulated market" and his concept of embeddedness; these in essence are consistent with the idea of context-bound rationality.

Parallels with Parsons's Institutionalism

Parsons sought to synthesize the institutionalist ideas associated with Emile Durkheim, Max Weber, Vilfredo Pareto, and Ferdinand Tönnies into a framework for modern sociology. The recent publication of "Prolegomena to a Theory of Social Institutions," written in 1934, shows that he regarded the construction of a theory of institutions as the central project for sociology. His outline there of a theory of institutions foreshadowed central themes in the new institutionalist paradigm. The idea of choice within institutional constraints is clearly specified in his observation that "the very concept of rational choice, pushed beyond the 'technological' application of means for a single end, to the case where there is also a choice of ends involved, has no meaning unless it is thought of in terms of an organized *system* of ends" (323, italics in original). He conceived of the institutional framework as an organized system of cultural beliefs—norms—common to most individuals composing a society. He argued that it is rules and values that constitute an institution, not the concrete pattern of behavior or social relationships. He maintained that rational action in "conformity with these norms, does not follow automatically from the mere acceptance of the ends as desirable" (325). And he viewed institutions as giving rise to socially structured interests, and hence to an organized system of incentives. It is useful to quote Parsons at length for his conception of how institutions structure interests:

> It is not to be supposed that the fact that it is to the personal advantage of the members of a community to conform to its institutional norms is proof that these norms depend primarily or exclusively on interest and sanctions for their effective enforcement. For the very strength of the moral attachment of the community to these norms will on the one hand tend to canalize interests in conformity with them. Thus the principal personal rewards, above all in social esteem, will tend to go to those who do conform with them. On the other hand, the same strength of moral attachment will tend to visit disapproval and sometimes overt punishment on those who violate them.
>
> But this very fact, of fundamental importance, means that, once really established, a system of institutional norms creates an interlocking of interests, both positive and negative, in its maintenance, and to a certain point its supports in the form of moral attachment may dissolve away and still leave it standing supported by the complex of interests, ultimately of sanc-

tions since once positive interests are diverted from conformity only sanctions can take their place.

North (1981, 185) acknowledges Parsons's "pioneering effort to come to grips with many of the issues" central to the new institutionalist paradigm. According to North, the problem with Parsons's institutionalism was that he failed to solve the free-rider problem and to produce a coherent theory of institutions. Coleman (1990b) makes essentially the same criticism in his commentary on Parsons's "Prolegomena" paper.[6] Coleman asserts (p. 327) that the failure of Parsons's "pioneering effort" to produce a theory of institutions has served to clarify what a theory of institutions must explain. A theory of institutions must specify the causal mechanisms through which norms and rules are produced and maintained.[7] It must explain the relationship between informal and formal regulatory norms. And it must explain institutional change. Related to this, a theory of institutions should address the question of how differences in cultural beliefs give rise to different institutional structures. These issues motivating research in the new institutionalist paradigm are taken up, in this volume, by Nee and Ingram; North; Ellickson; Greif; Knight and Ensminger; Brinton and Kariya; Ingram; and Hopcroft.

INSTITUTIONS AS A FORM OF CAPITAL

At the theoretical center of the new institutionalist paradigm is the concept of choice within constraints. Institutions, defined as webs of interrelated rules and norms that govern social relationships, comprise the formal and informal social constraints that shape the choice-set of actors. Conceived as such, institutions reduce uncertainty in human relations. They specify the limits of legitimate action in the way that the rules of a game specify the structure within which players are free to pursue their strategic moves using pieces that have specific roles and status positions. Norms are implicit or explicit rules of expected behavior that embody the interests and preferences of members of a close-knit group or a community. The institution of modern marriage, for example, encompasses social norms governing sexual conduct (monogamy), child-rearing (shared responsibility), property rights (equal), conflict, dissolution, and, upon divorce, the custody of children. The informal norms are monitored by family members, relatives, friends, and acquaintances, while the legal rules are formally monitored by the state. Insofar as norms help solve the problem of coordination and collective action, they enable actors to capture the gains from cooperation, which, in the case of marriage, entails sharing and thus lessening the costs of bearing and rearing children.

The idea of norms as a form of capital was first alluded to by Homans ([1961] 1974, 361) as "a moral code, especially a code supporting trust and confidence between men: a well-founded belief that they will not always let you down in favor of their private, short-term gain." Conformity to norms of a social group is what renders the norm a form of capital. Because norms are collectively maintained, and benefits gained by conforming are shared by members of the group, norms amount to a collective good (Coleman 1990a). An emphasis on norms as cultural beliefs that constrain opportunism distinguishes the new institutionalist approach from the instrumental view of network ties, which sees actors using their social ties to achieve private gain beyond that which could be obtained through their stock of human capital (Lin 1982). As in the network definition of social capital, individuals derive benefits from the norms, but such benefits are realized at the cost of short-term private gain by opportunists. In other words, norms become social capital to the extent they are able to solve social dilemmas that would otherwise result in suboptimal collective outcomes caused by individuals pursuing private advantage at the cost of collective goods. The idea of norms as social capital was given a stronger theoretical basis in Robert Ellickson's "welfare maximizing" hypothesis (1991, 167) for workaday norms: *"Members of a close-knit group develop and maintain norms whose content serves to maximize the aggregate welfare that members obtain in their workaday affairs with one another"* (italics in original). Consistent with Ellickson's hypothesis is the theory of social norms that builds on the proposition that *individuals jointly produce and uphold norms to capture the gains from cooperation* (Nee and Ingram in this volume).

The conception of norms as social capital has the advantage of making it possible to derive consistent predictions of their effects on individuals and group performance (Homans [1961] 1974; Ellickson 1991; Nee and Ingram in this volume). This allows social capital to be put on an analytical footing similar to that of other forms of capital. Human capital theory predicts a positive effect of education and work experience on an individual's income returns (Schultz 1961). Similarly, the workaday norm of a close-knit group can be expected to enhance the welfare of members who conform to the norm, by solving the problem of coordination and collective action. To be sure, zealots can induce a state of overconformity, resulting in negative effects on members of the group (Coleman 1990a). Overconformity is seen, for example, in religious cults, where it can produce such collective tragedies as the Jonestown and Heaven's Gate mass suicides. Such extreme examples of overconformity are uncommon, however. Generally, conformity to norms of a group produces a form of cooperation needed to achieve collective goods that otherwise could not be realized by individuals on their own in pursuit of private advantage. As noted, by constraining short-term private gains, norms facilitate cooperation that in turn enables actors to realize long-term benefits. It is in this sense that norms (and other cultural beliefs) constitute forms of capital. In sum, the social processes that give rise to conformity are causal mechanisms that enable cooperation to be sustained, and these in turn convert the norm into fungible capital realized by means of group performance.

The social mechanisms *through which* social norms are produced and maintained, not the norms themselves, give rise to social order. Informal norms are monitored by means of sanctions as common as social approval and disapproval, the by-products of social interactions in close-knit groups (Homans [1961] 1974). Universal preference for approval and aversion to ostracism contribute to maintaining the norms of a group. Formal rules are produced and maintained by such organizations as the state and the firm. When formal organizational rules are in conflict with interests and preferences embedded in social norms, customs, and conventions, they are costlier to monitor. On the other hand, when formal and informal norms are congruent, the monitoring of formal organizational rules is assumed to a larger extent by individual members of small groups and close-knit communities. This latter condition results in lower costs of monitoring and enforcement.

CONTEXT-BOUND RATIONALITY

The new institutionalist paradigm rests firmly within the choice-theoretic tradition. This raises the question of the place of rational choice theory in the new institutionalist sociology. Basic assumptions of rational choice theory become less and less tenable the more institutions are taken into account in causal models (see North, in this volume). In contrast to "thin" accounts of rational choice (Becker 1976; Coleman 1990a), the idea of context-bound rationality assumes a "thick" view of rationality. But this thick conception does not imply abandoning the assumption of rational action. As Herbert Simon (1957, xxiv) put it, humans are "intendedly rational, but only limitedly so." Although in this conception actors are seen to *meliorize* rather than maximize, the action of individuals is assumed to be purposive in the sense that self-interest and incentives matter. In thick accounts of rationality, understanding purposive action necessitates interpreting the choices made by actors according to benefits and costs embedded in the institutional environment.[8] The cultural heritage of a society is also important because custom, myths, and ideology matter in understanding the mental models of actors. For example, Jews and Arabs in Jerusalem employ sacred and profane symbols in defending collective identities and ethnic boundaries. It is thus impossible to understand the pattern of ethnic conflict in Jerusalem without examining the cultural beliefs and symbolic expressions of Arabs and Jews (Friedland and Hecht 1996).

As North remarks in his Nobel Prize acceptance speech (in this volume) pointing to the significance of recent breakthroughs in cognitive psychology for economics:

> It is necessary to dismantle the rationality assumption underlying economic theory in order to approach constructively the nature of human learning. History demonstrates that ideas, ideologies, myths, dogmas, and prejudices matter; and an understanding of the way they evolve is necessary for further progress in developing a framework to understand societal change. The rational choice framework assumes that individuals know what is in their self-interest and act accordingly. That may be correct for individuals making choices in the highly developed markets of modern economies, but it is patently false in making choices under conditions of uncertainty—the conditions that have characterized the political and economic choices that shaped (and continue to shape) historical change.

Context-bound rationality is not inconsistent with other formulations of rational action that have moved beyond the limits of rational choice theory. For example, the concept of emergent rationality extends evolutionary game theory to posit a backward-looking notion of rationality in which rules embody past experience of successful or rewarding adaptation (Macy 1997). Rather than calculating the future consequences of alternative sets of action, actors rely on rules of thumb and established routines. Both concepts assume limited cognitive ability on the part of actors. However, emergent rationality emphasizes adaptation based on unintended consequences of action not intentionally rational. Hence, actors may appear smarter than they are in following rules that have evolved through trial-and-error adaptation to the environment.

Central arguments in organizational new institutionalism are not inconsistent with context-bound rationality if actors are viewed as organizations. According to this interpretation, organizations conform to institutionalized myths to enhance their legitimacy and stability, and this promotes success and survival (Meyer and Rowan 1977). Because myths are external to the organization and do not emerge from the technical requirements of coordination and control, they often are at odds with the efficient execution of the organization's practical tasks. Consequently, although organizations behave rationally in conforming to the rules and expectations of the institutional environment, in doing so they construct an institutional environment that constrains their ability to change further (DiMaggio and Powell 1983).[9] The result is conformity but often without gains in efficiency in the aggregate. However, Meyer and Rowan (1977) predict that when myths and ceremonial functions are inconsistent with efficiency, organizations will decouple formal rules from their practical activities and comply with institutionalized myths ritualistically. Thus interpreted, the legitimacy/conformity story is clearly consistent with the mutual dependence of action and structure that is central to the idea of context-bound rationality.

A deepening interest in the implications of "thick" rationality for a theory of action provides an opening for intellectual trade between institutional theorists in organizational analysis and other new institutionalists. For new institutionalist sociology, the gain from trade with economics is an action theory that solves the problem of intentionality and interest posed by DiMaggio and Powell (1991). As Neil Fligstein (1996b, 397) remarks, organizational new institutionalism "has a limited theory of action because it generally focuses on how meanings become taken for granted." For economics, the gain is access to the theoretical and empirical findings specifying causal mechanisms at the organizational and environmental levels.

CONCLUSION

Methodological holism in sociology has been an obstacle to acceptance of the choice-theoretic approach underlying the new institutionalist paradigm. A consequence of this impasse has been sociology's growing isolation from allied social science disciplines at a time when rapid progress is being made in understanding and explaining the microfoundations of the social order. This need not be the case, because much of classical and modern sociology has sought to integrate utilitarian and structural accounts into a macrosociological theoretical framework. Indeed, a form of methodological individualism represents the mainstream of modern empirical sociology. It is this heritage that the new institutionalism in sociology seeks to build on. Periods of ascendancy in sociology have often followed open trade and engagement with economics. Rather than attempting to show how sociology relegates economics to the intellectual dustbin, the new institutionalism in sociology pursues a tack that is more consistent with the classical period of sociology. In this respect, the new institutionalist approach may be viewed as a neoclassical turn in sociology. The new institutionalism in sociology extends the intellectual legacies of classical sociologists and earlier sociological institutionalists who similarly engaged in productive intellectual trade with economics.

Sociology as a discipline has specialized in the study of humanly devised constraints. Although sociology does not have a theory of choice, it has pioneered a rich array of theoretical and empirical research on formal and informal constraints, their effects on individuals and organizations. From social exchange theory and network analysis to studies of organizational ecology and institutional environments, there is in sociology a growing accumulation of theory and evidence that pertain to the constraint side of the choice-within-constraint framework of analysis.

Until recently, however, sociologists have assumed but not explained the existence of constraints. Yet, as choice theorists have argued, the key to understanding and explaining large-scale collective action, the emergence of institutional structures, and the dynamics of institutional change—all issues of central interest to sociologists—resides in solving the free-rider problem (Olson 1965; North 1981; Hardin 1982). Recognition of the difficulty of doing this from within the explanatory framework of methodological holism has led sociologists to consider choice-theoretic arguments (Homans [1961] 1974; Coleman 1990b). But such pioneering efforts have stopped short of incorporating institutions into a coherent theoretical approach. Reformulating classical themes in sociology within a choice-theoretic framework—of context-bound rationality—opens the way to solving the free-rider problem while retaining the focus on institutional structures central to sociology.

I gratefully acknowledge the support of the College of Arts and Sciences at Cornell University and a fellowship from the National Science Foundation #SBR-9022192 during my year as a Fellow of the Center for Advanced Study in the Behavioral Sciences at Stanford. And I thank Mary Brinton, Rachel Davis, Brett de Bary, Neil Fligstein, Michael Macy, John Meyer, Neil Smelser, and Frank Young for their stimulating comments in the early stages of my thinking about this essay.

NOTES

1. Institutional theory is the most influential paradigm in sociological studies of organizations (Scott 1981; DiMaggio and Powell 1991). Sociologists often refer to this literature as the new institutionalism in sociology. This chapter is not about institutional theory in organizational analysis, although I do point out areas of convergence.

2. This is not as true of institutional theory in organizational analysis. Meyer and Rowan (1977), for example, assume the existence of myths. Organizational institutionalists are interested in studying the effect of isomorphic processes on organizations.

3. For example (to consider only one source of informational asymmetry), individuals calculate strategically to impose a definition of a situation that is in accord with their interests, and their behavior is frequently misunderstood by others, as Erving Goffman (1965, 6) observes:

Sometimes the individual will act in a thoroughly calculating manner, expressing himself in a given way solely in order to give the kind of impression to others that is likely to evoke from them a specific response he is concerned to obtain. Sometimes the individual will be calculating in his activity but be relatively unaware that this is the case. Sometimes he will intentionally and consciously express himself in a particular way, but chiefly because the tradition of his group or social status require this kind of expression and not because of any particular response (other than vague acceptance or approval) that is likely to be evoked from those impressed by the expression. Sometimes the traditions of an individual's role will lead him to give a well-designed impression of a particular kind and yet he may be neither consciously nor unconsciously disposed to create such an impression. The others in their turn, may be suitably impressed by the individual's efforts to convey something, or may misunderstand the situation and come to conclusions that are warranted neither by the individual's intent nor by the facts.

Goffman's microanalysis of social action indicates that actors engage routinely in strategic interactions modeled by game theorists. I am indebted to Neil Fligstein for this observation.

4. Institutional theory in organizational analysis is methodologically holist and rooted in Durkheim and the more phenomenological side of Weber through the influence of Alfred Schutz and Peter Berger and Thomas Luckmann. According to Meyer and Rowan (1977), in modern societies institutionalized rules "function as powerful myths." Such myths, defined as "classifications built into society as reciprocated typifications or interpretations," exercise an important causal effect on the formal structure of organizations and on their ability to survive. Myths become, in effect, the building blocks of formal organizational structures because "organizations must incorporate them to avoid illegitimacy." As extant myths are extended or new myths arise, defining "new domains of rationalized activity," existing organizations expand their formal structures accordingly and/or new organizations emerge.

5. The problem with Marx, according to North, is that he did not have a theory of the rate of technological change and that his overall theory put too much weight on the efficacy of class as the primary unit of action. Class assumes a community of interest when, in reality, conflicting interests exist within classes. Moreover, Marx's idea of class overlooked the free-rider problem. In other words, collective action in large groups is difficult to mobilize in the absence of selective incentives (Olson 1965). Because public goods are by definition nonexcludable, individuals have an incentive to "free ride" on the contributions of others.

6. According to Coleman, what led Parsons astray was the functionalist fallacy: "A serious fault in the theoretical structure that Parsons established in 'Prolegomena' is his failure to show how, and to define the conditions under which, the interest in or 'need for' an institutional norm actually results in the establishment of an institution" (336). Coleman also faulted Parsons for a reductio ad absurdum in claiming that action can be treated as social insofar as actors share common values.

7. Coleman emphasizes the need to explain the actual emergence of norms and institutions. This emphasis is misplaced, however, because the emergence of norms occurs mainly as an ad hoc process characterized by trial and error (Shibutani 1978). I am indebted to Russell Hardin on this point.

8. Purposive action is implicit in accounts of institutions viewed as constraints and opportunities (see Hamilton and Feenstra; Frank; Hopcroft; Western; and Szelényi and Kostello in this volume).

9. DiMaggio and Powell examine isomorphic institutional processes in order to account for the "startling homogeneity of organizational forms and practices." They explain this homogeneity as the outcome of three isomorphic mechanisms—coercive, mimetic, and normative—in the institutional environment. Organizations conform to political rules enforced by the state, mimic successful organizations in response to uncertainty, and comply with rules of professionalism fostered by schools and associations.

REFERENCES

Adams, Julia. 1996. "Principals and Agents, Colonialists and Company Men: The Decay of Colonial Control in the Dutch East Indies." *American Sociological Review* 61: 12–28.
Alexander, Jeffrey C., Bernhard Giesen, Richard Münch, and Neil J. Smelser, eds. 1987. *The Micro-Macro Link.* Berkeley, Calif.: University of California Press.
Bates, Robert H. 1989. *Beyond the Miracle of the Market: The Political Economy of Agrarian Development in Rural Kenya.* Cambridge, England: Cambridge University Press.
Becker, Gary. 1976. *The Economic Approach to Human Behavior.* Chicago, Ill.: University of Chicago Press.
Boudon, Raymond. 1987. "The Individualistic Tradition in Sociology." In *The Micro-Macro Link*, edited by Jeffrey Alexander, Bernard Giesen, Richard Münch, and Neil Smelser. Berkeley, Calif.: University of California Press.
Brinton, Mary. 1992. *Women and the Economic Miracle: Gender and Work in Postwar Japan.* Berkeley, Calif.: University of California Press.
Campbell, John L. and Leon N. Lindberg. 1990. "Property Rights and the Organization of Economic Activity by the State." *American Sociological Review* 55: 634–47.
Coase, Ronald. 1937. "The Nature of the Firm." *Economica* 4: 386–405.
———. 1960. "The Problem of Social Cost." *Journal of Law and Economics* 3: 1–44.
Coleman, James S. 1990a. *Foundations of Social Theory.* Cambridge, Mass.: Harvard University Press.
———. 1990b. "Commentary: Social Institutions and Social Theory." *American Sociological Review* 55: 333–39.
Collins, Randall. 1980. "Weber's Last Theory of Capitalism: A Systematization." *American Sociological Review* 45: 925–42.
Cook, Karen S., Richard M. Emerson, Mary R. Gillmore, and Toshio Yamagishi. 1983. "The Distribution of Power in Exchange Networks: Theory and Experimental Results." *American Journal of Sociology* 89: 275–305.
Cook, Karen Schweers, and Margaret Levi. 1990. *The Limits of Rationality.* Chicago, Ill.: University of Chicago Press.
DiMaggio, Paul J., and Walter W. Powell. 1983. "The Iron Cage Revisited: Institutional Isomorphism and Collective Rationality in Organizational Fields." *American Sociological Review* 48: 147–60.
———. "Introduction." 1991. In *The New Institutionalism in Organizational Analysis*, edited by Walter W. Powell and Paul J. DiMaggio. Chicago, Ill.: University of Chicago Press.
Ellickson, Robert. 1991. *Order Without Law.* Cambridge, Mass.: Harvard University Press.
Elster, Jon. 1985. *Making Sense of Marx.* Cambridge, England: Cambridge University Press.
England, Paula, and Barbara Stanek Kilbourne. 1990. "Markets, Marriages, and Other Mates: The Problem of Power." In *Beyond the Marketplace*, edited by Roger Friedland and A. F. Robertson. New York: Aldine de Gruyter.
Ensminger, Jean. 1992. *Making a Market: The Institutional Transformation of an African Society.* Cambridge, England: Cambridge University Press.
Evans, Peter. 1995. *Embedded Autonomy: States & Industrial Transformation.* Princeton, N.J.: Princeton University Press.
Fligstein, Neil. 1996a. "A Political-Cultural Approach to Market Institutions." *American Sociological Review* 656–73.
———. 1996b. "Social Skill and Institutional Theory." *American Behavioral Scientist* 40: 397–405.
Friedland, Roger, and Robert Alford. 1991. "Bringing Society Back In: Symbols, Practices, and Institutional Contradictions." In *The New Institutionalism in Organizational Analysis*, edited by Walter Powell and Paul DiMaggio. Chicago, Ill.: University of Chicago Press.
Friedland, Roger, and Richard Hecht. 1996. *To Rule Jerusalem.* Cambridge, England: Cambridge University Press.
Friedman, Debra, and Michael Hechter. 1988. "The Contribution of Rational Choice Theory to Macrosociological Research." *Sociological Theory* 6: 201–18.
Gibbons, Robert. 1992. *Game Theory for Applied Economics.* Princeton, N.J.: Princeton University Press.

Giddens, Anthony. 1984. *The Constitution of Society: Outline of the Theory of Structuration.* Cambridge, England: Polity Press.

Goffman, Erving. 1965. *The Presentation of Self in Everyday Life.* New York: Doubleday.

Granovetter, Mark. 1985. "Economic Action and Social Structure: The Problem of Embeddedness." *American Journal of Sociology* 91: 481–510.

Hamilton, Gary G., and Nicole Woolsey Biggart. 1988. "Market, Culture and Authority: A Comparative Analysis of Management and Organization in the Far East." *American Journal of Sociology* 94: 52–94.

Hardin, Russell. 1982. *Collective Action.* Baltimore, Md.: Johns Hopkins University Press.

Heckathorn, Douglas D. 1997. "The Emergence of Norms, Strategic Moves, and the Limits of Methodological Individualism." Paper presented at the Workshop on the Emergence of Norms, Russell Sage Foundation, New York (March 14, 1997).

Homans, George C. 1950. *The Human Group.* New York: Harcourt, Brace & World.

———. [1961] 1974. *Social Behavior: Its Elementary Form.* New York: Harcourt Brace Jovanovich.

Hopcroft, Rosemary. 1994. "The Social Origins of Agrarian Change in Late Medieval England." *American Journal of Sociology* 99: 1559–95.

Lin, Nan. 1982. "Social Resources and Instrumental Action." In *Social Structure and Network Analysis*, edited by Peter Marsden and Nan Lin. Beverly Hills, Calif.: Sage Publications.

Lindenberg, Siegwart. 1992. "An Extended Theory of Institutions and Contractual Discipline." *Journal of Institutional and Theoretical Economics* 148: 123–54.

Macy, Michael. 1997. "Identity, Interest, and Emergent Rationality: An Evolutionary Synthesis." *Rationality and Society* 4: 427–48.

Merton, Robert K. [1949] 1968. *Social Theory and Social Structure.* New York: Free Press.

Meyer, John W., and Brian Rowan. 1977. "Institutionalized Organizations: Formal Structure as Myth and Ceremony. *American Journal of Sociology* 83: 340–63.

Nee, Victor, and Peng Lian. 1994. "Sleeping with the Enemy: A Dynamic Model of Declining Political Commitment in State Socialism." *Theory and Society* 23: 253–96.

Nee, Victor, and Sijin Su. 1996. "Institutions, Social Ties, and Commitment in China's Corporatist Transformation." In *Reforming Asian Socialism: The Growth of Market Institutions*, edited by John McMillan and Barry Naughton. Ann Arbor, Mich.: University of Michigan Press.

North, Douglass C. 1981. *Structure and Change in Economic History.* New York: Norton.

———. 1986. "Is It Worth Making Sense of Marx?" *Inquiry* 29: 57–64.

North, Douglass C., and Bary W. Weingast. 1989. "The Evolution of Institutions Governing Public Choice in 17th Century England." *Journal of Economic History* 49: 803–32.

Olson, Mancur. 1965. *The Logic of Collective Action.* Cambridge, Mass.: Harvard University Press.

Ordeshook, Peter C. 1990. "The Emerging Discipline of Political Economy." In *Perspectives on Positive Political Economy*, edited by James Alt and Kenneth Shepsle. Cambridge, England: Cambridge University Press.

Parsons, Talcott. 1937. *The Structure of Social Action.* New York: McGraw-Hill.

———. 1990. "Prolegomena to a Theory of Social Institutions." *American Sociological Review* 55: 318–33.

Petersen, Trond. 1993. "Recent Developments in the Economics of Organization: The Principal-Agent Relationship." *Acta Sociologica* 36: 277–93.

Polanyi, Karl. [1944] 1957. *The Great Transformation: The Political and Economic Origins of Our Time.* Boston, Mass.: Beacon Press.

Roth, Guenther. 1968. "Introduction." In *Economy and Society*, by Max Weber, edited by Guenther Roth and Claus Wittich. New York: Bedminster Press.

Sanders, Jimy M., and Victor Nee. 1996. "Immigrant Self-Employment: Family-based Social Capital and Human Capital." *American Sociological Review* 61: 231–49.

Schultz, Theodore. 1961. "Investment in Human Capital." *American Economic Review* 51: 1–17.

Scott, Richard. 1981. *Organizations: Rational, Natural, and Open Systems.* Englewood Cliffs, N.J.: Prentice Hall.

Sewell, William H. Jr. 1992. "A Theory of Structure: Duality, Agency, and Transformation." *American Journal of Sociology* 98: 1–29.

Shibutani, Tamotsu. 1978. *The Derelicts of Company K: Study of Demoralization.* Berkeley, Calif.: University of California Press.

Simon, Herbert. 1957. *Administrative Behavior.* 2d ed. New York: Macmillan.

Smelser Neil, and Richard Swedberg. 1994. *The Handbook of Economic Sociology*. New York: Russell Sage Foundation.

Stinchcombe, Arthur L. 1975. "Merton's Theory of Social Structure." In *The Idea of Social Structure: Papers in Honor of Robert K. Merton*, edited by Lewis A. Coser. New York: Harcourt Brace & Jovanovich.

Weakliem, David. 1989. "The Employment Contract: A Test of Transaction Cost Theory." *Sociological Forum* 4: 203–326.

Weber, Max. [1922] 1968. *Economy and Society*. 3 vols. Edited by Guenther Roth and Claus Wittich. New York: Bedminster Press.

Williamson, Oliver E. 1975. *Markets and Hierarchies: Analysis and Antitrust Implications*. New York: Free Press.

Zelizer, Viviana A. 1994. *The Social Meaning of Money*. New York: Basic Books.

Part I

Institutions and Social Norms

2

Embeddedness and Beyond: Institutions, Exchange, and Social Structure

Victor Nee and Paul Ingram

S pecifying the mechanisms through which institutions shape the parameters of choice is important to an adequate sociological understanding of economic action.[1] These social mechanisms, we argue, involve processes that are built into ongoing social relationships—the domain of network analysis in sociology. Yet, how institutions and networks combine to determine economic and organizational performance is inadequately theorized in the sociological study of economic life. The ways in which institutions provide a framework for economic action and the role of network ties in structuring a wide array of economic phenomena are themes pursued by two rapidly growing—but separate—literatures in the social sciences. This essay aims to develop a theory of social norms that explains the relationship between institutions and networks.

We argue that the key to understanding that relationship is revealed at the level of face-to-face social interaction. An institution is a *web of interrelated norms*—formal and informal—governing social relationships. It is by structuring social interactions that institutions produce group performance, in such primary groups as families and work units as well as in social units as large as organizations and even entire economies. Networks of social relations are always in flux insofar as individuals respond to perceptions of costs and benefits in exchanges, and invest in or divest themselves of particular social ties. The production and monitoring of norms, standards of expected behavior that enjoy a high degree of consensus within a group or community, are rooted in such elementary forms of social behavior. Sociological research has focused mainly on norms that comprise informal constraints. Informal norms are rules of a group or community that may or may not be explicitly stated and that rely on informal mechanisms of monitoring, such as social approval and disapproval. Norms governing interpersonal relationships both constrain and facilitate behavior by defining the structure of incentives—material and nonmaterial—for individuals situated in a group. The same processes that account for conformity to informal norms apply to formal norms as well, for rarely, if ever, do formal norms, abstracted from social relationships, exercise a direct effect on individuals (Shibutani 1986). The main difference is that formal norms are explicit rules that rely, in addition, on formal mechanisms—the state and organizations—for their monitoring and enforcement, and the incentives backing compliance are often material, though never entirely so.

In the early stage of cross-disciplinary exchange, sociologists criticized the new institutional economics for overlooking the central role of social relationships in shaping economic action. We concur with Granovetter's assertion (1985) that economic behavior is almost always modified to some extent by personal connections. However, without incorporating institutional effects, this network-embeddedness perspective is limited in its explanatory power, even while its insight into the underpinnings of economic action remains of fundamental importance. Incorporating institutions into the new economic sociology requires going beyond network embeddedness. A firmer basis for intellectual trade between economics and sociology results from understanding how institutions and network ties are linked. Specifying the social mechanisms through which institutions affect behavior provides the missing link, integrating a choice-within-institutional-constraints approach with the network-embeddedness perspective.

THE CONVERGENT REASONING IN ECONOMICS AND SOCIOLOGY

Ronald Coase's seminal essays, "The Nature of the Firm" (1937) and "The Problem of Social Costs" (1960) introduced the core concepts of the new institutional economics. In these essays, Coase laid out the concept of transaction costs as costs stemming from dealing with social relationships in economic exchange and developed an innovative theory of the firm as an institutional domain in which market exchange is suppressed by a hierarchical authority as a means of economizing on these transaction costs. Rather than aligning themselves with the earlier American institutionalists such as Thorstein Veblen, John Commons, and Wesley Mitchell, new institutionalists in economics have instead positioned themselves as direct heirs of Adam Smith by incorporating the behavioral assumptions of microeconomics into a choice-within-institutional-constraints framework of empirical analysis. As Coase (1984, 230) succinctly put it, "What distinguishes the modern institutional economists is not that they speak about institutions . . . but that they use standard economic theory to analyze the working of these institutions and to discover the part they play in the operations of the economy."

From the start, new institutional economics emphasized analysis of the role of formal norms—contracts, property rights, laws, regulations, and the state—in structuring the framework of choice (Demsetz 1967; Cheung 1974; Alchian and Demsetz 1973; Williamson 1975, 1985; Matthews 1986; North 1981, 1990; Hodgson 1988; Eggertson 1990). Sociologists are most familiar with the writings of Oliver Williamson as a result of Granovetter's critical response (1985) to his transaction cost economics, in which he had extended Coase's theory, asserting that asset specificity and transaction cost economizing explain the boundaries of firms. Granovetter pointed out that this market and hierarchy framework overlooked the importance of social relationships in constraining opportunism and solving the problem of trust. Williamson's response (1994) to Granovetter's criticism was to incorporate network-embeddedness into Davis and North's concept (1971, 85) of the institutional environment: "Transaction cost economics and embeddedness reasoning are evidently complementary in many respects."

A convergence between new institutional economics and sociology is clearly evident in North's claim (1981, 1990) that institutions determine the structure of incentives and thereby the performance of economies. Institutions are important in economic life because they reduce uncertainty in human interactions and help solve the problem of coordination, especially in modern economies when specialization and the division of labor give rise to the need for sustaining complex exchanges over time and across space. Given the imperative in modern economies for increased reliance on impersonal exchange, institutions provide a basis for credible commitment, without which complex economic transactions become mired in high transaction costs. All societies rely on personalized exchanges to conduct economic transactions, but as specialization and the division of labor develop, so does the advantage of reliable institutions and third-party enforcement of contracts. Whether institutions foster credible commitment to long-term contracts determines to a large extent the economic performance of nations.

The "publish or perish" norm in research universities illustrates the way institutions reduce uncertainty and structure incentives. This norm dates back to the emergence of the American research university and was reinforced by new federal and state funding for research in the post–World War II expansion era. It leaves little uncertainty about what activities are most likely to be rewarded. In the absence of such a norm, assistant professors might not know how to balance the competing demands of teaching, research, committee work, and collegiality in the time leading up to the all-important tenure review. Consequently, it limits the choices of assistant professors striving to increase their chances of getting tenure, especially if senior colleagues at the university maintain a credible commitment to upholding the norm. A history of denying tenure to assistant professors with less than exemplary publication records can be expected to have a stiffening effect.

New institutionalists acknowledge that informal constraints stemming from personal relationships are critical to enforcing the rules of the game. In his analysis of disputes over trespassing cattle in rural California, Ellickson (1991) documents the importance of informal norms in the enforcement of property rights. Although Ellickson employs the reasoning of the new institutional economics, his substantive analysis of trespass-dispute resolution draws him closer to the law-and-society literature in sociology (Macaulay 1963). He argues that because transaction costs are high when formal institutional means are used to resolve trespass disputes—that is, the costs of legal research and litigation—the residents of Shasta County more commonly resort to informal norms of cooperation among neighbors and a live-and-let-live philosophy. They settle disputes over property rights informally, "beyond the shadow of the law." Ellickson's crucial insight is that people keep informal accounts of credits and debits along a number of fronts in multiplex relationships, and so long as the overall account is in balance, they overlook problems arising in any one area. Only when accounts get out of balance do tensions mount. Elinor Ostrom (1990) documents the role of informal constraints in the monitoring of rules that enable communities to successfully avoid the "tragedy of the commons" problem in managing communal resources. Such governance structures rely on long-standing social relationships within the community rather than on external authority to solve the collective action problem threatening the depletion of communal resources.

Although new institutionalists point to the importance of informal norms, North admits that economics does "not possess a good explanation for social norms." He maintains that game theory can at least predict the informal constraints that lead to cooperative behavior. However, the problem of multiple equilibria poses a difficult hurdle for game theorists in their attempt to develop a theory of norms. Axelrod (1986) employed computer simulation to demonstrate a variety of "norm games" but could not come up with an explanation from game theory for the emergence and persistence of norms. Although the application of game theory can lead to important insights, it is unlikely, as Ullmann-Margalit (1977, 14) points out, that the theory of games alone can "deliver the goods." The recognition that economics lacks a theory of social norms provides an opportunity for sociologists to specify the missing link in the theoretical synthesis integrating sociology and economics.

THE LIMITS OF NETWORK EMBEDDEDNESS

Economic sociologists have sought to demonstrate the centrality of social networks—from the cross-cutting ties that connect firms to the weak ties that join mutual acquaintances—in providing a framework for a wide variety of economic and organizational behavior (see Powell and Smith-Doerr 1994). Inspired by early breakthroughs in network studies of economic behavior by structural sociologists (White 1970; Granovetter 1974; Burt 1982; Baker 1984), and by Granovetter's seminal essay (1985) establishing the new economic sociology, they have documented the importance of networks of personal relationships in structuring diverse economic exchanges. In his 1985 essay, Granovetter directly challenged economists to provide realistic models of economic life. Whereas in an earlier assault on the neoclassical model, Polanyi (1944, 1957) had posited that economic exchanges are embedded in a matrix of institutions, Granovetter largely bypassed institutions—perhaps to distance himself from Williamson's new institutionalism—to establish the new sociology of economic life firmly on network ties, the bedrock concept of modern structural sociology. This decision led him to build economic sociology on the centrality of personal relationships, in contrast to the broader institutional focus of the Polanyi embeddedness framework that emphasized customs, laws, regulations, and the economic role of the state.

While Granovetter criticized the neoclassical model for building a house of cards on the fragile assumption of rationality, ironically, personal relationships as a basis present similar problems. Even the casual observer of social life can testify that personal relationships can be fragile as well as robust, and that they are often unpredictable, as reflected in the saying, "With a friend like you who needs an enemy?" When structural sociologists reify ongoing social exchanges, they assume a "harder" image of the fabric of social life than may be warranted. The imagery of network ties as a "hard" structural arrangement, for example, can lead an analyst to overlook their "softer," more elusive, and contradictory qualities.

The focus on personal relationships introduced an element of indeterminacy into economic sociology as an explanatory program of research. This indeterminacy stems from the difficulty of knowing *ex ante* whether, and to what extent, personal ties can cement trust between economic actors. As Granovetter (1985) concedes—indeed, even emphasizes—only those you trust are in a position to embezzle from you. It is well known that the risk of malfeasance and opportunism increases as the stakes involved in an exchange become larger. In the absence of a reliable third-party enforcer, there is often no firm basis for deciding whether an acquaintance or friend is trustworthy. That is why the new institutionalists among economists argue that formal institutional arrangements and their enforcement are necessary to back informal constraints in modern economies where the payoff from malfeasance and opportunism is high (North 1990; Greif, Milgrom, and Weingast 1994). The axiom "never lend money to a friend" stems from experiences on the flip side of the personal-relations-as-the-source-of-trust coin. Just as personal ties give rise to trust, so also do they foster wariness and distrust, often within the same set of relationships over time. This is evident, for example, in the recent case of the mole in the Central Intelligence Agency, in a context of long-standing intergenerational personal relationships characterized by "high network density," the condition that Granovetter argues promotes trust. The "clubby" atmosphere of the agency fostered trust to the extent that it resulted in a relaxation of counterintelligence procedures, the institutional arrangements established to guard against internal espionage. Trust based on long-standing personal relationships led to a devastating blow to the agency's counterespionage operations in the former Soviet Union. Thus, long-standing personal relationships can provide a basis for both secure transactions and malfeasance. The empirical studies Granovetter (1993) cites to illustrate embeddedness primarily discuss activities in "tribal and peasant societies." Yet the pervasive reliance on personal ties in such societies is uncontroversial to institutional economists who point to this phenomenon as one of the causes of underdevelopment (North 1990). But what about modern economies characterized by a complex division of labor and increasing specialization in which credible commitment to long-term contracts is essential? An economic sociology that in effect limits itself to the structure of personal relationships as its only explanatory variable cannot explain the role in such an economy of the formal constraints of the state, of laws, regulations, contracts, and property rights, and of organizations that buttress economic exchanges, in addition to informal constraints like social norms.

Comparing Genoese and Maghribi Jewish traders in the late medieval Latin world, Greif (in this volume) points to the development of impersonal formal institutions as a critical organizational innovation in the rise of the capitalist firm and suggests that reliance on personal ties to establish trust resulted in the segmentation of economic life within an ethnic group. Genoese traders constructed organizations capable of third-party enforcement, for addressing problems of agency relations. These integrated institutional structures employing nonkin agents proved to be a more effective institutional arrangement for trade than the ethnically bounded trading relationships of the Maghribi Jews, who relied on informal arrangements to resolve disputes and ensure compliance in agency relations between traders. Greif points out that the Maghribi Jewish traders eventually disappeared from the Mediterranean world, whereas Genoese traders flourished in late medieval Europe because they constructed enduring formal organizations.

The reliability of institutions provides an alternative basis of trust or credible commitment that is overlooked in the network embeddedness perspective. Investors purchase equity shares in companies or mutual funds not because they have personal ties with management but because a firm has a credible record of profitability and honest accounting. Similarly, the best high school seniors across the nation apply to top-ranked elite universities not primarily because they are children of alumni but because they are drawn by these universities' reputations (Frank and Cook 1995). Because college admissions offices in the United States maintain a credible commitment to meritocratic admissions, a high school senior is more apt to cram for the Scholastic Aptitude Test than channel time and resources into cultivating personal ties with admission officers. The opposite was true in Maoist China when institutions broke down in the wake of the Cultural Revolution and impersonal procedures were cast aside, and people in all walks of life were forced to resort to extensive reliance on personal connections. Under such conditions, it was impossible for the Chinese to maintain a semblance of meritocracy in their system of higher education.

Granovetter tried to build an institutional foundation for his network embeddedness approach by invoking the social constructionist institutional theory pioneered by Berger and Luckmann (1966). Yet, as he concedes, the phenomenological approach of *The Social Construction of Reality* offers a difficult framework for American empirical sociology insofar as it is oriented to interpretation rather than causal theory. Nevertheless, his understanding of the link between social networks and institutions is on the mark. Institutions, he argues, *"result from actions taken by socially situated individuals*, embedded in networks of personal relationship with non-economic as well as economic aims" [italics added] (forthcoming). Here Granovetter shifts the unit of analysis from the network structure to the behavior of *individuals* interacting in a group setting, the domain of social exchange theory. This is a useful reminder that networks of personal relationships are nothing but ongoing social interactions. Such networks entail dynamic social processes, rather than a static structure.

THE MISSING LINK

The theoretical groundwork for explaining the relationship between social networks and institutions was laid by social exchange theory (Homans 1958, [1961] 1974; Emerson 1962; Blau 1964). Through his case studies, Homans (1950) documented how individuals establish, monitor, and enforce norms as members of a social group.[2] He illuminated the manner in which informal norms shape the incentives of individuals in primary groups and specified how such constraints determine the behavior of individuals and give rise to group performance. The significance of Homans's ([1961] 1974, 76) theoretical contribution lay in locating the emergence of informal norms and their monitoring and enforcement by reference to mechanisms built into ongoing social relationships:[3]

> The great bulk of controls over social behavior are not external but built into the relationship themselves, in the sense that either party is worse off if he changes his behavior toward the other. This is what Malinowski (1959: 122–23) had in mind when he wrote down one of the most perspicacious statements ever made about society: "Law and order arise out of the very processes which they govern."

It is in this respect that social exchange theory differs from Hechter's theory of group solidarity (1987), which sees compliance as the outcome of more or less formal monitoring and enforcement mechanisms. In contrast to this Hobbesian approach to explaining social order, Homans views social order as a by-product of repeated social interactions and hence as an intrinsic feature of ongoing social relationships. Even in brief exchanges, elementary social processes are evident. This view of social order is the crucial insight that Ellickson's analysis (1991) of "order without law" builds on.

The most elementary exchange involves a dyadic relationship, say between Peter, a new employee, and Mary. Peter approaches Mary to ask for technical assistance on the job, which Mary provides at a cost of her time, which might have been spent on her own work. Peter reciprocates by conferring on Mary a higher grade of social approval. Both parties are rewarded by the exchange of assistance for approval and continue interacting. Their exchange builds up mutual expectations, an understanding that initially is unspoken. Even though Peter is dependent on Mary's help, he does not want Mary to tell their superior the extent to which he relies on her assistance. Mary may expect Peter to reciprocate with a greater willingness to support her in strengthening her position in the firm. *Such an implicit contract, an informal norm, may be sooner or later expressed verbally in statements of expected behavior.* Violation of the norm leads to such forms of punishment as anger or refusal to continue the interaction. By the principle of least interest, the one who is less dependent on the exchange has more power in the relationship and hence plays a greater part in defining its terms. In this case, Peter is more dependent on Mary's willingness to help than Mary is on Peter's approval. As illustrated by this example, informal norms arise in the course of social interactions as standards of expected behavior and are maintained when reward is expected to follow conformity and punishment, deviance. Members of a group reward conformity to norms by conferring social approval. Conversely, members punish failure to conform to norms through their social disapproval and, ultimately, through ostracism. In more complex exchanges, the same processes hold, but the pressure to conform also takes on a collective action dimension (Homans [1961] 1974; Hardin 1982).

Game theory illustrates the opportunity for norms to improve collective outcomes. Ullmann-Margalit (1977) identified two types of norms that emerge in response to problems of collective action and coordination: 1) Norms that arise in situations in which actors confront a prisoner's dilemma problem. The prisoner's dilemma norm alters the payoff matrix to reinforce cooperation and increase the cost of defection. 2) Norms that enable individuals to coordinate their activities. In situations where the interests of actors coincide, some coordination norms—conventions—are stable solutions to past recurrent coordination problems. Others—decrees—are stated at the outset as norms to solve novel but recurrent coordination problems. The emergence of coordination norms is simple to explain because it is easy to show that self-interested individuals who share a common interest can readily agree to rules to facilitate joint production. For example, tennis partners can quickly agree on a time and place to meet for their weekly game. The prisoner's dilemma norm, however, is more challenging to explain.

In the prisoner's dilemma game, two prisoners have the choice of keeping silent or confessing to their crime. Neither prisoner knows what the other will do—cooperate by refusing to confess or defect—because they are unable to talk with one another. Each is told that confession will result in a lighter sentence, while the refusal to confess to the crime will be penalized by a harsh sentence. If neither prisoner confesses, however, insufficient evidence will dictate that they are convicted only of a lesser crime. If both defect, then both receive the lighter sentence, yet both are worse off than if they had both cooperated by remaining silent. This is seen in the payoff matrix in figure 2.1 by comparing the payoffs in the lower right quadrant (both defect) with the upper left quadrant (both cooperate). The utility of the prisoner's dilemma game is that it presents a stylized account of a recurrent problem in which suboptimal outcomes result from the conjoint actions of self-interested individuals (Olson 1965; Axelrod 1984). The prisoner's dilemma game is widely applicable. As Hardin (1988) asserts, all social exchanges resemble it because of the temptation not to reciprocate a good or service received from another. Ullmann-Margalit (1977) argues that such social dilemmas are prone to generate norms that reward cooperation and punish opportunism or free riding.

The characteristic feature of prisoner's dilemma norms is that they involve higher transaction costs—monitoring—than coordination norms because it is always in the self-interest of individuals to free ride or defect. The definition of the prisoner's dilemma game is $T > R > P > S$. T is the temptation to defect; R is the reward for mutual cooperation; P is punishment for mutual defection; and S is the sucker's payoff (Axelrod 1984). As shown in figure 2.1, the reward for defecting is 5 if the other cooperates, but if both defect each player receives a lesser reward of 1. Both players are likely to defect since 5 is better than 3 and 1 is still better than 0—each player is better off defecting regardless of what the other player does—unless they can agree to a mutual contract that makes it costly to defect. The incentive to jointly produce the norm is the gains from cooperation represented in the upper left quadrant in figure 2.1. The total payoff of cooperation is greater than all other conjoint outcomes. In other words, both players are better off if they succeed in cooperating, so long as the costs of monitoring and enforcing a norm that induces cooperation are not too high. Algebraically this is shown as $2R - C > T + S$, where C is the cost of monitoring and enforcing the norm. Given the higher individual payoff, T, for defection, the joint production of prisoner's dilemma norms depends to a greater

Figure 2.1   The Prisoner's Dilemma

		Column Player	
		Cooperate	Defect
Row Player	Cooperate	R, R 3, 3	S, T 0, 5
	Defect	T, S 5, 0	P, P 1, 1

extent on the effectiveness of monitoring. Cooperation is contingent on C being less than 1. In small groups, *the only means to achieve a solution to the one-shot prisoner's dilemma situation is through mutual agreement;* otherwise the cost of monitoring and enforcement is likely to be too high to sustain cooperation. Largely for this reason, the PD norm cannot be imposed by the fiat power of one actor in the absence of mutual consent.

More generally, norms arise from the problem-solving activities of human beings in their strivings to improve their chances for success—the attainment of rewards—through cooperation. Norms have been around as long as humans beings have existed as a species. Language and norms evolved together: the first sentences were probably norms spoken to enable early man to coordinate group action, as in a hunting expedition. Most informal norms evolve gradually through trial and error, with the behavior that brings about success. Members of a group engage in collective problem solving by socially constructing a definition of a situation that optimizes the welfare of the group's members (Shibutani 1978, 431). When norms have a distributional consequence, the selection of norms involves bargaining—both implicit and explicit—among members. Powerful members of a small group or close-knit community have a greater say in specifying the terms of exchange (Knight and Ensminger in this volume). When a solution to a recurrent problem of collective action or coordination is found, it is repeated until mutual expectations become fixed.

Proposition 1.   Individuals jointly produce and uphold norms to capture the gains from cooperation.

This proposition is consistent with Ellickson's welfare-maximizing theory (1991) of norms. It shifts attention away from predicting the content of norms toward specifying instead the social mechanisms that give rise to and uphold norms. Ellickson's welfare-maximizing hypothesis predicts that norms in close-knit groups generally operate to maximize members' welfare, which "includes not only commodities but also other outcomes that people might value as much or more, such as parenthood, leisure, good health, high social status, and close personal relationships" (170). Ellickson applied this welfare-maximizing principle to predict the content of workaday norms. As a legal scholar, he was interested in demonstrating the pervasive reliance on informal norms as opposed to litigation in resolving property disputes in Shasta County. His field work there, however, did not include direct observation of how people actually monitored and enforced informal norms.

In the literature on collective action, the problem of establishing and enforcing the rules that induce cooperation is described as the second-order collective action problem (Taylor 1987; Elster 1989; Coleman 1990). Actors experience costs in applying sanctions and will only assume such costs if doing so results in a greater benefit to themselves. As Oliver (1993, 274) describes this problem, "somebody has to pay for the selective incentive, and paying for the selective incentive is, itself, a collective action in that it provides a benefit to everyone interested in the collective good, not just the people who pay for the incentive." Heckathorn's (1990) formal model of the emergence of compliance and opposition norms provides an explanation for second-order collective action. However, as Macy (1993, 820) points out, Heckathorn's theory of norms is computationally intensive: actors are required in the model "to make a highly sophisticated calculation of the marginal impact of second-order contributions on the level of first-order public goods." In any case, the problem of second-order contribution is overstated in Heckathorn's theory of norms. In small groups—from face-to-face networks to close-knit communities—the problem of second-order contribution is minimal because monitoring and enforcement are by-products of ongoing social interactions.

As demonstrated by Homans (1950) in his reanalysis of the Western Electric Bank Wiring Room study, monitoring and enforcement occurs spontaneously in the course of social interactions. His insights are crucial to understanding conformity to norms. He showed, first, that social approval and disapproval are routinely emitted by actors in the course of their everyday interactions. Conformity to the rules of a group is rewarded by social approval, and deviance is punished by social disapproval and ostracism. Hence, the monitoring of norms is a spontaneous by-product of social interactions. Second, not only do actors monitor behavior and enforce compliance to norms to capture the gains from cooperation, but they also attain higher status and power within the group by embodying the group's norms (see also Coleman 1990). Because the attainment of status and power is an individual outcome, it operates as a reward for complying with the group's norm. *Conformers have an interest in monitoring the norms of the group insofar as it reinforces the criteria upon which their higher status is based.* Rational choice theorists often overlook this social reward for second-order contributions when they address the "second-order free-rider problem" (Heckathorn 1988; Macy 1993). Third, information about individual actors is shared knowledge among all members of a small group. The cost of monitoring is lower when full information can be assumed for all members. Taken together, Homans's findings explain why in face-to-face networks and close-knit communities, a third-party "state-like" enforcer is not needed to monitor and enforce social norms. Thus:

Proposition 2. The more frequent the interactions between members of a group, the more effective the monitoring of its norms.

Flache and Macy (1996) suggest that under some circumstances social approval is exchanged not only for compliance but also for social approval, and that this form of exchange leads to noncompliance. Likewise, the pressure to conform in small groups can lead to excessive compliance when zealots dominate close-knit groups (Coleman 1990). However, *more frequent interactions give rise to conditions that lower the cost of monitoring.* In multiplex networks there are many opportunities to provide selective incentives to induce contributions that solve the second-order collective action problem. The variables that account for a group's capacity to use selective incentives to overcome that problem are probably features of social networks, such as centrality and connectivity, that are already the subject of extensive investigation. The multiple incentive opportunities of interpersonal relationships may also be useful in accounting for collective action efforts between organizations, where the relevant relations are not between the organizations per se but between the individuals that populate them (McGuire, Granovetter, and Schwartz 1993).

Returning to the example of the publish-or-perish norm, we note that although the focal point is often the formal review for promotion, social mechanisms enforcing the norm are manifest in everyday social interactions in the academic community. Through daily interactions, colleagues confer social approval and informally rank faculty members in a status order according to their perception of the members' academic productivity. Thus, although the publish-or-perish norm is backed by formal review procedures designed to gauge and reward research productivity, it is thoroughly embedded in ongoing social interactions in the academic community, so much so that the motivation for research productivity is only partly tied to monetary rewards and is also affected by such nonmaterial rewards as social approval and higher rank in the status order. The label "deadwood" reflects the cumulative withdrawal of social approval, while "active" connotes approval for continuing behavior in conformity with the norm. Conferring higher status on faculty members who conform to the publish-or-perish norm rewards those who contribute more to the department's success in securing valued resources and higher rank. A feature of institutional arrangements giving rise to high performance—as in elite research universities—is the close articulation between the informal norm that provides the criteria for conferring social approval and rank, and the formal institutional arrangements that buttress the informal constraints.

Thus, as elite universities and departments competed for research funding after World War II, they put a higher premium on the research productivity of their faculties. As the more productive faculty members were rewarded by higher social rank and monetary compensation, and became the objects of competitive bidding in the academic labor market, it gradually dawned on more traditional faculty members, who might have devoted more time and effort to teaching and academic citizenship, that the rules of the game had shifted from rewarding the gentleman scholar to rewarding research productivity (publish or perish). This change in norms enabled the university to compete more effectively for federal and state research funding, and also for the best students. The mechanism sanctioning the publish-or-perish norm is found in the actions of individual faculty members, whether in seeking tenure, social approval, higher rank, or better conditions of employment.

Norms are more likely to persist in a group to the extent that they result in the production of collective goods upon which members of the group depend. Success in solving long-standing collective action problems enables individuals to capture gains from cooperation and escape from suboptimal states. The evolutionary account of norms suggests that they emerge through a trial-and-error process by which members of a group negotiate and bargain over competing norms. In this view, the selection of a norm is governed by whether the members of the group are individually rewarded through their cooperation. Such rewards include the good feelings that come from membership in a group (Lawler 1997). The successful attainment of rewards reinforces the norm and provides the incentives for upholding it. Once a norm is established, self-reinforcing processes in the group lock it in, which makes it difficult to jettison and gives rise to "path dependence."

Proposition 3a.   The successful attainment of values by members of a group provides effective reinforcement for the joint production and maintenance of informal norms. The more frequently ego's compliance [noncompliance] to a norm is rewarded [met by disapproval] by alter, the more likely ego will uphold the norm.

Proposition 3b.   Competitive striving for social approval results in a self-reinforcing mechanism rewarding individuals for second-order contributions in upholding the norms of a group.

This proposition is derived from Homans's ([1961] 1974, 16) success proposition: "For all actions taken by persons, the more often a particular action of a person is rewarded, the more likely the person is to perform that action." And it is consistent with alternative choice-theoretic accounts of the evolutionary emergence of norms and the maintenance of social control (Akerlof 1976; Opp 1982; Axelrod 1986; Heckathorn 1988, 1990; Coleman 1990; Macy 1993; Lindenberg, 1994). It assumes that there are two sources of rewards. First, there are rewards from capturing the gains of cooperation. These rewards are available to all members of the group as a collective good. Second, there are second-order rewards attained from compliance and monitoring activity.

A norm originally selected to solve a collective action problem may later contribute to reentering a suboptimal state. This is due to lock-in and path dependence in the evolution of norms and institutions (David 1985; North 1990). Akerlof (1976, 617) explains by example the evolutionary dynamics of lock-in and path dependence in his model of India's caste order, which persists insofar as "the greatest rewards go to those who do not break social customs." If, however, adherence to a norm over time is consistently met by punishment from the environment, individuals are likely to seek to modify the norm (Shibutani 1986).

Group size affects a group's ability to establish, coordinate, and enforce effective incentives. When the social relationship is the vehicle for sanctioning, both sides are similarly affected: they lose all or some of the benefits they provide each other. In a dyad, this means that the costs to the sanctioner are great. However, as Simmel observed, the costs to the sanctioner are greatly reduced if the group is a triad or larger (Simmel 1950; see also Krackhardt 1994). If a member of a triad is ostracized, the remaining members are buffered by their interrelationships; they are not made isolates themselves as they would be if they had severed a dyadic relationship. As the group grows very large, however, new practical problems of coordinating collective action to establish institutions arise (Olson 1965). This is why formal norms and third-party enforcers are needed to solve problems of collective action when large numbers of actors—corporate and individual—are involved.

SOCIOLOGICAL NEW INSTITUTIONALISM

We now turn to the challenge of building a fully integrated model of institutions, embeddedness, and group performance. In developing our model, we assume that actors are rational in that they make decisions according to cost-benefit criteria.[4] However, we do not see humans as hyperrational—as does neoclassical economics—possessing perfect information and unbounded cognitive capacity. As North (in this volume) argues, the neoclassical assumption is "patently false" under conditions of uncertainty stemming from institutional change, which today characterize not only developing societies but also advanced industrial nations. Cognitive constraints make information imperfect and force decisionmakers to use heuristic devices. Moreover, cultural beliefs and cognitive processes embedded in institutions are key to understanding actors' perceptions of self-interest.

Figure 2.2   A Model for the New Institutionalism in Sociology

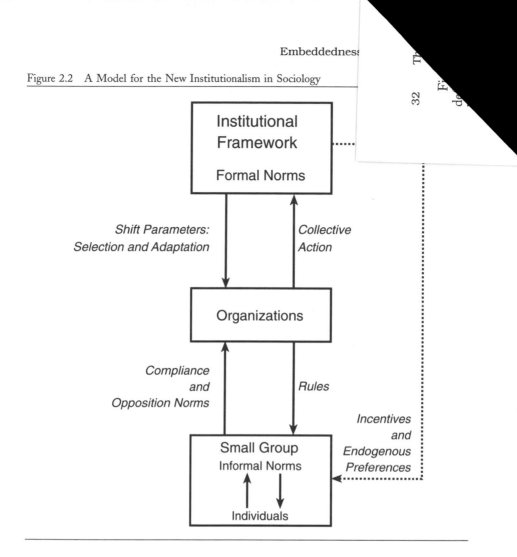

We also use a "thick" definition of interests wherein actors may value purely social goods such as status and the avoidance of social disapproval and ostracism.

Figure 2.2 adapts Williamson's (1994) synthesis of new institutional economics, with our modifications to address two limitations in his model. First, he assigns all constraints, formal and informal, to the same level of analysis. More specifically depicting the institutional environment by separating these, locating informal constraints in the domain of interacting individuals (figure 2.2), shows more clearly where these informal norms arise. Second, Williamson assumes an atomistic actor constrained by formal authority. Although he subsumes the embeddedness approach to the institutional environment, his model is unable to specify the social mechanisms through which norms affect individual performance. Such mechanisms are not simply formal governance structures, but rely overwhelmingly on informal norms and are embedded in ongoing social relationships.

gure 2.2 shows nested levels of constraints. Hierarchically superior levels ine structures of incentives and thus establish goals for social units at lower levels. Subordinate social units influence rules at the hierarchically superior level, and account for performance at that level. The two types of causal relationships are distinguished in the figure. The arrows pointing downward indicate constraints placed on one level by a hierarchically superior level. The institutional framework comprises the matrix of formal norms that constrain organizations; organizational rules—a type of formal norm—that constrain groups; and informal norms that constrain the members of groups. Institutions also affect individual action through endogenous preferences. The arrows pointing upward indicate that hierarchically superior levels are constituted and created by levels below. Individuals situated in networks or small groups create and enforce informal norms. Rules are determined by groups within the organization through a bargaining process (see Knight and Ensminger in this volume), and organizational performance is a function of group performance. Organizations in turn affect formal norms through political action, while their performance determines performance at the macro level.

In the new institutionalist paradigm, change in social organization results from path-dependent change in the institutional environment. Such parameter shifts, as Williamson (1991) argues, give rise to changes at the organizational level, as firms adapt their governance structure to capture new opportunities for profit and gain from trade opened up by institutional change and as firms that do not adapt are negatively affected by selection pressures. An example is the rise of local corporatism in China, a hybrid governance structure well-adapted to the needs of nonstate firms in the institutional environment of partial reform (Nee 1992). Failure to adapt to the changing institutional environment selects out large state-owned enterprises, not because they go bankrupt, since they are subsidized by the state, but because their share of industrial output declines relative to that of nonstate firms. Local corporatist firms represent hybrid organizational forms that embody characteristics better suited to an institutional environment shifting to a greater reliance on markets. Another example is the rise of multibank holding companies within the U.S. banking industry in recent decades (Mason 1996). The transformation of commercial banks from unit banks to multibank holding companies was driven by growing competition from alternative organizational forms in the financial services sector. In response to competitive pressures and declining market share, commercial bankers lobbied to change restrictive unit-bank rules in their state. After states relaxed their controls over commercial banks, the founding rate of the new hybrid organizational form—the multibank holding company—increased. Both examples highlight the importance of parameter shifts in the institutional environment for the comparative advantage of alternative governance structures and the emergence of new organizational forms.

Changes in formal norms stem from organizational actors. In North's view (1990), organizational actors, responding to changing relative prices or preferences, seek through collective action to bend and change formal rules in their favor. Corporate actors facing increased foreign competition in their domestic markets, for example, typically respond by lobbying their governments to intervene to provide domestic firms with protection from "unfair" competition. North emphasizes the capacity of organizational actors to change as they learn and adapt to change in the institutional environment. But, as organizational ecologists have demonstrated, the capacity of organizations to change through learning is limited by powerful inertial forces (Hannan and Freeman 1977), suggesting that pressures for institutional change may come from entrepreneurs championing new organizational forms rather than from dominant organizations (Ingram in this volume). These processes are shown schematically in figure 2.2 as the interactions between formal norms and organizations. Collective action directed at changing the formal rules of the game has been overlooked by organizational ecologists as a key causal mechanism in the emergence of new organizational forms. Economists, in focusing on learning behavior in the existing population of firms, have overlooked the importance of new organizational forms that emerge to exploit new knowledge or technologies as a mechanism of institutional change.

The Origin of Preferences

Although in rational choice theory preferences are critical to explaining action, the origin of preferences has been largely ignored. Economists, who rely most heavily on rational choice and therefore on preferences, have generally taken a complete set of well-ordered preferences as a starting assumption, leaving the explanation of preferences to others (DiMaggio 1990). Veblen (1899) explicitly recognized the relationship between preferences and social structure, and more recently sociologists have argued that preferences are socially constructed (DiMaggio 1990; Friedland and Alford 1991). Burt's model (1982) of the influence of social structure on action is a formal expression of this idea. Certainly, the status and social identity implications of objects explain much of their appeal to consumers. As noted, social approval and disapproval constitute the key mechanisms through which conformity to the norms of a group is achieved. Social approval is taken as an universal preference of human beings and is expressed as status, esteem, respect, and honor (Smith [1776] 1966; Lindenberg 1992).

Informal Norms and Formal Organizational Rules

Organizations solve problems of collective action through formal sanctions—by imposing costs on free riding and rewarding compliance. As with informal norms, individuals decide on the basis of accounts of past rewards and costs whether to contribute to the production of a collective good. The state provides the clearest example of a formal organizational structure that "raises the cost for individuals who refuse to join groups, pay membership dues, and generally refuse to participate in collective action" (Eggertsson 1990, 66). However, many other formal organizations use rules with a third-party to secure control.

In an organizational context, informal norms contribute with the realization of organizational goals through their effect on compliance to the formal rules of the game. The interaction between informal norms and formal organizations is complex. *When the formal norms of an organization are perceived to be congruous with the preferences and interests of actors in subgroups, the relationship between formal and informal norms will be closely coupled.* This close coupling of informal norms and the formal rules of the organization is what promotes high performance in organizations and economies. First, when the informal and formal rules of the game are closely coupled, they are mutually reinforcing. This is illustrated in the case of research universities in the congruence between formal review procedures gauging and rewarding research productivity and the informal norm of "publish or perish." It is also seen in the congruence between informal norms of fair play and formal rules in competitive games. In developed market economies, formal rules and regulations governing economic transactions are buttressed by informal norms of honesty and fair exchange. When formal and informal norms are closely coupled, it is often difficult to demarcate the boundaries between formal and informal social control. Second, the close coupling of formal and informal norms results in lower transaction costs because monitoring and enforcement can be accomplished informally. The cost of reliance on social rewards to achieve conformity to norms is low since it is produced spontaneously in the course of ongoing social interactions. By contrast, the greater the reliance on the state for monitoring, the higher the transaction cost. Litigation and policing are costly means to secure cooperation. Third, the close coupling between formal and informal norms reduces uncertainty in social transactions. Uncertainty increases when the formal rules of the game are inconsistent or at odds with the informal norms of subgroups. Thus:

Proposition 4.   The close coupling between informal norms and formal organizational rules results in high organizational performance.

The close coupling of informal and formal norms in organizational settings often stems from the responsiveness of organizational leaders to the interests and preferences of employees in seeking to improve productivity. For example, organizational leadership instituting and enforcing formal norms against sexual and racial harassment in the workplace may be responding to the increased representation of women and minorities in the modern firm and the perceived increase in transaction costs of not solving problems of coordination in an increasingly heterogenous workforce. Subsequently, feedback reinforces or alters preexisting informal norms about appropriate behavior governing gender and ethnic relations in the workplace. Similarly, firms conscious of the soaring cost of employee health insurance may reinforce the emergent expectation that nonsmokers have a right not to be exposed to indirect smoke by prohibiting smoking in the workplace. What may have originated as expected behavior among individuals interacting in face-to-face groups becomes instituted and enforced as formal rules that in turn reinforce the informal norm.

The significance of close coupling between informal and formal norms can be seen in the contradictory evidence regarding the effectiveness of formal organizational rules. Adler and Borys (1996) point out that formal organizational rules sometimes result in increased employee alienation, turnover, stress, and dissatisfaction, while in other cases formal rules have been shown to reduce the very same negative outcomes. This conflict occurs even when the nature of tasks and technologies in organizations is controlled for. Adler and Borys's explanation of this conflict corresponds with ours: sometimes formal organizational rules are aligned with the interests of employees, enabling them to do their jobs better, while at other times formal organizational rules merely coerce employees. When formal organizational rules reflect the interests of employees, they will also be consistent with the informal norms that evolve among employees to further the same interests, and close coupling will exist.

Contingency theorists of organizations point to the type of technology and the level of interdependence between work tasks as determinants of the appropriate level of formalization in an organization (Woodward, 1980; Thompson, 1967). Transaction-cost theorists point to the congruence of goals between employees and employers as influencing the relative effectiveness of formal and informal organizational rules (Ouchi, 1980). Our focus on close coupling does not deny either of these positions. We agree that the relative effectiveness of formal and informal norms depends on features of the task and the relationship between employees and employers, but we contend that in all but the most trivial organizations, high performance requires the close coupling of both formal and informal norms. In this view we join Barnard ([1938] 1964), who insisted that the informal organization was "indispensable" to the effective performance of the formal organization.

Proposition 5. When the formal rules are at variance with the preferences and interests of subgroups in an organization, a decoupling of the informal norms and the formal rules of the organization will occur.

According to Meyer and Rowan (1977), decoupling of the practical activities of organizations from their formal rules and myths "enables organizations to maintain standardized, legitimating, formal structures, while their activities vary in response to practical considerations" (58). For certain types of organizations, particularly those for which there is not a competitive market for their output (for example, schools and government agencies), formal organizational rules will be largely ceremonial, designed to satisfy external constituents that provide the organization with legitimacy. Independent of this ceremonial formal structure, informal norms will arise to guide the day-to-day business of the organization.

Blau's (1963) case study of a federal law enforcement agency provides an illustration of decoupling between informal norms and formal organizational rules. Since reporting attempts at bribery apparently weakened the agents' ability to secure the cooperation needed to complete their investigations, which was their raison d'être, it became the informal norm that agents in the agency ought not report such attempts. The norm against reporting bribery attempts was perceived to be so important to the agents' success that it was rarely violated. During Blau's field work, only one agent violated the norm, and he was subsequently ostracized. As Blau observed, the cost of violating an informal norm is to risk the social relationship itself, or at least to experience social disapproval and diminished status in the group.

Informal norms will evolve into "opposition norms" if institutions and organizational sanctions are weak relative to contradicting group interests. Opposition norms encourage individuals to directly resist formal norms. Of the three relationships between formal and informal norms that we identify, this has the most negative implications for performance. In state socialist societies where the state-managed economy was widely perceived to be inefficient and at odds with the interests of economic actors, opposition norms emerged to organize the informal economy (Stark 1990).

> **Proposition 6.** When the organizational leadership and formal norms are perceived to be at odds with the interests and preferences of actors in subgroups, informal norms opposing formal rules will emerge to "bend the bars of the iron cage" of the formal organizational rules.

Shibutani (1978), in his ethnography of Nisei soldiers, provides a vivid account of the emergence of opposition norms. Documenting the misadventures in World War II of a company of Japanese-American soldiers, he shows that even a coercive force as awesome as the U.S. Army can be rendered ineffective. The war record of Nisei soldiers was outstanding, and the men of Company K were drawn from the same manpower pool as the 442d Regimental Combat Team, which was legendary for its heroics. However, the record of Company K was very different. Trained as infantrymen, its members were assigned to the Military Intelligence Service Language School (MISLS) at Fort Snelling in Minnesota to learn Japanese so they could act as interpreters. They became known not for heroism on the battlefield, but for insubordination, incompetence, laziness, and violence against officers and each other.

From the beginning, the members of Company K refused to acknowledge the right of Nisei noncommissioned officers (NCOs) to give orders to other Nisei. They disobeyed other orders as well: they frequently left Fort Snelling without passes; they brought alcohol and women into the fort; they were rowdy in formation; and they talked back to officers. MISLS had strict regulations for classroom conduct backed by military authority, but the members of Company K disregarded them. Many falsely claimed that they knew no Japanese and refused to recite in class or to study; most slept in class. Rather than learning Japanese, they passed the time by administering "hotfoots" and "hot seats" to unsuspecting classmates.

Then there was their intramural violence. A small group of soldiers spent most nights drunk and looking for fights. One of them would pick a fight with almost anyone he encountered. His victim had the choice of taking a beating or fighting back and being set upon by the whole gang. Anyone who attempted to come to his rescue was also beaten. Even Company K's first sergeant was thus attacked (the perpetrator in that case was court-martialed).

This behavior persisted in the face of military rules because the informal norms of the company were more binding on soldiers than the military rules. Not all of the soldiers in Company K were embittered by the army, but all were forced to participate in these misdeeds. Peer pressure was powerful. "Dissidents are brought into line and heroes elevated through spontaneous expression of approval and disapproval, such as the show of displeasure through sarcastic remarks or changes of facial expression, ridicule, gossip, refusal to reciprocate favors, and sometimes ostracism" (Shibutani 1978, 433). Physical threats were also used, such as the application of hotfoots to the "eager beavers" who tried to pay attention in class. The soldiers went to great lengths to avoid censure from their comrades. For example, the company liked to torment its officers by marching so quickly that the officers could not keep up. Although many of the privates also had difficulty maintaining the pace, they pushed themselves to do so despite colds, blisters, and other impediments, often collapsing at the end of the march.

The opposition norms that developed among the Nisei soldiers have their analog in restriction-of-output norms. It is a common perception among workers paid under piece-rate systems that payment rates will be pushed downward if output is high. Thus, such workers share an interest in discouraging high output rates. In support of this interest, informal norms develop to punish "rate-busters" (Roy 1952). Roethlisberger and Dickson's study (1939) of a work group in the Western Electric Company documented a game called "binging" where a man would punch someone else in the upper arm as hard as he could, and the recipient of the punch would return it. Men were more likely to be binged when they exceeded the group's informal output norms. The slowest producers were often heckled and ridiculed. There were also positive sanctions, in the form of higher social status, for compliance with group norms. Homans's reanalysis (1950) of William Whyte's *Street Corner Society* (1943) recognized a similar relationship between status within the group and adherence to its norms.

COOPERATION AND PRODUCTIVITY AT CLEO

A case study from physics illustrates all the levels in the model presented in figure 2.2, and almost all the links between them. The Wilson Synchrotron is one of four high-energy physics laboratories in the United States. Its research scientists are members of Cornell's Large Experimental Organization (CLEO), consortium. As of the summer of 1997, CLEO consisted of about two hundred and fifty participants from twenty-three universities.

CLEO is a particularly successful research organization of its type. Some of its success is due to fortuitous circumstances. The accelerator was not considered to be state of the art at the time it was built but turned out to be well-suited for studying what is known as the "bottom quark," which was discovered in 1978 at Fermi National Accelerator Laboratory. However, much of the success of CLEO, and in some ways the success of all organizations of its type, is puzzling at first glance. The operation of CLEO seems to violate expectations in a competitive academic field: scientists who wish to join are welcomed; work proceeds without concern that jealous colleagues will steal ideas or sabotage results; and cooperation between the members is high. How do these features persist when an important finding can mean the difference between a successful career and failure?

The research scientists of course seek peer recognition, from which all other rewards derive (Merton 1957). The joint good they require is the data collected and perhaps the stimulating atmosphere available at the Wilson Synchrotron. Data collection, a stimulating atmosphere, and productivity require that there be a critical mass of active scientists at the facility. Because the group of scientists at the facility was initially small, and because there is a high attrition rate, CLEO must constantly admit new scientists to produce its joint goods. However, it may not be in the individual interest of the members of CLEO to admit new members. At any point in time, CLEO's scientists have exclusive access to the facility and the data. When they admit a new member, their own right to the data is reduced. It is possible that a potential member could choose to study a problem that an existing member might eventually have studied. Thus, CLEO members might rationally refuse to admit new entrants and simply reserve use of the Wilson Synchrotron exclusively for themselves. Sociologists who doubt that rational individuals might make that decision should think about the data in their own field that is underutilized because those who own it wish to maintain their exclusive right to it.

An organizational rule makes it possible to overcome the interest individuals would have in excluding new entrants—a rule concerning the authorship of papers using Wilson Synchrotron data. Although such papers are typically written by a smaller group of scientists, there is a rule here (as at other high-energy physics laboratories) that every member of the consortium must be listed as a coauthor, and that the coauthors must be listed in alphabetical order. As a result, those wishing to join CLEO are welcomed because they contribute to the production of joint goods, and they cannot take credit for an idea away from the existing CLEO members. If CLEO were considering a paper on a topic on which a potential entrant wishes to conduct research, the present members might decide to get around to the topic themselves eventually and put out a publication with all members, listed as coauthors, or they might decide to welcome the new member, with the idea that the paper will thus be published somewhat sooner, again with all CLEO members listed as coauthors. The reader might wonder why scientists do not simply break the rule and use data collected at Wilson in single-author papers. Such malfeasance is impossible. A scientist who "stole" data from Wilson to avoid adding two hundred and fifty names to his work would be quickly found out since there is no credible alternative source for the data.

The coauthorship rule explains why members of CLEO are happy to have extra help, but why is anyone willing to provide it? Certainly membership in this prestigious organization confers status, but why would a scientist choose to labor on the consortium's projects rather than simply free ride on the efforts of others? After all, the scientist's name will go on the published results regardless of his or her participation. The answer is that informal processes discourage free riding. Whereas publications shared with two hundred and fifty others say almost nothing about an individual scientist to outsiders on tenure review committees or in foundations, what such outsiders can do is ask his or her colleagues at CLEO about the participation of the scientist. *It is the reputation of the scientist among his or her immediate colleagues that counts.* This arrangement makes the participants highly dependent on the group and results in the extremely cooperative and collegial relationships that partially account for CLEO's success. To maintain the goodwill of their colleagues, and thereby to maintain critical social capital, CLEO members obey the normative controls on behavior that support the joint authorship rule.

Figure 2.3 shows how the CLEO case relates to the general model illustrated in figure 2.2. Formal norms affecting high-energy physics research, such as the tenure system and the research-funding process, influence the preferences of research scientists and determine the criteria for rewarding organizations. CLEO's joint authorship rule organizes incentives in such a way that the participants in CLEO are willing to admit the new blood that is a prerequisite for organizational success. Social exchange at the group level, particularly positive scholarly references and high status in the organization in return for hard work results in

Figure 2.3   The Model Applied to CLEO

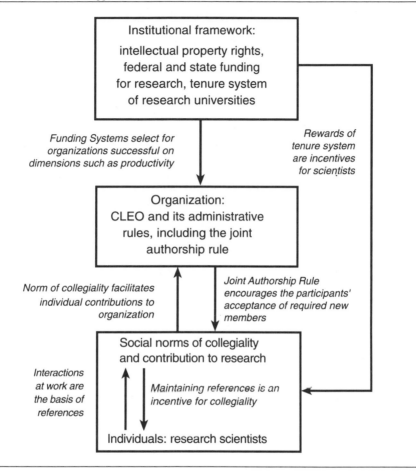

informal norms of collegiality and contributions to the joint goods the organization requires. These in turn facilitate the success of CLEO in meeting the criteria set out by the institutional environment. CLEO receives required funding, and its members can continue to work toward their goals. The correspondence between the organization's formal rules, informal norms, and the institutional framework of the modern research university results in high performance.

CONCLUSION

New institutionalists in economics have built a lively research program around the assumption that institutions matter in determining performance in organizations and economies. Without a theory of the origin of norms and the mechanisms through which institutions shape individual behavior, however, new institutionalists in economics cannot develop a satisfactory explanation for variation in economic performance. The formal normative framework of an economy accounts for only part of the story. Because economic performance entails cooperative behavior by individuals in groups, much of the variation in economic performance can be accounted for only by examining the effects of informal constraints on economic performance. Economic sociologists have studied the social network underpinning economic behavior. Yet without a theory that links networks of personal relationships to institutions, much of the economic life that characterizes modern economies eludes their explanation. Sociologists working in the social exchange tradition have contributed much to our understanding of exchange within network structures, but they have not sufficiently incorporated an institutional dimension in their work either.

By specifying the mechanisms that link norms to social networks, we supply the missing link that furthers the promise of mutually productive intellectual trade between economics and sociology. The production and maintenance of norms is a spontaneous byproduct of the interdependent activities of individuals. Social approval and disapproval provides the reward and punishment that uphold the norms of a group. Such positive and negative feedback built into ongoing social relationships provide the self-reinforcing mechanisms. New institutional economics is not imperialist insofar as its project is to elaborate a choice-within-constraints theory of economic. life. The constraints are institutions, involving the state, regulations, laws, property rights, organizations, ideology, and informal norms—all domains to which sociology has contributed a rich store of knowledge. These constraints, new institutionalists in economics maintain, are what shape the structure of incentives and thereby determine economic performance. Hence, constraints that sociology has been studying for many decades help explain economic performance. This view is quite different from that advocated by, for example, Gary Becker (1976), who argues that the neoclassical core explains all economic and social behavior. Such an assumption has been associated with the imperialist extension of rational choice theory into political science and sociology.

In sum, we have constructed a theory that provides a foundation for a sociological new institutionalism. We locate our actors in a network of personal relationships characterized by certain norms, in accordance with which they evaluate—and reward and punish—each other. High performance is determined by the extent to which institutions give rise to a structure of incentives that elicits cooperative behavior. The incremental rewards exchanged between individuals in permanent or semipermanent social relationships provide the social mechanisms essential to the conduct of economic life. Such rewards are mainly nonmaterial, motivated by the preference for social approval and rank, which often confer material benefits in turn.

Victor Nee gratefully acknowledges the support of the Russell Sage Foundation, the Center for Advanced Study in the Behavioral Sciences, and the National Science Foundation #SBR-9022192. We thank Robert K. Merton, Mary Brinton, Mark Granovetter, Richard Lempert, Siegwart Lindenberg, Michael Macy, Mark Mizruchi, Neil Smelser, Charles Tilly, and Oliver Williamson for their criticism of earlier drafts of this paper. Colleagues at Cornell, in particular Heather Haveman, Satoshi Kanazawa, Lisa Keister, Edward Lawler, and Rebecca Matthews, also provided useful comments. Earlier drafts of the paper benefited from comments from participants in the organizational workshop at Princeton University, the Bruce Mayhew Lecture Series at the University of South Carolina, the Workshop on the Place of Structuralism in New Institutional Sociology at Cornell University, the Rationality and Rational Choice Seminar at the Center for Advanced Study in the Behavioral Sciences, and the Workshop on the Emergence of Norms at the Russell Sage Foundation.

NOTES

1. We follow common usage by defining "economic" as pertaining to the allocation of scarce resources among competitive users (see Nicholson 1989). We apply this definition liberally, and our view of economic action is therefore more inclusive than that of some sociologists. Economic action includes not only market action, but allocative action within organizations of all types and even the allocation of nonmaterial scarce resources such as time, attention, and cognitive capacity.

2. Homans ([1961] 1974, 68–69) anticipated the embeddedness perspective of the new economic sociology and the link with the choice-within-institutional-constraints approach of new institutional economics:

> No doubt some persons do in fact trade regularly with others—the personal will keep breaking in—but economics can afford to disregard its effects. That is, classical economics does not concern itself with the permanent or semipermanent relationships, the repeated exchanges, between particular individuals or groups that make up so much of the subject matter of the other social sciences, including sociology. Economics can explain many features of behavior provided that it takes certain things called institutions—the market itself, for instance—as simply given. Yet these institutions, however difficult it often is to account for all their detailed characteristics, are at least the product of the very things economics disregards—the relatively permanent relationships between individuals or between groups, which form social structures. The general propositions of our present subject are not, we believe, different from those of economics, but we use them to try to explain just those features of social behavior which classical economics takes for granted.

3. Network analysis in its infancy at Harvard drew liberally from Homans's earlier work (1950), but veered away from his later work, turning to utilitarian social theory and methodological individualism. Yet that later work was entirely consistent with the Homans of *The Human Group* in its aim to explain, rather than to describe, the emergence of norms from concrete social relations and the manner in which norms provide a structure of incentives and thereby influence group performance.

4. It is hardly controversial that actors have preferences and that they consider their interests when choosing action. Likewise, most social scientists will accept that constraints are considered along with interests. That individuals have preferences and that these preferences compel them to act is the basic rational choice model. Despite its influence in all the social sciences, this model remains contentious. The problem is that it is easy to find examples of individuals failing to act rationally and difficult to believe that individuals can be as rational as the strictest rational choice model assumes. Refinements of the basic rational choice model, however, increase its application to sociology.

Frank (1988) argues that apparent failures of rationality, such as altruism, revenge, and honesty, can be explained with a commitment model. Generating credible commitment is a challenge actors constantly face. The familiar example of the commitment problem is provided by Schelling (1960): A kidnapper has a change of heart and would like to release his victim. If, in return for freedom, the victim had some way to make a credible commitment not to reveal the identity of the kidnapper, his life would be spared. However, the victim will have no incentive to keep any such promise once free, and the kidnapper reluctantly decides the victim must be killed. The victim is effectively doomed by his own rationality. Frank argues that many apparent failures of rationality are actually mechanisms to generate commitment. For example, many petty thefts occur because criminals realize that the cost of reporting a theft, filling out a police report, identifying the criminal, and appearing in court is greater than the cost of replacing many stolen items, and they therefore anticipate that victims will not pursue justice. This suggests that an individual known to have an irrational taste for vengeance will be less likely to be stolen from. Frank's work shows that some behavior that appears irrational can be seen as rational with a more sophisticated understanding of the commitment problems individuals are actually trying to solve.

There are other apparent deviations from rationality that cannot be so neatly explained. It appears that individuals often simply make mistakes in relation to the expectations of the rational choice model. Cognitive psychologists such as Tversky and Kahneman (1974, 1981) have investigated these failings of rationality. They have identified a number of systematic biases in decisionmaking behavior. For example, individuals appear to weigh losses heavier than gains and to value the components of pairs of events separately. So an individual might report being unhappy at coming home from a holiday and finding an unexpected gift of a hundred dollars and an unexpected bill for eighty dollars. People also overestimate the occurrence of events that are salient in memory, and underappreciate the importance of base rates in answering questions of the type "What is the likelihood that object A belongs to class B?" They also fail to properly disregard sunk costs (Thaler 1980). These and other examples of failings of rationality are systematic and thus show that the classic rational choice model is insufficient. But they suggest the possibility of developing a behavioral model of rational choice. By asserting that institutions matter, the new institutionalist paradigm maintains that a sufficient theoretic model of choice needs to incorporate the effects of institutions on individual and group performance.

REFERENCES

Adler, Paul S., and Bryan Borys. 1996. "Two Types of Bureaucracy: Enabling and Coercive." *Administrative Science Quarterly* 41: 61–89.

Akerlof, George. 1976. "The Economics of Caste and of the Rat Race and Other Woeful Tales." *Quarterly Journal of Economics* 90(4) 599–617.

Alchian, Armen, and Harold Demsetz. 1973. "The Property Rights Paradigm." *Journal of Economic History* 33: 16–27.

Axelrod, Robert. 1984. *The Emergence of Cooperation.* New York: Basic Books.

———. 1986. "An Evolutionary Approach to Norms." *American Political Science Review* 80: 1095–1111.

Baker, Wayne E. 1984. "The Social Structure of a National Securities Market." *American Journal of Sociology* 89: 775–811.

Barnard, Chester I. [1938] 1964. *The Functions of the Executive.* Cambridge, Mass.: Harvard University Press.

Becker, Gary. 1976. *The Economic Approach to Human Behavior.* Chicago, Ill.: University of Chicago Press.

Berger, Peter L., and Thomas Luckmann. 1966. *The Social Construction of Reality: A Treatise in the Sociology of Knowledge.* New York: Doubleday.

Blau, Peter. 1963. *The Dynamics of Bureaucracy.* 2d ed. Chicago, Ill.: University of Chicago Press.

———. 1964. *Exchange and Power in Social Life.* New York: Basic Books.

Burt, Ronald. 1982. *Toward a Structural Theory of Action: Network Models of Social Structure, Perception and Action.* New York: Academic Press.

Cheung, Steven. 1974. "A Theory of Price Control." *Journal of Law and Economics* 12: 53–71.

Coase, R. H. 1937. "The Nature of the Firm." *Economica* 4: 386–405.

———. 1960. "The Problem of Social Cost." *Journal of Law and Economics* 3: 1–44.

———. 1984. "The New Institutional Economics." *Journal of Institutional and Theoretical Economics* 140: 229–31.

Coleman, James. 1990. *Foundations of Social Theory.* Cambridge, Mass.: Harvard University Press.

David, Paul. 1985. "Clio and the Economics of QWERTY." *American Economic Review* 4: 386–406.

Davis, Lance E., and Douglass C. North. 1971. *Institutional Change and American Economic Growth.* Cambridge, England: Cambridge University Press.
Demsetz, Harold. 1967. "Towards a Theory of Property Rights." *American Economic Review* 57: 347–59.
DiMaggio, Paul. 1990. "Cultural Aspects of Economic Organization." In *Beyond the Market Place*, edited by Roger Friedland and A.F. Robertson. New York: Aldine de Gruyter.
Eggertsson, Thrainn. 1990. *Economic Behavior and Institutions.* Cambridge, England: Cambridge University Press.
Ellickson, Robert. 1991. *Order without Law.* Cambridge, Mass.: Harvard University Press.
Elster, Jon. 1989. *The Cement of Society: A Study of Social Order.* Cambridge, England: Cambridge University Press.
Emerson, Richard A. 1962. "Power-Dependence Relations." *American Sociological Review* 27: 31–41.
Flache, Andreas, and Michael W. Macy. 1996. *Journal of Mathematical Sociology.*
Frank, Robert H. 1988. *Passions within Reason.* New York: W. W. Norton and Company.
Frank, Robert H., and Robert J. Cook. 1995. *The Winner-Take-All Society.* New York: Free Press.
Friedland, Roger, and Robert Alford. 1991. "Bringing Society Back In: Symbols, Practices, and Institutional Contradictions." In *The New Institutionalism in Organizational Analysis*, edited by Walter Powell and Paul DiMaggio. Chicago, Ill.: University of Chicago Press.
Granovetter, Mark. 1974. *Getting A Job: A Study of Contacts and Careers.* Cambridge, Mass.: Harvard University Press.
———. 1985. "Economic Action and Social Structure: The Problem of Embeddedness." *American Journal of Sociology* 91: 481–510.
———. 1993. "The Nature of Economic Relationships." *Explorations in Economic Sociology*, edited by Richard Swedberg. New York: Russell Sage Foundation.
Greif, Avner, Paul Milgrom, and Barry R. Weingast. 1994. "Coordination, Commitment, and Enforcement: The Case of the Merchant Guild." *Journal of Political Economy* 102: 715–76.
Hannan, Michael T., and John Freeman. 1977. "The Population Ecology of Organizations." *American Journal of Sociology* 82: 929–64.
Hardin, Russell. 1982. *Collective Action.* Baltimore: Johns Hopkins University Press Resources for the Future.
———. 1988. *Morality Within the Limits of Reason.* Chicago, Ill.: University of Chicago Press.
Hechter, Michael. 1987. *Principles of Group Solidarity.* Los Angeles, Calif.: University of California Press.
Heckathorn, Douglas D. 1988. "Collective Sanctions and the Creation of Prisoner's Dilemma Norms." *American Journal of Sociology* 94: 535–62.
———. 1990. "Collective Sanctions and Compliance Norms: A Formal Theory of Group-Mediated Social Control." *American Sociological Review* 55: 366–84.
Hodgson, Geoffrey M. 1988. *Economics and Institutions: A Manifesto for a Modern Institutional Economics.* Cambridge, England: Polity Press.
Homans, George C. 1950. *The Human Group.* New York: Harcourt Brace Jovanovich.
———. 1958. "Social Behavior as Exchange." *American Journal of Sociology* 63: 597–606.
———. [1961] 1974. *Social Behavior: Its Elementary Form.* New York: Harcourt Brace Jovanovich.
Krackhardt, David. 1994. "Crisis in a Cluster: The Roles of Simmelian Ties in Organizations." Carnegie Mellon University. Manuscript.
Lawler, Edward J. 1997. "An Affect Theory of Social Exchange." Industrial and Labor Relations, Cornell University. Unpublished manuscript.
Lindenberg, Siegwart. 1992. "An Extended Theory of Institutions and Contractual Discipline." *Journal of Institutional and Theoretical Economics* 148: 123–54.
Macy, Michael W. 1993. "Backward-Looking Social Control." *American Sociological Review* 58: 819–36.
Macaulay, Stewart. 1963. "Non-Contractual Relations in Business: A Preliminary Study." *American Sociological Review* 55: 55–66.
Malinowski, Bronislaw. 1959. *Crime and Custom is Savage Society.* Patterson, N.J.: Littlefield, Adams.
———. 1994. "Norms and the Power of Loss: Ellickson's Theory and Beyond." *Journal of Institutional and Theoretical Economies* 150: 101–13.

Mason, James Eliot. 1996. "Transformation of Commercial Banking in the United States, 1956–1991." Ph.D. diss., Cornell University.

Matthews, R. C. O. 1986. "The Economics of Institutions and the Sources of Economic Growth." *Economic Journal* 96: 903–18.

McGuire, Patrick, Mark Granovetter, and Michael Schwartz. 1993. In *Explorations in Economic Sociology*, edited by Richard Swedberg. New York: Russell Sage Foundation.

Merton, Robert K. 1957. "Priorities in Scientific Discovery." *American Sociological Review* 22: 635–59.

Meyer, John W., and Brian Rowan. 1977. "Institutionalized Organizations: Formal Structure as Myth and Ceremony. *American Journal of Sociology* 83: 340–63.

Nee, Victor. 1992. "The Organizational Dynamics of Market Transition: Hybrid Forms, Property Rights, and Mixed Economy in China." *Administrative Science Quarterly* 37: 1–27.

Nicholson, Walter. 1989. *Microeconomic Theory*. New York: Dryden Press.

North, Douglass C. 1981. *Structure and Change in Economic History*. New York: Norton.

———. 1990. *Institutions, Institutional Change and Economic Performance*. Cambridge, England: Cambridge University Press.

Oliver, Pamela E. 1993. "Formal Models of Collective Action." *Annual Review of Sociology* 19: 271–320.

Olson, Mancur. 1965. *The Logic of Collective Action*. Cambridge, Mass.: Harvard University Press.

Opp, Karl-Dieter. 1982. "The Evolutionary Emergence of Norms." *British Journal of Social Psychology* 21: 139–49.

Ostrom, Elinor. 1990. *Governing the Commons: The Evolution of Institutions for Collective Action*. Cambridge, England: Cambridge University Press.

Ouchi, William G. 1980. "Markets, Bureaucracies, and Clans." *Administrative Science Quarterly* 25: 129–41.

Polanyi, Karl. 1944. *The Great Transformation: The Political and Economic Origins of Our Time*. Boston: Beacon Press.

———. 1957. "The Economy as Instituted Process." In *Trade and Market in Early Empires*, edited by Karl Polanyi, Conrad Arensberg, and Harry Pearson. Glencoe, Ill.: Free Press.

Powell, Walter W., and Laurel Smith-Doerr. 1994. "Networks and Economic Life." In *The Handbook of Economic Sociology*, edited by Neil Smelser and Richard Swedberg. New York: Russell Sage Foundation.

Roethlisberger, F. J., and W. J. Dickson. 1939. *Management and the Worker*. Cambridge, Mass.: Harvard University Press.

Roy, Donald. 1952. "Quota Restriction and Goldbricking in a Machine Shop." *American Journal of Sociology* 57: 427–42.

Schelling, Thomas C. 1960. *The Strategy of Conflict*. Cambridge, Mass.: Harvard University Press.

Shibutani, Tamotsu. 1978. *The Derelicts of Company K: A Study of Demoralization*. Berkeley, Calif.: University of California Press.

———. 1986. *Social Processes*. Berkeley, Calif.: University of California Press.

Simmel, Georg. 1950. *The Sociology of Georg Simmel*, edited by Kurt Wolff. Glencoe, Ill.: Free Press.

Smith, Adam. [1759] 1966. *A Theory of Moral Sentiments*. New York: Kelley.

Stark, David. 1990. "Bending the Bars of the Iron Cage: Bureaucratization and Informalization in Comparative Perspective." *Sociological Forum* 4: 637–64.

Taylor, Michael. 1987. *The Possibility of Cooperation*. Cambridge, England: Cambridge University Press.

Thaler, Richard. 1980. "Toward a Positive Theory of Consumer Choice." *Journal of Economic Behavior and Organization* 1: 39–60.

Thompson, James D. 1967. *Organizations in Action*. New York: McGraw-Hill.

Tversky, Amos, and Daniel Kahneman. 1974. "Judgment under Uncertainty: Heuristics and Biases." *Science* 185: 1124–31.

———. 1981. "The Framing of Decisions and the Psychology of Choice." *Science* 211: 453–58.

Ullmann-Margalit, Edna. 1977. *The Emergence of Norms*. Oxford, England: Clarendon Press.

Williamson, Oliver E. 1975. *Markets and Hierarchies: Analysis and Antitrust Implications*. New York: Free Press.

———. 1985. *The Economic Institutions of Capitalism*. New York: Free Press.

————. 1991. "The Analysis of Discrete Structural Alternatives." *Administrative Science Quarterly* 36(2): 269–96.

————. 1994. "Transaction Cost Economics and Organization Theory." In *The Handbook of Economic Sociology*, edited by Neil Smelser and Richard Swedberg. New York: Russell Sage Foundation.

White, Harrison C. 1970. *Chains of Opportunity*. Cambridge, Mass.: Harvard University Press.

Whyte, William F. [1943] 1993. *Street Corner Society*. 4th ed. Chicago, Ill.: University of Chicago Press.

Woodward, Joan. 1980. *Industrial Organization: Theory and Practice*. London, England: Oxford University Press.

Veblen, Thorstein B. 1899. *The Theory of the Leisure Class: An Economic Study of Institutions*. New York: Macmillan.

3

Of Coase and Cattle: Dispute Resolution Among Neighbors in Shasta County

Robert C. Ellickson

"I think the whole thing is good neighbors. If you don't have good neighbors, you can forget the whole thing."
—Chuck Searle, Shasta County cattleman

"My family believes in 'live and let live.' Have you heard of that?"
—Phil Ritchie, Shasta County farmer

This chapter reports the results of an investigation into how rural landowners in Shasta County, California, resolve disputes arising from trespass by livestock. The results provide an empirical perspective on one of the most celebrated hypothetical cases in the law-and-economics literature. In his landmark article, "The Problem of Social Cost,"[1] economist Ronald Coase invoked as his fundamental example a conflict between two neighbors—a rancher running cattle and a farmer raising crops. Coase used the Parable of the Farmer and the Rancher to illustrate what has come to be known as the Coase Theorem. This unintuitive proposition asserts, in its strongest form, that when transaction costs are zero, a change in the rule of liability will have no effect on the allocation of resources. For example, the theorem predicts that as long as its admittedly heroic assumptions are met, the imposition of liability for cattle trespass would not cause ranchers to reduce the size of their herds, erect more fencing, or keep closer watch on their livestock. The theorem has become the most fruitful, yet most controversial, proposition in the field of law and economics.[2]

Coase himself was fully aware that obtaining information, negotiating agreements, and litigating disputes are all potentially costly, and that thus his parable might not portray accurately how rural landowners would respond to a change in trespass law.[3] Some law-and-economics scholars, however, assume that transaction costs are indeed often trivial when only two parties are in conflict.[4] Therefore, these scholars might assume that Coase's parable faithfully depicts how rural landowners resolve cattle-trespass disputes.

To explore the realism of the assumptions underlying the Farmer-Rancher Parable, I searched for a jurisdiction that had imposed varying rules of liability in cattle trespass situations and had changed those rules with some frequency. After briefly surveying a half-dozen candidates in California, I settled on Shasta County. Since 1945, a specific California statute has authorized the Shasta County Board of Supervisors, the county's elected governing body, to determine where in the county an owner of cattle is liable for damages stemming from unintentional cattle trespass on unfenced land. Although most of Shasta County is "open range"—territory where a cattleman is not liable for trespass damages of that sort—the board has the authority to "close the range" in subareas of the county. A closed-range ordinance makes a cattleman strictly liable for any damage his livestock might cause while trespassing within the area affected by the ordinance.[5] The Shasta County Board of Supervisors has exercised this power to close the range on dozens of occasions since 1945, thus changing the exact rule of liability that Coase used in his famous example.[6] I traveled to Shasta County to determine whether these legal changes had had any impact.[7]

This study presents findings that cast doubt on many of the assumptions undergirding the Coasean parable. It also strives to help bridge the chasm lying between the law-and-economics and law-and-society movements,[8] perhaps the two most significant social-scientific schools of legal research. On the whole, the law and society scholars have gathered the better field data on dispute resolution practices, and the law and economics scholars have developed the more explicit, rigorous, and testable theories of human behavior. Although one might think that members of these two schools would perceive irresistible benefits from collaboration, these two groups have worked largely in isolation from one another. They have separate journals.[9] They gather at separate conferences. They rarely read, much less cite, work by scholars in the other camp. This absence of cross-fertilization stems not only from lack of familiarity with the working language of the other group, but also from a mutual lack of respect, even a contempt, for the kind of work that the other group does. To exaggerate only a little, the law-and-economics scholars believe that the law-and-society group is deficient in both sophistication and rigor, and the law-and-society scholars believe that the law-and-economics group is not only out of touch with reality but also short on humanity.

In conducting this study, I placed a foot squarely within each of the two camps. Law and economics, the tradition within which I have mainly labored, provided the parable that inspired the study. By undertaking "microscopic"[10] field research into the resolution of a narrow class of disputes, however, I followed the methods of pioneering law-and-society scholars such as Stuart Macaulay and H. Laurence Ross.[11] After reading in both literatures, I confess my disloyal suspicion that law-and-society scholars would generally be more successful than law-and-economics scholars in predicting the essentials of the story to come.

The Shasta County evidence indicates that Coase's Farmer-Rancher Parable correctly anticipates that a change in the rule of liability for cattle trespass does not affect, for example, the quality of fences that separate ranches from farms. The parable's explanation for the allocative toothlessness of law is, however, exactly backward. The parable's explanation is that transaction costs are low and that parties respond to a new rule by agreeing to an exchange of property rights that perpetuates the prior (efficient) allocation of resources. The field evidence I gathered suggests that a change in animal trespass law indeed fails to affect resource allocation, *not because transaction costs are low, but because transaction costs are high.* Legal rules are costly to learn and enforce. Trespass incidents are minor irritations between parties who typically have complex continuing relationships that enable them readily to enforce informal norms. The Shasta County evidence indicates that under these conditions, potential disputants ignore the formal law. As Coase probably suspected,[12] the Parable of the Farmer and the Rancher therefore ill-describes how rural landowners actually interact with one another.

This chapter introduces the relevant residents of Shasta County and their techniques of cattle ranching and boundary fencing. It describes how the rural residents of Shasta County resolve their cattle-trespass disputes. The chapter concludes with a summary of the principal findings and implications.

SHASTA COUNTY AND ITS CATTLE INDUSTRY
Physical Environment

Shasta County lies at the northern end of the four-hundred-mile-long Central Valley of California (see figure 3.1). The Sacramento River, which drains the northern half of the Central Valley, bisects the county. Redding, Shasta County's county seat and largest city, is situated at an elevation of five hundred feet at the spot where the Sacramento River emerges from the mountains north of the Valley to begin its trip south toward San Francisco Bay. High mountain peaks lie within sight of Redding in all directions except south. The Trinity Mountains lie to the west; the towering cone of Mount Shasta stands fifty miles due north, in Siskiyou County; and to the east lie other peaks of the volcanic Cascade Range—notably Mount Lassen, which sits in Shasta County's southeastern corner. To the east, north, and west of Redding, foothills rise irregularly toward these distant mountain peaks.

Weather dictates Shasta County's ranching practices. Like the rest of California, the county has a wet season and a dry season. Redding receives an average annual rainfall of 38.74 inches, most of it concentrated in the winter months.[13] Little rain falls between mid-May and November. During the summer months intense sunlight bakes Redding, and the surrounding mountains block cooling winds.[14] In the spring, the grasslands near Redding are green from the heavy winter rains; by summer, the extreme heat has turned the groundcover brown.

Most of Shasta County's terrain is too mountainous and its soils too poor to support significant agricultural activity. The majority of the land area in the county is commercial-quality forest, most of which the United States Forest Service and a handful of private timber companies own.[15] Census data describe 16 percent of the county as "land in farms."[16] The bulk of this agricultural land is unirrigated and used only as seasonal pasture for livestock—principally cattle, the county's major agricultural product. Only 1 percent of the county's land is used for raising harvested crops,[17] and a majority of this field-crop acreage is devoted to alfalfa or other hay grown as livestock feed.[18]

In 1973, the Shasta County Board of Supervisors voted to "close the range" in a fifty-six-square-mile rectangle of territory around Round Mountain, a rural hamlet situated thirty miles northeast of Redding (see figure 3.2). This ordinance, which county cattlemen now call "Caton's Folly" to embarrass John Caton, the supervisor who helped pass it, provided the best opportunity in Shasta County to test the effects of an *actual* change in the rule of liability for cattle trespass. Nine years later, in 1982, the Board of Supervisors considered, but rejected, a petition to close the range in the Oak Run area immediately southwest of Caton's Folly. The Oak Run controversy promised to reveal the effects of a *threatened* change in liability rules. Residents of the Oak Run and Round Mountain areas were interviewed to shed more light on these effects. The general area northeast of Redding—what I call the Northeastern Sector—thus warrants closer description.

Figure 3.1   Map of Northwestern California

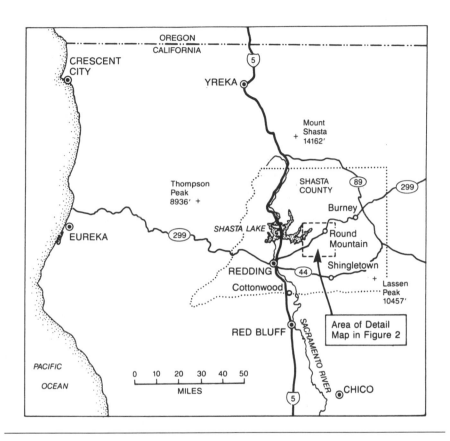

The Northeastern Sector consists of three ecological zones: grassy plains, foot-hills, and mountain forest. The elevation of the land largely determines the boundaries of these zones; the higher the terrain, the more rain it receives, and the cooler its summer weather.

The zone between five hundred and fifteen hundred feet in elevation, the zone closest to Redding, consists of grassy plains. This idyllic, oak-dotted country provides natural pasture during the spring and, if irrigated, can support a herd year-round. A water supply adequate for irrigation is available, however, only near the streams that flow through the area. Moreover, the soil in much of the grassy plains is infertile hardpan. Because of these natural constraints, the full-time ranchers who operate in this zone typically need at least several square miles of pasture.

The foothills lie between fifteen hundred and thirty-five hundred feet in ele-vation. Both Caton's Folly and the Oak Run area fall within this transition zone. Much of the foothill area has a mixed natural treecover of pine and oak. In open areas the natural ground cover is less likely to be grass than an unpalatable chaparral of manzanita, buckbrush, and like shrubs. To foothill ranchers this brush is almost as repulsive a thought as the importation of Australian beef; the more enterprising foothill ranchers spend much of their energies grappling with this foe.

Mountain forest, the third zone, starts at about thirty-five hundred feet. Ponderosa pine, Douglas fir, and other conifers that have supplanted the deciduous oaks cover the mountainsides at this elevation. The mountain forests remain green year-round, but most are too cold in winter and too hard to clear to be suitable sites for cattlemen's base ranches. The Roseburg Lumber Company owns much of the mountain forest in the Northeastern Sector.[19] Like other private timber companies in the county, Roseburg has not shown any interest in subdividing its lands for development. For many decades, however, Roseburg and its predecessors in ownership have leased their forests to Shasta County cattlemen for summer range.

Social Environment

The volatility of population change may affect how people resolve their disputes. Shasta County has experienced rapid population growth. Between 1930 and 1980, the number of county residents increased ninefold,[20] and in the decade from 1970 to 1980, total county population rose from 78,000 to 116,000.[21] The county's population growth rate of 49.0 percent in the 1970s was substantially higher than the overall state rate (18.5 percent), and was somewhat higher than the aggregate rate for California's nonmetropolitan counties (36.4 percent).[22] Redding's location at the northern end of the Central Valley makes it a natural transportation hub. It serves as the gateway to mountain recreation areas lying in three directions, and it has emerged as the major regional center on Interstate 5 between Sacramento, California, and Eugene, Oregon. Many migrants to Shasta County have come from the San Francisco and Los Angeles areas. Indications of social instability have accompanied the influx of migrants. In 1981, Shasta had the highest divorce rate of any county in California,[23] and in 1980, the county's unemployment rate was twice that of the state as a whole.[24]

Precise figures on population trends within the Northeastern Sector are not available. It appears, however, that during the 1970s, the sector's population grew by an even larger percentage than did the county's.[25] Not surprisingly, the recent demographic histories of the three ecological zones within the sector are rather different.

Residential patterns in the grassy plains have not changed much in recent years. Beyond the suburbs of Redding most of the acreage in the grasslands and lower foothills remains divided into ranches at least several square miles in size. Approximately half of these ranches are owned by descendants of families that have been in the county for several generations.[26] Although many of these ranches have a current market value of one million dollars or more, the ranchers typically have modest annual incomes. For decades, ranchlands in Shasta County have generated an annual cash return of only 1 or 2 percent of market value.[27] The cattlemen who own and operate the large family ranches tend to follow self-imposed seven-day-a-week work schedules and live in houses less imposing than

Figure 3.2   Map of the Oak Run/Round Mountain Area

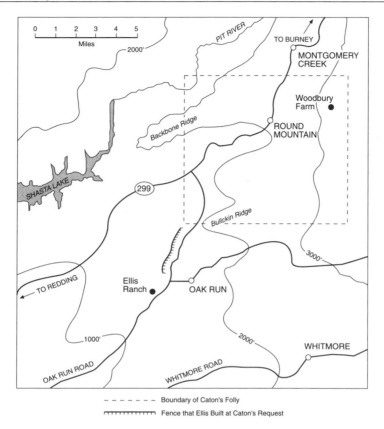

those one would find in an average American suburb. When estate taxes or property taxes have squeezed them financially, ranching families have either conveyed their entire holdings to other ranchers or to investors seeking tax shelters or, more commonly, they have sold tree-covered pieces of their ranches to developers for subdivision into ranchettes.

The foothills have seen more subdivision activity and absolute population growth than have the grassy plains. Both supply and demand conditions explain this pattern. Because the foothills are somewhat less suited than the grasslands for agriculture, foothill landowners are more likely to consider subdividing their holdings. Most homebuyers would also prefer the foothills to the grasslands as a residential location because the higher elevations are cooler in summer and offer more tree cover. As a result, the foothills within commuting distance of

Redding have experienced a multifold increase in population over the past twenty years.[28]

Many of the recent settlers in the foothills are either retirees or younger migrants from California's major urban areas. These newcomers tend to live on minimally improved lots of from five to forty acres, either in owner-built houses or mobile homes. Many of these ranchettes have sprung up near hamlets, such as Oak Run and Round Mountain, that contain a general store, a post office, an elementary school, and other basic community facilities. Despite these clusters of growth, development in the foothills has been rather diffuse. Especially since the mid-1960s, small-scale real estate operatives have subdivided forested areas in every sector of the foothills.[29] Thus virtually all foothill ranchers have some ranchette owners as neighbors. Ranchette owners may keep a farm animal or two as a hobby, but few of them make significant income from agriculture. The ranchette owners nevertheless admire both the cattlemen and the folkways traditionally associated with rural Shasta County.

Work Environment: Modes of Cattle Ranching

Despite their long hours of work, few ranchers in Shasta County find raising beef cattle a road to prosperity. The typical rancher runs a cow-and-calf operation. When his calves are seven to twelve months old, he[30] trucks them a dozen miles south of Redding to the Shasta County Auctionyard at Cottonwood, where each Friday some three thousand head change hands. Agents for feedlot operators and pasture owners buy the calves, take them to feedlots and pastures outside the county, and feed and fatten them for a few months to prepare them for slaughter. In 1982, a six-hundred-pound yearling sold at auction in Cottonwood for about $375, compared to the $500 it would have brought in 1979, the year that nominal beef prices peaked.[31] Not only have beef prices recently failed to match the rate of inflation, but in the 1970s per capita consumption of beef in the United States began to fall.[32] Shasta County is at best marginal cattle country, and some cattlemen there understandably fear that they may be among the casualties in their beleaguered industry's continuing shakeout.

Shasta County cattlemen may be loosely grouped into two categories: the traditionalists and the modernists.[33] Traditionalists tend to be more marginal economically, and have a greater stake in fighting "closed range" ordinances.

The Traditionalists   Traditional Shasta County cattlemen continue to follow the husbandry practices that were nearly universal in the county as late as the 1920s. A traditionalist's trademark is that he lets his cattle roam, essentially untended, in unfenced mountain areas during the summer.[34] This customary practice evolved in response to the severity of Shasta County's dry season. In the area northeast of Redding, a rancher lacking irrigated pasture needs about ten to twenty acres per animal unit[35] for winter and spring pasture. Thus, to support two hundred cattle—a substantial herd by Shasta County standards—a rancher without irrigated pasture needs at least two thousand acres, or just over three square miles of land. During the dry season the brutal heat makes unirrigated grasslands almost worthless. To feed his animals during the summer, a lowland cattleman must therefore either have access to irrigated pasture or be able to move his animals to the high foothills and mountains where cooler dry season temperatures enable natural forage to survive. The traditionalist solution is a summer grazing lease on a large tract of mountain forest.

The United States Forest Service, the Bureau of Land Management (BLM),[36] and major private timber companies have regularly entered into grazing leases with county cattlemen. Although the timber-company grazing leases typically have only a one-year term, the companies have allowed cattlemen to renew them as a matter of course.[37] Federal leases may run for any period up to ten years,[38] and they also tend to be automatically renewable.[39] A cattleman who has been leasing a tract of forest for summer range thus tends to regard the leased tract as a normal part of his operations. Although the forest areas remain green in summer, they contain too few open meadows to support many cattle. Traditionalists may have to lease three hundred acres of forest per animal unit: Thus, a traditionalist with a herd of only one hundred animals may lease during the summer a forest equal in area to the city of San Francisco.

The fencing of these far-flung forest leaseholds has never been cost-justified in the eyes of either the timber owners or their traditionalist lessees. To reduce the risk of livestock trespassing on contiguous lands, forest leasehold boundaries are often drawn to follow natural barriers such as ridges and gulches. But adroit boundary drawing is hardly a foolproof method for controlling strays. Mountain cattle tend to drift down the drainage areas to lower elevations, especially when the weather turns cold or a drought dries the upland creeks. Lessees occasionally erect drift fences across mountain valleys to block the most obvious migration routes. Because drift fences are easily destroyed by winter snows, however, traditionalists often let their animals roam at will in the mountains. Even a forest lessee who has ridden his leasehold periodically during the summer risks being unable to find part of his herd when he gathers his livestock in mid-October. After the October gathering, a traditionalist returns his animals to a base ranch at a lower elevation and feeds them hay or other stored feed for a few months until the winter rains revive the natural grasses on the base ranch pastures.[40]

The Modernists   Modernists among the Shasta County cattlemen keep their livestock behind fences at all times in order to increase their control over their herds. To satisfy the need for summer forage that originally caused traditionalist cattlemen to enter into forest leases, modernists install ditches and sprinklers to irrigate base ranch pastures. One acre of irrigated pasture can support a cow and calf for an entire summer. A modernist who can irrigate about 10 percent of his lands is usually able to run a year-round, fenced operation.[41]

Modernists are more active than traditionalists in managing ranchland vegetation. If not controlled, the native brush that thrives in the foothill zone would consume much of the scarce groundwater and soil nutrients that competing grasses need. Modernist foothill ranchers fight the brush by setting controlled burns, spreading herbicides, and dragging chains from tractors to uproot the larger plants.[42] Using these clearing techniques, leading modernist cattlemen have transformed unproductive foothill areas into valuable pasturelands.

Modernists tend to be younger than traditionalists, have more formal education, and be more active in the Cattlemen's Association. Some modernists view the traditionalists as old-fashioned and primitive. Traditionalists, however, see themselves as the "real" cattlemen—the ones who can recognize a cow at half a mile and sleep out under the stars in the tradition of the nineteenth-century cowboy.

Despite their stylistic differences, modernists and traditionalists have much in common. Members of both groups believe that the life of the cattleman is the best possible in western America. They enjoy riding horses and regularly wearing blue jeans, cowboy hats, and cowboy boots. They regard the late John Wayne as their kind of guy. Although traditionalists have a much greater stake than modernists do in keeping the Board of Supervisors from closing the range, modernist cattlemen typically join the traditionalists in opposing proposed legal changes that would increase the liabilities of owners of stray cattle.

The Benefits and Costs of Boundary Fences

The study of cattle trespass incidents is inevitably a study of fencing. A fence demarcates boundaries, keeps out human and animal trespassers, and keeps in the fencebuilder's own animals. In the Farmer-Rancher Parable, Coase perceived the sole benefit of a fence to be the reduction of trespass damages to crops.[43] In fact, cattlemen enclose their lands largely to prevent damage to their own livestock. Predators, rustlers, winter snows, and poisonous plants such as larkspur all pose potentially lethal threats to cattle roaming unfenced countryside.[44] Cattlemen also worry that a wandering cow will be impregnated by a bull of worthless pedigree. Furthermore, fencing makes it easier for a rancher to provide salt and other useful diet supplements, and to prevent the weight loss likely to occur when cattle walk long distances.

The prices of grazing leases reflect the value that ranchers place on fences. In 1982, fenced land in the Northeastern Sector rented for about ten dollars per animal unit month, whereas unfenced land rented for about three dollars.[45] Because both arrangements yield the same quantity of forage, the rent differential provides a rough measure of how much ranchers value the protection and control that boundary fences provide.[46]

Since 1874, the year J. F. Glidden took out the first patent on barbed wire, the barbed-wire fence has been the standard American technology for enclosing livestock.[47] California's statutory standard for a "lawful fence" was set at the turn of the century. It calls for three tightly stretched strands of barbed wire stapled to posts situated sixteen and one half feet (one rod) apart.[48] Today, Shasta County ranchers tend to use at least four strands of barbed wire[49] and they employ steel posts instead of the cedar posts customarily used earlier in the century.[50]

In 1982, the materials for a new four-strand, barbed-wire fence in Shasta County cost about two thousand dollars per mile. Fence contractors charge at least as much for labor and overhead.[51] Both ranchers and ranchette owners customarily build their own fences and thereby drastically reduce out-of-pocket labor expenditures.[52]

Barbed-wire fences require periodic maintenance, especially in Shasta County, where many natural forces conspire against fence wire. The extreme summer heat loosens the wire while the winter cold pulls it taut. The deer that migrate through the foothills during the wet season are generally able to jump cattle fences; but when a jumping deer fails to clear a fence cleanly, its hoof may break a tightly stretched top wire.[53] Heavy winter rains, rotting posts, downed trees, unruly bulls, or wayward automobiles may also create a breach. A rancher or his hand therefore must spend a few days each spring, either on horseback or in a pickup truck, riding fence. A conscientious rancher also inspects his fences in the fall after the deer season, in part to see what damage trespassing hunters may have inflicted.[54] With emergency repairs needed frequently, fence maintenance chores weigh constantly on a rancher's mind.[55]

Ranchers believe that the many benefits of perimeter barriers outweigh fence construction and maintenance costs. Cattlemen with permanent ranches in either the grasslands or foothills almost invariably have perimeter fences as well as cross fences to divide their spreads into separate pastures. A ranchette owner, however, is unlikely to fence the boundary of his land unless he has livestock. In forest pastures, one observes either no fencing or only an occasional drift fence.[56]

Traditionalists running herds in unfenced mountain forests have provoked most of the closed-range political movements in Shasta County.[57] During the summer months mountain cattle sometimes wander onto rural highways and ravage hay fields and gardens in the settled parts of the foothills. The recent proliferation of ranchettes in the foothills has aggravated these two risks and heightened opposition to the practice of running cattle at large.

THE RESOLUTION OF ANIMAL TRESPASS DISPUTES IN SHASTA COUNTY

This part of this chapter reports the frequency of cattle trespass incidents in Shasta County, discusses residents' knowledge of relevant California trespass law, and recounts how Shasta County neighbors actually resolve their trespass disputes. In the Coasean parable of the farmer and the rancher, the two neighbors both know and honor applicable legal rules. Much of law-and-economic scholarship has similarly assumed that law is efficacious in this way.[58] This part suggests that the assumption of efficacious law is more heroic than certain scholars have realized.

Animal Trespass Incidents

Every landowner interviewed, including all thirteen ranchette owners, reported at least one instance in which his lands had been invaded by someone else's livestock. Hay farmers grow what cattle especially like to eat, and thus expect frequent trespasses.[59] Owners of large ranches are also common victims because they cannot keep their many miles of aging perimeter fence cattle-tight. Thus, when a rancher gathers his animals on his fenced pastures each spring, he is not startled to find a few head carrying his neighbor's brand.

Because cattle eat almost incessantly, a trespass victim's vegetation is always at risk.[60] Nevertheless, a victim usually regards the loss of grass as trivial so long as the owner removes the animals with reasonable promptness—that is, within a day or two if the animals are easy to corral. Trespassing livestock occasionally do cause more than nominal damage. Several ranchette owners reported incidents in which wayward cattle had damaged their fences and vegetable gardens; one farmer told of the ravaging of some of his ornamental trees.

The most serious trespasses reported were ones involving either at-large cattle or bulls. A ranchette owner narrated how mountain cattle had once invaded his house construction site, broken the windows, and contaminated the creek. A part-time horsebreeder told of buying seven tons of hay and stacking it on an unfenced portion of his fifty-acre ranchette near Oak Run. The hay was then eaten by roaming cattle belonging to Frank Ellis, who by the late 1970s was running the largest open-range herds in the foothills.

Rural residents especially fear trespasses by bulls. In a modern beef cattle herd, roughly one animal in twenty-five is a bull, whose principal function is to impregnate cows during their brief periods in heat.[61] Bulls are twice as heavy as the other herd animals,[62] and tend to be much more ornery. Several respondents had vivid memories of bull trespasses. A farmer who owned irrigated pasture was amazed at the depth of the hoof marks that an entering bull made. A ranchette owner and a rancher told of barely escaping goring while attempting to corral invading bulls.[63] Because an alien bull often enters in pursuit of cows in heat, owners of female animals fear illicit couplings that might produce offspring of an undesired pedigree. Although no cow owner reported actual damages from misbreeding, several mentioned that this risk especially worried them.

Knowledge of Animal Trespass Law

Before examining how Shasta County landowners actually resolve their cattle trespass disputes, I describe their working knowledge of the formal rules of trespass law. The extent of their knowledge is relevant for at least two reasons. First, Coase's parable is set in a world of zero transaction costs, where everyone has perfect knowledge of legal rules. In reality, legal knowledge is imperfect because legal research is costly and human cognitive capacities are limited. The following overview of the working legal knowledge of Shasta County residents provides a glimpse at how people behave in the face of these constraints. Analysts interested in designing legal rules to achieve specific instrumental goals must heed data of this sort, because rules cannot have instrumental effects unless they are communicated to the relevant actors. Second, most residents resolve trespass disputes by applying lower-level norms that are consistent with an overarching norm of cooperation among neighbors. To the extent that residents understand that their lower-level norms are inconsistent with formal legal rules, the more notable it is that the norms prevail.

Laymen's Knowledge of Animal Trespass Law   To apply formal legal rules to a specific trespass incident, a Shasta County resident would first have to know whether it had occurred in an open-range or closed-range area of the county. Ideally, the resident would either have or know how to readily locate the map of closed-range areas published by the county's Department of Public Works. Second, a legally sophisticated person would have a working command of the rules of trespass law. In general, in a closed-range area an owner of domestic livestock is strictly liable (that is, liable even in the absence of negligence) for property damage that his animals cause while trespassing. In open-range areas by contrast, a victim of unintentional animal trespass can recover damages only if the victim had protected his lands with a lawful fence.

I found no one in Shasta County—layman or professional—with a complete working knowledge of the formal trespass rules just described. The persons best informed are, interestingly enough, two public officials without legal training: Brad Bogue, the animal control officer, and Bruce Jordan, the brand inspector.[64] Their jobs require them to deal with stray livestock on almost a daily basis. Both have striven to learn applicable legal rules, and both sometimes invoke formal law when mediating disputes between county residents. Both Bogue and Jordan possess copies of the closed-range map and relevant provisions of the California Code. What they do *not* know is the case law; for example, neither is aware of the rule that an intentional trespass is always tortious, even in open range. Nevertheless, Bogue and Jordan, both familiar figures to the cattlemen and (to a lesser extent) the ranchette owners of rural Shasta County, have done more than anyone else to educate the populace about formal trespass law.

What do ordinary rural residents know of that law? To a remarkable degree the landowners I interviewed did know whether their own lands were within open or closed range. Of the twenty-five I asked to identify whether they lived in open or closed range, twenty-one provided the correct answer, including two who were fully aware that they owned land in both.[65] This level of knowledge is probably atypically high.[66] Most of the landowner interviews were conducted in the Round Mountain and Oak Run areas. The former was the site in 1973 of the Caton's Folly closed-range battle. More importantly, Frank Ellis's aggressive herding had provoked a furious closed-range battle in the Oak Run area just six months before I conducted the interviews. Two well-placed sources—the Oak Run postmaster and the proprietress of the Oak Run general store—estimated that this political storm had caught the attention of perhaps 80 percent of the area's adult residents. In the summer of 1982, probably no populace in the United States was more alert to the legal distinction between open and closed range than the inhabitants of Oak Run.[67]

What do laymen know of the substance of trespass law? In particular, what do they know of how the rules vary from open to closed range? Laymen tend to conceive of these legal rules in black-and-white terms: Either the livestock owners or the trespass victims "have the rights." In fact, the law of animal trespass in open range is quite esoteric. Even there, an animal owner is liable, for example, for intentional trespass, trespass through a lawful fence, or trespass by a goat. Only a few rural residents of Shasta County know anything of these subtleties. "Estray" and "lawful fence," central terms in the law of animal trespass, are not words in the cattlemen's everyday vocabulary. Neither of the two most sophisticated open-range ranchers that I interviewed was aware that enclosure by a lawful fence elevates a farmer's rights to recover for trespass. A traditionalist, whose cattle had often caused mischief in the northeastern foothills, thought estrays could never be seized in open range, although a lawful fence gives a trespass victim exactly that entitlement. No interviewee believed that Frank Ellis's intentional herding on his neighbors' lands in open range might have been in excess of his rights.

As most laymen in rural Shasta County see it, trespass law is clear and simple. In closed range, an animal owner is strictly liable for trespass damages. (They of course never used, and would not recognize, the phrase "strict liability.") In open range, their basic premise is that an animal owner is never liable. When I posed hypothetical fact situations designed to put their simple rules under stress, the lay respondents sometimes backpedaled a bit, but they ultimately stuck to the notion that cattlemen have the rights in open range and trespass victims the rights in closed range.

Legal Specialists' Knowledge of Trespass Law   The laymen's penchant for simplicity enabled them to identify correctly the rule of strict liability for cattle trespass that formally applies in closed range. In that regard, the laymen outperformed the "legal specialists"—the judges, attorneys, and insurance adjusters. Although I sought out specialists who I had reason to believe would be knowledgeable about rural legal problems, I found that in two important respects the legal specialists had less working knowledge of trespass and estray rules than did the lay landowners.[68] First, in contrast to the landowners, the legal specialists immediately invoked *negligence* rules when asked to analyze rights in trespass cases. In general, they thought that a cattleman would not be liable for trespass in open range (although about half seemed aware that this result would be affected by the presence of a lawful fence), and that he would be liable *only when negligent* in closed range. The negligence approach has so dominated American tort law during this century that legal specialists—insurance adjusters in particular—may fail to identify narrow pockets where strict liability rules, such as the English rule on cattle trespass, formally apply.[69]

Second, unlike the lay rural residents, the legal specialists knew almost nothing about the location of the closed-range districts in the county.[70] For example, two lawyers who lived in rural Shasta County and raised livestock as a sideline, were ignorant of these boundaries; one incorrectly identified the kind of range in which he lived, and the other admitted he did not know what areas were open or closed. The latter added that this did not concern him because he would fence his lands under either legal regime.

I interviewed four insurance adjusters who settle trespass-damage claims in Shasta County. These adjusters had little working knowledge of the location of closed-range and open-range areas or of the legal significance of those designations. One incorrectly identified Shasta County as an entirely closed-range jurisdiction. Another stated that he did not keep up with the closed-range situation because "closed-range" just signifies places where there are fences, and the fence situation changes too rapidly to be worth following. The other two adjusters knew a bit more about the legal situation. Although neither possessed a closed-range map, they were able to guess how to locate one. On the other hand, both implied that they would not bother to find out whether a trespass incident had occurred in open or closed range before settling a claim. The liability rules that these adjusters apply to routine trespass claims seemed largely independent of formal law.[71]

The Settlement of Trespass Disputes

If Shasta County residents were to try to settle their trespass disputes[72] like the farmer and the rancher in Coase's parable, they would act in the following way.[73] First, they would look to the formal law to determine who had what entitlements. They would then regard those substantive rules as beyond their influence ("exogenous" to use the economists' adjective). When they faced a potentially costly interaction, such as a trespass risk to crops, they would resolve it "in the shadow of"[74] the formal legal rules. Because transactions would be costless, enforcement would be complete: no violation of an entitlement would be ignored. For the same reason, two neighbors who interacted on a number of fronts would resolve their disputes front by front, rather than globally. My findings cast doubt on the realism of each of these implications of the parable. Because Coase himself was fully aware that transactions are costly and thus that the parable was no more than an abstraction, my findings in no way diminish his monumental contribution.[75] The findings may, however, serve as a valuable caution to other law-and-economics scholars who may have underestimated the impact of transaction costs on how the world works.[76]

Norms, Not Legal Rules, Are the Basic Sources of Entitlements
In rural Shasta County, trespass conflicts are generally resolved not "*in* the shadow of the law" but, rather, *beyond* that shadow. Most rural residents are consciously committed to an overarching norm of cooperation among neighbors.[77] In trespass situations, their salient lower-level norm, adhered to by all but a few deviants, is that an owner of livestock is responsible for the acts of his animals. Allegiance to this norm seems wholly independent of formal legal entitlements. Most cattlemen believe that a rancher should keep his animals from eating a neighbor's grass, regardless of whether the range is open or closed. Cattlemen typically couch their justifications for the norm in moral terms:

> Marty Fancher: "Suppose I sat down [uninvited] to a dinner your wife had cooked." Dick Coombs: It "isn't right" to get free pasturage at the expense of one's neighbors. Owen Shellworth: "[My cattle] don't belong [in my neighbor's field]." Attorney-rancher Pete Schultz: A cattleman is "morally obligated to fence" to protect his neighbor's crops, even in open range.

In what follows, I describe in greater detail how the norms of neighborliness operate and how deviants who violate these norms are informally controlled. I also identify another set of deviants: trespass victims who actually invoke their formal legal rights.

Incomplete Enforcement: The Live-and-Let-Live Philosophy
The norm that an animal owner should control his stock is modified by another norm that holds that a rural resident should "lump" minor damage stemming from isolated trespass incidents. The neighborly response to an isolated infraction is an exchange of civilities. A trespass victim should notify the animal owner that the trespass has occurred and assist the owner in retrieving the stray stock. Virtually all residents have telephones, the standard means of communication. A telephone report is regarded not as a form of complaint, but rather as a service to the animal owner, who, after all, has a valuable asset on the loose. Upon receiving a telephone report, a cattleman who is a good neighbor will quickly retrieve the animals (by truck if necessary), apologize for the occurrence, and thank the caller. The Mortons and the Shellworths, two ranching families in the Oak Run area particularly esteemed for their neighborliness, are known for promptly and apologetically responding to their neighbors' notifications of trespass.[78]

Several realities of rural life in Shasta County help explain why residents are expected to "lump" trespass losses. First, it is commonplace for a country land-owner to lose a bit of forage or to suffer minor fence damage. The area northeast of Redding lies on a deer migration route. During the late winter and early spring thousands of deer and elk move through the area, easily jumping the barbed wire fences.[79] Because wild animals trespass so often, most rural residents come to regard minor damage from alien animals not as an injurious event, but as an inevitable part of life.

Second, most residents expect to be on both the giving and receiving ends of trespass incidents. Even the ranchette owners have, if not a few hobby livestock, at least several dogs, which they keep for companionship, security, and pest con-trol. Unlike cattle, dogs that trespass may harass, or even kill, other farm animals. If trespass risks are symmetrical, and if residents lump all trespass losses, accounts balance in the long run. Under these conditions, the advantage of reciprocal lumping is that each person is made whole without having to expend time or money to settle disputes.

The norm of reciprocal restraint that underlies "live-and-let-live" also calls for ranchers to lump the costs of boarding another person's animal, even for months at a time. A cattleman often finds in his herd an animal wearing someone else's brand. If he recognizes the brand he will customarily inform its owner, but the two will often agree that the simplest solution is for the animal to stay put until the trespass victim next gathers his animals, an event that may be weeks or months away. The cost of "cutting" a single animal from a larger herd seems to underlie this custom. Thus, ranchers often consciously provide other people's cattle with feed worth perhaps as much as ten dollars to a hundred dollars per animal. Although Shasta County ranchers tend to regard themselves as finan-cially pinched, even ranchers who know that they are legally entitled to recover feeding costs virtually never seek monetary compensation for boarding estrays. The largest ranchers northeast of Redding who were interviewed reported that they had never charged anyone, or been charged by anyone, for costs of that sort. Even when they do not know to whom a stray animal belongs, they put the animal in their truck the next time they take a load of animals to the auctionyard at Cottonwood, and drop it off without charge so that the brand inspector can locate the owner.[80]

The Complexity of Interneighbor Relations: Comprehensive Mental Accounts of Who Owes Whom   Residents with few animals may of course not perceive any average reciprocity of advantage in a live-and-let-live approach to animal trespass incidents. What if, for example, a particular rancher's livestock repeatedly caused minor mischief in a particular farmer's fields? In that situation, Shasta County norms call for the farmer to keep track of those minor losses in a mental account. Eventually, the norms entitle him to act to remedy any imbal-ance.

A fundamental feature of rural society makes this enforcement system feasible: *Rural residents deal with one another on a large number of fronts, and most residents expect those interactions to continue far into the future.* In sociological terms, their relationships are "multiplex," not "simplex."[81] They interact on water supply, con-trolled burns, fence repairs, social events, staffing the volunteer fire department, and so on. Where population densities are low, each neighbor looms larger. Thus any trespass dispute with a neighbor is almost certain to be but one thread in the rich fabric of a continuing relationship.

A person in a multiplex relationship can keep a rough mental account of the outstanding credits and debits in each aspect of that relationship.[82] Should the aggregate account fall out of balance, tension may mount because the net creditor may begin to perceive the net debtor as an overreacher. On the other hand, so long as the aggregate account is in balance, neither party need be concerned that particular subaccounts are not. For example, if a rancher were to owe a farmer in the trespass subaccount, the farmer can be expected to remain content if that imbalance were to be offset by a debt he owed the rancher in, say, the watersupply subaccount.[83]

The live-and-let-live norm also suggests that neighbors should put up with minor imbalances in their aggregate accounts, especially when they perceive that their future interactions will provide adequate opportunities for settling old scores. Creditors may prefer having others in their debt. For example, when Larry Brennan lost six to seven tons of baled hay to Frank Ellis's cattle in open range, Brennan (although he did not know it) had a strong legal claim against Ellis for intentional trespass. Brennan estimated his loss at between $300 and $500, hardly a trivial amount. When Ellis learned of Brennan's loss he told Brennan to "come down and take some hay" from his barn. Brennan declined this offer of compensation, partly because he thought he should not have piled the bales in an unfenced area, but also because, to paraphrase his words, he would rather have Ellis in debt to him than be in debt to Ellis. Brennan was willing to let Ellis run up a deficit in their aggregate interpersonal accounts because he thought that as a creditor he would have more leverage over Ellis's future behavior.

The Control of Deviants: The Key Role of Self-help

The rural Shasta County population includes deviants who do not adequately control their livestock and do not adequately balance their informal accounts with their neighbors. Frank Ellis, for example, seemed to care little about his reputation among his neighbors. In general, the traditionalists who let their animals loose in the mountains during the summer are less scrupulous than the modernists are in honoring the norms of neighborliness, perhaps because the traditionalists have less complex, and shorter-lived, interrelationships with the persons who encounter their range cattle.

To discipline deviants, the residents of rural Shasta County use the following four types of countermeasures, listed in escalating order of seriousness: (1) self-help retaliation; (2) reports to county authorities; (3) claims for compensation informally submitted without the help of attorneys; and (4) formal legal claims to recover damages. The law starts to gain bite as one moves down this list.

Because most trespass disputes in Shasta County are resolved according to extralegal rules, the fundamental enforcement device is also extralegal. A measured amount of self-help—just enough to "get even," to invoke a marvelously apt phrase—is the predominant and ethically preferred response to someone who has not taken adequate steps to prevent his animals from trespassing.[84]

The mildest form of self-help is negative gossip.[85] This usually works because only the extreme deviants are immune from the general obsession with neighborliness. Although the Oak Run–Round Mountain area is undergoing a rapid increase in population, it remains distinctly rural in atmosphere. People tend to know one another, and they value their reputations in the community. Some ranching families have lived in the area for several generations and plan to stay indefinitely. Members of these families seem particularly intent on maintaining their reputations as good neighbors. Should one of them not promptly and courteously retrieve an estray, he might fear that any resulting gossip would permanently besmirch the family name.

Residents of the northeastern foothills seem quite conscious of the role of gossip in their system of social control. One longtime resident, who had also lived for many years in a suburb of a major California urban area, observed that people in the Oak Run area "gossip all the time," much more than in the urban area. Another reported intentionally using gossip to sanction a traditionalist who had been "impolite" when coming to pick up some stray mountain cattle; he reported that application of this self-help device produced an apology, an outcome itself presumably circulated through the gossip system.

The furor over Frank Ellis's loose cattle in the Oak Run area induced area residents to try a sophisticated variation of the gossip sanction. The ranchette residents who were particularly bothered by Ellis's cattle could see that he was utterly indifferent to his reputation among them. On the other hand, they thought that a large rancher such as Ellis would worry about his reputation among the large cattle operators in the county. They therefore reported Ellis's activities to the Board of Directors of the Shasta County Cattlemen's Association. This move proved unrewarding, for Ellis was also surprisingly indifferent to his reputation among the cattlemen. As the association president later explained in a hearing before the county Board of Supervisors, the problem was that Ellis, a county resident for a decade, "hasn't been [in the County] all that long."

When milder measures such as gossip fail, a person is regarded as being justified in threatening to use, and perhaps even actually using, tougher self-help sanctions. Particularly in unfenced country, a victim may respond to repeated cattle trespasses by herding the offending animals to a location extremely inconvenient for their owner.[86] Another common response to repeated trespasses is to threaten to kill a responsible animal should it ever enter again. Although the killing of trespassing livestock is a crime in California,[87] six landowners—not noticeably less civilized than the others—unhesitatingly volunteered that they had issued death threats of this sort. These threats are credible in Shasta County, because victims of recurring trespasses, particularly if they have first issued a warning, feel justified in killing or injuring the mischievous animals. Despite the criminality of the conduct (a fact not necessarily known to the respondents), I learned the identity of two persons who had shot trespassing cattle. Another landowner told of running the steer of an uncooperative neighbor into a fence. The most intriguing report came from a rancher who had had recurrent problems with a trespassing bull many years ago. This rancher told a key law enforcement official that he wanted to castrate the bull—"to turn it into a steer." The official replied that he "would have deaf ears" if that were to occur. The rancher asserted that he then carried out his threat.

It is difficult to estimate how frequently rural residents actually resort to violent self-help. Nevertheless, fear of physical retaliation is undoubtedly one of the major incentives for order in rural Shasta County. Ranchers who run herds at large freely admit that they worry that their trespassing cattle might meet with violence. One traditionalist reported that he is responsive to complaints from ranchette owners because he fears they will poison or shoot his stock. A judge for a rural district of the county asserted that a vicious animal is likely to "disappear" if its owner does not control it. A resident of the Oak Run area stated that some area residents responded to Frank Ellis's practice of running herds at large by rustling Ellis's cattle. He suggested that Ellis prepare a T-shirt with the following inscription: "Eat Ellis Beef. Everyone in Oak Run Does!"

The long-time ranchers of Shasta County pride themselves on being able to resolve their problems on their own.[88] Except when they lose animals to rustlers, they do not seek help from public officials. Although ranchette owners also use the self-help remedies of gossip and violence, they, unlike the cattlemen, sometimes respond to a trespass incident by contacting a county official who they think will remedy the problem. These calls are usually funneled to the animal control officer or brand inspector, who report that most of their callers are ranchette owners with limited rural experience. These calls do produce results. The county officials typically contact the owner of the animal, who then arranges for its removal. Brad Bogue, the animal control officer, reported that in half the cases the caller knows whose animal it is. This suggests that callers often think that requests for removal have more effect when issued by someone in authority.

Mere removal of an animal may provide only temporary relief if its owner is a mountain lessee whose cattle repeatedly descend upon the ranchettes. County officials therefore use mild threats to caution repeat offenders. In closed range, they may mention both their power to impound the estrays and the risk of criminal prosecution. These threats appear to be bluffs; the county never impounds stray cattle when it can locate an owner, and it rarely prosecutes cattlemen (and then only when their animals have posed risks to motorists). In open range, county officials may deliver a more subtle threat: not that they will initiate a prosecution, but that, if the owner does not mend his ways, the Board of Supervisors may face insuperable pressure to close the range in the relevant area. Because cattlemen perceive that a closure significantly diminishes their legal entitlements in situations where motorists have collided with their livestock, this threat can catch their attention.

A trespass victim's most effective official protest is one delivered directly to his elected county supervisor—the person best situated to change stray-cattle liability rules. Many Shasta County residents are aware that traditionalist cattlemen fear the supervisors more than they fear law enforcement authorities. Thus in 1973, alfalfa farmer John Woodbury made repeated phone calls about mountain cattle not to Brad Bogue but to Supervisor John Caton. When a supervisor receives many calls from trespass victims, his first instinct is to mediate the crisis. Former Supervisor Norman Wagoner's standard procedure was to assemble the ranchers in the area and advise them to put pressure on the offender or else risk the closure of the range. Wagoner's successor, Supervisor John Caton, similarly told Frank Ellis that he would support a closure at Oak Run unless Ellis built three miles of fence along the Oak Run Road. If a supervisor is not responsive to a constituent's complaint, the constituent may respond by circulating a closure petition.

Because Shasta County residents tend to settle their trespass disputes beyond the shadow of the law, one might expect that the norms of neighborliness would include a norm against the invocation of formal legal rights. And this norm is indeed strongly established.[89] Owen Shellworth: "I don't believe in lawyers [because there are] always hard feelings [when you litigate]." Tony Morton: "[I never press a monetary claim because] I try to be a good neighbor." Norman Wagoner: "Being good neighbors means no lawsuits." Although trespasses are frequent, *Shasta County's rural residents virtually never file formal trespass actions against one another.* John Woodbury, for example, made dozens of phone calls to Supervisor John Caton but never sought monetary compensation from the traditionalists whose cattle had repeatedly marauded his alfalfa field. Court records and conversations with court clerks indicate that in most years not a single private lawsuit is filed in the county's courts seeking damages for either trespass by livestock or the expense of boarding estrays.[90] The residents of the northeastern foothills not only refrain from filing formal lawsuits, but they are also strongly disinclined to submit informal monetary claims to an owner of trespassing animals or that owner's insurance company.[91]

The landowners who were interviewed clearly regard their restraint in seeking monetary relief as a mark of virtue. When asked why they did not pursue meritorious legal claims arising from trespass or fence-finance disputes, various landowners replied: "I'm not that kind of guy"; "I don't believe in it"; "I don't like to create a stink"; "I try to get along." The landowners who attempted to provide a rationale for this forbearance all implied the same one, a long-term reciprocity of advantage. Ann Kershaw: "The only one that makes money [when you litigate] is the lawyer." Al Levy: "I figure it will balance out in the long run." Pete Schultz: "I hope they'll do the same for me." Phil Ritchie: "My family believes in 'live and let live.'"

Mutual restraint saves parties with long-term relationships the costs of going through the formal claims process. Adjoining landowners who practice live-and-let-live are both better off whenever the negative externalities from their activities are roughly in equipoise. Equipoise is as likely in closed-range as in open. Landowners with property in closed-range—the ones with the greatest formal legal rights—were the source of half of the quotations in the prior two paragraphs.

Shasta County landowners regard a monetary settlement as an arms-length transaction that symbolizes an unneighborly relationship. Should your goat happen to eat your neighbor's tomatoes, the neighborly thing for you to do would be to help replant the tomatoes; a transfer of money would be too cold and too impersonal.[92] When Kevin O'Hara's cattle went through a break in a fence and destroyed his neighbor's corn crop (a loss of less than a hundred dollars), O'Hara had to work hard to persuade his neighbor to accept O'Hara's offer of money damages. O'Hara insisted on making this payment because he "felt responsible" for his neighbor's loss, a feeling that would not have been in the least affected had the event occurred in open instead of closed range. There can also be social pressure against offering money settlements. Bob Bosworth's father agreed many decades ago to pay damages to a trespass victim in a closed-range area just south of Shasta County; other cattlemen then rebuked him for setting an unfortunate precedent. The junior Bosworth, currently president of the Shasta County Cattlemen's Association, could recall no other out-of-pocket settlement in a trespass case.

Trespass victims who sustain an unusually large loss are more likely to take the potentially deviant step of making a claim for monetary relief. I interviewed adjusters for the two insurance companies whose liability policies would be most likely to cover losses from animal trespass. The adjusters' responses suggest that in a typical year these companies receive fewer than ten trespass damage claims originating in Shasta County. In the paradigmatic case, the insured is not a rancher, but rather a ranchette owner whose family's horse escaped and trampled a neighboring homeowner's shrubbery. The claimant is typically not represented by an attorney—a type of professional these adjusters rarely encounter. The adjusters also settle each year two or three trespass claims that homeowners or ranchette owners have brought against ranchers. Ranchers who suffer trespasses virtually never file claims against others' insurance companies. An adjuster for the company that insures most Shasta County ranchers stated that he could not recall, in his twenty years of adjusting, a single rancher's claim for compensation for trespass damage.

The landowners, particularly the ranchers, express a strong aversion to hiring an attorney to fight their battles. To hire an attorney is to escalate a conflict. A good neighbor does not do such a thing because the "natural working order" calls for two neighbors to work out their problems between themselves. The files in the Shasta County courthouses reveal that the ranchers who honor norms of neighborliness—the vast majority—are simply not involved in cattle-related litigation of any kind.

My field research uncovered two instances in which animal trespass victims in the Oak Run–Round Mountain area had turned to attorneys. In one of these cases the victim actually filed a formal complaint. Because attorney-backed claims are so unusual, these two disputes deserve elaboration.

The first dispute involved Tom Hailey and Curtis McCall. For three generations, Hailey's family has owned a large tract of foothill forest in an open-range area near Oak Run. In about 1978 Hailey discovered McCall's cattle grazing on some of Hailey's partially fenced land. Hailey suspected that McCall had brought the animals in through a gate in Hailey's fence. When Hailey confronted him, McCall, who lived about a mile away, acted as if the incursion had been accidental. Hailey subsequently found a salt block on the tract—an object he could fairly assume that McCall had put there to service his herd. Hailey thus concluded that McCall had not only deliberately trespassed but had also aggravated the offense by untruthfully denying the charge. Hailey seized the salt block and consulted an attorney, who advised him to seek compensation from McCall. The two principals eventually agreed to a small monetary settlement.

Hailey is a semiretired government employee who spends much of his time outside of Shasta County; he is regarded as reclusive and eccentric—certainly someone outside the mainstream of Oak Run society. McCall, a retired engineer with a hard-driving style, moved to Shasta County in the late 1970s to run a small livestock ranch. The Haileys refer to him as a "Texan"—a term that connotes someone who is both an outsider and lacks neighborly instincts.

The second dispute involved Doug Heinz and Frank Ellis. Heinz had the misfortune of owning a ranchette near Ellis's ranch. After experiencing repeated problems with Ellis's cattle, Heinz unilaterally seized three of the animals that had broken through his fence. Heinz boarded these animals for three months without notifying Ellis. Heinz later asserted he intended to return them when Ellis next held a roundup. According to Heinz, Ellis eventually found out that Heinz had the animals and asked for their return. Heinz agreed to return them if Ellis would pay pasturage. When Ellis replied, "You know I'm good for it," Heinz released the animals and sent Ellis a bill. Ellis refused to pay the bill, and he further infuriated Heinz by calling him "boy" whenever Heinz brought up the debt.

On January 8, 1981, Heinz filed a small-claims action against Ellis to recover $750 "for property damage, hay and grain ate [sic] by defendant's cattle, boarding of animals."[93] Acting through the attorney he kept on retainer, Ellis responded eight days later with a separate civil suit against Heinz.[94] Ellis's complaint sought $1,500 compensatory and $10,000 punitive damages from Heinz for the shooting deaths of two Black Brangus cows that Ellis had pastured on BLM lands; it also sought compensation for the weight loss Ellis's three live animals had sustained during the months Heinz had been feeding them. The two legal actions were later consolidated. Heinz, who called Ellis's allegation that Heinz had killed two cows "100 percent lies" and "scare tactics," hired a bright young Redding attorney to represent him. This attorney threatened to pursue a malicious prosecution action against Ellis if Ellis persisted in asserting that Heinz had slain the Black Brangus cows. In December 1981, the parties agreed to a settlement under the terms of which Ellis paid Heinz $300 in damages and $100 for attorney fees. Ellis's insurance company picked up the tab. By that time Heinz was spearheading a political campaign to close the range Ellis had been using.

The Heinz-Ellis and Hailey-McCall disputes share several characteristics. Although both arose in open range, in each instance legal authority favored the trespass victim: Hailey, because McCall's trespass had been intentional; and Heinz, because Ellis's animals had broken through an apparently lawful fence.[95] In both instances, the victim, before consulting an attorney, had attempted to obtain informal satisfaction but had been rebuffed. Each victim perceived that the animal owner had not been honest. Each dispute was ultimately settled in the victim's favor. In both instances, neither the trespass victim nor the cattle owner was well-socialized in rural Shasta County norms. Thus other respondents tended to refer to the four individuals involved in these two claims as "bad apples," "odd ducks," or otherwise as people not aware of the natural working order. Ordinary people, it seems, do not often turn to attorneys to help resolve disputes.[96]

SUMMARY AND IMPLICATIONS

Coase's Parable of the Farmer and the Rancher, like most writing in law and economics, implies that disputants look solely to formal legal rules to determine their entitlements. In rural Shasta County, California, residents instead typically look to informal norms to determine their entitlements in animal trespass situations. In open-range areas, the norm that a livestock owner should supervise his animals dominates the legal rule that a cattleman is not legally liable for unintentional trespasses on unfenced land. Trespass victims mainly employ negative gossip and physical reprisals against trespassing stock to discipline cattlemen who violate this norm.

In Shasta County, the law of trespass had no apparent feedback effects on trespass norms. In no instance did the legal designation of an area as open (or closed) range affect how residents resolved a trespass or estray dispute. Thus rancher Kevin O'Hara paid a neighbor for the loss of a corn crop because he "felt responsible," a feeling he said would not have been influenced by formal trespass law. Being located in closed range did not appear to make a trespass victim more likely to perceive a grievance or to exercise self-help. Insurance adjusters paid virtually no attention to the distinction between open range and closed range when settling trespass claims.

Other findings suggest the unreality of other literal features of the Coasean parable. Victims of stray cattle did not treat the formal legal rules as exogenous; they were aware that one way to use limited resources is to lobby for legal change. Victims' enforcement of their norm-based entitlements was far from complete; they ignored some trespasses altogether and used others to offset outstanding informal debts. Victims tended to shun monetary settlements and instead preferred in-kind transfers, including ones effected through self-help. Although these findings are at odds with the literal features of the Coasean parable, they are fully consistent with Coase's central idea that, regardless of the specific content of law, people tend to structure their affairs to their mutual advantage.

The Shasta County evidence suggests that law-and-economics scholars need to pay more heed to how transaction costs influence the resolution of disputes. Because it is costly to carry out legal research and to engage in legal proceedings, a rational actor often has good reason to apply informal norms, not law, to evaluate the propriety of human behavior. Contracts scholars have long known that norms are likely to be especially influential when disputants share a continuing relationship.[97] A farmer and a rancher who own adjoining lands are enduringly intertwined, and therefore readily able to employ nonlegal methods of dispute resolution. Law-and-economics scholars misdirect their readers and students when they invoke examples—such as the Parable of the Farmer and the Rancher—that greatly exaggerate the domain of human activity upon which the law casts a shadow.

My debts are many. Jerry Anderson, Thomas Hagler, and Keith Kelly were able research assistants. Participants in workshops at the Boston University, Harvard, Stanford, and Yale Law Schools provided helpful suggestions. Financial support was received from the Stanford Legal Research Fund, made possible by a bequest from the estate of Ira S. Lillick, and by gifts from Roderick E. and Carla A. Hills and other friends of the Stanford Law School. Dozens of people in Shasta County were of immeasurable assistance. I especially thank Bob Bosworth, the President of the Shasta County Cattleman's Association, and Walt Johnson, the county Farm Advisor, for easing immersion into Shasta County life.

NOTES

This is an abridged version of an article originally published in the *Stanford Law Review* (vol. 38, February 1986). Sections II and III of the article ("The Politics of Cattle Trespass in the Northeastern Foothills" and "Research Methods") and their accompanying footnotes have been deleted from this version, as has the subsection, "Animal Trespass Law," of the chapter's original Section IV ("The Resolution of Animal Trespass Disputes in Shasta County").

A few stylistic notes are in order. Except for public figures the names used are pseudonyms. To reduce clutter, and sometimes to protect privacy, I have generally refrained from footnoting references to individual interviews. The present tense usually denotes the situation in Shasta County in 1982, the year in which I conducted most of my interviews.

1. Coase, *The Problem of Social Cost*, 3 J.L. & Econ. 1 (1960).

2. Some recent landmarks in the Coase Theorem literature are Cooter, *The Cost of Coase*, 11 J. Legal Stud. 1 (1982); Hoffman & Spitzer, *The Coase Theorem: Some Experimental Tests*, 25 J.L. & Econ. 73 (1982); Regan, *The Problem of Social Cost Revisited*, 15 J.L. & Econ. 427 (1972). A central theme of these articles is that Coase should have explicitly recognized the possibility that disputants may act strategically and thereby fail to carry out mutually advantageous exchanges. An unusually complete review of the literature is provided by Zerbe, *The Problem of Social Cost in Retrospect*, 2 Research in J. L. & Econ. 83 (1980).

3. *See* Coase, *supra* note 1, at 15–19 (titled "The Cost of Market Transactions Taken into Account").
   Ronald Coase has in fact been a militant for the cause of empiricism. In recent years, he seems to have become increasingly frustrated with the sterility of the abstract debates over his theorem:

   > [W]hile considerations of what would happen in a world of zero transaction costs can give us valuable insights, these insights are, in my view, without value except as steps on the way to the analysis of the real world of positive transaction costs. We do not do well to devote ourselves to a detailed study of the world of zero transaction costs, like augurs divining the future by the minute inspection of the entrails of a goose.

   Coase, *The Coase Theorem and the Empty Core: A Comment*, 24 J.L. & Econ. 183, 187 (1981).

   The central finding of the present work is that the residents of Shasta County often succeed, without the involvement of the state, in coordinating with one another in a mutually advantageous way. Coase's Parable of the Farmer and the Rancher sounds this same general theme of cooperative interaction. This finding is generally consistent with what Coase found in his own microscopic investigation of the supply of lighthouses in England. *See* Coase, *The Lighthouse in Economics*, 17 J.L. & Econ. 357 (1974).

4. Several of Coase's colleagues at the University of Chicago wedded themselves to this assumption in the 1960s. *See*, for example, W. Blum & H. Kalven, Public Law Perspectives on a Private Law Problem: Auto Compensation Plans 58–59 (1965); Demsetz, *When Does the Rule of Liability Matter*, 1 J. Legal Stud. 13, 16 (1972) (transaction costs "would seem to be negligible" when a baseball player negotiates with his club).
   The current consensus, even among Chicagoans, is that negotiations in bilateral monopoly situations can be costly because the parties may act strategically. *See*, for example, R. Posner, Economic Analysis of Law 45 (2d ed. 1977); Cooter, Marks & Mnookin, *Bargaining in the Shadow of the Law: A Testable Model of Strategic Behavior*, 11 J. Legal Stud. 225, 242–44 (1982) ("The obstacle to agreement is the strategic nature of bargaining, not the cost of communicating"); Landes & Posner, *Salvors, Finders, Good Samaritans, and Other Rescuers: An Economic Study of Altruism*, 7 J. Legal Stud. 83, 91 (1978) ("transaction costs under bilateral monopoly are high"). *See also* sources cited at note 2 *supra*.

5. The terms "closed-range" and "open-range" can be a source of confusion. I use the terms throughout this article as they are ordinarily used in Shasta County, to denote the *legal regime* applicable to a particular territory. The potential confusion arises because the terms might be construed as indicating a *method of husbandry*—that is, whether in a particular area it is the custom of cattlemen to run their animals at large or to keep them behind fences. In Shasta

County, the correlation between legal regime and method of husbandry is rather weak. For example, most ranchers in the open-range areas of the county keep their herds behind fences.

6. To invoke Calabresi & Melamed's fruitful typology, a closed-range ordinance essentially shifts the legal regime from property-rule protection of the rancher to liability-rule protection of the trespass victim. *See* Calabresi & Melamed, *Property Rules, Liability Rules, and Inalienability: One View of the Cathedral,* 85 Harv. L. Rev. 1089, 1105–1115 (1972). Hoffman & Spitzer, note 2 *supra,* at 84, deserve credit for noting that Coase had contrasted asymmetrical legal positions.

7. A number of other law-and-economics scholars have investigated empirically the impact of transaction costs on interneighbor coordination. *See,* for example, Cheung, *The Fable of the Bees: An Economic Investigation,* 16 J.L. & Econ. 11 (1973); Crocker, *Externalities, Property Right, and Transactions Costs: An Empirical Study,* 14 J.L. & Econ. 451 (1971). The study closest to mine in its substantive focus, although not its methodology, is Vogel, *The Effect of Changes in Property Rights Entitlements on Production: The Coase Theorem and California Animal Trespass Law,* 15 J. Legal Stud.—(1986) (forthcoming) (regression analysis of effects of various closed-range ordinances on agricultural production in California counties between 1850 and 1877).

   In recent years Elizabeth Hoffman and Matthew Spitzer have been the most persistent and creative transaction costs empiricists. *See,* for example, Hoffman & Spitzer, *supra* note 2 (report on a series of laboratory experiments in which subjects could achieve gains by cooperating); Spitzer & Hoffman, *A Reply to Kelman's "Consumption Theory, Production Theory, and Ideology in the Coase Theorem,"* 53 S. Cal. L. Rev. 1187 (1980) (study of the effect of the elimination of the Reserve Clause on the movement of baseball players between clubs).

8. Any discussion of a chasm between academic subcultures brings to mind C.P. Snow's classic 1959 lecture on "The Two Cultures." Snow used as his polar opposites literary intellectuals and physical scientists, and speculated on whether social scientists represented yet a third culture. C.P. Snow, The Two Cultures: and a Second Look 70–71 (1964). The chasm that I identify is a division *between* groups of social scientists. It suggests that Snow was understandably in a quandary about how to classify members of the social scientific disciplines.

9. The core journals are the Journal of Law and Economics and the Law & Society Review.

10. I borrow the term "microscopic" from Clifford Geertz, an anthropologist noted for his devotion to "thick descriptions" of human interaction. *See,* for example, C. Geertz, The Interpretation of Cultures 3–30 (1973).

11. In preparing his classic article, *Non-Contractual Relations in Business: A Preliminary Study,* 28 Am. Soc. Rev. 55 (1963), Macaulay interviewed business executives and lawyers to find out how Wisconsin manufacturing firms resolve contractual disputes. Ross's best known work is H. Ross, Settled Out of Court (rev. ed. 1980), which describes how insurance adjusters process claims covered under automobile liability policies. Notable also is Ross & Littlefield, *Complaint as a Problem Solving Mechanism,* 12 Law & Soc'y Rev. 199 (1978), a study of how a large appliance retailer in Denver handles consumer complaints.

   Law-and-society scholars have done relatively little field work on dispute resolution between adjoining landowners. *But see,* for example, Baumgartner, *Social Control in Suburbia,* in 2 Toward a General Theory of Social Control 79 (D. Black ed. 1984); Ruffini, *Disputing over Livestock in Sardinia,* in The Disputing Process: Law in Ten Societies 209 (L. Nader & H. Todd eds. 1978) (finding that shepherds in Sardinia rely on self-help, not formal legal processes, to resolve rustling disputes). Economists have also done little field work on relations among neighbors. *But see* sources in the first paragraph of note 7 *supra.*

   There is a broad interdisciplinary perception that progress in understanding conflict resolution depends upon more low-level empirical work. *See,* for example, R. Hardin, Collective Action 229–30 (1982) (comments of a philosopher-game theorist). *See also* Felstiner, *Influences of Social Organization on Dispute Processing,* 9 Law & Soc'y Rev. 63, 86 n.28 (1974) ("Ironically, we have better data about dispute processing in Indian villages, Mexican towns, and East African tribes than we have about that process in American communities." (comments of a law-and-society scholar)).

12. *See* note 3 *supra* and accompanying text.

13. *Record Searchlight* (Redding, Cal.), Aug. 11, 1982, at 15, col. 1.

14. In July, the city's average daily high temperature is 98 degrees. *Id.* at 14, col. 3.

15. Of the 2.4 million acres of land in Shasta County, 1.3 million have been identified as "commercial forest." Cal. Dep't of Finance, Cal. Statistical Abstract 2, 129 (1983). The United States Forest Service owns 35 percent of this commercial forest, and forest industry companies own 46 percent. *Id.* at 129.

16. *Id.* at 111 (citing data from the 1978 U.S. Census of Agriculture).

17. *Id.* at 2, 111.

18. E. Peterson, In the Shadow of the Mountain: A Short History of Shasta County, California 110 (1965).   Coase's parable involves a pasture adjoining a field of annually harvested crops. These land uses are rarely contiguous in Shasta County. The lessons of the parable, however, in no way depend on how the rancher's neighbor uses his land.

19. The Roseburg Lumber Company is a closely held corporation based in Roseburg, Oregon. It is controlled by Kenneth Ford, a self-made man whom *Forbes* magazine has listed as one of the forty wealthiest persons in the United States. *San Francisco Chronicle*, Aug. 28, 1982, at 14, col. 4. When Roseburg purchased its forests in the Northeastern sector in 1979 from the Kimberly-Clark Corporation, it became the fourth timber company to own these lands since the early 1940s.

20. In 1930, the county's population was 13,927. U.S. Dept. of Commerce, Bureau of the Census, 15th Census of the United States, vol. 3, pt. 1, at 284 (1932).

21. U.S. Dept. of Commerce, Bureau of the Census, 1980 Census of Population, vol. 1, pt. 6, ch. A. table 4 (1982). In 1980, 42,000 people lived in the city of Redding. *Id.* By 1984, the city's estimated population exceeded fifty thousand, and Shasta County achieved the status of a Standard Metropolitan Statistical Area.

22. Calculated from data in the 1980 Census of Population.

23. In 1981, Shasta County had 8.7 dissolutions and nullities of marriage per one thousand estimated persons, compared to a statewide figure of 5.8 per thousand. State of Cal. Dep't of Health Servs., Vital Statistics of California—1981, at 128 (1983).

24. Census data put the county's unemployment rate at 13.8 percent, compared to the state's 6.5 percent. U.S. Dep't of Commerce, Bureau of the Census, 1980 Census of Population and Housing, Advance Estimates of Social, Economic, and Housing Characteristics. The timber industry, an important factor in the Shasta County economy, was in a deep slump in 1980, a factor that no doubt contributed to this disparity.

25. The population of what the Census Bureau calls the Central Shasta division increased from 3,049 in 1970 to 6,784 in 1980, or by 122 percent. U.S. Dep't of Commerce, Bureau of the Census, 1980 Census of Population, vol. 1, pt. 6, ch. A, table 4, n.41 (1982). This division includes both the Northeastern Sector and larger rural territories to the north, south, and southeast.

26. The first pioneers to settle east and northeast of Redding used the grasslands and lower foothills to raise livestock. The descendants of the nineteenth century pioneer families—Coombs, Donaldson, Wagoner—still hold a special place in rural Shasta County society. Oldtimers are quick to identify their roots in the county, and sometimes refer to families who arrived a generation ago as "people who haven't been here very long."
     Prior to the 1920s, the Southern Pacific Railroad owned alternate sections in the grassy plains—a reward from the United States for laying track to Redding. The government grant consisted of alternate sections for a distance of 20 miles on both side of the track. S. Daggett, Chapters on the History of the Southern Pacific 50, 122 (1922). During the 1920s, the Southern Pacific sold off most of its grassland sections at the then market price of $2.50 to $5.00 per acre, thereby enabling the pioneer ranching families to consolidate their holdings. Abandoning their prior practice of running their herds at large, these families erected fences around their multi-thousand-acre spreads, cleared patches of brush, and began to irrigate their better pastures.

27. Interview with Robert Shaw, Redding-based appraiser (July 19, 1982). Mr. Shaw attributed the low returns to tax benefits and psychic income that ranching confers.

    Cattle ranching is noted for skimpy financial returns. *See* Arthur D. Little, Inc., Final Environmental Statement, Proposed Livestock Grazing Program, BLM Cerbat/Black Mountains Planning Units II-139 to -142 (1978) (returns to cattle ranching in Arizona range from negative to a positive 1 to 2 percent; ranchers do it for love); Charlier, *Home on the Range is a Part-Time Deal for Many Cowboys. Wall Street Journal*, Jan. 8, 1985, at 1, col. 4.

28. Some of the new development has been for second homes. Celebrities such as baseball pitcher Vida Blue, actor Clint Eastwood, country singer Merle Haggard, and ex-congressman Pete McCloskey are among those who have purchased properties in the rural areas east of Redding.

29. John Williams of the Redding office of the Title Insurance & Trust Co. generously permitted me to use the firm's tract indexes. These indexes showed that in 24 sections near the southern border of Caton's Folly, the number of land parcels increased from 61 in 1930, to 145 in 1972, to 295 in 1982.

    Countywide, the number of land parcels quadrupled between 1967 and 1982. Interview with Tony Estacio, Chief, Administrative Services, Assessor's Office of Shasta County (July 8, 1982). These recent rates of parcelization appear atypically high for rural land markets. *See* R. Healy & J. Short, The Market for Rural Land 22 (1976) (in only one of five counties studied did the number of rural land parcels double between 1954 and 1976).

30. Although women own, manage, and provide most of the physical labor on a number of the ranches in Shasta County, rural culture generally supports the differentiation of sex roles. Thus a woman rancher who wishes to be active in the county Cattlemen's Association is likely to participate only in the CowBelles, the women's auxilliary. The National Cattlemen's Association did recently elect its first woman president, JoAnn Smith, but she had come to prominence by serving as president of the Florida CowBelles. *New York Times*, Apr. 24, 1985, at C1, col. 1.

31. *See San Francisco Chronicle*, Aug. 26, 1982, at 38, col. 2.

32. Per capita beef consumption peaked at 95.7 lbs. in 1976, and by 1981 had fallen to 78.3 lbs., as consumers shifted toward poultry and pork. *New York Times*, Aug. 9, 1981, § IV, at 22, col. 3.

33. These categories inevitably oversimplify. For example, Dick Coombs and Chuck Searle employ modernist land-management and husbandry practices, yet continue the traditionalist practice of leasing mountain forest for summer range.

34. The classic study of cattlemen operating on unfenced range is E. Osgood, The Day of the Cattleman (1929) (emphasizing practices in Wyoming and Montana during the latter part of the Nineteenth Century). On the history of traditionalist practices in California, see R. Cleland, The Cattle on a Thousand Hills (2d ed. 1951); D. Dary, Cowboy Culture 44–66 (1981).

35. An "animal unit" is a mature cow plus calf, or the equivalent in terms of forage consumption. A horse converts to 1.25 animal units, a sheep to 0.2 animal units, and so on. An "animal unit month" (AUM) is the amount of forage an animal unit consumes in one month of grazing. H. Heady, Rangeland Management 117 (1975).

36. These two agencies manage most of the vast federal holdings in the county. Altogether, federal agencies own 42 percent of the county's acreage. Walter H. Johnson, *Agriculture as a Competitor for Land*, in Economic Competition for Land: Shasta County 48 (Univ. of Cal., Agric. Extension Serv. 1966).

37. A specialist in brokering private grazing leases stated that most of his landowner-lessee relationships had endured for decades. Interview with Jim Cochran, Wm. Beatty & Assocs., in Redding, Ca. (July 21, 1982).

38. *See* 43 U.S.C.A. §§ 315b, 1752 (Supp. 1983).

39. Interviews with Terry Brumley of the U.S.F.S., in Redding, Ca. (Aug. 9, 1982), and Paul McClain of the B.L.M., in Redding, Ca. (July 9, 1982).

40. Untimely grazing may damage rangeland. If grazing occurs too early, it may kill immature grass; if it occurs too late, the livestock may eat seeds needed for the following year's forage. Grazing leases therefore regulate entry and exit dates.

41. A cattleman needs at least ten acres of unirrigated land per AUM for winter range. If he were to irrigate 10 percent of this acreage, he would have enough irrigated pasture for summer range. Instead of irrigating, a modernist who prefers operating behind fences may move his herds to fenced summer grasslands located in the high mountain valleys of Superior California. ("Superior California" is a regionally popular geographical designation that, unlike "Northern California," distinguishes the northernmost counties from the Bay Area.)

42. *See generally* H. Heady, *supra* note 35, at 253–55, 258, 280–329. On controlled burns, see also Cal. Pub. Res. Code §§ 4475–94 (West Supp. 1981) (delineating the role of the State Department of Forestry); L. Stoddart & A. Smith, Range Management 383–94 (1943) (describing the effects of burning upon various types of rangeland).

43. *See* Coase, note 1 *supra*, at 3, 5.

44. Rancher Dick Coombs, the epitome of honor in rural Shasta County, counseled that "[I]f you don't fence, your neighbors get your cattle, and their cattle get your feed."

    During the nineteenth century, when cattlemen let their stock loose on the Great Plains during the winter, even the best managers were likely to lose 5 percent of their mature animals each grazing season. D. Boorstin, The Americans: The Democratic Experience 10 (1973). In the Northwest during the same time period, losses ran about 10 percent. J. Oliphant, On the Cattle Ranges of the Oregon Country 240–41 (1968). In Wyoming and Montana, during the disastrous winter of 1885–86, blizzards killed 85 percent or more of the livestock in some herds. E. Osgood, note 34 *supra*, at 216–18.

45. These are rough averages of figures that ranchers and grazing-lease specialists offered in interviews. For the definition of "animal unit month," see note 35 *supra*.

46. The quality of forage of course varies from pasture to pasture, and is apt to be better where a landowner has deliberately tried to cultivate his grasses.

47. D. Dary, *supra* note 34, at 308–31, recounts the impact of the advent of barbed wire on ranching practices nationally. Before barbed wire, the fencing-in of cattle was generally not economical in California. R. Cleland, *supra* note 34, at 62.

    A standard barbed-wire fence will not contain sheep or hogs. To fence in those animals, Shasta County landowners use woven wire (which they variously refer to as "netting," "hog-wire," or "field fence") for the bottom 39 or 47 inches of fence, and top it off with one to three strands of barbed wire. Because many ranchers in Shasta County owned sheep and swine a half century ago, many boundary fences there still contain woven wire.

    Other types of boundary fences, such as electrified fence, are uncommon. However, an owner of horses may use board fencing, rather than barbed wire, to eliminate the risk that barbs pose to the coats of show animals. A natural barrier such as a gulch or a dense growth of brush may obviate the need for any type of boundary fencing. On fence technology, see generally U.S. Dep't of Agric., Farmers' Bull. No. 2247: Fences for the Farm and Rural Home (1971).

48. Cal. Agric. Code § 17121 (West 1968).

49. Because he believed his existing three-strand fence to be inadequate, rancher Dick Coombs persuaded his neighbor Ed Donaldson to join him in adding a fourth strand to their common boundary fence. Walt Johnson, the County Farm Advisor, recommends that barbed wire fences have five strands, and this is what Al Levy installed on the long stretch of new fence on the southern boundary of his mammoth ranch.

    A rancher often erects "cross" or "division" fences to subdivide his own pastureland into separate fields. These fences enable a rancher to rest a pasture that would be damaged by further grazing, to control breeding, and to keep livestock away from a controlled burn.

    Ranchers tend to invest less time and money in their cross fences than in their boundary fences, in part because a breach in a cross fence is less likely to result in the loss of an animal. Al Levy admitted to using only four strands for his cross fences and to not maintaining them quite as well as his five-strand boundary fences.

50. A half-century ago, most Shasta County ranchers made their own fence posts by splitting logs. Should his own ranchland have lacked an adequate supply of logs, a rancher would have

contracted with a private timber company to obtain the right to split downed cedar trees in the mountain forests.

Today, farm supply stores offer ready-made steel and wooden posts. Ranchers typically prefer the steel posts because they are less expensive, easier to drive into rocky soil, and more likely to survive a controlled burn. Wooden posts are still essential at corners, gates, stretch panels, and other places where extra strength is needed.

51. Interview with Carl Yokum of Northwest Fence, in Palo Cedro, Cal. (Aug. 11, 1982).

Technological advances—particularly the invention of barbed wire—have made fencing much less expensive relative to land and labor than it was in Abraham Lincoln's log-splitting days. Today, a newcomer to rural Shasta County would spend in the neighborhood of $40,000 to purchase a forty-acre ranchette, but for one-tenth of that sum he could hire a contractor to fence it with barbed wire. In the 1850s, "[i]t was certainly a rare farm-maker who had not to invest more capital—or its equivalent in labor in the case of forested areas—in his fence than in land." Danhof, *Farm-Making Costs and the "Safety Value": 1850–60,* 49 J. Pol. Econ. 317, 345 (1941). Fencing costs in California during the 1850s are estimated to have been $300 to $600 per mile in the currency of the time. *Id.* at 345 n.78. *See also Meade* v. *Watson,* 67 Cal. 591, 595, 8 P.311, 313 (1885) (complaint asserted "value" of a stone boundary fence to be $1.75 per rod or $560 per mile). In the latter part of the nineteenth century, mean family income in the United States was on the order of $600 to $800 per year. *See* Bureau of the Census, U.S. Dep't of Commerce, 1 Historical Statistics of the United States: Colonial Times to 1970 322 (1975). Before the arrival of barbed wire, a mile of fence thus cost about as much as an average family's annual income. In 1981, the mean family income in the United States was $24,000. *See* Bureau of the Census, U.S. Dep't of Commerce, Statistical Abstract of the United States 1982–1983, at 435 (1982). That income would have then been sufficient to purchase the installation of at least five miles of barbed wire fence in Shasta County.

52. I found only one rancher, and no ranchette owner, who admitted having contracted-out fencing work. The fence contractors of Shasta County agreed that the vast majority of rural fencing is done on a do-it-yourself basis. Walt Johnson, the astute farm advisor for Shasta County, could not identify the name of a single fence contractor.

53. To quality as "lawful," a barbed wire fence in California must have its top strand at least forty-eight inches above the ground. Cal. Agric. Code § 17121 (West 1968). Farm experts recommend that the top wire of a five-strand fence be elevated fifty-two inches. *See* Fences for the Farm and Rural Home, *supra* note 47, at 17. The risk of damage from jumping deer has induced some fence contractors to warn against placing the top strand too high.

54. Veteran rancher and ex-supervisor Norman Wagoner estimated that a cattleman working alone can inspect and repair a fence at a rate of about two miles per day.

55. Rancher Owen Shellworth estimated that he spent 25 percent of his work on fences, including corral fences.

56. I did not learn of a single instance in which a forest owner, or a traditionalist cattleman who leased a forest for summer range, had fenced a forest boundary.

57. But they have not provoked all of them. Farm Advisor Walt Johnson could recall several instances in which the trigger had been a rancher, ostensibly operating behind fence, who had deliberately turned out his animals onto neighboring lands.

58. *See,* for example, Calabresi & Melamed, note 6 *supra,* at 1090–91 (assuming that the "state" is the sole source of entitlements).

59. John Woodbury suffered almost weekly incursions into his alfalfa field in 1973. Although the situation improved when many of the mountain lessees subsequently declined to renew their leases, Woodbury was still experiencing a couple of cattle trespasses a year in the early 1980s. Another hay farmer, Phil Ritchie, identified six neighbors whose cattle had trespassed on his lands in recent years.

60. Beef cattle eat feed equal to about 2-1/2 percent of their body weight each day. Division of Agric. Sci., Univ. of Cal., Leaflet No. 21184, Beef Production in California 12–13 (Nov. 1980).

61. *Cf.*, Cal. Agric. Code § 16803 (West 1968) (cattlemen grazing herds on open range must include at least one bull for every thirty cows). The refinement of artificial insemination techniques has enabled some ranchers to reduce the fraction of bulls in herds kept behind fences.

62. A Hereford bull has a mature weight of 2,000 pounds, compared to 1,100–1,200 pounds for a mature Hereford cow. Steers (castrated male cattle) are typically slaughtered when they weigh between 1,000 and 1,150 pounds. Beef Production in California, note 60 *supra*, at 3, 5.

63. I learned of no cattle trespasses that had resulted in personal injury. Two insurance adjusters who frequently had been called upon to settle dog-bite claims could remember, between them, only one personal-injury claim arising from cattle—an instance in which a cow had stepped on someone's foot.

64. Bogue is a Shasta County employee; Jordan is an employee of the California Bureau of Livestock Identification.

65. Eleven correctly stated they lived in open-range; eight correctly stated they lived in closed-range; one gave a flatly wrong answer; one, a partially wrong answer; and two "didn't know."

66. My interviewees were disproportionately active in local politics; two had obtained copies of the Department of Public Works closed-range map in conjunction with their political endeavors.

67. Of 11 respondents asked, only three stated that they had known when they bought their land what kind of "legal range" it lay in.

68. This startling finding can be attributed to the fact that trespass and estray claims are virtually never processed through the formal legal institutions of Shasta County.

69. Some legal specialists conceivably may also believe that the negligence principle is in every application normatively superior to the principle of strict liability.

70. Additionally, neither of the two fence contractors interviewed had any notion of these boundaries. The county tax assessor assigned to the Oak Run–Round Mountain area was equally unfamiliar with the closed-range map.

71. In his study of the settlement of automobile-liability claims, Ross found the law-in-action to be simpler and more mechanical than the formal law, but he did not find it to be quite as disconnected as I found it in trespass cases. *See* H. Ross, note 11 *supra*, at 134–35, 237–40. One might expect formal liability law to be particularly toothless when it applies to situations—such as animal trespass incidents—that generate few insurance claims and for which the claims are almost always for paltry monetary amounts.

72. The scholars involved in the Civil Liability Research Project have attempted to standardize the vocabulary of dispute resolution. They use "grievance" to describe a perceived entitlement to pursue a claim against another, "claim" to describe a demand for redress, and "dispute" to describe a rejected claim. *See*, for example, Miller & Sarat, *Grievances, Claims, and Disputes: Assessing the Adversary Culture*, 15 Law & Soc'y Rev. 525, 527 (1980–81). I am less precise and employ these terms loosely, as they tend to be employed in ordinary speech.

73. *See* Coase, *supra* note 1, at 15.

74. This now-familiar phrase originated in Mnookin & Kornhauser, *Bargaining in the Shadow of the Law: The Case of Divorce*, 88 Yale L.J. 950 (1979).

75. *See* notes 3, 12 *supra* and accompanying texts.

76. Law-and-economics scholars often employ models that explicitly assume that actors have perfect knowledge of legal rules. *See*, for example, A. Polinsky, An Introduction to Law and Economics 37–49 (1983) (assuming drivers and pedestrians know personal injury law); Shavell, *An Analysis of Causation and the Scope of Liability in the Law of Torts*, 9 J. Legal Stud. 463, 471 (1980).

77. Although the rural landowners were emphatic about the importance of neighborliness and could offer many specific examples of neighborly behavior, they never articulated a general formula for how a rural resident should behave. In my book on Shasta County I hypothesize that the specific norms they honored were wealth maximizing, and explore how wealth-maximizing norms might evolve.

For other discussions of the role of nonlegal norms in dispute settlement, see Eisenberg, *Private Ordering Through Negotiation: Dispute-Settlement and Rulemaking*, 89 Harv. L. Rev. 637, 638–65 (1976); Macaulay, note 11 *supra*, at 61–62.

78. A trespass victim who cannot recognize the brand of the intruding animal—a quandary more common for ranchette owners than for ranchers—may telephone county authorities. Calls of this sort are eventually referred to the brand inspector or animal control officer, who then regard their main priority to be return of the animal to its owner.

79. One rancher reported that during the winter he expects to find thirty to forty deer grazing in his hayfield each night. The owner of a particularly large ranch estimated that about five hundred deer winter there—a condition he likes, because deer are "part of nature." John Woodbury, an alfalfa farmer and key lobbyist for the passage of the Caton's Folly ordinance, stated that elk and deer had eaten more of the grass in his alfalfa field than mountain cattle ever had.

80. Brand Inspector Bruce Jordan estimated that ranchers drop off approximately three hundred head of stray livestock at the auctionyard each year and that these ranchers typically decline to seek compensation from the owners of the strays.

81. *See* R. Kidder, Connecting Law and Society 70–72 (1983). The law-and-society literature has long emphasized that law is not likely to be important to parties enmeshed in a continuing relationship. For example, Marc Galanter has observed:

> In the American setting, litigation tends to be between parties who are strangers. Either they never had a mutually beneficial continuing relationship, as in the typical automobile case, or their relationship—marital, commercial, or organizational—is ruptured. In either case, there is no anticipated future relationship. In the American setting, unlike some others, resort to litigation is [usually] viewed as an irreparable breach of the relationship.

Galanter, *Reading the Landscape of Disputes: What We Know and Don't Know (and Think We Know) About Our Allegedly Contentious and Litigious Society*, 31 U.C.L.A. L. Rev. 4, 24–25 (1983) (brackets in original).

82. *Cf.* A. Vidich & Bensman, Small Town in Mass Society 34 (rev. ed. 1968):

> To a great extent these arrangements between friends and neighbors have a reciprocal character: a man who helps others may himself expect to be helped later on. In a way the whole system takes on the character of insurance. Of course some people are more conscious of their premium payments than others and keep a kind of mental bookkeeping on "what they owe and who owes them what," which is a perfectly permissible practice so long as one does not openly confront others with unbalanced accounts.

83. *See* O. Williamson, Markets and Hierarchies 256–57 (1975) (a party to a continuing relationship seeks to achieve a favorable balance in the overall set of interactions, not in each separate interaction).

84. *See generally* Black, *Crime as Social Control*, 48 Am. Soc. Rev. 34 (1983) (a trenchant assessment of the phenomenon of self-help).

85. *See* Merry, *Rethinking Gossip and Scandal*, in 1 Toward a General Theory of Social Control 271 (D. Black ed. 1984).

86. Two respondents admitted that they had done this.

87. Cal. Penal Code § 597(a) (West Supp. 1985); *People v. Dunn*, 39 Cal. App. 3d 418, 114 Cal. Rptr. 164 (1974).

88. *Cf.* Engel, *Cases, Conflict, and Accommodation: Patterns of Legal Interaction in an American Community*, 1983 Am. B. Found, Research J. 803, 821 (role of complaints to public officials in a rural Illinois county).

89. Investigators have found norms against litigation in other social environments. *See* Engel, note 88 *supra*, at 816–22, 851–56 (rural Illinois county); Macaulay, note 11 *supra*, at 64 (Wisconsin businessmen).

90. In the Burney Justice Court, the 1980 small claims files showed no animal trespass cases, and the clerks could recall no such cases in their four years on the job.

    In the Central Valley Justice Court, no small claims for the 8/81 to 6/82 period involved animal trespass, and the civil clerk who had worked there for eleven years could not remember any. The index of defendants for the 1975 to 1982 period indicated that Frank Ellis was the only large rancher to become the target of any kind of legal action.

91. I did hear several secondhand reports of informally settled claims for the costs of boarding estrays. Only one rancher told of paying such a claim; he regarded the claimant's pursuit of the money as a "cheap move."

92. A donor who wishes to symbolize an intimate relationship typically gives, not currency, but a gift that apparently required special effort to prepare. *See* Landa, *The Enigma of the* Kula Ring: *Gift-Exchanges and Primitive Law and Order*, 3 Int'l Rev. L. & Econ. 137, 152 (1983) (Melanesians return armshells for necklaces because to return a necklace for a necklace would be interpreted as a rejection of friendship). *See generally* M. Mauss, The Gift (1967).

93. *Heinz v. Ellis*, No. 81 SC 7 (Cent. Valley Just. Ct. filed Jan. 8, 1981).

94. *Ellis v. Heinz*, No. 81 CV 6 (Cent. Valley Just. Ct. filed Jan. 16, 1981).

95. Heinz had technically imperiled his statutory claim for damages under the Estray Act when he failed to notify the proper authorities promptly that he had taken up Ellis's animals. *See* Cal. Agric. Code §§ 17042, 17095 (West 1967).

96. *See also* W. Nelson, Dispute and Conflict Resolution in Plymouth Colony, Massachusetts 1725 to 1825 (1981) (Plymouth's particularly litigious individuals during the 1725 to 1774 period tended to be people who were poorly socialized); Todd, *Litigious Marginals: Character and Disputing in a Bavarian Village*, in The Disputing Process: Law in Ten Societies, note 11 *supra*, at 86, 118 (socially marginal people were disproportionately represented in civil and criminal litigation).

97. *See*, for example, Macaulay, note 11 *supra*; Macneil, *The Many Futures of Contracts*, 47 S. Cal. L. Rev. 691, 715 (1974).

4

Cultural Beliefs and the Organization of Society: A Historical and Theoretical Reflection on Collectivist and Individualist Societies

Avner Greif

The organization of a society—its economic, legal, political, social, and moral enforcement institutions, together with its social constructs and information transmission and coordination mechanisms—profoundly affects its economic performance and growth. It determines the cost of various feasible actions as well as wealth distribution. Although this theme goes back at least to Adam Smith, it has recently been the focus of historical and theoretical studies. For example, North (1991) attributed the growth performance of nations throughout history to differences in their enforcement mechanisms. North and Weingast (1989) claimed that England's unique political institutions encouraged economic growth. Marimon (1988) examined the growth rate attainable under various enforcement mechanisms, and others (for example, Banerjee and Newman 1993) explored the relations between wealth distribution and growth due to credit market imperfections and investment in human capital.

Indeed, social psychologists have found societal organization to be highly correlated with per capita income in contemporary societies: most of the developing countries are "collectivist," whereas the developed West is "individualist." In collectivist societies the social structure is "segregated" in the sense that each individual socially and economically interacts mainly with members of a specific religious, ethnic, or familial group in which contract enforcement is achieved through "informal" economic and social institutions, and members of collectivist societies feel involved in the lives of other members of their group. At the same time, noncooperation characterizes the relations between members of different groups. In individualist societies the social structure is "integrated" in the sense that economic transactions are conducted among people from different groups and individuals shift frequently from one group to another. Contract enforcement is achieved mainly through specialized organizations such as the court, and self-reliance is highly valued.[1]

Economic anthropologists, economic historians, and theorists have long conjectured that cultural variations account for intersociety differences in societal organizations. Yet, little is known about the origins of various systems of societal organization and the factors that make these systems path dependent.[2] Thus we cannot address a question that seems to be at the heart of developmental failures: why do societies fail to adopt the organization of more economically successful ones?

This chapter presents a historical and game-theoretical analysis of the relations between culture and societal organization by examining the cultural factors that have led two premodern societies to evolve along distinct trajectories of societal organization. It examines two traders' groups that operated during the late medieval period, an era that had a profound impact on the evolving European (post-Roman) societal organization. The Maghribi traders of the eleventh century were part of the Muslim world, and the Genoese traders of the twelfth century were part of the Latin world. These two historical case studies provide the base for an examination of differences in societal organization.

Analytically, the chapter models an economic transaction central to these two trading societies to examine the relations between culture and societal organization in the related multiple equilibria game.[3] The theoretical and historical analyses indicate the importance of a specific cultural element—*cultural beliefs*—in being an integral part of institutions and in affecting the evolution and persistence of diverse societal organizations. Differences in the societal organization of the two trading societies can be consistently accounted for as reflecting diverse cultural beliefs. It is interesting to note that the societal organization of traders from the Muslim world resembles modern collectivist societies, whereas that of the traders from the Latin world resembles individualist societies. Hence my findings suggest the theoretical and historical importance of culture in determining societal organizations, in leading to path dependence of institutional frameworks, and in forestalling successful intersociety adoption of institutions.

CULTURAL BELIEFS AND THE ORGANIZATION OF SOCIETY

Sociologists and anthropologists consider the organization of society to be a reflection of its culture—an important component of which is cultural beliefs. Cultural beliefs are the ideas and thoughts common to several individuals that govern interaction—between these people, and between them, their gods, and other groups—and differ from knowledge in that they are not empirically discovered or analytically proved. In general, cultural beliefs become identical and commonly known through the socialization process by which culture is unified, maintained, and communicated (see, for example, Davis 1949, 52 ff., 192 ff.; Bandura 1977). That cultural beliefs influence economic outcomes is intuitive, but formal examination of the relations between cultural beliefs and societal organization is subtle. If we arbitrarily define cultural beliefs, a variety of phenomena can be generated. How should cultural beliefs be restricted, and what are their sources? Should they be considered rational?

The historical analysis of this chapter indicates the importance of a specific subset of cultural beliefs, namely, rational cultural beliefs that capture individuals' expectations with respect to actions that others will take in various contingencies. Since cultural beliefs are identical and commonly known, when each player plays his best response to these cultural beliefs, the set of permissible cultural beliefs is restricted to those that are self-enforcing. Hence this specific subset of cultural beliefs can be formalized as a set of probability distributions over an equilibrium strategy combination. Each probability distribution reflects the expectation of a player with respect to the actions that would be taken on and off the path of play.

Yet if each player expects others to play a self-enforcing and hence an equilibrium strategy, is there any analytical benefit from distinguishing between strategies and cultural beliefs? Unlike strategies, cultural beliefs are qualities of individuals in the sense that cultural beliefs that were crystallized with respect to a specific game affect decisions in historically subsequent strategic situations. Past cultural beliefs provide focal points and coordinate expectations, thereby influencing equilibrium selection and society's enforcement institutions.

These enforcement institutions are composed of cultural beliefs and the rules of the game. In the long run, the (nontechnologically determined) rules of the game may be changed endogenously as individuals attempt to improve their lot by establishing organizations. These organizations alter the rules of the game by, for example, introducing a new player (the organization itself), by changing the information available to players, or by changing payoffs associated with certain actions. Examples of organizational innovations of this nature are the court system, the credit bureau, and the firm. The introduction of a new organization reflects an increase in the stock of knowledge, which may be the outcome of an intentional pursuit or unintentional experimentation.

A necessary condition for an organizational change, however, is that those able to initiate it expect to gain from it. Their expectations depend on their cultural beliefs, and hence diverse cultural beliefs lead to a distinct trajectory of organizational development. The distinctiveness of each trajectory is reinforced by the process of modifying and refining "microinventions," which follows an "organizational macroinvention."[4] Diverse paths of organizational development, in turn, further affect the historical process of equilibrium selection. Once a specific organization is introduced, it influences the rules of historically subsequent games and hence the resulting societal organization.

Cultural beliefs also influence societal organization since strategic interactions occur within a specific social and historical context. Diverse cultural beliefs can lead to differential economic behavior toward individuals with diverse social characteristics such as wealth or "membership" in a specific social group. For example, different cultural beliefs may imply diverse social constructs—diverse social patterns of economic interactions—each of which entails different dynamics of wealth distribution. Different cultural beliefs may also imply different relations between efficiency and profitability in intrasociety and intersociety economic interactions. Some cultural beliefs can render efficient intersociety relations unprofitable, leading to an economically inefficient social structure.

Various social patterns of economic interactions further affect societal organization by, for example, the process examined by the eminent sociologist George Homans (1950). Frequent economic interactions among the same individuals give rise to "friendliness," and satisfaction from friendliness motivates them to interact further, socially as well as economically. These repeated interactions and the resulting social networks for information transmission facilitate informal collective economic and social punishments for deviant behavior (see also Dawes and Thaler 1988).

Finally, social and economic patterns of interactions also affect moral enforcement mechanisms, that is, enforcement based on the tendency of humans to derive utility from acting according to their values. Although this tendency seems to be universal, different patterns of social and economic interactions lead to the development of distinctive value systems as individuals attempt to find moral justification for their behavior through cognitive dissonance (Davis 1949, 52; Homans 1950).[5] Different values, in turn, entail the moral enforcement mechanism that reinforces distinct behavior.

AGENCY RELATIONS AND CULTURAL BELIEFS

The Italian city-states of the late medieval period were the forerunners of the emerging post-Roman, European economy. Among these cities, Genoa stands out for its commercial importance and excellent historical records from as early as the late eleventh century, when the city was incorporated. These records enable examining the emergence of its societal organization. The examination is facilitated by the fact, reflected in the saying *genuensis ergo mercator* (Genoese, therefore merchant), that long-distance overseas trade was central to Genoa's economy. Similarly, trade was central to a group of eleventh-century traders from the Muslim world known as the Maghribi traders. These Jewish merchants were involved in large-scale, long-distance trade all over the Muslim Mediterranean.[6]

The Maghribis and the Genoese faced a similar environment, employed comparable naval technology, and traded in similar goods. The efficiency of their trade depended, to a large extent, on their ability to mitigate an organizational problem related to a specific transaction, namely, the provision of the services required for handling a merchant's goods abroad.[7] A merchant could either provide these services himself by traveling between trade centers or hire *overseas* agents in trade centers abroad to handle his merchandise. Employing agents was efficient, since it saved the time and risk of traveling, allowed diversifying sales across trade centers, and so forth.[8] Yet without supporting institutions, agency relations could not be established since an agent could embezzle the merchant's goods. Anticipating this behavior, a merchant would not hire an agent to begin with.

For agents to be employed, the organization of society had to enable them to commit themselves ex ante to be honest ex post, after receiving the merchant's goods. The societal organization of the Maghribis and the Genoese enabled them to mitigate this commitment problem, and in both groups trade was based on agency relations among nonfamily members. For example, the first Genoese historical source reflecting agency relations, the cartulary of Giovanni Scriba (1155–1164), indicates that in its approximately 612 contracts reflecting trade, only 5.3 percent did not entail agency relations, and only 6.45 percent of the sum sent abroad through agents was entrusted to family members.

To examine how each group mitigated the merchant-agent commitment problem, consider the following perfect and complete information One-Side Prisoner's Dilemma (OSPD) game, which captures the essence of the problem. (Extensions are discussed later.) There are M merchants and A agents in the economy, and (in accordance with the historical evidence) it is assumed that $M < A$. Players live an infinite number of periods, agents have a time discount factor β, and an unemployed agent receives a reservation utility per period of $\phi_u \geq 0$. In each period, an agent can be hired by only one merchant, and a merchant can employ only one agent. Matching is random, but a merchant can restrict the matching to a subset of the unemployed agents that contains the agents who, according to the information available to the merchant, have previously taken particular sequences of actions. A merchant who does not hire an agent receives a payoff of $\varkappa > 0$. A merchant who hires an agent decides what wage ($W \geq 0$) to offer the agent. An employed agent can decide whether to be honest or to cheat. If he is honest, the merchant's payoff is $\gamma - W$, and the agent's payoff is W. Hence the gross gain from cooperation is γ, and it is assumed that cooperation is efficient, $\gamma > \varkappa + \phi_u$. The merchant's wage offer is assumed credible, since in reality the agent held the goods and could determine the ex post allocation of gains. For that reason, if the agent cheats, the merchant's payoff is zero and the agent's payoff is $\alpha > \phi_u$. Finally, a merchant prefers receiving $\varkappa$ over being cheated or paying $W = \alpha$, that is, $\varkappa > \gamma - \alpha$.

After the allocation of the payoffs, each merchant can decide whether to terminate his relations with his agent or not. There is a probability σ, however, that a merchant is forced to terminate agency relations, and this assumption captures merchants' limited ability to commit to future employment because of the need to shift commercial operations over places and goods and the high uncertainty of commerce and life during that period. For similar reasons, the merchants are assumed to be unable to condition wage on past conduct (indeed, merchants in neither group did so). Finally, in neither group was wage a function of political or legal considerations. Wages were not determined by the court or politically supported guild. Accordingly, and as is customary in similar efficiency wage models (for example, Shapiro and Stiglitz 1984), the analysis assumes that no subgroup is organized in a manner that affects wage determination. Furthermore, attention is restricted to equilibria in which wages are constant over time.[9]

Suppose for the moment that the history of the game is common knowledge. What is the minimum (symmetric) wage for which, if it is offered by all merchants, an agent's best response is to be honest under the threat of firing if he cheats and the promise of being rehired if he is honest (unless forced separation occurs)? To find this wage, one has to fully specify the merchants' strategies. Yet to analyze the impact of different strategies in the same framework, the analysis initially concentrates on probabilities that are a function of the strategies. Denote as an *honest agent* an unemployed agent who was honest in the last period he was employed, and by h_h the probability that he will be hired in that period. Denote as a *cheater* an agent who cheated in the last period he was employed, and by h_c the probability that he will be hired. Proposition 1, which is proved in the appendix, specifies the minimum wage that supports cooperation.

Proposition 1. Assume that $\beta \in (0, 1)$, and $h_c < 1$. The *optimal wage*, the lowest wage for which an agent's best response is to play honest, is $W^* = w(\beta, h_h, h_c, \sigma, \phi_u, \alpha) > \phi_u$, and w is monotonically decreasing in β and h_h and monotonically increasing in h_c, σ, ϕ_u, and α.

A merchant induces honesty by the carrot of a wage higher than the agent's reservation utility and the stick of terminating their relations. For a wage high enough, the difference between the present value of the lifetime expected utility of an unemployed and employed agent is higher than what an agent can gain by one-period play of cheating, and hence the agent's best response is to be honest. The minimum wage that ensures honesty decreases in the factors that increase the lifetime expected utility of an honest agent relative to that of a cheater (that is, β and h_h) and increases in the factors that increase the relative lifetime expected utility of a cheater (that is, h_c, σ, ϕ_u, and α).

How can differences between collectivist and individualist societies manifest themselves in agency relations? Intuitively, in collectivist societies everyone is expected to respond to whatever has transpired between any specific merchant and agent, whereas the opposite holds for individualist societies. Two strategy combinations formalize this difference: the *individualist* and the *collectivist* strategies. In each strategy a merchant hires, for a wage W^*, an unemployed agent whom he rehires as long as cheating or forced separation does not occur. Under the individualist strategy, however, a merchant randomly hires an unemployed agent, whereas under the collectivist strategy a merchant randomly hires only from among the unemployed agents who have never cheated. An agent's strategy is to play honest if and only if he is offered at least the W^* relevant to him given the history of the game. Note that W^* is lower under the collectivist strategy. Each of these strategies is a subgame perfect equilibrium as established in proposition 2 (proved in the appendix).

Proposition 2.   Assume that under both the *individualist* and the *collectivist* strategy combinations $\gamma - \varkappa \geq W^*$; then each strategy combination is a subgame perfect equilibrium of the OSPD game.

The individualist strategy is a subgame perfect equilibrium because merchants are not expected to take into account the agent's past behavior when making hiring decisions. Hence each merchant perceives the probability that an unemployed agent who cheated in the past will be hired to equal that of an unemployed honest agent. According to proposition 1, this implies that each merchant is indifferent whether to hire a cheater or an honest agent. (As discussed below, when the decision to acquire information is endogenous, under individual equilibrium the merchant would not have the related information.)

Under the collectivist equilibrium, because each merchant expects others not to employ a cheater, the perceived probability that a cheater will be hired is lower than that of an honest agent. According to proposition 1, this implies that a higher wage is required to keep him honest, and hence the merchant strictly prefers to hire an honest agent. The merchant's expectations are self-enforcing, although cheating does not convey any information about future behavior; the agent's strategy does not call for cheating any merchant who violates the collective punishment; and merchants do not "punish" any merchant who hires a cheater.

The preceding analysis assumed that the history of the game is common knowledge. Acquiring and transmitting information during the late medieval period was costly, and hence the model should incorporate a merchant's decisions to acquire costly information. Since merchants gathered information by being a part of an informal information-sharing network, suppose that each merchant can either "invest" or "not invest" in "getting attached" to a network before the game begins, and his action is common knowledge. Investing requires paying Λ

each period, in return for which the merchant learns the private histories of all the merchants who also invested. Otherwise, he knows only his own history. Intuitively, under the individualist equilibrium, history has no value, since an agent's wage does not depend on it. Hence no merchant will invest in information. In contrast, under the collectivist equilibrium, history has value since the optimal wage is a function of an agent's history. Merchants will invest since an agent who cheated in the past will cheat if hired and paid the equilibrium wage. Although on the equilibrium path cheating never occurs, merchants are motivated to invest, since this action is common knowledge and hence one who does not invest is cheated if he pays the equilibrium W^*. This intuition is verified in proposition 3, which is proved by inspection.

Proposition 3. W^*_{-i} is the minimum wage that merchant i has to pay his agent if only he does not invest; W^*_c is the equilibrium wage under the collectivist strategy is an equilibrium iff $W^*_{-i} - W^*_c \geq Y$. Not to invest and the individualist strategy is an equilibrium whereas invest and the individualist strategy is not an equilibrium.

Reality may also be characterized by incomplete information; that is, some agent may have an unobservable "bad" attribute and thus be more likely to cheat. The analysis above holds when the proportion of the bad type is "high" or "low." Under a collectivist equilibrium, incomplete information reinforces investment in information. Under an individualist equilibrium, the value of information may still be zero (if the proportion of the bad type is high) or may not be high enough to induce investment in information (if the proportion of the bad type is low). Hence this chapter uses the complete information model, which highlights the role of expectations with respect to actions and abstracts away from expectations with respect to types (see the discussion in Greif 1989, 1993a).

This section relates two societal organizations and different cultural beliefs, that is, different expectations with respect to actions that will be taken off the path of play. In an individualist equilibrium, players are expected to be indifferent, and in a collectivist equilibrium players are expected to respond to whatever transpires between others. Since these cultural beliefs correspond to an equilibrium, they are self-enforcing, and each entails a different wage, enforcement institution (second- vs. third-party enforcement), and investment in information.

On the equilibrium path, the individualist and collectivist cultural beliefs entail the same *actions* with respect to agents: merchants randomly hire unemployed agents and agents never cheat. By assuming complete information, the discussion above and the next section's analysis enable concentration on cultural beliefs concerning actions that never actually transpire, thereby emphasizing the implications for societal organization of diverse expectations regarding actions rather than the actions themselves. Hence the following analysis identifies cultural beliefs with probability distributions over the off-the-path-of-play portion of a strategy combination generating an observed path of play.[10] Historically, imperfect monitoring is a likely cause of the observed punishment phases, and thus, historically, it is not feasible to distinguish between cultural beliefs relating to on and off the path of play, and no attempt to do so is made.[11]

THE MAGHRIBIS AND GENOESE: ORIGIN AND MANIFESTATIONS OF DIVERSE CULTURAL BELIEFS

Are there historical reasons to believe that the Maghribis and the Genoese held diverse cultural beliefs? The historical records do not provide any reason to believe that a particular theory of equilibrium selection is relevant in this case. They indicate, however, that cultural "focal points" as well as social and political events in the early development of these societies were likely to be instrumental in shaping diverse cultural beliefs and the related equilibria in these groups. When the Maghribis began trading in the Mediterranean early in the eleventh century and when the Genoese began trading toward the end of that century, they had already internalized different cultures and were in the midst of different social and political processes. Their cultural heritage and the nature of these processes suggest that among the Maghribis a collectivist equilibrium was a natural focal point, whereas among the Genoese an individualist equilibrium was the natural focal point.

The Maghribis were *musta'ribun*, that is, non-Muslims who adopted the values of the Muslim society. Among these values is the view that they were members of the same *umma*. This term, although translated as "nation," is derived from the word *umm*, meaning "mother," reflecting the basic value of mutual responsibility among the members of that society (see, for example, Cahen 1970). Further, members of the *umma* share the fundamental duty not only to practice good but also to ensure that others do not practice sin (B. Lewis 1988). In addition, the Maghribis were part of the Jewish community, within which it is a prominent idea that "All Israel is responsible for every member." Furthermore, as is common among immigrant groups, the Maghribis, who migrated from Iraq to Tunisia, retained social ties that enabled them to transmit the information required to support a collectivist equilibrium. The associated collectivist cultural beliefs in turn encouraged retaining an affiliation with this information network.

In contrast, Christianity during that period placed the individual rather than his social group at the center of its theology. It advanced the creation of "a new society based not on the family but on the individual, whose salvation, like his original loss of innocence, was personal and private" (Hughes 1974, 61). Indeed, the contract through which the Genoese established their city shortly before 1099 was a contract between individuals, not between families or other social groups. Furthermore, for political reasons the number of Genoese active in trade rose dramatically toward the end of the twelfth century. Instead of a few dozen traders who had previously been active in each trade center abroad, hundreds of Genoese began trading. At the same time, Genoa experienced a high level of immigration. For instance, Genoa's population increased from 30,000 to 100,000 between 1200 and 1300. In the absence of appropriate social networks for information transmission, the individualist equilibrium was likely to be selected. Once it was selected, individualist cultural beliefs discouraged investment in information. In the absence of a coordinating mechanism, a switch to a collectivist equilibrium was not likely to occur.

Collectivist cultural beliefs were a focal point among the Maghribis, and individualist cultural beliefs were a focal point among the Genoese. Does the historical evidence indicate the existence of the related societal organizations? That is, was there high investment in information and collective punishment among the Maghribis and low investment in information and individualist punishment among the Genoese?

The historical evidence indicates that the Maghribis invested in sharing information and the Genoese did not. Each Maghribi corresponded with many other Maghribi traders by sending informative letters to them with the latest available commercial information and "gossip," including whatever transpired in agency relations among other Maghribis. Important business dealings were conducted in public, and the names of the witnesses were widely publicized (Goitein 1967, 1973; Greif 1989). Information transmission was probably facilitated by the relatively small size of the Maghribi traders' group (although, as discussed below, this size was endogenously determined). In 175 documents, for example, 330 different names are mentioned.[12] Although, most likely, not every Maghribi trader was familiar with all the others, belonging to the Maghribis was easily verifiable through common acquaintances, and extensive network of communication, a common religion, and a common language (Judaeo-Arabic).

The historical records indicate the use of collective punishment among the Maghribis, although it was rarely used.[13] For example, in the first decade of the eleventh century, Samhun ben Da'ud, a prominent trader from Tunisia, sent a long letter to his business associate, Joseph ben 'Awkal of Fustat. The letter says that Joseph made his future dealings with Samhun conditional on his record: "If your handling of my business is correct, then I shall send you goods." It happened, however, that Samhun did not handle Joseph's business to his satisfaction: Joseph believed that Samhun had intentionally not remitted his revenues on time. Joseph's response was to ignore Samhun's request to pay two of Samhun's creditors in Fustat. By the time Samhun found out about it, "their letters filled with condemnation had reached everyone." The contents of these letters caused Samhun to complain that "my reputation (or honor) is being ruined" (David Kaufmann Collection, Hungarian Academy of Science, Budapest [document 13, side a, lines 26 ff., 41]; Stillman 1970, 267 ff.; Goitein 1973, 26 ff.).[14]

In contrast, the Genoese seem to have held an opposite attitude regarding information sharing. Lopez (1943) noted the efforts of the Genoese to conceal information and conjectured that the "individualistic, taciturn, and reserved Genoese" were not "talkative" about their businesses and were even "jealous of their business secrets" (168). For example, when the Vivaldi brothers attempted in 1291 to sail from Genoa to the Far East through the Atlantic, their commercial agreements were drawn for trade in "Majorca, even for the Byzantine Empire" (169). Genoa's historical records are not explicit about the nature of punishment. Yet they suggest the lack of collective punishment and informal communication. For example, despite the fact that it was known that a Genoese merchant, Daniel Fontanella, gained at least 50 percent on the capital entrusted to him as an agent, he declared a loss of 20 percent (Lopez 1943, 180; De Roover 1965; 88–89).

Cultural factors that coordinated expectations and social and political factors that slightly altered the relevant games in the formative period seem to have directed the Maghribis and the Genoese toward different cultural beliefs. As these various cultural beliefs were a part of the institutional framework of each group, they determined the costs and benefits of various actions and hence efficiency. For example, since collectivist cultural beliefs reduce the optimal wage, they can sustain cooperation in situations in which it cannot be sustained by individualist cultural beliefs (Greif 1993a). Even if each member of the society recognizes the inefficiency caused by individualist cultural beliefs, a unilateral move by an individual or a (relatively) small group would not induce a change. Expectations about expectations are difficult to alter, and thus cultural beliefs can make Pareto-inferior institutions and outcomes self-enforcing. (Responding to this constraint, however, individuals may strive to change the rules of the game, as discussed later.)

WITHIN THE BOUNDARIES OF THE GAME:
CULTURAL BELIEFS, SOCIAL PATTERNS OF AGENCY
RELATIONS, AND WEALTH DISTRIBUTION

What are the implications of different cultural beliefs on social patterns of economic relations and the dynamics of wealth distribution? Can different cultural beliefs manifest themselves in distinct social structures? Examining this issue requires extending the theoretical analysis to allow each merchant to serve as an agent for another merchant.[15] Accordingly, the collectivist cultural belief should be redefined to include the expectations that merchants will not retaliate against someone who cheats a merchant who has cheated any other merchant. That is, whoever is hired by a merchant who cheated in the past is not expected to be subjected to collective punishment if he cheats that merchant. Indeed, the historical evidence indicate that Maghribis shared such expectations. For example, a Maghribi merchant who was accused in 1041 to 1042 of cheating complains that when it became known, "people became agitated and hostile and whoever owed [me money] conspired to keep it from [me]" (Bodleian Library, Oxford, MS Hebrew, a 2 f. 17, sec. D; Goitein 1973, 104).[16]

In this extended game, two social patterns of agency relations and associated dynamic patterns of wealth distribution can emerge. The first is a vertical social structure in which merchants (find it optimal and therefore) employ only agents and hence an individual functions as either a merchant or an agent. The second is a horizontal social structure in which merchants employ only other merchants, and thus an individual functions as an agent *and* a merchant, providing and receiving agency services. What are the relations between cultural beliefs and these social patterns of agency relations?

Intuitively, under collectivist cultural beliefs a merchant's capital functions as a bond that reduces the optimal wage required to keep him honest. If a merchant cheats while functioning as an agent, he is no longer able to hire agents under the threat of collective punishment and thus either has to operate without agents or, to keep an agent honest, has to pay the agent a wage higher than the one that prevails under collectivist cultural beliefs. Hence, cheating by a merchant while he functions as an agent reduces the future rate of return on his own capital. This implies that a merchant who had cheated while functioning as an agent had to bear a cost that an agent (who does not have capital of his own) would not have to bear. Hence a lower wage is required to keep a merchant honest, and each merchant is motivated to hire another merchant as his agent leading to a horizontal social structure. This is not the case, however, under individualist cultural beliefs. Past cheating does not reduce the rate of return on a merchant's capital. But having capital to invest de facto increases a merchant's reservation utility relative to that of an agent thereby increasing the wage required to keep him honest. Merchants are discouraged from hiring other merchants as their agents, leading to a vertical social structure.[17]

It can be concluded that merchants' capital serves as a bond that encourages their employment under collectivist cultural beliefs. Merchants' higher reservation utilities, however, discourage their employment under individualist cultural beliefs (and possibly collectivist cultural beliefs). Hence under individualist cultural beliefs, a society reaches a vertical social structure for a larger set of initial conditions than under collectivist cultural beliefs, whereas under collectivist cultural beliefs a society reaches a horizontal social structure for a larger set of initial conditions than under individualist cultural beliefs.

Differences in social structure are indeed observed among the Maghribis and the Genoese. The Maghribi traders were, by and large, merchants who invested in trade through horizontal agency relations. Each trader served as an agent for several merchants while receiving agency services from them or other traders. Sedentary traders served as agents for those who traveled, and vice versa. Wealthy merchants served as agents for poorer ones, and vice versa. Among the Maghribis there was not a "merchants' class" and an "agents' class." The extent to which the Maghribis' social structure was horizontal can be quantified by examining the related distributions of "agency measure." Agency measure is defined as the number of times a trader operated as an agent divided by the number of times a trader operated as either a merchant or an agent. It equals one if the trader was only an agent, zero if he was only a merchant, and some intermediate value in between if he was both a merchant and an agent. In 175 letters written by Maghribi traders and in which 652 agency relations are reflected, 119 traders appear more than once, and almost 70 percent of them have an agency measure between zero and one. Furthermore, the more a trader appears in the documents, the more likely he is to have such agency measure.[18]

The horizontal social structure of the Maghribis is also reflected in the forms of business associations through which agency relations were established among the Maghribis, mainly partnership and "formal friendship." In partnership two or more traders invested capital and labor in a joint venture and shared the profit in proportion to their capital investment. In "formal friendship" two traders who operated in different trade centers provided each other with agency services without receiving pecuniary compensation (Goiten 1967, 214 ff.; Stillman 1970; Gil 1983b, vol. 1, 200 ff.).[19]

In contrast, agency relations among the Genoese traders were vertical. Wealthy merchants who rarely if ever functioned as agents hired relatively poor agents who rarely if ever functioned as merchants (De Roover 1965, 51 ff.). Byrne (1916, 159) concluded that during the late twelfth century, "as a rule" the Genoese agents were "not men of great wealth or of high position." (p. 159) Agency measures calculated from specific cartularies reflect this assertion. For example, only 21 percent of the 190 trader families mentioned more than once in the cartulary of Giovanni Scriba (1155–1164) have an agency measure between zero and one, and in value terms only 11 percent have this agency measure.[20] The vertical character of the Genoese social structure is also reflected in the forms of business associations through which agency relations were established. They mainly used *commenda* contracts, which were, by and large, established between two parties, one providing capital and the other providing work in the form of traveling and transacting overseas. The difference in forms of business associations between the two merchant groups does not reflect diverse knowledge.[21]

Diverse cultural beliefs not only affect social patterns of economic interactions but also lead to diverse dynamics of wealth distribution. *Ceteris paribus*, a vertical society provides better opportunity for "upward" mobility to wealthless individuals (in a partial equilibrium framework). Since under individualist cultural beliefs an agent's ability to commit is negatively related to his wealth, wealthless individuals are better able to capture the rent (above the reservation utility) available to agents. In a horizontal society, wealthless individuals are not able to capture the rent available to agents, since under collectivist cultural beliefs one's commitment ability is positively related to one's wealth.

The historical sources are mute with respect to the dynamics of wealth distribution among the Maghribis, but the Genoese sources reflect a dynamics of wealth distribution that conforms to the theoretical prediction. Wealth transfer is reflected in a declining concentration of trade investment and the increase, over time, of trade investment made by commoners (that is, nonnobles). In the cartulary of Giovanni Scriba (1155–1164) trade was concentrated, by and large, in the hands of a few noble families, and less than 10 percent of the merchants invested 70 percent of the total. In the cartulary of Oberto Scriba (1186), 10 percent of the families invested less than 60 percent. In 1376, the only year for which, to the best of my knowledge, data are available in the secondary literature, commoners who paid customs in Genoa exceeded nobles (295 versus 279), and the share of the latter amounted to only 64 percent of the total (Kedar 1976, 51–52).[22] That agency relations shifted wealth distribution is reflected, for example, in the affairs of Ansaldo Baialardo, who was hired in 1156 by the noble Genoese merchant Ingo do Volta. From 1156 to 1158, Ansaldo sailed abroad as Ingo's agent, and by investing only his retained earnings he accumulated the sum of 142 lire. (A house in Genoa cost about 40 lire [see *Giovanni di Guiberto, 1200–1211*, nos. 260, 261].)[23]

An indirect indication of the growing wealth of the commoners is reflected in the political history of Genoa. A relative increase in the wealth possessed by a subgroup within a society is likely to lead them to demand a greater say in political matters. Indeed, the *popoli* of Genoa revolted during the thirteenth century against the nobility and changed the political organization of Genoa to reflect and protect their growing wealth (for example, Vitale 1955).

TRANSCENDING THE BOUNDARIES OF THE GAME: SEGREGATED AND INTEGRATED SOCIETIES

The Maghribis and the Genoese experienced over time a specific alteration in the merchant-agent game. Following various military and political changes in the Mediterranean, both groups had the opportunity to expand their trade to areas previously inaccessible to them (see, for example, A. R. Lewis 1951).[24] Commercially, both groups responded similarly and expanded their trade from Spain to Constantinople. From the perspective of societal organization, however, their responses differed. The Genoese responded in an "integrated" manner, but the Maghribis responded in a "segregated" manner.

The Maghribis expanded their trade employing other Maghribis as agents. They emigrated from North Africa to other trade centers, and for generations the descendants of Maghribis continued to cooperate with the descendants of other Maghribis (Goitein 1967, 156–59, 186–92; Gil 1983b, vol. 1, 200 ff.). For example, in the letters of Naharay ben Nissim, the most important Maghribi trader in Fustat around the midcentury, 97 different traders are mentioned but only two were Muslims.[25] This segregated response was not a result of the Maghribis being a religious minority, as they did not establish agency relations with other Jewish traders even when these relations were (ignoring agency cost) perceived by the Maghribis as very profitable. This was true, in particular, with respect to Italian Jewish merchants (Greif 1989, 1993a; Goitein 1973, 44, 211). That this segregation is endogenous is reflected in the Maghribis' later history when, toward the end of the twelfth century, they were forced by the ruler of Egypt to cease trading. At this point they integrated with the Jewish communities and vanished from the stage of history.

The Genoese also responded to the new opportunities by emigrating abroad, and their cartularies indicate that agency relations between Genoese prevailed. Yet although the cartularies were written in Genoa and hence are biased toward reflecting agency relations among Genoese, they nevertheless clearly indicate the establishment of agency relations between Genoese and non-Genoese. For example, in the cartulary of the Genoese Giovanni Scriba (1155–1164), at least 18.3 percent of the total sent abroad through agents was sent or carried by a non-Genoese.[26]

The rationale behind the Maghribis' and the Genoese's different responses to the same exogenous change in the rules of the game is clear once one considers the impact of cultural beliefs on equilibrium selection.[27] The change altered the OSPD game in a specific manner. As trade with more remote trade centers became possible, a merchant could either hire an agent from his own economy who would sail or move abroad, or hire an agent native to the other trade center. Such intereconomy agency relations are likely to be more efficient than intraeconomy agency relations, since they enhance commercial flexibility and a native agent does not need to immigrate and is likely to possess a better knowledge of local conditions.

In deciding whether to establish intereconomy agency relations, however, a merchant's concern is profitability, not efficiency. The relations between efficiency and profitability are influenced by cultural beliefs that had crystallized before intereconomy agency relations became possible. Individualist cultural beliefs lead to an "integrated" society in which intereconomy agency relations are established if they are efficient. Collectivist cultural beliefs create a wedge between efficient and profitable agency relations, leading to a "segregated" society in which efficient intereconomy agency relations are not established. Whenever there is uncertainty whether collectivist or individualist cultural beliefs will be practiced in intereconomy agency relations, these more efficient agency relations are less profitable to collectivist merchants since it increases the agents' wages.

To see why this is the case, suppose that two *identical* economies, within which either individualist cultural beliefs or collectivist cultural beliefs prevail, become a *joint economy* in which players can identify members of their previous economy but intereconomy agency relations are possible. What will the patterns of hiring agents in the joint economy be as a function of the players' cultural beliefs? (For ease of presentation, assume that past actions are common knowledge. Letting players invest in information greatly strengthens the results presented below.)

Intuitively, when players project their cultural beliefs on the new game—that is, when their expectations concerning others' actions in the postchange game are the prechange expectations—these prechange cultural beliefs constitute the initial conditions for a dynamic adjustment process.[28] For example, if the prechange economies were collectivist, players expect each merchant to hire agents from his own economy and expect that merchants of the same economy will retaliate against an agent who has cheated one of them. Yet the prechange cultural beliefs are insufficient to calculate best responses in the postchange game. They do not stipulate a complete strategy for a player, since the same prechange behavior implies off-the-path-of-play situations in the postchange game that did not exist before. For example, the prechange cultural beliefs do not specify how merchants from one economy would react to actions taken by an agent from their economy in intereconomy agency relations. As the others' strategies are not specified, a player cannot find his best response.

To find his best response, a merchant has to form expectations about the response of the merchants from the other economy to actions taken in intereconomy agency relations. Although the merchants from the agent's economy can be expected to respond in various ways, two responses predominate. For any agent's action in intereconomy agency relations, the merchants from the agent's economy can regard him either as one who cheated one of them or as one who did not cheat one of them. For example, in a collectivist economy the merchants may consider an agent who cheated in intereconomy agency relations as a cheater subject to collective retaliation, or they may ignore his cheating. There is nothing in the prechange cultural beliefs, however, that indicates which of these responses will be selected for each action. Accordingly, the best that can be done analytically is to assume that in intereconomy agency relations any probability distribution over these two responses is possible.[29] Considering the prechange cultural beliefs and any such probability distributions as initial conditions enables examination of the merchants' best response (while not imposing any differences between the prechange economies apart from their cultural beliefs).

What would the merchants' best response be as a function of their cultural beliefs? It is easier to present the related analysis, assuming initially that there is no efficiency gain from intereconomy agency relations. Intuitively, when intereconomy agency relations become possible between two collectivist economies, the initial cultural beliefs specify collective punishment in intraeconomy agency relations. But if there is some doubt whether collective punishment also governs intereconomy agency relations, the optimal wage in intereconomy agency relations is higher than in intraeconomy relations. It is higher because the uncertainty about collective punishment in intereconomy relations reduces the probability that an agent who cheats in such relations will be punished, and, as established in proposition 1, this increases the optimal wage. As the merchants' cost of establishing intereconomy agency relations is higher than the cost of establishing intraeconomy agency relations, only the latter will be initiated, and segregation is the end result. If intereconomy agency relations are more efficient, the analysis implies that merchants will initiate them only if the efficiency gains are sufficiently large.

The foregoing analysis does not hold when intereconomy agency relations become possible between two individualistic economies. Although similar uncertainty is likely to exist, the intereconomy and intraeconomy optimal wages are the same. Individualist cultural beliefs make this uncertainty irrelevant for the determination of the optimal wage. Hence any efficiency gains from intereconomy agency relations will motivate merchants to establish them.

While a similar analysis can be conducted when a collectivist and an individualist society interact, the preceding discussion indicates the mechanism through which cultural factors manifested through economic institutions support the emergence of distinct social structures which, in turn, reinforce the original cultural factors and economic institutions. Finally, the preceding discussion assumes that information regarding agents' histories can be obtained without any cost. Clearly, relaxing this assumption strengthens the results discussed above. In particular, if merchants do not learn about the actions taken by an agent in intereconomy agency relations, they cannot be expected to retaliate by imposing a collective punishment.

This section examines the relations between different cultural beliefs, the endogenous emergence of segregation and integration, and economic efficiency. Pareto-inferior segregation may prevail because of the structure of expectations and the absence of a mechanism able to alter them in a manner that makes this alteration common knowledge. Thus, the extent of trade expansion of a collectivist society is limited by the initial expectations regarding the boundaries of the society. Different cultural beliefs determine directions of trade expansion since individualist merchants are likely to penetrate collectivist societies but not the other way around. Indeed, during the period under consideration, trade expansion was based on Latin merchants' penetration into the Muslim world. Finally, as discussed in the next section, segregation and integration influence the relations between individuals and their society and hence affect the evolution of organizations that govern collective actions and facilitate exchange.

TRANSCENDING THE BOUNDARIES OF THE GAME: ORGANIZATIONAL EVOLUTION

Among the Maghribis, collectivist cultural beliefs led to a collectivist society with an economic self-enforcing collective punishment, horizontal agency relations, segregation, and an in-group social communication network. In a collectivist society, individuals can be induced to forgo "improper" behavior through a credible threat of informal collective economic punishment. Suppose, for example, that every Maghribi expects everyone else to consider a specific behavior as "improper" and punishable in the same manner as cheating in agency relations. This punishment is self-enforcing for the same reasons as the self-enforcing collective punishment in agency relations and is feasible because there is a network for information transmission. Furthermore, this punishment is likely to be reinforced by social and moral enforcement mechanisms that, as discussed earlier, emerge as a result of frequent economic interactions within a small segregated group. Clearly, to make the threat of collective punishment credible, there is a need to coordinate expectations by defining what constitutes "improper" behavior. In a collectivist society, this coordination is likely to be based on informal mechanisms such as customs and oral tradition.

Among the Genoese, individualist cultural beliefs led to an individualist society with a vertical and integrated social structure, a relatively low level of communication, and no economic self-enforcing collective punishment. In such a society a relatively low level of informal economic enforcement can be achieved because of the absence of economic self-enforcing collective punishment and networks for information transmission. Furthermore, the integrated social structure and the low level of communication hinder social and moral enforcement mechanisms. To support collective actions and to facilitate exchange, an individualist society needs to develop formal legal and political enforcement organizations. Further, a formal legal code is likely to be required to facilitate exchange by coordinating expectations and enhancing the deterrence effect of formal organizations.

During the period under consideration, both the Genoese and the Maghribis were establishing a governmental system. Genoa had just been incorporated into a city and liberated de facto from the rule of the Holy Roman Empire (see, for example, *Annali Genovesi*, vol. 1, 1162; Vitale 1955; Airaldi 1986). The Maghribis immigrated to and operated within the Fatimid caliphate, in which "the administration of their own affairs was left to themselves" (Goitein 1971, 1). Hence both groups were in a position to devise their own form of authority and jurisdiction. Yet it was the Genoese who developed formal organizations to support collective actions and exchange; the Maghribis did not develop such organizations and seem not to have used the ones available to them.

During the twelfth century the Genoese ceased to use the ancient custom of entering contracts by a handshake and developed an extensive legal system for registration and enforcement of contracts. Furthermore, the customary contract law that governed the relations between Genoese traders was codified as permanent courts were established (Vitale 1955). In contrast, despite the existence of a well-developed Jewish communal court system, the Maghribis entered contracts informally, adopted an informal code of conduct, and attempted to resolve disputes informally (Goitein 1967; Greif 1989, 1993a).

The relations between cultural beliefs and organizational development are reflected not only in these general processes but also in organizations that served specific economic aims. For example, in medieval trade, the need for enforcement organizations to support collective action was likely to manifest itself in relations between traders and rulers. The medieval ruler could abuse the property rights of *alien* traders visiting his territory. As long as the number of traders was low, the relatively high value for the ruler of each trader's future trade was sufficient to motivate the ruler to respect their rights. When the number of traders was large, however, this was no longer the case. A mechanism that might provide protection to traders at the higher volume of trade is for (sufficiently many) traders to respond—in the form of a trade embargo—to transgressions by the ruler against any trader. Once an embargo is declared, however, some traders can benefit from ignoring it and selling their goods in the prohibited area in times of shortage.

Hence, some enforcement mechanism is required to assure that each trader will indeed respect a collective decision to impose an embargo.[30] In collectivist societies, one would expect that informal enforcement mechanisms would be sufficient to ensure traders' compliance with embargo decisions. In individualist societies, however, one would expect organizations specializing in embargo enforcement to emerge.

Indeed, the historical evidence concerning the Maghribis and the Genoese is consistent with this prediction. Among the Maghribis, compliance was assured through informal means. After the Muslim ruler of Sicily abused the rights of some Maghribi traders, the Maghribis responded by imposing, circa 1050, an embargo on Sicily. It was organized informally. Maymun ben Khalpha wrote a letter to Naharay ben Nissim of Fustat (old Cairo) from Palermo (Sicily), in which he informed Naharay about the abuse and asked him to "hold the hands of our friends [that is, Maghribi traders] not to send to Sicily even one dirham [a low-value coin]." Indeed, the Maghribis sailed that year to Tunisia and not to Sicily, and a year later the abuse was remedied (David Kaufmann Collection, Hungarian Academy of Science, Budapest [no. 22, side a, lines 29–31; side b, lines 3–5]; Taylor-Schechter Collection, University Library, Cambridge [no. S 10 J 12, f. 26, side a, lines 18–20]; Michael 1965, vol. 2, 85; Gil 1983a, 97–106). There is no evidence that compliance was supported by any formal enforcement organization, although the Maghribis could have used the Jewish court system or a communal organization to this end.

In sharp contrast, the city of Genoa functioned as a formal enforcement organization to make the threat of collective retaliation credible. After the authorities had declared that a certain area was a *devetum*, any merchant found there was subject to legal prosecution. For example, in 1340 the ruler of Tabriz (an important trade center between the Black Sea and the Persian Gulf) abused many Genoese traders, and Genoa responded by declaring a *devetum* against the city. In 1343, during the *devetum*, a Genoese merchant named Tommaso Gentile was on his way from Hormuz to China. Somewhere in the Pamir plateau he fell sick and had to entrust his goods to his companions and head back to Genoa by the shortest route. His way, however, passed through Tabriz. When this became known in Genoa, Tommaso's father had to justify the transgression before the court, which accepted the claim of an act of God and acquitted Tommaso without penalty (Lopez 1943, 181–83).

The history of the modern bill of lading provides another example of a development of formal organizations among the Genoese but not among the Maghribis. This bill combines an earlier version of the bill of lading with a so-called bill of advice. The former was the ship's scribe's receipt for the goods the merchant deposited on the ship. This receipt was sent by the merchant to his overseas agent, who then claimed the goods on the basis of the scribe's own signature. The letter of advice was sent after the ship arrived at its destination by the ship's scribe to the consignee, who did not come to claim the goods. The bill of lading and the letter of advice surmounted an organizational problem related to the shipping of goods abroad.

The earliest known European bill of lading and letter of advice date from the 1390s and relate to the trade of Genoa, whereas the Maghribi traders hardly ever used the bill of lading even though it was known to them.[31] Why did the

Genoese advance the use of the bill and the Maghribis abandon it? The Maghribis rejected the bill because they had solved the related organizational problem by using their informal collective enforcement mechanism. Maghribis entrusted their goods to other Maghribis traveling on board the ship that carried their merchandise. For example, in a letter sent early in the eleventh century by Ephraim, son of Isma'il from Alexandria, to Ibn ʿAwkal, a prominent merchant who lived in Fustat, Isma'il mentions the names of the men in four different ships entrusted "to watch carefully the 70 bales and one barqalu [containing the goods] until they will deliver them safely into the hands of Khalaf son of Ya ʿqub" (Taylor-Schechter Collection, University Library, Cambridge [no. 13 J 17, f. 3]; Goitein 1973, 313).[32]

Instead of solving the organizational problem between the merchant and the ship's operator, the Maghribis circumvented it. This fact is forcefully illustrated in a letter sent from Sicily in 1057 that describes what happened to loads of merchandise whose covers were torn during a voyage. The ship arrived in port, and the owner (operator?) of the ship started to steal merchandise. The writer of the letter remarked that "unless my brother had been there to collect [the goods], nothing that belonged to our friends [that is, the Maghribi traders] would have been collected" (Bodleian Library, Oxford, MS Hebrew [no. c28, f. 61, side a, lines 12–14]; Gil 1983a, 126–33). The fact that the ship's owner did not consider himself, and was not considered by the traders, responsible for protecting the goods is clear from this letter. Similarly, if goods of unknown ownership were unloaded from the ship or if the ship did not reach its destination, it was not the captain but the Maghribi traders who took care of the goods of their fellow traders (Bodleian Library, Oxford, MS Hebrew [no. c28, f. 61, side a, lines 9–17]; Gil 1983a, 126–33). The Genoese traders, lacking an equivalent informal enforcement mechanism, could not rely on fellow traders to protect their goods and solved the organizational problem associated with shipping goods by using the bill of lading, the letter of advice, and the legal responsibility they entail.

The differences between collectivist and individualist societies are also likely to manifest themselves in the development of organizations related to agency relations. For example, recall that proposition 1 established that a reduction in the probability of forced separation, σ, reduced the optimal wage. That is, the more likely it is that there will be future relations between a specific agent and merchant, the less that merchant has to pay his agent. Yet the magnitude of this reduction is a function of cultural beliefs. This is so because the gains from reducing the probability of forced separation depend on the probability that a cheater will be rehired and the probability that an honest agent will be rehired. The lower the probability that a cheater will be rehired and the higher the probability that an honest agent will be rehired, the lower the gain from changing the probability of forced separation. Furthermore, when an unemployed honest agent will be rehired with probability one, the gain from changing the probability of forced separation is zero. That is, $\partial^2 W(\cdot)/\partial h_c d\sigma > 0$ (for $\beta > h_c$), $\partial^2 W(\cdot)/\partial h_h \partial\sigma < 0$, and finally, $\partial W/\partial\sigma = 0$ when $h_h = 1$.

Collectivist cultural beliefs and the resulting segregation and collective punishment increase, and may bring to one, the probability that an honest agent will be rehired. Furthermore, these factors are likely to bring to zero the probability that a cheater would be rehired. Thus, under collectivist beliefs and segregation, a merchant's incentive to reduce the probability of forced separation is marginal, or even absent. In contrast, under individualist cultural beliefs and the resulting integration and second-party punishment, merchants are motivated to establish an organization that reduces the likelihood of forced separation.

The evolution of family relations and business organization among the Maghribis and the Genoese suggests that the latter but not the former introduced an organization that changed the probability of forced separation. When the Maghribi and the Genoese merchants first began trading in the Mediterranean, it was common in both groups for a trader's son to start operating independently during his father's lifetime. The father would typically help the son until he was able to operate on his own. After the father's death, his estate was divided among his heirs and his business dissolved.[33] Later development of family relations and business organization, however, differs substantially. During the thirteenth century the Genoese traders adopted the family firm, the essence of which was a permanent partnership with unlimited and joint liability. This organization preserved the family wealth undivided under one ownership, and a trader's son, reaching the appropriate age, joined his family's firm (see De Roover 1965, 70 ff.; Rosenberg and Birdzell 1986, 123–24). The Maghribi traders, after being active in trade at least as long as the Genoese, did not establish a similar organization.

The analysis above indicates the sources of this uneven development. Given the collectivist cultural beliefs of the Maghribis and the resulting segregation, collective punishment, and horizontal relations, a merchant could not gain much by introducing an organization that reduced the likelihood of forced separation. Among the Italian traders, however, individualist cultural beliefs motivated merchants to increase the security of the employment they offered their agents. The family firm seems to have been the manifestation of this desire. In the Italian family firm, several traders combined their capital and formed an organization with an infinite life span and a lower probability of bankruptcy that replaced each individual merchant in his relationship with agents.[34]

The preceding historical examples illustrate that collectivist and individualist cultural beliefs are likely to motivate the introduction of different organizations. Once an organization is introduced for specific reasons, it is likely, as discussed in section II, to lead to other organizational innovations through learning and experimentation and as existing organizations direct responses to (historically) subsequent contractual problems. For example, the organizational "macroinvention" of the family firm led to organizational "microinventions" among the Italians. Family firms began to sell shares to non-family members. The capital of the Bardi Company consisted of 58 shares: six members of the family owned the majority of the shares, and five outsiders owned the rest. In 1312, the capital of the Peruzzi Company was distributed among eight members of the family and nine outsiders. In 1331, the Peruzzi family lost control of the company when more than half the capital belonged to outsiders (De Roover 1963, 77–78; De Roover 1965). Tradable shares required a suitable market, and "stock markets" were developed. Furthermore, the separation between ownership and control introduced by the family firm motivated the introduction of organizations able to surmount the related contractual problems, such as improvement in information transmission techniques, accounting procedures, and the incentive scheme provided to agents.

CONCLUSIONS

Constrained by the same technology and environment and facing the same organizational problem, the Maghribis and the Genoese had divergent cultural heritages and political and social histories that gave rise to different cultural beliefs. Theoretically, their cultural beliefs are sufficient to account for their diverse trajectories of societal organization, indicating how these forces may have had a lasting impact despite their temporary nature. Collectivist cultural beliefs constituted part of the Maghribis' collective enforcement mechanism and induced investment in information, segregation, horizontal economic interactions, and a stable pattern of wealth distribution. The endogenous partition of society restricted economic and social interactions to a small group and further facilitated in-group communication and economic and social collective punishments. Collectivist cultural beliefs led to a societal organization based on the group's ability to use economic, social, and, most likely, moral sanctions against deviants.

In contrast, individualist cultural beliefs constituted a part of the second-party enforcement mechanism of the Genoese and induced a low level of communication, a vertical social structure, economic and social integration, and wealth transfer to the relatively poor. These manifestations of individualist cultural beliefs weakened the dependence of each individual on any specific group, thereby limiting each group's ability to use economic, social, and moral sanctions against individual members. Individualist cultural beliefs led to a societal organization based on legal, political, and (second-party) economic organizations for enforcement and coordination.

The analysis demonstrates how the interactions between institutions, exogenous changes, and the process of organizational innovation govern the historical development of societal organization and the related economic, political, legal, and social constructs. Each of these elements complements the others to generate a self-sustained system, and each of the two systems analyzed in this paper has different efficiency implications. The collectivist system is more efficient in supporting intraeconomy agency relations and requires less costly formal organizations (such as law courts), but it restricts efficient intereconomy agency relations. The individualist system does not restrict intereconomy agency relations but is less efficient in supporting intraeconomy relations and requires costly formal organizations. Furthermore, each system entails different patterns of wealth distribution, each of which is likely to have different efficiency implications. This implies that the relative efficiency of individualist and collectivist systems depends on the magnitude of the relevant parameters. Hence although in the long run the Italians drove the Muslim traders out of the Mediterranean, the historical records do not enable any explicit test of the relative efficiency of the two systems.

Yet it is intriguing that the Maghribis' societal organization resembles that of contemporary developing countries, whereas the Genoese societal organization resembles the developed West, suggesting that the individualistic system may have been more efficient in the long run. The analysis in this chapter enables conjecturing about the possible long-run benefits of the individualistic system. To the extent that the division of labor is a necessary condition for long-run sustained economic growth, formal enforcement institutions that support anonymous exchange facilitate economic development. Individualist cultural beliefs foster the development of such institutions and hence enable society to capture these efficiency gains. Further, an individualist society entails less social pressure to conform to social norms of behavior and hence fosters initiative and innovation. Indeed, Genoa was well known among the Italian city-states for its individualism and was a leader in commercial initiative and innovation (Greif 1993b). Historically, then, the medieval Latin individualist society may have cultivated the seeds of the "Rise of the West."[35]

Although the conjectures discussed above await further research, this chapter points to factors that make trajectories of societal organization—and hence economic growth—path dependent. Given the technologically determined rules of the game, institutions—the nontechnological constraints on human interactions—are composed of two interrelated elements: cultural beliefs (how individuals expect others to act in various contingencies) and organizations (the endogenous human constructs that alter the rules of the game and, whenever applicable, have to be an equilibrium). Thus, the capacity of societal organization to change is a function of its history, since institutions are combined of organizations and cultural beliefs, cultural beliefs are uncoordinated expectations, organizations reinforce the cultural beliefs that led to their adoption, and past organizations and cultural beliefs influence historically subsequent games, organizations, and equilibria.

Understanding the sources of institutional path dependence indicates the factors that forestall successful intersociety adoption of institutions for which there are many historical and contemporary examples. North (1991) pointed out that the adoption of the U.S. Constitution by South American countries did not lead to democracy, and Litwack (1991) pointed to the failure of "Western" organizational reforms in the Soviet Union to generate any economic benefit. The view of institutions developed in this chapter indicates why it is misleading to expect that a beneficial organization of one society will yield the same results in another. The effect of organizations is a function of their impact on the rules of the game *and* the cultural beliefs of the society within which this game is embedded. Analyzing economic and political institutions and the impact of organizational modifications requires the examination of the historical development and implications of the related cultural beliefs.

Past, present, and future economic growth is not a mere function of endowment, technology, and preferences. It is a complex process in which the organization of society plays a significant role. The organization of society itself, however, reflects historical, cultural, social, political, and economic processes. Comparative historical analysis is likely to enhance our comprehension of the evolution of diverse societal organization, since this process is historical in nature. Furthermore, such an analysis provides the historical perspective and diversity required to examine institutional evolution and the interrelations between culture, the organization of society, and economic growth.

APPENDIX
Proof of Proposition 1

For a given h_c and h_h, to show that playing honest is optimal for the agent, it is sufficient to show that he cannot gain from cheating one period if offered W^*. Accordingly, denote by V_h the present value of lifetime expected utility of an employed agent who, whenever hired, is honest. Denote by V_h^u the present value of the lifetime expected utility of an unemployed honest agent. Denote by V_c^u the lifetime expected utility of an unemployed cheater (who will be honest in the future if hired). These lifetime expected utilities are

$$V_h = W^* + \beta(1 - \sigma) V_h + \sigma V_h^u,$$
$$V_i^u = \beta h_i V_h + \beta(1 - h_i)(\phi_u + V_i^u), \ i = h, c.$$

Cheating once yields $\alpha + V_c^u$ as the agent's present value of his lifetime expected utility. Thus an agent will not cheat if $V_h \geq \alpha + V^u c$. Substituting and rearranging yield the result that an agent's best response is being honest if and only if

$$W \geq (\Sigma - \beta \sigma H_h) \left[\frac{\alpha}{1 - \beta H_c} + \beta \, \phi_u \left(\frac{P_c}{1 - \beta H_c} - \sigma P_h \right) \right] = W^*,$$

where $\Sigma = 1 - \beta(1 - \sigma)$; $H_i = h_i / [1 - \beta(1 - h_i)]$, $i = h, c$, and

$$P_i = \frac{1 - h_i}{1 - \beta(1 - h_i)}, i = h, c.$$

The properties of W can be derived from this expression using the fact that $h_c \leq h_h$. Q.E.D.

Proof of Proposition 2

Under both strategies, the merchants act in accordance with the strategy assumed in proposition 1.[36] Under the individualist strategy, $h_c = h_h > 0$, whereas under the collectivist strategy, $h_h > 0$ and $h_c = 0$ after every history. Hence, proposition 1 holds, and given W^*, an agent cannot do better by deviating. This implies that on the equilibrium path a merchant's strategy is a best response. The only nontrivial part of the proof regarding off-the-path-of-play events is verifying the optimality of the merchant's hiring procedures after cheating under the collectivist strategy. Denote the probability that a cheater (honest agent) will be hired by h_c^c (h_h^c) under the collectivist strategy. Note that under this strategy $h_c^c = 0$ (since a cheater is not expected to be rehired), but along the equilibrium path, $h_h^c = \sigma M/[A - (1 - \sigma)M] > 0$ (since an honest agent will be hired in the future). According to proposition 1, the optimal wage for a cheater is $W_c^* = w(\cdot, h_h^c = 0, h_c^c = 0)$ and the optimal wage for an honest agent is $W_h^* = w(\cdot, h_h^c > 0, h_c^c = 0)$. Since the function w decreases in h_h, $W_c^* > W_h^*$, and a merchant strictly prefers to hire an agent who has always been honest rather than an agent who has cheated. Thus firing a cheater and hiring only from the pool of honest agents are optimal for the merchant. Note that this implies that in another off-the-path-of-play event in which a merchant did not fire an agent who cheated him, there is no wage for which it is profitable for the merchant to employ the agent. The merchant should pay this agent at least W_c^*, implying that even if this agent will be honest, the best response of the merchant is to fire him in the next period. Hence, for any $W \neq \alpha$, the agent's best response is to cheat. Q.E.D.

I gratefully acknowledge the support of National Science Foundation grants 9009598 and 9223974. This paper was written when I was a National Fellow at the Hoover Institution, Stanford, California, and completed when I was a fellow at the Center for Advanced Study in the Behavioral Sciences, Stanford, whose hospitality greatly facilitated this research. I have elaborated on similar ideas previously (Greif, in press). I wish to thank Partha Dasgupta for encouraging me to undertake this project and Masahiko Aoki, Paul David, Stanley Engerman, W. Bentley MacLeod, Paul Milgrom, Jeroen Swinkels, Julie Schaffner, Gavin Wright, two anonymous referees, and an editor of the *Journal of Political Economy* for helpful remarks. A previous version of this chapter benefited from the comments of participants in the Von Gremp Workshop in Economic and Entrepreneurial History at the University of California at Los Angeles, the Uncertainty Seminar at the University of Chicago Business School, the All Department Seminar at Tel Aviv University, the 1993 Tokyo Center for Economic Research conference on economic theory, and the applied micro seminar at the University of British Columbia.

NOTES

This is a much abridged version of an article originally published in the *Journal of Political Economy* 102(5): 912–50. It is reprinted with permission from the University of Chicago.

1. Clearly, any society has individualistic and collectivist elements, and categorization is a matter of their relative importance. For discussions, see Bellah et al. (1985), Reynolds and Norman (1988), and Triandis (1990).

2. See, for example, Polanyi (1957), North (1981, 1990), and Cole, Mailath, and Postlewaite (1992). Regarding path dependence, see Arthur (1988) and David (1988). On path dependence and institutions, see North (1990, 1991) and David (1992).

3. Game theory has been employed to examine social norms and status (for example, Schotter 1981; Okuno-Fujiwara and Postlewaite 1990; Kandori 1992) as well as conventions and focal points (for example, Schelling 1960; D. Lewis 1969; Sugden 1989; Kreps 1990).

4. Mokyr (1990) introduced this terminology with respect to technological change.

5. This view of culture as a "legitimizing" mechanism is fundamental in Karl Marx and Emile Durkheim. For recent economic analyses, see Sugden (1989) and Rabin (in press).

6. For a general introduction to Genoa's history, see Vitale (1955). For a general introduction to the Maghribis' history, see Goitein (1967), Gil (1983b, vol. 1), and Greif (1989, 1993a).

7. Williamson (1985) calls attention to the importance of using transaction as a unit of analysis.

8. For the superiority of trading systems that employ agents, see, for example, De Roover (1965).

9. For an efficiency wage model in which this result is derived endogenously, see MacLeod and Malcomson (1989).

10. In Greif (in press) this subset is referred to as "behavioral beliefs." In a perfect information extensive form game, denote by P a path of play, and define $S(P)$ to be the set of all strategy combinations for which the path of play is P. Denote the cultural beliefs of player i by CB_i $(S(P))$ defined as a probability distribution over $S(P)$. Note that diverse cultural beliefs differ

only in terms of expectations concerning behavior off the path of play. When it is common knowledge that

$$CB_i(P(S)) = \{prob(s^*(P) = 1)\} \ \forall \ i \text{ for some } s^*(P)$$

and

$$U_i(s_i^*, CB_i(S(P))) \geq U_i(s_i, CB_i(P(S))) \ \forall \ i \text{ and } s_i \in S_i,$$

then s^* is a Nash equilibrium. Hence $s^*(P)$ is an equilibrium and the associated cultural beliefs are self-enforcing.

11. For a discussion of imperfect monitoring models, see Pearce 1992. Under imperfect monitoring, agents will be punished on the equilibrium path. This does not qualitatively alter the results of this chapter.

12. These letters are those available regarding the trade with Sicily and Israel during the mid-eleventh century and the trade of Naharay ben Nissim (see Michael 1965; Gil 1983b; Ben-Sasson 1991).

13. In the 175 contracts mentioned here that reflect at least 652 business ventures, only three cases of alleged cheating are mentioned.

14. For other examples and a discussion, see Greif (1989, 1993a).

15. To shorten the presentation, this extension is not made explicit here.

16. See also Greif (1989, 1993a). Regarding the Italian merchants not holding such beliefs, see, for example, De Roover (1965, 88–89).

17. For formal presentation and further elaboration of this discussion, see Greif (1994, 925–27).

18. This data set is defined in note 12. The nature of the sources precludes calculating a value-based agency measure for the Maghribis.

19. For business associations, see Goitein (1973, 11 ff.); Gil (1983b, vol. 1, 216 ff.); Goitein (1964, 316), concluded that about half of the business dealings reflected in the Geniza are formal friendships.

20. Krueger (1957) concluded that only 6 percent (36 traders) in of those mentioned in Giovanni Scriba's cartulary functioned as both agents and merchants.

21. See Krueger (1962). For general discussion, see, for example, De Roover (1965). Knowledge: Lieber (1968).

22. De Roover (1965) argued that agency relations in Italy facilitated wealth transfer.

23. De Roover (1965, 51–52).

24. Among these changes were the disintegration of the Muslim caliphate in Spain, the rise of the Fatimids in North Africa, and the decline of the Byzantine naval power.

25. Al Qasim and Muhammad. Based on the thirty-seven documents published by Michael (1965).

26. For non-Genoese in other cartularies see, for example, *Oberto Scriba de Mercato 1186*, nos. 9, 38; *Oberto Scriba de Mercato, 1190*, 138, 139; *Guglielmo Cassinese (1190–1192)*, nos. 418, 1325, and *Lanfranco (1202–1226)*, no. 524. The ease of hiring non-Genoese is reflected in their use to circumvent a politically unfavorable situation in Sicily (see Abulafia 1977, 201 ff.).

27. For a formal presentation of the following discussion, see Greif (1994), section VI.

28. For references and results regarding this type of convergence, see Milgrom and Roberts (1990). For a sociological discussion regarding the tendency of human beings to feel that culture patterns of behavior *ought* to be followed and the tension between this feeling and the actual behavior, see Davis (1949, 52–53). For a recent economic analysis, see Geanakoplos, Pearce, and Stacchetti (1989).

29. This probability distribution can also be thought of as reflecting a merchant's uncertainty regarding the agent's expectations concerning the responses of the merchants from the agents' economy.

30. For a theoretical exposition of the traders-ruler relations, the associated commitment problem, and the role of the European merchant guild in assuring collective action, see Greif, Milgrom, and Weingast (1994).

31. For information on Genoa, see Bensa (1925). For the use of the bill of lading by the Maghribi traders and possible bias in the historical records, see Goitein (1973, 305 ff).

32. For the generality of this practice, see Goitein (1967).

33. Regarding the Maghribis, see Goitein (1967, 180 ff.) and Gil (1983b, vol. 1, 215 ff). Regarding the Genoese, see *Il Cartolare di Giovanni Scriba, 1154–1164*, nos. 236, 575, 946, 1047.

34. Additional theoretical and historical work is required to establish whether and how the family firm achieved a level of commitment above that of each of its individual members. It should be noted that agency relations in the Italian family firms were not confined to family members (see De Roover 1963, 1965).

35. See Greif (in press) regarding the extent to which the Maghribis' experience represents that of other groups in the Muslim world.

36. For technical reasons, it is assumed that if a merchant offers $W = 0$, employment is de facto not taking place and the merchant receives ξ and the agent receives ϕ_u; that the collectivist strategy also calls for ignoring cheating by more than one agent; and that under the individualist strategy in the off-the-path-of-play event in which a merchant did not fire an agent who cheated him, the agent's strategy specifies cheating for every wage and the merchant's strategy specifies offering $W = 0$.

REFERENCES

Abulafia, David. 1977. *The Two Italies: Economic Relations between the Norman Kingdom of Sicily and the Northern Communes*. Cambridge, England: Cambridge University Press.

Airaldi, Gabriella. 1986. *Genova e la liguria nel medioevo*. Turin, Italy: Utet Libreria.

Annali genovesi di Caffaro e dei suoi continuatori, 1099–1240. 4 vols. 1923–29. Translated by Ceccardo Roccatagliata Ceccardi and Giovanni Monleone. Genoa, Italy: Municipio di Genova.

Arthur, W. Brian. 1988. "Self-Reinforcing Mechanisms in Economics." In *The Economy as an Evolving Complex System*, edited by Philip W. Anderson, Kenneth J. Arrow, and David Pines. Redwood City, Calif.: Addison-Wesley.

Bandura, Albert. 1977. *Social Learning Theory*. Englewood Cliffs, N.J.: Prentice-Hall.

Banerjee, Abhijit V., and Andrew F. Newman. 1993. "Occupational Choice and the Process of Development." *Journal of Political Economy* 101 (April): 274–98.

Bellah, Robert N., Richard Madsen, William M. Sullivan, Ann Swidler, and Steven M. Tipton. 1985. *Habits of the Heart: Individualism and Commitment in American Life*. Berkeley, Calif.: University of California Press.

Bensa, Enrico. 1925. *The Early History of Bills of Lading*. Genoa, Italy: Stabilimento d'Arti Grafiche.

Ben-Sasson, Menahem. 1991. *The Jews of Sicily, 825–1068*. Jerusalem, Israel: Ben Zvi Institute.

Byrne, Eugene H. 1916. "Commercial Contracts of the Genoese in the Syrian Trade of the Twelfth Century." *Quarterly Journal of Economics* 31 (November): 128–70.

Cahen, Claude. 1970. "Economy, Society, Institutions." In *The Cambridge History of Islam*. Vol. 2B, *Islamic Society and Civilization*, edited by P. M. Holt, Ann K. S. Lambton, and Bernard Lewis. Cambridge, England: Cambridge University Press.

Il Cartolare di Giovanni Scriba, 1154–1164. 1935. Edited by Mario Chiaudano and Mattia Moresco. Torino, Italy: Lattes & Editori.

Cole, Harold L., George J. Mailath, and Andrew Postlewaite. 1992. "Social Norms, Savings Behavior, and Growth." *Journal of Political Economy* 100 (December): 1092–1125.

David, Paul A. 1988. "Path-Dependence: Putting the Past into the Future of Economics." Stanford University. Unpublished paper.
———. 1992. "Why Are Institutions the 'Carriers of History'?" Stanford University. Unpublished paper.
Davis, Kingsley. 1949. *Human Society.* New York: Macmillan.
Dawes, Robyn M., and Richard H. Thaler. 1988. "Anomalies: Cooperation." *Journal of Economic Perspectives* 2 (summer): 187–97.
De Roover, Raymond A. 1963. *The Rise and Decline of the Medici Bank, 1397–1494.* Cambridge, Mass.: Harvard University Press.
———. 1965. "The Organization of Trade." In *Cambridge Economic History of Europe.* Vol. 3, *Economic Policies in the Middle Ages,* edited by M. Michael Postan, E. E. Rich, and Edward Miller. Cambridge, England: Cambridge University Press.
Geanakoplos, John, David Pearce, and Ennio Stacchetti. 1989. "Psychological Games and Sequential Rationality." *Games and Economic Behavior* 1 (March): 60–79.
Gill, M. 1983a. "The Jews in Sicily under the Muslim Rule in the Light of the *Geniza* Documents." Tel Aviv University. Manuscript. Also in Italian in *Italia Judaaica.* Rome, Italy: Instituto Poligrafico e Zecca dello Stato.
———. 1983b. *Palestine during the First Muslim Period (634–1099).* 3 vols. Tel Aviv, Israel: Ministry Defence Press and Tel Aviv University Press.
Giovanni di Guiberto, 1200–1211. 1939–40. Documents 17–18. Edited by M. W. Hall-Cole and R. G. Reinert. Turin, Italy: Editrice Libraria Italiana.
Goitein, S. D. 1964. "Commercial and Family Partnerships in the Countries of Medieval Islam." *Islamic Studies* 3 (September): 315–37.
———. 1967. *A Mediterranean Society.* Vol. 1, *Economic Foundations: The Jewish Communities of the Arab World as Portrayed in the Documents of the Cairo Geniza.* Berkeley, Calif.: University of California Press.
———. 1971. *A Mediterranean Society.* Vol. 2, *The Community.* Berkeley, Calif.: University of California Press.
———. 1973. *Letters of Medieval Jewish Traders.* Princeton: Princeton University Press.
Greif, Avner. 1989. "Reputation and Coalitions in Medieval Trade: Evidence on the Maghribi Traders." *Journal of Economic History* 49 (December): 857–82.
———. 1993a. "Contract Enforceability and Economic Institutions in Early Trade: The Maghribi Traders' Coalition." *American Economic Review* 83 (June): 525–48.
———. 1993b. "On the Political Foundations of the Late Medieval Commercial Revolution: Genoa During the Twelfth and Thirteenth Centuries." Stanford University. Unpublished paper.
———. 1994. "Cultural Beliefs and the Organization of Society: A Historical and Theoretical Reflection on Collectivist and Individualist Societies." *Journal of Political Economy* 102 (October): 912–50.
———. In press. "Cultural Beliefs as a Common Resource in an Integrating World: An Example from the Theory and History of Collectivist and Individualist Societies." In *The Economics of Transnational Commons,* edited by Partha Dasgupta, K.-G. Mäler, and A. Vercelli. Oxford, England: Caldamon Press.
Greif, Avner, Paul Milgrom, and Barry Weingast. 1994. "Coordination, Commitment, and Enforcement: The Case of the Merchant Guild." *Journal of Political Economy* 102 (4): 745–76.
Guglielmo Cassinese (1190–1192). 1938. In *Notai liguri del sec. XII,* edited by Margaret W. Hall, Hilmar C. Krueger, and Robert L. Reynolds. Torino: Editrice Libraria Italiana.
Homans, George. 1950. *The Human Group.* New York: Harcourt.
Hughes, Diane Owen. 1974. "Toward Historical Ethnography: Notarial Records and Family History in the Middle Ages." *Historical Methods Newsletter* 7 (March): 61–71.
Kandori, Michihiro. 1992. "Social Norms and Community Enforcement." *Review of Economic Studies* 59 (January): 63–80.
Kedar, Benjamin Z. 1976. *Merchants in Crisis: Genoese and Venetian Men of Affairs and the Fourteenth-Century Depression.* New Haven, Conn.: Yale University Press.
Kreps, David. M. 1990. "Corporate Culture and Economic Theory." In *Perspectives on Positive Political Economy,* edited by James E. Alt and Kenneth A. Shepsle. Cambridge, England: Cambridge University Press.

Krueger, Hilmar C. 1957. "Genoese Merchants, Their Partnerships and Investments, 1155 to 1164." In *Studi in onore di Armando Sapori*. Milan, Italy: Instituto Editoriale Cisalpino.

———. 1962. "Genoese Merchants, Their Associations and Investments 1155 to 1230." In *Studi in onore di Amintore Fanfani*. Vol. 1, *Antichità e alto medioevo*. Milan, Italy: Giuffrè.

Lanfranco, 1202–1226. 1952–54. In *Notai liguri del sec. XII e del XIII*, edited by Hilmar C. Krueger and Robert L. Reynolds. Genoa, Italy: Società Ligure di Storia Patria.

Lewis, Archibald R. 1951. *Naval Power and Trade in the Mediterranean, A.D. 500–1100*. Princeton, N.J.: Princeton University Press.

Lewis, Bernard. 1988. *The Political Language of Islam*. Chicago, Ill.: University of Chicago Press.

Lewis, David K. 1969. *Convention: A Philosophical Study*. Cambridge, Mass.: Harvard University Press.

Lieber, Alfred E. 1968. "Eastern Business Practices and Medieval European Commerce." *Economic History Review* 21 (August): 230–43.

Litwack, John M. 1991. "Legality and Market Reform in Soviet-Type Economies." *Journal of Economic Perspectives* 5 (fall): 77–89.

Lopez, Robert Sabatino. 1943. "European Merchants in the Medieval Indies: The Evidence of Commercial Documents." *Journal of Economic History* 3 (November): 164–84.

MacLeod, W. Bentley, and James M. Malcomson. 1989. "Implicit Contracts, Incentive Compatibility, and Involuntary Unemployment." *Econometrica* 57 (March): 447–80.

Marimon, Ramon. 1988. "Wealth Accumulation with Moral Hazard." Hoover Institution, Stanford University. Unpublished paper.

Michael, M. 1965. "The Archives of Naharay ben Nissim, Businessman and Public Figure in Eleventh Century Egypt." Ph.D. diss., Hebrew University.

Milgrom, Paul R., and John Roberts. 1990. "Rationalizability, Learning, and Equilibrium in Games with Strategic Complementarities." *Econometrica* 58 (November): 1255–77.

Mokyr, Joel. 1990. *The Lever of Riches: Technological Creativity and Economic Progress*. Oxford, England: Oxford University Press.

North, Douglass C. 1981. *Structure and Change in Economic History*. New York: Norton.

———. 1990. *Institutions, Institutional Change, and Economic Performance*. Cambridge, England: Cambridge University Press.

———. 1991. "Institutions." *Journal of Economic Perspectives* 5 (winter): 97–112.

North, Douglass C., and Barry R. Weingast. 1989. "Constitutions and Commitment: The Evolution of Institutions Governing Public Choice in Seventeenth-Century England." *Journal of Economic History* 49 (December): 803–32.

Oberto Scriba de mercato, 1186. 1940. Documents 11 and 16. Edited by Mario Chiaudano and R. Morozzo Della Rocca. Turin, Italy: Deputazione di Storia Patria per la Liguria Genoa.

Oberto Scriba de mercato, 1190. 1938. Edited by Mario Chiaudano and R. Morozzo Della Rocca. Turin, Italy: Deputazione di Storia Patria per la Liguria Genoa.

Okuno-Fujiwara, Masahiro, and Andrew Postlewaite. 1990. "Social Norms and Random Matching Games." Working Paper 90–18. Philadelphia, Penn.: Center for Applied Research in Economics and Social Science, University of Pennsylvania.

Pearce, David. G. 1992. "Repeated Games: Cooperation and Rationality." In *Advances in Economic Theory, Sixth World Congress*. Vol. 1, edited by Jean-Jacques Laffont. Cambridge, England: Cambridge University Press.

Polanyi, Karl. 1957. *The Great Transformation*. Boston, Mass.: Beacon Hill.

Rabin, Matthew. In press. "Cognitive Dissonance and Social Change." *Journal of Economic Behavior and Organization*.

Reynolds, Charles H., and Ralph V. Norman, eds. 1988. *Community in America: The Challenge of Habits of the Heart*. Berkeley, Calif.: University of California Press.

Rosenberg, Nathan, and Luther E. Birdzell, Jr. 1986. *How the West Grew Rich: The Economic Transformation of the Industrial World*. New York: Basic Books.

Schelling, Thomas C. 1960. *The Strategy of Conflict*. Cambridge, Mass.: Harvard University Press.

Schotter, Andrew. 1981. *The Economic Theory of Social Institutions*. Cambridge, England: Cambridge University Press.

Shapiro, Carl, and Joseph E. Stiglitz. 1984. "Equilibrium Unemployment as a Worker Discipline Device." *American Economic Review* 74 (June) 433–44.

Stillman, Norman Arthur. 1970. "East-West Relations in the Islamic Mediterranean in the Early Eleventh Century." Ph.D. diss., University of Pennsylvania.

Sugden, Robert. 1989. "Spontaneous Order." *Journal of Economic Perspectives* 3 (fall): 85–97.

Triandis, Harry C. 1990. "Cross-Cultural Studies of Individualism and Collectivism." In *Nebraska Symposium on Motivation*. Vol. 37, edited by John J. Berman. Lincoln, Neb.: University of Nebraska Press.

Vitale, Vito. 1955. *Breviario della storia di Genova*. Genoa, Italy: Società Ligure di Storia Patria.

Williamson, Oliver E. 1985. *The Economic Institutions of Capitalism: Firms, Markets, Relational Contracting*. New York: Free Press.

— 5 —

Conflict over Changing Social Norms: Bargaining, Ideology, and Enforcement

Jack Knight and Jean Ensminger

S ocial norms are the foundation of social life. They govern social relations and establish expectations as to how we are to act in our everyday affairs. They facilitate continuity across generations and among changing populations, and constitute an ongoing record of the history of social practices in a community. They structure social interactions in ways that allow social actors to gain the benefits of joint activity. And they determine in significant ways the distribution of the benefits of social life.

These effects of social norms are the focus of much of the work in the social sciences, including among economists, who, for example, have increasingly recognized the importance of social norms in contributing to economic performance (North 1990). While this work differs widely as to how norms substantively affect social behavior, most of it conceives of norms, at least in part, as rules. From one perspective, Coleman (1990), among others, treats norms as rules that structure strategic behavior. In his account, norms constrain behavior by affecting the incentives for various actions. They are treated as analogous to any other informal rule: people comply with norms when it is in their self-interest to do so. From a far different perspective, Bourdieu (1977) emphasizes nonconsequentialist motivations as the main explanation of norm compliance: people comply with norms because such rules define the appropriate form of behavior in a specific context. In Bourdieu's conception, when an individual acts pursuant to a social norm, that action is governed by a rule and the individual will act according to the dictates of the rule even if it is not in his or her narrow self-interest to do so.

In our analysis here we share with both perspectives the basic view that norms are informal rules that structure social interactions in ways that promote the benefits of cooperative behavior. Although we rely primarily upon strategic considerations in explaining why social actors comply with norms, we reject any narrow conception that limits compliance to self-interest and accept other non-self-interested motivations as possible reasons for compliance.[1] But explanations of social norms must do more than merely acknowledge the constraining effects of normative rules on social action. Such explanations must address the process that culminates in the establishment of one of these rules as the common norm in a community. One of the keys to the establishment of a new norm is the ability of those who seek to change norms to enforce compliance with the new norm.

We propose an approach to explain the emergence of and changes in social norms that draws on the rational choice tradition. Rational choice theorists have produced a number of accounts of the evolution of social norms.[2] Each starts from the premise that social actors pursue some set of preferences in a rational way. This means that social actors seek to achieve their most-preferred outcome in the least costly manner. But from this initial assumption, rational choice theorists develop different explanations about how social norms emerge and change. We argue elsewhere (Ensminger and Knight 1997) that whenever norms have distributional consequences for the actors involved, bargaining is the primary mechanism for the emergence and change of social norms.

Here we use a bargaining framework to analyze how social conflict is associated with changing social norms. Social norms have important distributional effects on who gets what from social interactions. Social actors will differ over the form that the norm should take, with each preferring that norm that best favors his or her individual interests and preferences. With respect to norms governing economic behavior, the implications for a bargaining mechanism are clear: bargaining over norms is a conflict among economic actors motivated by conflicting material interests. But with respect to norms that govern noneconomic behavior, the benefits derived from such behavior are nonmaterial. Thus, as actors seek to determine which norms are best for them, they are not motivated by a desire for material gain. Rather they are motivated by ideological values and nonmaterial preferences. Yet conflicts of interest are potentially just as likely to occur over ideologically motivated norm changes as over materially motivated ones. Thus, we argue here that ideology is compatible with a bargaining approach: bargaining power has an important role to play in instances of ideologically motivated change.

In the bargaining account we offer here, the question of which norm will be established is resolved by asymmetries in bargaining power: the norm most likely to be established will be the one that manifests the interests of those actors who enjoy a relative bargaining advantage. We define bargaining power as superiority in resource endowments. There are many factors that can determine the relative bargaining power of the actors. One important factor that affects the ability of those who are well-endowed to impose their preferred norms upon others is access to and control over methods of enforcement. If enforcement is centralized, such control may stem from privileged access to the state or other enforcement bodies. When enforcement is decentralized, it may be realized through rewards and negative sanctions embodied in such crosscutting ties as those of the clan or kinship network.

In this chapter we develop explanations of how superior bargaining power produces social norms. We show that, contrary to various sociological criticisms of the rational choice approach (Zald 1987; Oberschall and Leifer 1986; March and Olsen 1989), explanations grounded in rational decisionmaking can incorporate power asymmetries, distributional consequences, and ideological motivations not based upon economic interests. We present the basic logic of bargaining over social norms and offer an extended example of how social conflict produces norms of marriage in an African society. This first case is a relatively straightforward instance of bargaining over distributional gains. Then we consider the role of ideology in conjunction with bargaining power as a motivation for changing social norms. Although rational choice accounts usually borrow the neoclassical habit of assuming preferences rather than examining them, here we highlight conflict over ideologically defined preferences. Finally, we consider the complex issue of enforcement. New behaviors do not achieve the status of new norms until they are widely practiced. Therefore, we consider the evidence from a number of case studies on the role of enforcement in the process of changing social norms, giving special emphasis to factors that complicate enforcement efforts and diminish the likelihood of success for those who seek to change existing norms.

BARGAINING OVER NORMS FOR DISTRIBUTIONAL ADVANTAGE

The bargaining approach explains the emergence of social norms primarily in terms of the distributional effect of the possible norms (Knight 1992). In the classic bargaining account, social norms are a by-product of strategic conflict: actors produce social norms in the process of seeking distributional advantage in the conflict over substantive benefits. In some cases they will create norms consciously; in other cases the norms will emerge as unintended consequences of the pursuit of strategic advantage. In each case the main focus is on the substantive outcome; the development of the norm is merely a means to that substantive end. As in any bargaining situation, there are some factors that distinguish the actors and thus influence the bargaining outcome in favor of one of the parties. In our analysis, asymmetries in resource ownership serve as a proxy for bargaining power. These factors are what we usually refer to when we speak of bargaining power (Bachrach and Lawler 1981; Raiffa 1982). Asymmetries in resource ownership affect the willingness of rational self-interested actors to accept the bargaining demands of other actors. Social actors suffer significant costs for the failure to coordinate on social outcomes, yet those costs need not be suffered uniformly. Those actors who have either fewer alternatives or less beneficial ones will be more inclined to respect the commitments of those who have substantial resources. In this way, the existence of resource asymmetries in a society can significantly influence the choice of a social norm. The task of a bargaining theory of norm emergence is to identify those factors that are most likely to explain (1) how bargaining gets resolved in a single interaction and (2) how a particular outcome gets enforced and generalized for the community as a whole.

To better understand how bargaining power affects this process, it is helpful to analyze the way in which norms structure social interactions. Norms establish expectations about what people will do in common social situations and thus guide us to act in particular ways in those situations. We comply with social norms in order to gain the benefits of coordinated social activity. In analytical terms, norms structure social situations that are characterized by the existence of multiple equilibria; that is, there is more than one way of coordinating our behavior in a particular setting, but we need to establish shared expectations as to which of those ways we will actually choose. Norm creation involves the establishment of shared expectations, while norm change involves changing those expectations.

Bargaining power affects norm creation and change in those situations in which social actors differ in their preferences over which form of behavior should be embodied in the norm. Bargaining over the establishment of a norm consists of an assessment of the credibility of various claims made by the actors (either explicitly through negotiations or implicitly through their previously demonstrated behavior) about their commitments to various forms of behavior. For example, an actor might make the following claim: "I am going to act in a particular way regardless of what anybody else does." Other actors might then respond by either asserting a similarly adamant commitment to a different form of behavior, offering a compromise that is different from any of their most preferred forms of behavior or agreeing to the first actor's demand. A bargaining explanation of norm creation and change rests on the idea that relative bargaining power will ultimately determine whose commitments will be embodied in the dictates of the social norm.

It is important to note that the bargaining model is a simplification of a wide variety of social interactions, ranging from formal negotiations of the whole community to implicit strategic behavior that converges over time to form a common norm of behavior. Central to all of these various social interactions is the common feature of multiple equilibria in the social interaction, conflict in preferences over the range of possible norms of behavior, and asymmetries in the possession of relevant resources. The explanation of norm emergence and change rests primarily on the effects of these asymmetries on the acceptance or rejection of the various commitments that people claim to have to the alternative ways of acting in common social situations.

If everyone in a community had complete knowledge of how each person assessed the benefits and costs involved in committing to the different possible ways of behaving, then bargaining over social norms would be a fairly simple and straightforward process. People could rather quickly assess the extent to which their own preferred behavior was shared by others in the community and thus determine the relative benefits of sticking to their own approach versus adopting an alternative way of acting. The establishment of a social norm would occur as members of the community made this assessment and then adjusted their own actions to the form of behavior on which most of the community converged. But there are many features of social life that complicate this bargaining process. And most of these factors affect the ways in which social actors assess the long-run effects of committing to a particular way of acting.

In this chapter we focus on two such factors: ideology and the complexity of norm enforcement. We have already suggested some of the ways in which these factors can affect bargaining over norms, and it may be helpful to clarify how these factors enter into our analytical account. First, ideological beliefs affect how people assess the relative merits of various forms of behavior. To the extent that norms structure behavior and thus affect the outcomes of social interactions, they lead to significant consequences for various ways of living. For most people their ideological beliefs are grounded in their assessment of which consequences are best for themselves and their community. Thus, when ideological beliefs enter into the consideration of the relative merits of various possible norms, they will complicate the task of assessing the costs and benefits of the different alternatives. In so doing, ideology can alter the bargaining process in many ways, the most important of which involves the willingness of both the powerful and the powerless to both maintain existing commitments and accept proposals for change.

Second, the complexity and diversity of enforcement mechanisms affect the costs of maintaining commitments to various forms of behavior.[3] Sanctions are an important source of the costs of acting. Social actors employ many forms of sanctions as a way of forcing people to keep their commitments and to comply with social norms. When people are confronted with a choice between two forms of behavior, they must take account of the costs they might incur in selecting the different alternatives. The task of assessing these costs is especially acute when the issue is one of norm compliance versus norm change. There are the straightforward costs created by those who seek to enforce compliance with existing norms, but there are also the potential enforcement costs involved in seeking to change norms. Since the task of norm change involves changing established social expectations, the process of undertaking a change in an existing norm entails a process of coordination among those actors who share an interest in the change. To the extent that the interests of each member of this group depends on the cooperation of the other members, the members will seek to establish their own sanctioning mechanisms to ensure that the reform group will abide by their new commitments to the changed form of behavior. The success of reform efforts will depend in large part on the ability of such groups to establish and maintain these alternative enforcement mechanisms.

Before turning to our analysis of the relationship between bargaining over norms and the complicating factors of ideology and enforcement, we should briefly address a potential source of confusion in our conceptualization, with its emphasis on enforcement, of social norms. We treat norms as rules that stabilize social expectations and thus establish commitments to particular ways of acting in common social situations. From a purely behavioral perspective this leads to the following problem: what distinguishes a social norm and the behavior that it induces from a mere behavioral regularity or social practice? This is an especially difficult thing for a social scientist to discern because once a social norm has been firmly established in a community, the only thing that we should observe is the regularity in behavior embodied in the norm.[4] But there is an important distinction that lies in the differences in the reaction of the other members of the community to deviations from the regularity in the social practice.

To clarify the distinction, we must look at the problem from the internal perspective of the members of the community (Hart 1994). When an individual deviates from his normal behavior, those social actors with whom he interacts may be surprised or disappointed, but they do not feel either the need or the right to sanction him for the change in behavior. On the other hand, when an individual deviates from compliance with a social norm, the other members of the community generally feel that their expectations have been inappropriately violated and that they have a right to employ whatever means of informal sanctioning are at their disposal so as to make sure that the act of noncompliance will not be repeated.[5] This difference in internal perspective suggests that the task of the social scientist who seeks to distinguish social norms from mere regularities in behavior is to focus on the behavior manifest in the community when deviations from regular social practices are observed. When we observe sanctioning after deviant behavior, we have evidence to support a claim that a social norm exists. To better illustrate how the bargaining approach works we turn to an analysis of changes in social norms among the Galole Orma of northeastern Kenya.

THE CASE STUDY

The Galole Orma[6] of the Tana River District, Kenya, are a pastoral population, still partly nomadic, who live primarily off the products of their livestock (cattle, sheep, and goats). But like most pastoralists in Africa, the Orma are increasingly market-oriented and in recent years have had to adapt to considerable changes in their economic and political systems (see Ensminger 1992). Today, less than a third of the Galole Orma continue to attempt a subsistence-based nomadic existence, living off dairy products exclusively whenever milk yields will allow it and resisting the sale of their stock in order to maximize their herd size. The vast majority of Orma are now sedentary and sell stock on a regular basis to purchase their daily foodstuffs and household needs. They are effectively commercial ranchers, harvesting their annual off-take much as farmers harvest their crops. Large numbers of Orma also derive the majority of their income from wage labor and trade.

Bargaining over Political and Economic Advantage

We can begin to demonstrate the explanatory power of the bargaining approach by examining changes in norms requiring marriage outside the clan (clan exogamy) and marriage payments from the family of the groom to that of the bride (bridewealth). These examples allow us to show how a bargaining mechanism can explain the emergence of norms when either nonmaterial or material interests are involved. In each of these examples, we focus primarily on the following explanatory factors central to the bargaining approach: First, we look at how the norm affects the distribution of economic resources, power, or other benefits. For example, does the norm of clan exogamy or bridewealth distribute the benefits of marriage and family in a manner different than other marriage norms would? To the extent that a norm distributes these resources in unequal ways, there is evidence of a potential conflict of interest in the establishment of the norm that we would expect to see resolved in favor of those with the most bargaining power. Second, we look for evidence of asymmetries in bargaining power as the source of the emergence of a particular norm. Here it is important to ask whether there is a correlation between the distribution of asymmetries in bargaining power and the distribution of interests over the different alternative norms. For example, do those who disproportionately benefit from clan exogamy or bridewealth hold an advantage in the relevant resources that constitute bargaining power in the community? To the extent that there is evidence of the anticipated correlation between power and interests, the plausibility of the bargaining explanation is enhanced. And finally, we look to the method of enforcement of both existing and potentially new norms to see how it affects the capacity of those with a relative bargaining advantage to enforce compliance with their preferred norms.

Like many patrilineal African societies, the Orma have historically practiced clan exogamy; all marriages within the clan were forbidden. Here we can see how the conflict over norms governing marriage can explain the emergence of clan exogamy as well as how they are currently changing among the Orma.

While everyone in the community would benefit from some norm that structured marriages, the members differed over the nature of the particular rule. For example, clan exogamy is in the interests of elders to gain alliances, but it is not necessarily in the interests of youths who might wish to marry some of the potential spouses who are being defined as off-limits. Assuming that the bargaining power of the elders far exceeded that of the youth, perhaps by right of ownership of the cattle necessary for bridewealth payments, youth would have had little choice in the matter. Similarly, even some elders may not have been happy with the original practice of clan exogamy. Those elders who were anticipating their own marriage or that of their sons to the daughters who were originally "married out" from their group may not have been at all happy with the emergence of a norm of clan exogamy. If there was such a conflict of interest among the elders, then the norm of clan exogamy may have been initiated by the entrepreneurial behavior of some elder or elders who had the political and economic force to deny daughters in marriage to those who had most reason to expect such unions. Those most able to have made such a change would have been the elders who could "compensate" the wife-losers for their loss and thereby realize a net gain in political relations with outsiders that did not cost them equally in worsened relations with nearer groups. Enforcement could have been achieved by the refusal of elders to support in any way marriages within the clan. Because bridewealth is often accumulated from a wide circle of an individual's kin and members of the clan, such a refusal would have had a marked effect upon people's choices. Elders might also have refused to engage in marriages with families that did not practice clan exogamy. Because marriages to economically powerful families are highly desirable, even such uncoordinated and decentralized enforcement could have rapidly led to compliance throughout the society.

Within recent memory, the Orma practiced strict clan exogamy, but this norm is rapidly eroding. Orma clans are nonterritorial and responsible primarily for dispute resolution within the clan, for arranging marriages, and for such general assistance as help following droughts and contributions to bridewealth and funeral payments. All of these clan functions were in decline at the time of the first breaches of clan exogamy. The earliest remembered cases of marriage within the clan date to approximately 1980 and occurred simultaneously in the southern part of the region and in Galole.

Orma tradition recognizes three forms of marriage: by arrangement (*kadda*), elopement (*adaban*), and force (*buta*). Until recently, arranged marriages were by far the most numerous, though young women commonly eloped to avoid arranged marriages to old men. Older women, often grandmothers, were helpful in arranging for young girls to "run away" with young men in order to avoid undesirable matches. Forced marriage, where the young man literally captures the girl in the bush and rapes her with the intent of forcing a marriage, is still rare.[7] Today, elopement is greatly on the rise. In the past, elopement did not involve intraclan marriages, but today it is sometimes the means by which young men and women of the same clan manage to get consent for their union from their parents.

At least since their conversion to Islam in the 1920s, the Orma have placed great emphasis upon virgin marriage. In the past, the fact that a boy and girl "eloped" did not necessarily mean that the marriage was consummated. Nevertheless, the parents often consented to the union after heavy persuasion on the part of the couple's supporters. The threat was ever present that if the parents did not consent, the couple could always run away together again and consummate the marriage, thus "forcing" the issue, as the woman's marriageabilty would then be considerably reduced. Today, young men and women of the same clan who elope are more likely to consummate the marriage prior to informing their parents of the elopement. They may even stay away as long as three days to convince their parents of their determination. The consequence of such actions is that the parents almost always relent, and marriages within the clan are now quite common. This change in behavior also represents a change in attitude among the young regarding female virginity. Women feel less ashamed of losing their virginity prior to marriage than was the case in the past. Much to the chagrin of the elders, young men and women are marrying for love without concern for clan.

We hold that this change in norms is a direct result of the increasing bargaining power of young men and women vis-à-vis elders. There are a number of factors that have contributed to the change in bargaining power. Young men are earning a larger share of the household's income, which means that they are less dependent on their fathers for help with marriage payments and other financial assistance. If fact, sons in many cases are supporting their fathers. This is a complete reversal of past practice, where old men had complete control over cattle dispersal (the only significant form of wealth or income) until their death. In addition, joint extended families are splitting up more frequently prior to the death of the father, which contributes to independent decisionmaking. Moreover, marriage payments are also declining.

These changes in the relative bargaining power of young men also work to the benefit of the interests of young women. For their part, women also have a desire to marry for love. And sedentary women report that they seek to avoid at all costs a marriage to a nomad or a very old man. If such a marriage has been arranged for a sedentary woman, she is at great risk for elopement. The Islamic courts (*kadi*) have also enhanced young women's bargaining power by supporting a woman's right to resist a marriage that she does not wish to enter into. A virgin, commonly referred to as "a girl," can still be legally married against her will according to Orma practice, but if a "woman" is prepared to admit publicly that she is not a virgin, the Islamic *kadi* will not agree to allow a marriage against her will. More women are prepared to at least threaten such action in order to marry the men of their choice and resist the marriages that have been arranged for them. The fact that sedentary women are restricting their choice to young sedentary men also reduces the size of the marriage pool and thereby increases the chances of them desiring to marry within the clan.

For all of these reasons, the bargaining power of young men and young women has increased sufficiently for them to make more of their own marriage choices. They appear not to be concerned with the consequences of intraclan marriage that worry their elders. One source of support they have mustered comes from the Koranic teachers. The Koran does not require clan exogamy and permits marriage between first cousins. Young Orma can and do sometimes point to the well-known fact that Arabs in the district commonly marry their cousins. And Islamic leaders have felt it necessary to mention in the mosque that the Koran does not prohibit intraclan unions. There are in fact now cases among the Galole Orma of first cousin patrilateral marriage. The elders have given up trying to fight marriage within the clan, but they still maintain that it is a bad thing. They warn that domestic disputes that arise from such unions will cause conflict within the clan among people who should always be cooperating. They also cite the example of the Somali, who though putatively clan exogamous, do have territorial clans and a high incidence of clan endogamy (Kelly 1992, 50), and as the world has recently learned, the Somali are known for inter-clan fighting. Orma elders fear that the Orma too may get to the point where they *prefer* to marry within the clan, which will lead to the sort of hostilities between clans that they see as the root of the recent ethnic clashes in Somalia. In short, some Orma elders subscribe to Tylor's analysis (1889) of the function of clan exogamy in maintaining political alliances and peace. We do not dispute this function, but eschew Tylor's functionalist extension that imputes origin from function. We instead look more to bargaining power to explain the norm's emergence and change.

The bargaining approach effectively explains the development and decline of clan exogamy among the Orma. It is a fairly straightforward case of the initial emergence of a norm that benefits the dominant members of the community, followed by the possibility of changes in that norm as the relevant asymmetries in bargaining power change in the community. We find a similarly straightforward example in the origin and maintenance of bridewealth systems of marriage payments.

Most explanations of the institution of bridewealth and the level of payments assume some form of supply-and-demand relationship. One of the more common arguments explaining bridewealth is that it relates to the value of women's labor: the higher the productive value of women's labor, the higher the bridewealth (Borgerhoff Mulder 1988; Boserup 1970, 46; Hakansson 1988, 93). Another argument is that bridewealth is related to women's fertility, or to descent group rights in children of the union (Goody 1973). Mair (1969) suggests that brideprice be thought of as "child price." Still other scholars have argued that bridewealth is related to the relative scarcity of women in society, which may be exacerbated by polygyny: the fewer women there are, the higher the bridewealth demanded (Goldschmidt 1974). Schneider (1964, 1979), Borgerhoff Mulder (1995), and Hakansson (1988) also argue that the general level of wealth in society can explain historical fluctuations in bridewealth payments.

These hypotheses concerning bridewealth payments are by no means mutually exclusive, and indeed there is interesting evidence among the Orma to support almost all of them. For example, in the wealthiest and southernmost third of Orma territory (Chaffa), bridewealth in the early 1980s was approximately double that in the poorer Galole area (Ensminger's field notes; Hilarie Kelly, personal communication). In the area immediately to the north of Galole, which is poorer yet, bridewealth was less than half that of Galole and dwindled to nothing among some very poor Boran families (with whom the Orma married) farther north. There was a wealth gradient from north to south paralleled by a bridewealth gradient and a flow of women from north to south. Goldschmidt (1974) noted a similar flow of women to the wealthiest portion of Sebei territory. This is consistent with the notion that bridewealth varies according to the wealth of society (see also Kelly 1992, 336). Kelly (1992, 341) also argues that women were in short supply in the southern part of Orma territory and that this contributed to the higher rates of bridewealth there. Historically, when Orma rates of bridewealth were high, they also practiced levirate marriage (inheritance of the widow by the deceased husband's brother) and had virtually no divorce. All of these factors are consistent both with Schneider's (1964) cross-cultural patterns and with his argument that high bridewealth correlates with a high degree of rights in women and offspring.

What is striking about all of these factors is that they can be incorporated in a bargaining account of the emergence of bridewealth. This follows from the fact that bridewealth as an institution or norm has significant distributional consequences; as such, bargaining power was almost certainly an agent in its creation. The institution of bridewealth, when coupled with polygyny and arranged marriages, provided an extremely effective mechanism for the concentration of women in fewer hands. In particular, it provided a powerful means by which older men (who controlled most of the wealth in pastoral societies) could attract disproportionately large numbers of spouses for themselves and their sons. In the absence of the institution of bridewealth and other coercive norms, there is reason to believe that young women would more often choose mates closer to their own age and less often choose to join polygynous unions.[8] For these reasons we argue that bridewealth originated because it served the interests of those with more economic resources. Although there may be a tendency in many societies for women to prefer marriages to older and richer men, the institution of bridewealth greatly facilitates the practice at rates beyond that which would be voluntarily chosen by young women.

Given the significant distributional effects of bridewealth in the allocation of women, we find the bargaining explanation of the emergence of bridewealth a compelling one. And this structures our analysis of subsequent changes in the norm. Rates of bridewealth have been in decline for the Galole Orma over at least the last sixteen years. There is also talk of abandoning the practice in favor of indirect dowry (payments from the groom's family to the bride). As with any norm that was initially the product of asymmetries in bargaining power, in attempting to explain the potential decline of bridewealth, we should look initially at some restructuring of the bargaining situation.

If our argument that bridewealth served the interests of the elite by allowing wealthy old men to disproportionately monopolize women is correct, why did the older elite acquiesce in the decline of this institution? We speculate that changes in the political economy have shifted more of the income into young men's hands and, furthermore, that it is more equitably distributed among them.[9] As young men increasingly earn their own livings in trade, civil service jobs, and wage labor, they are less dependent upon their elders for marriage arrangements and bridewealth. If their fathers refuse to allow them to marry when they are ready to do so, they have the financial means to set up independent households. What is more, young women report that they will eagerly marry young men in preference to even rich old men. Young men do not need to attract young women by offering their fathers large bridewealth payments. And given that the income disparity among young men is not as great as it is among old men, they have less reason to compete among themselves through an institution such as bridewealth. This change is also driven in part by the shift in bargaining power in favor of young women noted earlier, who are now finding support in both the civil and Muslim courts against "forced" marriages. This undermines the ability of their fathers to hold out for marriages with high bridewealth to less desirable spouses. In 1994, a small sample of the ten most recent marriages indicated that four were elopements in which the young man and the young woman chose each other and "ran away together." The Galole predict that elopement and love marriages are becoming the norm.

But while this scenario of increasing bargaining power on the part of young men and women may explain the demise of bridewealth, it does not explain the potential rise of indirect dowry. Many cases, like the change to indirect dowry, are more complicated than the clan exogamy and bridewealth origin stories. Next we turn to the question of what the introduction of more complicated factors does to the conflict over social norms. When economic and political interests are at stake, it seems natural to assume a role for superior bargaining power based upon material advantage in access to resources. When the struggle over different social norms is about ideological differences or preferences less tied to material interest, the role for bargaining power is less obvious but, we would argue, equally potent.

Bargaining over Ideological Commitment: Whose Preferences Become the Social Norm?

We can analyze the effects of ideology on the conflict over social norms by examining the recent changes in the practices of marriage payments and attitudes toward female circumcision. In these cases we identify two major categories of ideological effects: (1) the effects on the preferences of powerful actors who seek to change existing norms, and (2) the effects of ideological commitments to existing norms on the level of resistance offered by social actors who prefer the status quo. Ideological belief can hasten change through its effect on the preferences of the more powerful members of a community. In our cases we focus on how ideology can (1) expand the set of possible forms of behavior that can be embodied in a norm, and (2) alter the ways in which social actors assess the relative merits of the existing possibilities. As to the issue of how ideology can inhibit change, we focus on how ideology can reinforce commitments to existing norms and, in doing so, make the task of changing social expectations more difficult.

Consider first the transition to indirect dowry as an example of how ideology can expand the set of possible norms. Bridewealth consists of payments from the groom's family to that of the bride. Following Goody (1973), indirect dowry is the term used for payments from the groom's family to the bride herself. As in many East African pastoral societies (Schneider 1979), the Orma have historically had high rates of polygyny and bridewealth. Among the Orma, after years of pressure on the rate of bridewealth payments, the institution of bridewealth itself may be under threat. This threat highlights how ideological factors may affect conflict over social norms.

The rate of Orma bridewealth has been declining from at least 1978 to the present, as has the incidence of levirate marriage; meanwhile, divorce has been on the rise. Simultaneously, an even more interesting story is unfolding among the Orma, involving the transition from bridewealth to indirect dowry. Unlike bridewealth, indirect dowry has been associated in the literature with an enhanced status for women (Goody 1990, 468; Schlegel and Eloul 1988, 306); it is also an Islamic institution.

The Galole Orma converted to Islam in the 1920s and 1930s. Their Orma neighbors to the north preceded them slightly in this conversion. The Orma to the north currently practice considerably different patterns of marriage payments than do the Galole or the southern Orma, and these are related to their interpretation of Islamic law. While the Koran does not forbid bridewealth, it does mandate the payment of indirect dowry from the husband to the wife (*mahr*). The Orma to the north of the Galole tend to pay little or no bridewealth and abide by the Islamic prescription to pay dowry, set by the Orma at four cattle. In the case of divorce, these dowry cattle need not be repaid.

Some northern elders have been resident among the Galole for many years and continue to practice their northern custom of indirect dowry rather than bridewealth, which they hold to be truer to Islamic law. One elder, described as a particularly "polite" and devout man, has never accepted bridewealth for his daughters' marriages, but insists upon *mahr*, which his daughters keep. Another group of brothers from the north have also refused bridewealth for their daughters over the past twenty years and insists upon four cattle for dowry instead. However, at least one of these elders does not turn their "dowries" over to his daughters, keeping them, supposedly "on their behalf." (Mir-Hosseini [1989, cited in Goody 1990, 376], notes that this practice is found in other Islamic societies as well.) There is considerable "talk" in the village these days that the practice of forgoing bridewealth and accepting indirect dowry instead is a good one, although to date this is merely at the level of discussion. A similar trend is reported among the Kikuyu (Worthman and Whiting 1987). What we may be seeing in these cases, including that of the Orma, is the adoption of a new norm of indirect dowry.

To date, the instances of indirect dowry are far too few to reach any conclusions about this, but there is sufficient evidence to suggest possible causes for the change. One possible explanation is that elite fathers are contemplating using indirect dowry rather than bridewealth to increase the probability of attracting more desirable sons-in-law. In the Orma case, however, the transition would not be about hypergamy (wealthy but low-status families marrying their daughters to high-status, perhaps poorer, families) but, rather, about building endogenous class relations. A father may wish to marry his daughter to another wealthy family in order to increase ties to economically and politically useful families. This perspective is of course perfectly consistent with our general thesis that bargaining power plays a role in directing the course of changing norms; it also falls in the usual category of bargaining over substantive economic advantages. But to completely explain the newfound interest in indirect dowry, we find ideology and the possibility of a preference change to be helpful supplements to the basic bargaining account.

As noted, a few religiously motivated men had utilized indirect dowry and kept the norm "out there" as yet another alternative in the feasible set. The men from the north continued to practice the norm they were raised with, reflecting an ideological commitment for which they were prepared to pay a rather high price. In 1978, bridewealth was frequently on the order of twelve to sixteen cattle, while dowry was four. It would therefore be difficult to make the case that in the early days of this changing norm economic or political gains were motivating these elders. The costs in cattle forgone relative to the value of beneficial afffinal ties appear to be too great. Significantly, this norm was not adopted by the Galole population at large when it would have represented a large economic cost and bridewealth served the interests of those with bargaining power in the society. But the existence of a possible alternative norm was preserved because of the presence of a small number of ideologically motivated people.

We would argue that this example illustrates the manner in which ideologically motivated behavior can create new "focal points" or alternative norms (Schelling 1960). Ideology may motivate a small subset of a population to engage in some form of deviant behavior and by doing so expand the set of salient forms of behavior. However, we do not believe that this alone leads to a *resolution* of the problem of norm convergence within a society. While ideologically motivated behavior may effectively increase the feasible set of alternative norms, we would hold that these new norms will not be adopted broadly in the society until they are of reasonable cost and serve the interests (material or ideological) of those with bargaining power. In the case of indirect dowry, we see evidence that both of these conditions are close to being met. In 1994, by which point the "talk" of adopting the norm of indirect dowry had intensified, it was not uncommon for bridewealth to be as little as four cattle. This means that a change from bridewealth to dowry would represent minimal loss to a father, especially if he kept the dowry cattle "on behalf" of his daughter. Part of the attraction of receiving dowry instead of bridewealth is also that dowry does not have to be repaid upon divorce, while bridewealth does. In a time of rising divorce rates, this has not gone unnoticed by fathers.

Ideology can also hasten a change in social norms by affecting the ways in which social actors assess the existing set of possible forms of behavior. The beginnings of opposition to female circumcision among the Orma may be explained by the effects of outside ideological influences. Female circumcision has received a great deal of public and scholarly attention recently, much of it motivated by human rights concerns. Both human rights groups and scholars have commented upon the great difficulty involved in changing this practice, which appears to meet with more resistance than many other norms.

The Orma practice one of the more radical forms of female circumcision, involving infibulation of young girls at about the age of eight. The operation consists of the removal of all of the female genitalia. Infibulation involves stitching the wound in such a way that only a small opening remains for urination and menstruation. Among the Orma today there is universal compliance with this norm, but there is also discussion of change.

Some young educated men claim to be against the practice and say they wish not to circumcise their own daughters. This change in preference seems to be associated with young men who have gone to school, read newspapers, and traveled more widely where they have contact with other ethnic groups and are aware of the controversial nature of this practice. They cite the medical complications associated with the operation (even including the potential for the spread of AIDS during the operation) and are aware that it reduces women's sexual pleasure. This is an example of a change in preference caused by an introduction of new information that has caused some of the Orma to change their evaluation of the benefits of the existing norm. As in other societies (Assaad 1980), it is in fact Orma women and elders who most staunchly defend the practice.

One scene observed by Ensminger during fieldwork in 1987 speaks to the process by which preferences change. Three well-educated young men were relaxing in the evening reading the national newspaper, which happened to have an unusually long and sophisticated article about the practice and medical implications of female circumcision. The young men read the article with absolute attentiveness. One looked up from the paper after finishing the piece and said, "I had no idea there were so many harmful medical complications associated with female circumcision. I don't want my daughters circumcised." The other two young men agreed, and a lengthy discussion ensued. When one of these young men later reported his new beliefs to his wife, she laughed, at first believing that he was not serious. Then, realizing that he was, she remarked that his mother would never allow it, the assumption being that she had the final word. And indeed in this case, she did.

This vignette about changing attitudes toward female circumcision also calls attention to the inhibiting effects of ideology on social change. When people are prepared to pay a price for noncompliance with those holding bargaining power, it is more difficult for the powerful to achieve compliance with their preferred norms. In two of our cases this was not a problem, and those cases illustrate the relative ease with which compliance can be "bought" in the absence of strong ideological commitment. In the case of bridewealth, wealthy elders can effectively increase their monopoly on women (as measured by the polygyny rate) by bidding up the price of bridewealth. The same principle applies to clan exogamy: wealthy elders can refuse to cooperate or marry with families who do not comply and reward those who do with more economic help (including bridewealth contributions) and more desirable marriages. As the price moves up and down, so does the incidence of these behaviors, eventually converging on something recognized as a norm.

The case of female circumcision, however, is more complicated. While one might hypothesize that the norm originated as part of a market-driven process—that, for example, wealthy men demanded the practice as verification of female virginity—this does not explain the dismantling of the norm. The wealthy elites of the 1990s, armed with information that makes female circumcision an undesirable norm from their point of view, cannot so easily use their status to favor uncircumcised women. Such a market mechanism might facilitate a change if there was a supply of uncircumcised women. But a pool of uncircumcised women does not yet exist because there is an asymmetry of information within their own families concerning the effects of female circumcision, and this leads to different preferences concerning the practice. Generally, women and more senior uneducated elders from elite families still prefer to have young girls circumcised.

Women raise two points in defense of circumcision. First, they mention that no uncircumcised girl would be able to marry, and second they note that infibulation is used to check upon the virginity of their daughters, and thus of course to certify their purity. Even those who are against circumcision are consistently won over by the marriageability argument. No parents wish to be the first and take the chance that their daughters will not be able to marry. This of course prevents the creation of a supply of uncircumcised women with whom willing educated males could marry, thus signaling the erroneousness of the belief that uncircumcised girls will be unmarriageable. It is a catch-22. Another source of pressure to continue the practice comes from the uncircumcised young girls themselves, who are ridiculed by their age-mates as "silly little girls" once the age-mates have themselves undergone circumcision. As a marker of maturity and membership in an exclusive society, young girls may actually plead with their parents to let them be circumcised if they fall behind their age group.

Until relatively recently, whenever rumors surfaced that a young Orma girl was engaging in sexual activity, other young girls in the village were "inspected" to ensure that their virginity was intact. Such quasi-public inspections by a few old women in the village have now ceased. Young mothers explain that it is unfair to put innocent girls through such humiliation merely because one young girl is believed to have transgressed. Now mothers are expected to examine only their own daughters. Although it is still thought that a woman who is not a virgin has little chance of a desirable first marriage, in fact these days there are many first marriages between such young women and desirable young men. Young women often elope with their boyfriends. This is important, as one of the primary arguments by women in favor of maintaining circumcision is to be able to "police" the sexual activity of their daughters. Once virgin marriage is no longer the standard practice for women, the need for verification (served by infibulation) is undermined.

But the problem of disentangling the association between circumcision and marriageability remains emotionally potent. Who will dare to test its symbolic demise? Two young Orma men reported a public discussion that took place in front of senior elders. One married young man with daughters commented that he did not see the purpose of female circumcision and no longer approved of it. The old men quickly retorted that his daughters would then never marry and he had better not even discuss such a thing. One brazen young man then proclaimed in front of the old men, "I'll marry your daughters." This young man later explained that he in fact would rather marry an uncircumcised women, as he would rather have a sexual partner who enjoyed sex.[10] A quantitative survey of three hundred Sudanese husbands who had both circumcised and uncircumcised wives (Lightfoot-Klein 1989, 7), provides support for this young Orma man's perspective. This study found that all of the husbands preferred their noninfibulated wives to their infibulated wives as sexual partners. Holy (1991, 170, cited in Hicks 1993, 79) provides corroborating evidence from Sudan that men prefer a milder form of circumcision to infibulation. Other scholars have also reported that the custom is most strongly defended by women (Assaad 1980). The enthusiasm of young Orma men for this change raises the possibility that uncircumcised Orma girls would not have difficulty marrying, but it is a big chance for them to take.

It is a chance that four Orma men chose to take together. In the late 1980s, four well-educated and comfortably employed men with families made a pact to not circumcise their daughters and to marry among themselves. This was a serious agreement made among extremely close friends. Significantly, three of the four men involved lived outside the district at the time, although their families frequently returned home and sometimes lived there. Of the four men, three have failed to prevent their own parents from having the operation performed on their daughters in their absence and against their wishes. The fourth succeeded two years longer than the others but eventually failed. As he put it, "What am I to do? I can't take my own parents to court."

The role of bargaining power on the part of the young men fighting for a change in this norm is highly evident. It is in fact the most financially independent young men who are pushing for a change. These young men of independent means still respect their fathers and clan elders, but they have less concern for the economic sanctions of senior men. These young men are driven in part by sincere concern for their daughters' well-being and are campaigning for a change that meets with strong opposition from everyone: their wives, their parents, their in-laws, and their senior elders. This campaign has costs for the innovators, though the daughters themselves potentially suffer the most no matter what the outcome. It is important to note in this example that while a new preference is the motivation for change, only the powerful are likely to be able to effect such change. Daughters of wealthy men will have the greatest chance of overcoming the initial stigma associated with being uncircumcised, as they are particularly desirable marriage partners. But even for the powerful, this change in norm is constrained by the continuing will of the population to enforce the old norm and the inability of the young men to establish a new norm that they could subsequently enforce. We turn now to this crucial aspect of norm change: enforcement.

ENFORCEMENT

Bargaining power clearly plays an important role in changing social norms. However, superior bargaining power does not guarantee a quick, nor even necessarily a successful, change in norms. Social actors wishing to establish a new norm must undertake the task of re-coordinating social expectations. They must find a way of shifting the focus of the expectations of the community from the existing norm to their preferred alternative. The complexity of the task varies with the interests of the different community members. For those whose interests would be enhanced by the new norm once it is established throughout the community, reformers face a task of assuring those people that others will also shift their behavior. This involves a process of coordinating expectations and enforcing new commitments. To be successful they must resolve the collective action problems necessary to assure these people that their interests will not be harmed by shifting to the new form of behavior. This requires a mechanism to enforce promises to comply with the new norm. Given the effects of norm uncertainty on individual benefits, any attempt to change existing norms is risky. Reformers must establish sanctions that make it costly to renege on promises to join the reform effort, otherwise the temptation to revert to the known benefits of the existing norm may fatally undermine their efforts.

The difficulty of the task of social change is further complicated by the enforcement problems that primarily involve those members of the community who are either indifferent to or opposed to the change. The task facing reformers vis-à-vis these people is akin to the more general problem of norm enforcement in a community. Any system of social norms must be reinforced by mechanisms of sanction that create costs for noncompliance. Unless such mechanisms are established, community members whose interests would be enhanced by forms of behavior other than those embodied in the norm will have an incentive to deviate from established social expectations. The success of any effort to change social norms rests on the ability of reformers not only to momentarily change the focus of social expectations but also to maintain the change in those expectations.

We address issues related to both categories of enforcement problems. First, we look at a feature of many efforts to coordinate the expectations and behavior of those who prefer a change in an existing norm: a long time lag between the change in the norm and the realization of the costs and benefits of that change. Second, we consider a characteristic of sanctioning mechanisms that can significantly affect the creation and maintenance of new social norms: decentralized versus centralized enforcement.

One of the most important insights from the female circumcision example is the degree of coordination necessary to effect a change. We believe that the exceptional persistence of this norm is due in large part to the long time lag between a change in the norm (at the age of eight when circumcision is carried out) and evidence of the costs associated with change (at marriage, which may be at sixteen to twenty years of age). Thus, the norm of female circumcision is unlike the other cases in which the consequences of a change in the norm are proximate to the change, thus allowing both a reasonable assessment of the relative costs of the different norms and, more important, an assessment of the credibility of the commitments of others to a change in that norm. There are many years during which parents, close relatives, and friends can rethink their decision and reverse it. And this is indeed what happened among the four families whose male heads formed a pact. This extended time lag exacerbates the task of enforcement for those seeking to put an end to female circumcision.

The time lag also seriously heightens the uncertainty for any member of the community who seeks to challenge the existing norm. Even if a father is unconcerned about the immediate economic sanctions that he might suffer from noncompliance, he will have a difficult time assessing the probabilities regarding the severity of the potential consequences suffered by his daughters in the future. The existence of a time lag between the initiation of change and the experience of the consequences of that change may therefore be crucial to explaining the resilience of norms in the face of changing bargaining power and changing preferences. The time lag exacerbates the problem for original innovators of assessing the costliness of a norm change. Parents must act before there is any evidence to suggest what effect lack of circumcision will have upon their daughters' marriageability. While some young men profess to prefer to marry uncircumcised women, to date such promises remain untested. Parents must calculate the odds that the families of willing young men may refuse to help with the bridewealth in such marriages or otherwise make it clear to the young man that sanctions, such as a refusal to cooperate in the pooling of labor or to provide aid in crisis, may be imposed.

A second issue that can mitigate the ability of those with bargaining power to effect change in social norms is the degree of decentralization in the enforcement process. While decentralized enforcement may work against the interests of the powerful by exacerbating the coordination problems faced by those who seek to solidify a change in norms, centralized enforcement often works to their advantage, as they may be in the position to harness the enforcement apparatus of the government toward their own ends. This may be seen in the abortion debate in the United States where each side attempts to capture the state and impose its preferences through the executive, legislature, and/or judicial branches of government. In Kenya, the debate over female circumcision could very well take this form in the end. One Orma woman expressed the fear that the government was becoming more motivated to use enforcement toward this end. She speculated that men's attitudes toward circumcision were changing because they were weak and afraid of going against the government's stated preferences to eradicate the practice.

The Orma elite have already turned to centralized enforcement to push through another change in norms that could not be accomplished through decentralized enforcement. In the 1980s the Orma turned over to the government responsibility for maintaining their borders, thereby effectively hastening the demise of their common grazing system of property rights (see Ensminger 1992). More restrictive property rights were definitely in the interest of the more powerful members of the community but could not be enforced against the norm of common grazing when they were dependent upon decentralized enforcement. This is not to say that whenever the government or other centralized enforcement bodies mandate compliance with a norm that their actions are necessarily effective. For example, the government of Kenya has tried to discourage female circumcision, but its failure to *enforce* such a preference renders it virtually meaningless all over the country, including among the Orma. Similarly, primary education was made mandatory in Kenya in 1978, but a year later only 3 percent of school age Galole Orma girls and only 30 percent of schoolage boys were in school. By 1994, the numbers were far higher, but they were still well below 50 percent.

In the example of female circumcision we see perhaps the ultimate in decentralized enforcement: different preferences within the family create struggles between husbands and wives, and between elders and juniors. In an interview on this subject with a husband and wife, the husband (whose wives knew him to be opposed to female circumcision) learned for the first time that his eight-year-old daughter had been circumcised without his knowledge approximately six months earlier. The wife was quite open with him about the fact that the rest of the family had had it done in his absence specifically because they knew he would not approve.

In the case of indirect dowry in lieu of forgone bridewealth, it is quite likely that one inhibition, even in those ideologically motivated to make the change, results from the pressure of kin who would be the recipients of some of the forgone bridewealth. Just as bridewealth is acquired by seeking help from one's kin and clan, so too must much of it be distributed to clearly specified individuals upon receipt. These individuals have an incentive to discourage the "altruistic" tendencies of those who would wish to forgo bridewealth for indirect dowry and greater adherence to Islamic law.

The common theme of these various examples is that the existence of a change in relative bargaining power does not guarantee a change in social norms. Once a norm has captured the attention of a community and has garnered the compliance of some of its members, the effort to change it must still overcome the pressures to enforce the status quo. A significant part of this pressure will come from those members of the community whose interests will be adversely affected by the change. But another distinct source of pressure will derive from the inertia of stable expectations: even if someone would benefit as an individual from a change in the norm, she will not adopt the change unless she is confident that those in the community with whom she interacts will also comply with the change. Both time lags and decentralized enforcement will reinforce the effects of pressure in support of the status quo. However, this is not to say that relative bargaining power does not (all other things being equal) afford greater ability to enforce new norms and to resist the sanctions of those who persist in maintaining the status quo.

CONCLUSION

Social norms have traditionally been the main purview of sociological analysis. As we suggested in the introduction to this chapter, an interest in the importance of norms has spread through the other social sciences as we have come to understand an important fact about social life: our formal institutions, such as property rights, some forms of economic organization, and political institutions, are significantly affected by the network of informal institutions (social conventions and norms) in which the formal institutions are created. For example, norms governing economic interactions affect the capacity of property rights and other economic institutions to enhance economic performance (North 1990). Similarly, norms governing day-to-day political interactions affect the ability of a community to effectively employ institutions of democratic decisionmaking (Putnam 1993).

Given the significant effects produced by social norms, it is understandable that social conflict will arise over efforts to establish particular norms. The main focus of this chapter has been an effort to explain how this conflict affects the changing nature of these norms. Our analysis employs a bargaining model grounded in rational choice theory. The fact that such a model can accurately explain how conflicts of interest and bargaining power generate norm emergence and norm change undermines various criticisms of rational choice accounts of social institutions. More specifically, our analysis calls into question the criticism of those who have suggested that rational choice accounts of social norms are unable to incorporate power asymmetries and distributional consequences into their analysis (Oberschall and Leifer 1986; March and Olsen 1989). To the contrary, bargaining over the distributional effects of social norms is the primary explanation in our account.

But our analysis illustrates more than this. Conflict over social norms is a complex process. We have developed here two important characteristics of that complexity. First, we have highlighted the effects of ideological commitments and nonmaterial preferences in bargaining over changing norms. Our analysis shows that conflict is an important feature of normative change even when change is motivated by ideology. In such cases ideological commitment can serve both to motivate and to resist efforts to change norms. Second, we emphasized the problem of enforcement. In doing so, we identified conditions under which change will be hampered even when it is motivated by those social actors who enjoy a relative bargaining advantage. The main reason why these conditions inhibit change is that they exacerbate a problem inherent in efforts to change norms: change must not only be initiated, but it must also be solidified over time through efforts to enforce compliance. As the bargaining process becomes more complex, so does the task of enforcement.

We share equal credit for any insights and equal responsibility for any errors in this essay. The empirical evidence in this chapter is based on Ensminger's fieldwork with the Orma from July 1978 to February 1981, and from April–December 1987, June–July 1994, and July 1996. This chapter builds upon the theoretical framework and empirical case studies discussed in more detail in Ensminger and Knight 1997. The research presented in this chapter was sponsored by the Beijer International Institute of Ecological Economics, the Royal Swedish Academy of Sciences, Stockholm, with support from the World Environment and Resources Program of the John D. and Catherine T. MacArthur Foundation and the World Bank. It was conducted as part of the research program, Property Rights and the Performance of Natural Resource Systems. We also wish to thank the Office of the President, Government of Kenya, for granting Ensminger clearance on three occasions to carry out the field research upon which this chapter is based. Ensminger also wishes to acknowledge the intellectual support and institutional affiliation provided by the members of the Institute for Development Studies, University of Nairobi. The chapter has been much improved by the comments of participants in a conference sponsored by the Russell Sage Foundation, "The New Institutionalism in Economic Sociology." In particular, we wish to thank Ted Bestor, Mary Brinton, Gary Hamilton, Paul Ingram, and Victor Nee.

NOTES

1. Here we are in agreement with Nee and Ingram's argument (in this volume) that analyses of the effects of social norms on social action must go beyond a narrow self-interest conception of institutional effects.

2. For a review of these alternatives see Knight (1995) and Ensminger and Knight (1997).

3. See Nee and Ingram (in this volume) for a related discussion of the factors that affect the capacity of groups to effectively enforce social norms.

4. Knight (1992, ch. 3) addresses a range of questions related to the similarities and differences between the concepts of behavioral regularity, social rules, and institutions.

5. See Taylor 1982 for an excellent discussion of the range of informal mechanisms that might be employed to enforce social norms.

6. The Orma are split into three divisions, with the Chaffa in the southern, the Galole in the middle, and the Hirman in the northern part of the region. This study is based upon Ensminger's four years of residence and research with the Galole Orma (in 1978 to 1981, 1987, and, briefly, in 1994 and 1996), and although this intermediate group is usually representative of the entire population, this should not be assumed.

7. There may be an increasing tendency for young men and women who wish to elope to do so but to *call* it a marriage by force. In this way, the girl appears to her parents to be an innocent victim who has been forced into an unapproved marriage that she in fact wishes to enter.

8. This is supported by numerous testimonials of young girls.

9. While wealth, measured in livestock, was *less* equitably distributed in 1987 than in earlier periods, *income* was more equitably distributed among households (Ensminger 1992). This anomaly is explained largely by the increasing significance of income from wage labor and trade. Although the analysis did not include a comparison of incomes among young men still

dependent upon their fathers, there is reason to believe that even more equity would be apparent in such a comparison because, with the exception of the most elite young men (those in trade and holding civil service jobs), there is little difference in the income earning capabilities of sons of rich and poor men. This pattern is quite likely to change in the future as education and commerce become more significant.

10. The Orma have had considerable contact with, and there has been some intermarriage between, two neighboring groups who do not circumcise women, the Pokomo and the Arabs who live in the district headquarters.

REFERENCES

Assaad, Marie Bassili. 1980. "Female Circumcision in Egypt: Social Implications, Current Research, and Prospects for Change," *Studies in Family Planning* 11: 3–16.

Bachrach, Samuel B., and Edward J. Lawler. 1981. *Bargaining: Power, Tactics and Outcomes.* San Francisco, Calif.: Jossey-Bass.

Borgerhoff Mulder, M. 1988. "Kipsigis Bridewealth Payments." In *Human Reproductive Behaviour*, edited by L. L. Betzig, M. Borgerhoff Mulder, and P. W. Turke. Cambridge, England: Cambridge University Press.

———. 1995. "Bridewealth and Its Correlates: Quantifying Changes over Time." *Current Anthropology* 36(4): 573–603.

Boserup, E. 1970. *Women's Role in Economic Development.* London, England: Allen and Unwin.

Bourdieu, Pierre. 1977. *Outline of a Theory of Practice.* Cambridge, England: Cambridge University Press.

Coleman, James. 1990. *The Foundations of Social Theory.* Cambridge, Mass.: Harvard University Press.

Ensminger, Jean. 1992. *Making a Market: The Institutional Transformation of an African Society.* Cambridge, England: Cambridge University Press.

Ensminger, Jean, and Jack Knight. 1997. "Changing Social Norms: Common Property, Bridewealth, and Clan Exogamy." *Current Anthropology* 38(1): 1–24.

Goldschmidt, W. 1974. "The Economics of Bridewealth among the Sebei in East Africa." *Ethnology* 13: 311–33.

Goody, Jack. 1973. "Bridewealth and Dowry in Africa and Eurasia." In *Bridewealth and Dowry*, edited by Jack Goody and S.J. Tambish. Cambridge, England: Cambridge University Press.

———. 1990. *The Oriental, the Ancient, and the Primitive.* Cambridge, England: Cambridge University Press.

Hakansson, Thomas. 1988. *Bridewealth, Women and Land.* Stockholm, Sweden: Almqvist and Wiksell International.

Hart, H.L.A. 1994. *The Concept of Law.* Oxford, England: Clarendon Press.

Hicks, Esther K. 1993. *Infibulation: Female Mutilation in Islamic Northeastern Africa.* New Brunswick, N.J.: Transaction Publishers.

Holy, L. 1991. *Religion and Custom in a Muslim Society: The Berti of Sudan.* Cambridge, England: Cambridge University Press.

Kelly, Hilarie Ann. 1992. "From 'Gada' to Islam: The Moral Authority of Gender Relations among the Pastoral Orma of Kenya." Ph.D. diss., University of California, Los Angeles.

Knight, Jack. 1992. *Institutions and Social Conflict.* Cambridge, England: Cambridge University Press.

———. 1995. "Models, Interpretations and Theories: Constructing Explanations of Institutional Emergence and Change." *Explaining Social Institutions*, edited by Jack Knight and Itai Sened. Ann Arbor, Mich.: University of Michigan Press

Lightfoot-Klein, H. 1989. *Prisoners of Ritual: An Odyssey into Female Genital Circumcision.* Binghamton, N.Y.: Harrington Park Press.

Mair, L. 1969. *African Marriage and Social Change.* London, England: Frank Cass.

March, James G., and Johan P. Olsen. 1989. *Rediscovering Institutions: The Organizational Basis of Politics.* New York: Free Press.

Mir-Hosseini. Ziba. 1989. "Some Aspects of Changing Marriage in Rural Iran: The Case of Kalardasht, a District in the Northern Provinces." *Journal of Comparative Family Studies* 20(2): 215–30.

North, Douglass. 1990. *Institutions, Institutional Change and Economic Performance*. New York: Cambridge University Press.

Oberschall, Anthony, and Eric M. Leifer. 1986. "Efficiency and Social Institutions: Uses and Misuses of Economic Reasoning in Sociology." *American Review of Sociology* 12: 233–53.

Putnam, Robert D. 1993. *Making Democracy Work: Civic Traditions in Modern Italy*. Princeton, N.J.: Princeton University Press.

Raiffa, Howard. 1982. *The Art and Science of Negotiation*. Cambridge, Mass.: Harvard University Press.

Schelling, Thomas C. 1960. *The Strategy of Conflict*. Cambridge, Mass.: Harvard University press.

Schlegel, Alice, and Rohn Eloul. 1988. "Marriage Transactions: Labor, Property, Status." *American Anthropologist* 90(2): 291–309.

Schneider, Harold K. 1964. "A Model of African Indigenous Economy and Society." *Comparative Studies in Society and History* 7: 37–55.

Schneider, Harold K. 1979. *Livestock and Equality in East Africa*. Bloomington, Ind.: Indiana University Press.

Taylor, Michael. 1982. *Community, Anarchy, and Liberty*. Cambridge, England: Cambridge University Press.

Tylor, E.B. 1889. "On a Method of Investigating the Development of Institutions: Applied to Laws of Marriage and Descent." *Journal of the Royal Anthropological Institute* 18: 245–72.

Worthman, C. M., and J.M.W. Whiting. 1987. "Social Change in Adolescent Sexual Behavior, Mate Selection and Premarital Pregnancy Rates in a Kikuyu Community." *Ethnos* 15: 145–65.

Zald, Mayer. 1987. "The New Institutional Economics." *American Journal of Sociology* 93: 701–8.

6

Embeddedness and Immigration: Notes on the Social Determinants of Economic Action

Alejandro Portes and Julia Sensenbrenner

One of the most exciting developments in economic sociology is the recent work that promises to vindicate the heritage of Max Weber in the analysis of economic life and, by the same token, to rescue this vast field from the exclusive sway of the neoclassical perspective. Spearheaded by Mark Granovetter's critique (1985) of a pure "market" approach to economic action, the sociological perspective has been reinforced by the introduction and subsequent use of the concept of "social capital" (Bourdieu 1979; Bourdieu, Newman, and Wàcquant 1991; Coleman 1988), the emphasis on the predictive power of contextual variables in addition to individual characteristics (Wellman and Wortley 1990), and extensive research on the structure and dynamics of social networks (Marsden 1990; Laumann and Knoke 1986; Mintz and Schwartz 1985; White 1970).

Granovetter's treatment of the concept of "embeddedness" represents a veritable manifesto for those whose sociological cast of mind has led them to question individualistic analyses of such phenomena as socioeconomic attainment and the cultural arguments that neoclassical economists sometimes invoke when their own perspective can go no further. The concept was originally coined by Karl Polanyi and his associates (Polanyi, Arensberg, and Pearson 1957) in their analysis of trades and market, but in its more recent formulation it has sparked renewed interest in what sociology has to say about economic life.

The purpose of this chapter is to contribute to this emerging perspective by: 1) delving into the classical roots of recent theoretical developments so as to refine the concepts invoked by present-day economic sociologists; 2) fleshing out the concepts of embeddedness and, in particular, social capital; 3) using the resulting typology as the basis for a series of hypotheses amenable to empirical research; and 4), showing how this theoretical program relates to and may be advanced by recent literature on immigration and ethnicity.

The existing concepts of the new economic sociology represent a broad programmatic statement in need of further specification. Embeddedness, for example, provides a very useful standpoint for criticizing neoclassical models but suffers from theoretical vagueness. The observation that outcomes are uncertain because they depend on how economic action is embedded in social structures does not help us meet the positivistic goals of predictive improvement and theoretical accumulation. To fulfill these goals, we must better specify how social structure constrains, supports, or derails individual goal-seeking behavior. Our attempt to move in this direction takes two forms.

First, we try to arrive at a more systematic understanding of the sources of what is now called social capital by tracing the roots of the concept in the sociological classics. Second, we utilize contemporary research on immigration to document the operation of some of these sources and their effects. In keeping with the goal of theoretical specificity, our strategy is to use knowledge about immigrant economic adaptation to generate propositions of more general applicability.

The following analysis focuses on the concept of social capital, introduced in the recent sociological literature by Pierre Bourdieu and developed in English by James Coleman, since we believe it is more suitable to the enterprise of theoretical fleshing out than the more general notion of embeddedness. Coleman (1988, S98) defines social capital as a variety of entities with two characteristics in common: "They all consist of some aspect of social structures, and they facilitate actions within that structure." The facilitation component is highlighted by Coleman, who likens social capital to "material" and "human" capital—resources available to individuals to attain their ends. The main difference is that social capital is more intangible than the other forms, since it inheres in the structure of relations within which purposive action takes place.

Although insightful, Coleman's contribution suffers from two shortcomings: first, a theoretical indefiniteness that leaves open the question of what those social entities facilitating individual goal attainment are and where they come from; and second, a marked instrumentalist orientation that views social structural forces only from a positive perspective. This positive bent sacrifices the insight (present in Granovetter's broader analysis of embeddedness) that social structures can advance as well as constrain individual goal seeking and that they can even redefine the content of such goals. We can at this point respecify the purpose of our own analysis as an attempt to further refine the concept of social capital by: a) attempting to identify its different types and sources; b) clarifying conditions under which it can not only promote but also constrain or derail economic goal seeking.

Before plunging into this task, we should say a word about the source of the empirical material used in this chapter. This source—immigration studies—has been frequently, albeit haphazardly, mined by writers of the theoretical literature on economic sociology. Coleman (1988), for example, uses Asian immigrant families as an illustration of what he labels "closure" in social relations, and both he and Granovetter (1985) highlight the significance of the immigrant rotating credit association as an example of either embeddedness or social capital. This frequent utilization of immigration research is not surprising in that foreign-born communities represent one of the clearest examples of the bearing contextual factors can have on individual economic action. With skills learned in the home country devalued in the receiving labor market and with a generally poor command of the receiving country's language, immigrants' economic destinies depend heavily on the structures in which they become incorporated and, in particular, on the character of their own communities. Few instances of economic action can be found that are more embedded. The task before us is to review this empirical literature more systematically with an eye to developing propositions of general applicability.

SOCIAL CAPITAL AND ITS TYPES

The effervescent intellectual atmosphere following the reconceptualization of economic sociology in recent years has somewhat obscured the fact that many of the ideas now being floated have been present all along in the sociological tradition and are, in a sense, central to the founding of the discipline. Our purpose here is not historical exegesis but the investigation of classical sources for clues to the various mechanisms through which social structures affect economic action. We begin by redefining "social capital" as those expectations for action within a collectivity that affect the economic goals and goal-seeking behavior of its members, even if these expectations are not oriented toward the economic sphere.

This definition differs from Coleman's, where the emphasis is on social structures facilitating individual rational pursuits. This positive emphasis is only half of the story because the same constellation of forces can have the opposite effect. As redefined here, social capital seems sufficiently general to encompass most uses of the term in the recent sociological literature. However, by its very generality, the concept encompasses so many situations as to make its empirical application difficult. Thus, we must further specify what those collective expectations are, their sources, and how they are likely to affect economic behavior.

It is possible to distinguish four specific types of economically relevant expectations. The first, *value introjection*, takes its cue from Durkheim ([1893] 1984) and a certain interpretation of Weber to emphasize the moral character of economic transactions that are guided by value imperatives learned during the process of socialization (Parsons 1937; Parsons and Smelser 1956). The central role accorded to this process in American functionalist sociology draws its inspiration from passages such as the following from Weber's ([1904] 1958, 54) analysis of Puritan values:

One's duty in a calling is what is most characteristic of the social ethic of capitalist culture and is, in a sense, the fundamental basis of it. It is an obligation which the individual is supposed to feel and does feel towards the content of his professional activity, no matter in what it consists.

Value introjection is a source of social capital because it prompts individuals to behave in ways other than out of naked greed; such behavior then becomes a resource appropriable by others or by the collectivity. Although criticized later as an "oversocialized" conception of human action (Wrong 1961), this source of social capital remains central to the sociological perspective and figures prominently in contemporary examples of the effects of social structure on economic action (Swedberg 1991). Economists bent on dismissing the "sociological approach" to economic behavior also tend to aim their criticisms against this first source (Leff 1979; McCloskey and Sandberg 1971; Baker and Faulkner 1991).

The second source of social capital, which takes its cue from the classic work of Georg Simmel ([1908] 1955), derives from the dynamics of group affiliation. As elaborated by exchange theorists, social life consists of a vast series of primary transactions where favors, information, approval, and other valued items are given and received. Social capital arising from such *reciprocity transactions* consists of an accumulation of "chits" earned through previous good deeds to others, backed by the norm of reciprocity. In contrast to the first type of social capital, individuals are not expected to behave according to a higher group morality but rather to pursue selfish ends. The difference between this behavior and regular market behavior is that transactions center not on money and material goods but on social intangibles (Gouldner 1960; Blau 1964; Hechter 1987). Nevertheless, the analogy between social capital and money capital is nowhere closer than in these exchange analyses of group life.

The third source of social capital, *bounded solidarity*, relates to situational circumstances leading to the emergence of principled group-oriented behavior quite apart from any early value introjection. Its classic sources are best exemplified by Marx and Engels's analysis of the rise of proletarian consciousness and the transformation of workers into a class for themselves (Marx and Engels [1848] 1948, 17–18). The weapon of the working class is its internal solidarity, born out of its common awareness of capitalist exploitation. This emergent collective sentiment transforms what had hitherto been individual market encounters between employer and employee into a group affair where subordinates have the advantage of numbers. Starting from an analysis of pure market competition, Marx hence arrives at sociability. It is not, however, the sociability underlying the "noncontractual elements of the contract," or that arising out of Puritan values, but the defensive banding together of the losers in the market struggle. Their individual self-interests are welded together into a higher form of consciousness.

As a source of social capital, bounded solidarity arises not out of the introjection of established values or from individual reciprocity exchanges but out of the situational reaction of a class of people faced with common adversities. If sufficiently strong, this emergent sentiment will lead to the observance of norms of mutual support, a resource appropriable by individuals in their own pursuits.

The fourth source of social capital, *enforceable trust*, is captured in Weber's ([1922] 1947) classic distinction between formal and substantive rationality in market transactions. Formal rationality is associated with transactions based on universalistic norms and open exchange; substantive rationality involves particularistic obligations in monopolies or semi-monopolies benefiting a particular group. With substantive rationality, we are, of course, in the realm of embeddedness, because group goals govern economic behavior. The significant point, however, is that individual members subordinate their present desires to collective expectations in anticipation of what Weber designates as "utilities," that is long-term market advantages by virtue of group membership (Weber [1922] 1947, 165).

Social capital in this instance is generated by individual members' disciplined compliance with group expectations. However, the motivating force is not value convictions but the anticipation of rewards associated with "good standing" in a particular collectivity. As with reciprocity exchanges, the predominant orientation is utilitarian, except that the actor's behavior is not oriented to a particular other but to the web of social networks of the entire community.

For the sake of clarity, table 6.1 formalizes the typology of social capital elaborated so far. The table summarizes the processes through which individual maximizing behavior is constrained in ways that lead to reliable expectations by

Table 6.1   Social Capital: Collective Expectations Affecting Individual Economic Behavior

Sources	Operating Principle	Individual Motivation for Compliance	Classical Referents	Modern Applications
Value introjection	Socialization into consensually established beliefs	Principled	Durkeim's ([1893] 1984) analysis of the social underpinnings of legal contracts	Functionalist economic sociology (Parsons and Smelser 1956)
Reciprocity exchanges	Norm of reciprocity in face-to-face interaction	Instrumental	Simmel's ([1908] 1955) analysis of exchanges in dyads and trials	Exchange and power in social life (Blau 1964)
Bounded solidarity	Situational reactive sentiments	Principled	Marx and Engels's ([1848] 1948; [1846] 1947) analyses of the emergence of working-class consciousness	Solidarity bonds in immigrant and ethnic communities (Tilly 1990; Yancey et al. 1976).
Enforceable trust	Particularistic rewards and sanctions linked to group membership	Instrumental	Weber's ([1922] 1947) analysis of substantive rationality in economic transactions	Dynamics of ethnic entrepreneurship (Light 1972; Aldrich and Zimmer 1986)

others; under certain conditions these expectations can be appropriated as a resource. While the first two sources of social capital in the table are the core of entire schools of sociological thought, the last two have been less theorized. These last sources depend on a heightened sense of community and hence have the greatest affinity to the experience of immigrant groups. As the examples we offer in this chapter will illustrate, it is the particular circumstance of "foreignness" that often best explains the rise of these types of social capital among immigrants. This linkage is highlighted in table 6.1, in which examples of modern analyses of the last two sources are drawn from the literature on immigrant adaptation.

The next goal of our analysis is to develop specific propositions based on the last two sources of social capital as a way of fleshing out the theoretical implications of this concept. These propositions are presented in table 6.2. The following sections illustrate the rationale for each. The material presented is not intended to "prove" these formal propositions but rather to demonstrate their plausibility. As we indicated at the start, our goal is to examine the possible reach of general concepts rather than to provide a definitive test of their implications.

Table 6.2   Determinants and Consequences of Bounded Solidarity and Enforceable Trust

Sources of Social Capital	
Bounded Solidarity	Enforceable Trust
I. The more distinct a group is in terms of phenotypical or cultural characteristics from the rest of the population, the greater the level of prejudice associated with these traits, and the lower the probability of exit from this situation, then the stronger the sentiments of in-group solidarity among its members and the higher the appropriable social capital based on this solidarity.	III. As a source of social capital, enforceable trust is directly proportional to the strength of outside discrimination and inversely proportional to the available options outside the community for securing social honor and economic opportunity.
II. Social capital arising out of situational confrontations is strongest when the resulting bounded solidarity is not limited to the actual events but brings about the construction of an alternative definition of the situation based on reenactment of past practices and a common cultural memory.	IV. The greater the ability of a community to confer unique rewards on its members and the more developed its internal means of communication, then the greater the strength of enforceable trust and the higher the level of social capital stemming from it.

V. The greater the social capital produced by bounded solidarity and community controls, then the greater the particularistic demands placed on successful entrepreneurs and the more extensive the restrictions on individual expression.

VI. The longer the economic mobility of a group has been blocked by coercive non-market means, then the more likely the emergence of a bounded solidarity that negates the possibility of advancement through fair market competition and that opposes individual efforts in this direction.

BOUNDED SOLIDARITY

In 1989, a riot was triggered in Miami by the shooting of two African-American cyclists by a Colombian-born policeman. The officer, William B. Lozano, was suspended without pay from the Miami police force and found himself facing the wrath of the entire black community. To defend himself in the face of the hostility of much of the local population, he hired one of Miami's best criminal attorneys. As his legal bills mounted, the unemployed Lozano found that he had no other recourse but to go to the local Spanish-language radio stations to plead for help from his fellow Colombians and other Latins. Lozano had no means of verifying his claims to innocence and, as a potential felon, he should have received little sympathy from most citizens. However, he counted on the emergent feeling among Colombians that he was being turned into a scapegoat and on the growing sympathy toward that position in the rest of the Latin community. After his first radio broadcast, Lozano collected $150,000 for his legal bills; subsequent appeals also yielded substantial sums.[1]

The mechanism at work in this case is called bounded solidarity because it is limited to members of a particular group who find themselves affected by common events in a particular time and place. As in Marx's ([1894] 1967) description of the rise of class consciousness, this mechanism depends on an emergent sentiment of "we-ness" among those confronting a difficult situation. And as a result of this sentiment, forms of altruistic conduct emerge that can be tapped by other group members to obtain privileged access to various resources. The resulting behaviors are, of course, not well-explained by utility-maximizing models of economic action. The fundamental characteristic of this source of social capital is that it does not depend on its enforceability but on the moral imperative felt by individuals to behave in a certain way. In this sense, it is akin to value introjection, except that it represents the emergent product of a particular situation.

The confrontation with the host society has historically created solidary communities among immigrants. Nee and Nee (1973), Boswell (1986), and Zhou (1992) describe the plight of nineteenth-century Chinese immigrants in New York and San Francisco who were subjected to many forms of discrimination and lacked the means to return home. Barred from factory employment by nativist prejudice and prevented by the Chinese Exclusion Act from bringing their wives and other family members into the country, these hapless seekers of the "Mountain of Gold" had no recourse but to band together in tightly knit communities that were the precursors of today's Chinatowns (Zhou 1992). Solidarity born out of shared adversity is reflected in the "clannishness" and "secretiveness" that outsiders were later to attribute to these communities. Such communities also provided the basis for the rapid growth of fledgling immigrant enterprises. Today, Chinese immigrants and their descendants have one of the highest rates of self-employment among all ethnic groups, and their enterprises are, on the average, the largest among both native and foreign-born minorities (U.S. Bureau of the Census 1991; *Wall Street Journal* 1991).

All immigrant groups do not experience equal levels of confrontation, which accounts, in part, for differences in the strength of reactive solidarity among them. The cultural and linguistic distance between home country and receiving society, and the distinctness of immigrants relative to the native-born population govern, to a large extent, the magnitude of the clash between the two groups. A second factor critical to forging solidarity is the possibility of "exit" from the host society to return home. Immigrants for whom escape from nativist prejudice and discrimination is but a cheap ride away are not likely to develop as high levels of bounded solidarity as those whose return is somehow blocked. Turn-of-the-century Chinese immigrants are an example of the latter, as are the Russian Jews who came to American to escape czarist persecution at home (Rischin 1962; Dinnerstein 1977). Today, blocked return is characteristic of many political refugees, and higher levels of internal solidarity have indeed been noted among such groups (Gold 1988; Forment 1989; Perez 1986). The dynamics at play are summarized in the first proposition in table 6.2.

In addition to charitable contributions, like those solicited by Officer Lozano, a more common use of this source of social capital is in the creation and consolidation of small enterprises. A solidaristic ethnic community represents, simultaneously, a market for culturally defined goods, a pool of reliable low-wage labor, and a potential source for start-up capital. Privileged access to these resources by immigrant entrepreneurs is not easily explainable on the basis of economic models focused on individual human capital and atomized market competition (Baker and Faulkner 1991). Aldrich and Zimmer (1986, 14) make essentially the same point when they note that "conditions that raise the salience of group boundaries and identity, leading persons to form new social ties and action sets, increase the likelihood of entrepreneurial attempts by persons within that group and raise the probability of success."

However, reactions to cultural differences and outside discrimination alone cannot account fully for the observed differences in the strength of bounded solidarity among different immigrant communities. We find such differences among groups subjected to similar levels of discrimination and even among those whose exit is equally blocked. The missing element seems to be the ability of certain minorities to activate a cultural repertoire, brought from the home country, which allows them to construct an autonomous portrayal of their situation that goes beyond a mere adversarial reaction.

German and Russian Jews arriving in America in the nineteenth and early twentieth centuries represent the paradigmatic example of a group whose situational solidarity, when confronted with widespread native prejudice, was not limited to an adversarial stance but went well beyond it by taking advantage of a rich cultural heritage. Jewish-American society developed its own autonomous logic governed not so much by what "natives were thinking of us" as by concerns and interests springing from the group's distinct religious and cultural traditions (Howe 1976; Rischin 1962). Chinese-Americans were not far behind in this. According to Nee and Nee (1973), the "bachelor society" of San Francisco's Chinatown was organized along lines that reproduced in close detail the influence of Kwangtung Province, where most immigrants originated.[2] As in Kwangtung, the basis of social organization in Chinatown was the kinship group or clan that incorporated males who claimed descent from a common ancestor:

> The Wong, Lee, and Chin families were the largest and most powerful clans in Chinatown. Basic everyday needs were dealt with within the framework of the clan unit in which a sense of shared collective responsibility and mutual loyalty were central values. (64)

The reproduction of Chinese practices and values to deal with adverse circumstances continues to our day (Zhou 1992). The opening chapter of Amy Tan's (1989) autobiographical novel tells of the re-creation in San Francisco of a weekly club that originated in Kweilin [Guilin] during the Japanese invasion of China. Organized by immigrant women, the Joy Luck Club was meant to ease the difficulties of poverty and cultural adjustment by providing an atmosphere of camaraderie and familiar food and games. A generation later the club was still functioning, its members discussing joint investments in the stock market while they sat around the Mah Jong table.

The reenactment of many cultural practices after immigration does not come about spontaneously but usually results from the clash with the host society. Such practices are, in this sense, an emergent product. The fundamental source of solidarity is still situational, since it is the reality of discrimination and minority status that activates dormant home customs (Yancey, Ericksen, and Juliani 1976).

Because of its relatively recent establishment, the Nicaraguan immigrant community of Miami provides an excellent example of the birth of bounded solidarity and the reactivation of a cultural repertoire brought from the home country. In the words of one community leader, Nicaraguan refugees are resentful because "people think we're all uneducated, poor people without documents" (Branch 1989, 20). To reassert their own identity and distinctness, Nicaraguans have resorted to a variety of practices including the revival of near-forgotten folk items. Ethnic stores, for example, do a brisk business selling Nicaraguan products such as *cotonas* (a cotton shirt usually worn only by Nicaraguan Indians) to well-to-do refugees. As one store owner put it, "The people who always wore American brands and European clothes in Nicaragua now come shopping for a *cotona* to wear to parties" (Veciana-Suarez 1983).

Although most contemporary immigrants have a clear sense of national identity, in exceptional circumstances they are prevented from reenacting their cultural practices. Peasant refugees from the remote highlands of Southeast Asia who have resettled in American cities, for example, are unable to reimplement cultural practices from a preindustrial past in the vastly different environment in which they find themselves and, as a result, often lapse into despair and suffer from emotional disorders (Rumbaut and Ima 1988). The following statement from a Hmong refugee in southern California illustrates a situation reminiscent of those recorded by Thomas and Znaniecki (1984) among Polish peasant immigrants at the turn of the century:

In our old country, whatever we had was made or brought in by our own hands; we never had any doubts that we would not have enough for our mouth [*sic*]. But from now on to the future, that time is over. So you see, when you think these things over, you don't want to live anymore. . . . Don't know how to read and write, don't know how to speak the language. My life is only to live day by day until the last day I live, and maybe that is the time when my problems will be solved. (Rumbaut 1985, 471–72)

These contrasting experiences provide the basis for the second proposition in table 6.2.

ENFORCEABLE TRUST

The fourth source of social capital is also based on the existence of community, except that in this case it is not the sense of solidarity drawn from outward confrontation but the internal sanctioning capacity of the community itself that plays the central role. Coleman (1988, S107–8) identifies this mechanism as the difference between open and closed social structures: "Closure of the social structure is important not only for the existence of effective norms but also for another form of social capital: the trustworthiness of social structures that allows the proliferation of obligations and expectations. . . ."

Shared experiences of departure from the home country and at arrival in the United States create bonds among immigrants and give rise to social networks that frequently lead to tightly knit ethnic communities. The social capital emerging from the monitoring capacity of these communities is referred to as enforceable trust.

Bounded solidarity shares with the first source of social capital (value introjection) an element of moral obligation. Individuals behave in certain ways because they must—either because they have been socialized in the appropriate values or because they enact emergent sentiments of loyalty toward others like themselves. Such behavior can occur even in the absence of reward or punishment. Enforceable trust shares with the second source of social capital (reciprocity exchanges) a strong instrumental orientation. In both cases, individuals behave according to expectations not only because they must but out of fear of punishment or in anticipation of rewards. The predictability of the behavior of members of a group is in direct proportion to its sanctioning capacity. Hence, the oxymoron enforceable trust: *trust* exists in economic transactions because it is *enforceable* by means that transcend the individuals involved.

It has already been noted in the literature of economic sociology that while the rewards and sanctions administered by ethnic communities are generally nonmaterial in character, they can have serious material consequences in the long run. The latter largely depends on whether such communities have access to resources for capitalizing small enterprises. This is a prime instance of the utility of the economic sociological approach as compared with individualistic accounts of economic attainment.

Dominicans in New York City

The Dominican immigrant community in New York City has been characterized until recently as a working-class ghetto composed mostly of illegal immigrants working for low wages in sweatshops and menial service occupations. A study conducted under the auspices of the U.S. Congressional Commission for the Study of Immigration contradicts this description and points to the emergence of a budding entrepreneurial enclave among Dominican immigrants (Portes and Guarnizo 1991). The city-within-a-city that one encounters when entering the Washington Heights area of New York, with its ethnic restaurants and stores, Spanish-language newspapers, and travel agencies is, to a large extent, a Dominican creation built on the strength of skills brought from the Dominican Republic, ready access to a low-wage labor pool, and the development of informal credit channels.[3]

While New York City hosts several formally registered Dominican finance agencies (*financieras*), networks of informal loan operations also grant credit with little or no paperwork. And although some of the Dominican capital represents profits from the drug trade, it also comes from established ethnic firms and from the savings of workers who obtain higher interest rates from the ethnic finance networks than from formal banking institutions. These sources are reinforced by flight capital from the Dominican Republic. Money circulates within community networks and is made available for business start-ups because recipients are expected to repay the loans made to them. This expectation is based on the reputation of the recipient but also on the knowledge that there will be swift retribution against those who default. Such punishment may include coercive measures but is more often based on ostracism from ethnic business circles.

These patterns can be illustrated by the experiences of a Dominican entrepreneur interviewed in the course of fieldwork in New York. This man, whom we shall call Nicolas, is thirty-eight years old and already owns five shops in New York City and a *financiera* in the Dominican Republic. He employs a staff of thirty, almost all of whom are Dominican relatives or friends of relatives. To finance his businesses, he relies exclusively on the informal system of Washington Heights. He has earned a reputation that enables him to collect thousands of dollars to invest in his businesses in New York and Santo Domingo, generally from other immigrants who do not yet have enough capital to initiate businesses themselves. As a borrower, he seems to enjoy ample credit. At the time he was interviewed, Nicolas had two active loans—one for $125,000 and the other for $200,000, only one of which was accompanied by some signed papers—on which he was paying interest at the rate of 2.6 percent a month.[4]

Cubans in Miami

Early conventional accounts of business success among exiles from Castro's Cuba in South Florida attributed their advance to the material capital brought by the earlier arrivals. However, later studies revealed the inadequacy of this explanation in that few of the businesses that formed the core of the Miami enclave were capitalized in this fashion (Wilson and Portes 1980; Wilson and Martin 1982). By the mid-1960s, a few small banks in Miami were owned by wealthy South American families who began hiring unemployed Cuban exile bankers, first as clerks and then as loan officers. Once they were secure in their jobs, these bankers started lending small sums—from $10,000 to $30,000—to fellow exiles for business start-ups. These loans were made without collateral on the basis of the personal reputations of the recipients when they lived in Cuba.[5]

This source of credit became known as "character" loans. Its effect was to allow penniless refugees who had no standing in the American banking system to gain a foothold in the local economy. A banker who took part described the process as follows:

> At the start, most Cuban enterprises were gas stations; then came grocery shops and restaurants. No American bank would lend to them. By the mid-sixties we started a policy at our bank of making small loans to Cubans who wanted to start their own business, but did not have the capital. These loans of $10,000 or $15,000 were made because the person was known to us by his reputation and integrity. All of them paid back; there were zero losses. With some exceptions they have continued being clients of the bank. People who used to borrow $15,000 on a one-time basis now take $50,000 in a week. In 1973, the policy was discontinued. The reason was that the new refugees coming at that time were unknown to us. (Portes and Stepick 1993, 133).

Bounded solidarity clearly had something to do with the initiative since fellow exiles were preferred to other potential recipients. However, this mechanism was not enough. The exiles arriving in the 1960s to whom these loans were made available, in contrast to those who came after 1973 and were ineligible for them, were members of a prerevolutionary community of business people in Cuba in which personal reputation and social ties were a precondition for success. Once in Miami, these connections became all the more valuable because penniless refugees had little else on which to rebuild their careers.

The Cuban bankers could make these loans in good conscience since they were certain that their clients would pay them back. Anyone defaulting or otherwise violating the expectations built into such deals would be excluded from the Cuban business community in Miami. As with the Dominicans in New York, there was little else in Miami in the way of economic opportunity. Character loans were backed, therefore, by much more than sentiments of loyalty or a written promise to repay: by the sanctioning capacity built into the business networks of the enclave. That there was more at work here than bounded solidarity is demonstrated by the exclusion of Cubans who came after the exodus of the prerevolutionary business elite was over.[6]

Community Resources   As a source of social capital, enforceable trust varies greatly with the characteristics of the community. Since the relevant behaviors are guided by utilitarian expectations, the likelihood of their occurrence is conditioned by the extent to which the community is the sole or principal source of certain rewards. When immigrants can draw on a variety of valued resources—from social approval to business opportunities—from their association with outsiders, the power of their ethnic community becomes weaker. Conversely, when outside prejudice denies them access to such rewards, observance of community norms and expectations becomes much more likely. After reviewing studies of business behavior among the overseas Chinese in the Philippines and Asian Indians in Kenya, Granovetter (1995, 149–50) arrives at essentially the same conclusion, noting that "the discrimination that minority groups face can actually generate an advantage. . . . Once this discrimination fades, intergenerational continuity in business is harder to sustain." These observations provide the basis for the third proposition in table 6.2.

What happens outside the community must be balanced, however, with the resources available within the ethnic community itself. It may be that the second- or third-generation Chinese American or Jewish American faces no great prejudice in contemporary American society, yet he or she may choose to preserve ties to his or her ethnic community because of the opportunities available through such networks. The durability of institutions created by successful immigrant groups may have less to do with the long-term persistence of outside discrimination than with the ability of these institutions to "compete" effectively with resources and rewards available in the broader society. Conversely, a resource-poor immigrant community will have trouble enforcing normative patterns even if its members continue to face severe outside discrimination.

An ongoing study of second-generation Haitian students in Miami high schools illustrates this point.[7] Like the members of other immigrant groups before them, Haitian parents want their children to preserve their culture and language as they adapt to the American environment. However, most Haitian parents lack the means to send their children to private schools, and, in any event, there are none such in Miami that conduct classes in French or foster Haitian culture. As a result, many Haitian-American students must attend the same high school that serves the inner-city area known as Liberty City. There, Haitian students are socialized in a different set of values, including the futility of trying to advance in life through education. Their culture is denigrated by native-born minority students who often poke fun at the Haitians' accents and their docility. Since immigrant parents have very little material wealth to show for their efforts, and the Haitian community as a whole is poor and politically weak, second-generation Haitian students have few incentives to stay within the community. Many opt to melt into the mainstream. In this instance, "mainstream" does not mean white society, but the impoverished black community of Liberty City.[8]

Finally, the effectiveness of collective sanctions through which enforceable trust is built depends on the group's ability to monitor the behavior of its members and its capacity to publicize the identity of deviants. Sanctioning capacity is increased by the possibility of bestowing public honor or inflicting public shame after certain deeds are committed. Means of communication, in particular the ethnic media, play a crucial role in this regard (Olzak and West 1991). Foreign-language newspapers, radio stations, and television spots exist not only to entertain the respective communities but also to uphold collective values and highlight their observance or violation (Forment 1989, 63–64). The existence of well-developed media channels within an ethnic community therefore represents a powerful instrument of social control. These observations are summarized in the fourth proposition in table 6.2.

By failing to take into account the differential presence of resources giving rise to enforceable trust, those who develop orthodox economic models of minority poverty and mobility deprive themselves of a crucial analytical tool. Recent research shows that levels of entrepreneurship vary significantly among ethnic minorities and that such differences are positively associated with average incomes (Fratoe and Meeks 1985; Aldrich and Zimmer 1986; Light and Bonacich 1988; Borjas 1990). Other analyses indicate that neither the origins of ethnic entrepreneurship nor its average higher levels of remuneration are fully explained by human capital differences (Portes and Zhou 1995). The social capital arising from enforceable trust may well account for the remaining differences.

NEGATIVE EFFECTS

Coleman's analysis of social capital sounds a note of consistent praise for the various mechanisms that lead people to behave in ways different from naked self-interest. Indeed, it is our sociological bias to see good things emerging out of social embeddedness; bad things are more commonly associated with the behavior of *homo economicus*. Many examples could be cited in support of the sociological position in addition to those presented by Coleman (see Hechter 1987; Uehara 1990). To do so, however, would only belabor the point. Instead, we wish to consider the other side of the question. When social capital is put on a par with money capital and human capital, an instrumentalist analysis of it is necessarily biased toward emphasizing its positive uses—from capitalizing minority enterprises to cutting down the number of lawyers required for enforcing contracts.

It is important, however, not to lose sight of the fact that the same social mechanisms that give rise to appropriable resources for individual use can also constrain action or even divert it from its original goals. At first glance, the term "social debit" might seem appropriate in order to preserve the parallel with money capital. However, this term is inadequate because the relevant phenomena do not reflect the *absence* of the forces that give rise to social capital but their other, less desirable, manifestations. The following examples illustrate these alternative facets.

Costs of Community Solidarity

The existence of a measure of solidarity and trust in a community represents a precondition for the emergence of a network of successful enterprises. However, the exacerbation of these sentiments and obligations can conspire against such a network. In his study of the rise of commercial enterprises in Bali, Geertz (1963) observed how successful entrepreneurs were constantly assaulted by job- and loan-seeking kinsmen. These claims were buttressed by strong norms enjoining mutual assistance within the extended family and among community members in general. Balinese social life is based on groups called *seka*, and individuals typically belong to several of these. According to Geertz, "The value of *seka* loyalty, putting the needs of one's group above one's own is, along with caste pride, a central value of Balinese social life" (84). Although entrepreneurship is highly valued in this community, successful businessmen face the problem of numerous claims on their profits based on the expectation that economic decisions "will lead to a higher level of welfare for the organic community as a whole" (123). The result is to turn promising enterprises into welfare hotels, checking their economic expansion.

Granovetter (1995), in calling attention to this phenomenon, notes that it is the same problem that classic economic development theory identified among traditional enterprises and that modern capitalist firms were designed to overcome. Hence, cozy intergroup relationships of the sort frequently found in solidaristic communities can give rise to a gigantic free-riding problem. Less diligent group members can enforce on successful members all types of demands backed by the same normative structure that makes the existence of trust possible.

In the indigenous villages surrounding the town of Otavalo in the Ecuadoran Andes, male owners of garment and leather-artisan shops are often Protestant (or "Evangelicals" as they are known locally) rather than Catholic. The reason for this is not that the Protestant ethic spurred them to greater entrepreneurial achievement or that they found Evangelical doctrine to be more compatible with their own beliefs, but a more instrumental one. By shifting religious allegiance, these entrepreneurs removed themselves from the host of social obligations for male family heads associated with the Catholic Church and its local organizations. The Evangelical convert becomes, in a sense, a stranger in his own community, which insulates him from free riding by others who follow Catholic-inspired norms.[9]

Among present-day immigrant communities in the United States, scattered instances of this phenomenon appear to be operating. In the course of fieldwork in Orange County, California, Rumbaut interviewed a successful Vietnamese electronics manufacturer who employed approximately three hundred workers in his plant. Not one of them was Vietnamese. The owner had anglicized his name and cut most of his ties to the immigrant community. The reason was less a desire for assimilation than fear of the demands of other Vietnamese, especially the private "security services" organized by former members of the Vietnamese police.[10]

Constraints on Freedom

A second manifestation of negative effects consists of the constraints that community norms put on individual action and receptivity to the outside culture. This is an expression of the age-old dilemma between community solidarity and individual freedom in the modern metropolis, already analyzed by Simmel (1964). The dilemma becomes acute in the case of tightly knit immigrant communities since they usually find themselves in the core of the metropolis yet are simultaneously upholding a foreign culture. The city-within-a-city sustained by the operation of solidarity and trust creates unique economic opportunities for immigrants but often at the cost of fierce regimentation and limited contacts with the outside world.

Until a few years ago, San Francisco's Chinatown was a tightly knit community where the family clans and the Six Companies ruled supreme. These powerful associations regulated the business and social life of the community, guaranteeing its normative order and privileged access to resources for its entrepreneurs. However, such assets came at the cost of restrictions on most members' scope of action and access to the outside world. In their study of Chinatown, Nee and Nee (1973) report on the continuing power of the clans and the Chinese companies and their strong conservative bent. What put teeth in the clans' demands was their control of land and business opportunities in the Chinese enclave and their willingness to exclude those who violated normative consensus by adopting a "progressive" stance. One of the Nees' informants described the situation as follows:

> And not only the Moon Family Association, all the family associations, the Six Companies, any young person who wants to make some changes, they call him a communist right away. He's redcapped right away. They use all kinds of tricks to run him out. You see, in old Chinatown, they didn't respect a scholarly person or an intelligent person. . . . They hold on to everything the way it was in China, in Kwangtung. Even though we're in a different society, a different era. (190)

Like Chinatown in San Francisco, the Korean community of New York is undergirded by a number of associations—from traditional extended family groups and various types of *gye* (rotating credit associations) to modern businesses and professional organizations. The role of this associational structure in generating social capital for collective advancement follows closely the pattern of enforceable trust already described. The flip side of this structure, however, takes a peculiar form among Koreans. As described by Illsoo Kim (1981), the South Korean government, represented by its consulate general, has played a very prominent role in the development of the ethnic community: "Partly because Korean immigrants have a strong sense of nationalism and therefore identify with the home government, the Korean Consulate General in New York City . . . has determined the basic tone of community-wide politics" (227).

This position has, in the past, enabled the South Korean government to promote its own interests by rewarding "loyal" immigrants to the United States with honors and business concessions and by intimidating its opponents. Especially during the government of Park Chung-hee, the Korean central intelligence agency was active in the community, rooting out anti-Park elements and silencing them with threats of financial ruin or even physical harm. In the American context, this heavy political hand became excessive, leading other community organizations to mobilize in order to weaken its hold. However, the consulate remains an integral part of this community and a significant institutional factor in it.

The solidarity and enforcement capacity that promote ethnic business success also restrict the scope of individual expression and the extent of extra community contacts. Combined with the first negative effect of community solidarity, these examples illustrate the fifth proposition in table 6.2.

Leveling Pressures

The previously mentioned negative effects are not intrinsically at odds with economic mobility but represent its marginal costs as it were: successful individuals are beset by fellow group members relying on the strength of collective norms, and highly solidaristic communities restrict the scope of personal action as the cost of privileged access to economic resources. There is, however, a negative effect that does conspire directly against efforts toward individual mobility: leveling pressures to keep members of downtrodden groups in the same situation as their peers. The mechanism at work in this instance is the fear that a solidarity born out of common adversity would be undermined by the departure of members who achieved success.

This conflict is experienced by the Haitian-American teenagers discussed previously, who are torn between parental expectations of success through education and an inner-city youth culture that denies that such a thing is possible. Assimilation to American culture for these immigrant children thus often means their giving up the dream of making it in America through individual achievement.[11] The neologism "wannabe," arguably the latest contribution of the inner city to the cultural mainstream, captures succinctly this process. Calling someone by this name is a way of ridiculing his or her aspiration to move above his or her present station and of exercising social pressure on the person to remain in it. In his ethnographic research among Puerto Rican crack dealers in the Bronx, Bourgois (1991, 32) calls attention to the local version of the "wannabe" among second-generation Puerto Rican youngsters—the "turnover." He reports the views of one of his informants:

When you see someone go downtown and get a good job, if they be Puerto Rican, you see them fix up their hair and put some contact lens in their eyes. Then they fit in. And they do it! I have seen it! . . . Look at all the people in that building, they all turn-overs. They people who want to be white. Man, if you call them in Spanish it wind up a problem. I mean like take the name Pedro—I'm just telling you this as an example—Pedro be saying (imitating a whitened accent) "My name is Peter." Where do you get Peter from Pedro?

In their description of what they label the "hyperghetto" of Chicago's South Side, Wàcquant and Wilson (1989) speak of a similar phenomenon in which solidarity cemented by common adversity discourages individuals from seeking or pursuing outside opportunities. Notice that in each such situation, social capital is still present, but its effects are exactly the opposite of those found among other immigrant communities. Whereas among Asian, Middle-Eastern, and other foreign groups, social capital based on bounded solidarity is one of the bases for the construction of successful enterprises, in the inner city it has the opposite effect.

This contrast is all the more telling because it often involves groups from the same broad cultural origins. In this regard, the use of Spanish in Miami and in the Bronx is instructive. In the Bronx, an individual who shifts to English and anglicizes his or her name is signaling that he or she aspires to move up by leaving the ethnic community behind. In Miami, the same behavior would bring exclusion from the business networks of the enclave and the unique opportunities for upward mobility that they make available. In both instances, public use of Spanish signals membership in the ethnic community, but the socioeconomic consequences are very different.

It is beyond the scope of this chapter to explore the contextual forces leading to the widely different outcomes of ethnic solidarity. However, the existing literature suggests a common strand in every manifestation of this last type of negative effect based on downward leveling norms. Each such instance has been preceded by extensive periods of time, sometimes generations, in which the upward mobility of the group has been blocked (Marks 1989; Barrera 1980; Nelson and Tienda 1985). This has led to the emergence of collective solidarity based on opposition to the existing conditions and an accompanying explanation of the group's social and economic inferiority as having been caused by outside oppression. Although correct historically, this position frequently produces negative consequences for individual mobility through the operation of the mechanism discussed here. These observations support the final proposition in table 6.2.

The six propositions discussed in this essay can also be graphically summarized, as in figure 6.1, which attempts to formalize our discussion of the antecedents and effects of bounded solidarity and enforceable trust. The present state of knowledge does not allow a more refined analysis of the character of relationships between antecedent and consequent factors including whether, for example, they involve additive or interactive effects. Such refinements and possible corrections to the set of hypothesized relationships must await additional research and theoretical work.

At first glance, our sixth proposition contradicts others concerning the positive effects of bounded solidarity (propositions II, III, and IV). In fact, it supports them: the reactive mechanism giving rise to bounded solidarity in response to outward discrimination is the same. The crucial difference lies in the extent of discrimination and its duration: protracted periods of oppression undermine the cultural and linguistic resources available to a group for constructing an alternative definition of the situation (proposition II). A situation of permanent subor-

Figure 6.1 Antecedents and Effects of Two Types of Social Capital Among Immigrant Communities

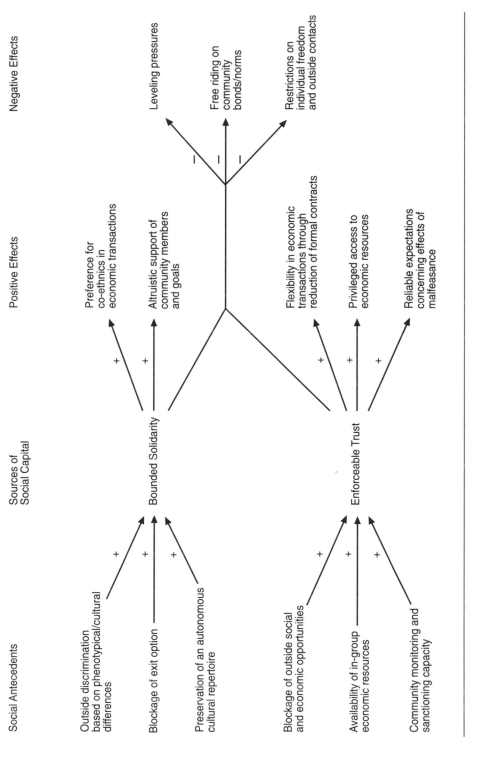

dination also deprives a collectivity of the resources necessary to sanction its members independently (proposition IV), so that its enforcement capacity is entirely dependent on outside discrimination that forces its members to band together (proposition III). The downward leveling pressures reviewed here are a reaction to the partial breakdown of this source of sanctioning capacity, as fissures in the barriers confronting the group allow some of its members—"wannabes" or "turnovers"—to escape its hold.

SUMMARY AND CONCLUSION

In this chapter, we have attempted to contribute to the reemerging field of economic sociology by delving into its classical roots and by using empirical examples from the immigration literature to explore the different forms in which social structures can affect economic action. "Embeddedness" provides a suitable conceptual umbrella for this exploration, although to analyze its specific manifestations we have focused on the concept of social capital. We believe that previous analyses of this concept have been too vague concerning its origins and too instrumentalist with respect to its effects. Accordingly, the aim of this analysis has been to identify the various mechanisms leading to the emergence of social capital and to highlight their consequences, positive and negative.

Economic sociology traces its origins not only to Max Weber and other sociological classics but to economists such as Joseph Schumpeter, who saw in this field a needed corrective to the simplifications of classical economic theory. Schumpeter (1954) and other "historical school" economists in Germany, along with Veblen and later institutionalist economists in the United States, struggled mightily to stem the growing propensity to think of individuals as "mere clotheslines on which to hang propositions of economic logic" (Schumpeter 1954, 885). The effort to highlight the economic significance of what Schumpeter called "social institutions" collapsed, however, under the relentless expansion of rational utilitarian models, to the point that these perspectives have begun to make significant inroads into sociology itself (Swedberg 1991).

In this context, the efforts of Granovetter (1985, 1990), Block (1990), and others to reopen space for social structures in the analysis of economic life represent a commendable, if still fragile, venture. In our view, such efforts will not prosper if they are limited, as in the past, to a critique of neoclassical theories, with nothing being proposed to replace them. A viable strategy for filling this gap is to ground the sociological response in established bodies of empirical knowledge. The rapidly growing immigration research literature, which has been mined but not exhausted in these pages, offers a rich source for such efforts.

NOTES

This chapter is a revised version of an article originally published in the *American Journal of Sociology* 98, no. 6 (May 1993): 1320–50. It is reprinted with permission from the University of Chicago.

1. Officer Lozano was initially convicted by a Miami jury, but an appeals court threw out the conviction on the grounds that he could not get a fair trial in the city. The venue of the retrial was first changed to Orlando, later to Tallahassee, and then back to Orlando. In 1994, an Orlando jury found the police officer not guilty, reversing the original verdict. Throughout this

protracted legal struggle, Lozano continued to make appeals for financial support through the Spanish-language radio stations ("Lozano Gets 7 Years," *Miami Herald*, January 25, 1990; "Lozano Wins a Manslaughter Retrial," June 26, 1991; and Portes's fieldwork).

2. Nee and Nee use the Wade-Giles spelling system for Chinese place names. In Pinyin, the romanization system now used in China, the name of the province is spelled Guangdong.

3. According to the Federation of Dominican Industrialists and Merchants of New York, the city hosts some twenty thousand Dominican-owned businesses, including about 70 percent of all of the city's Spanish grocery stores or bodegas, 90 percent of the gypsy (unlicensed) cabs in Upper Manhattan, three chains of Spanish supermarkets, and several newspapers and radio stations. Allowing for a measure of prideful exaggeration in these figures, they still point to the diversity of business initiatives in which Dominican immigrants participate (Guarnizo 1992).

4. From field interviews conducted in New York by Luis Guarnizo in 1989.

5. Material gathered by Portes during fieldwork conducted in Miami and included in the book on that city (Portes and Stepick 1993).

6. For a periodization of the Cuban exodus, see Diaz-Briquets and Perez (1981) and Pedraza-Bailey (1985).

7. Study in progress titled, "Children of Immigrants: The Adaptation Process of the Second Generation." The material presented herein comes from fieldwork conducted by Portes and Alex Stepick in South Florida during the summer of 1990. (See Portes and Zhou 1993.)

8. Ibid. On the condition of Haitians in South Florida, see also Stepick (1982) and Miller (1984).

9. Preliminary results of an ongoing study of indigenous entrepreneurship in the Andes being conducted by the Latin American School of Social Sciences (FLACSO) in Quito. Personal communication with the study director, Dr. Jorge Leon, June 1991.

10. This interview was conducted in June 1985 and is reported in Portes and Rumbaut (1990, 3–4).

11. For a description of a similar situation confronting Mexican and Central American immigrant children in California schools, see Suarez-Orozco (1987).

REFERENCES

Aldrich, Howard E., and Catharine Zimmer. 1986. "Entrepreneurship through Social Networks." In *The Art and Science of Entrepreneurship*, edited by D. L. Sexton and R. W. Smilor. Cambridge, Mass.: Ballinger.

Baker, Wayne E., and Robert R. Faulkner. 1991. "Role as Resource in the Hollywood Film Industry." *American Journal of Sociology* 97: 279–309.

Barrera, Mario. 1980. *Race and Class in the Southwest: A Theory of Racial Inequality*. Notre Dame, Ind.: Notre Dame University Press.

Blau, Peter M. 1964. *Exchange and Power in Social Life*. New York: Wiley.

Block, Fred. 1990. *Postindustrial Possibilities: A Critique of Economic Discourse*. Berkeley, Calif.: University of California Press.

Borjas, George. 1990. *Friends or Strangers*. New York: Basic Books.

Boswell, Terry E. 1986. "A Split Labor Market Analysis of Discrimination Against Chinese Immigrants, 1850–1882." *American Sociological Review* 52: 352–71.

Bourdieu, Pierre. 1979. "Les trois états du capital culturel." *Actes de la Recherche en Sciences Sociales* 30: 3–5.

Bourdieu, Pierre, Channa Newman, and Loïc J.D. Wàcquant. 1991. "The Peculiar History of Scientific Reason." *Sociological Forum* 6: 3–26.

Bourgois, Philippe. 1991. "In Search of Respect: The New Service Economy and the Crack Alternative in Spanish Harlem." Paper presented at the Conference on Poverty, Immigration, and Urban Marginality in Advanced Societies, Maison Suger. Paris, France (May 10–11, 1991).

Branch, Karen. 1989. "Nicaraguan Culture: Alive and Growing in Dade." *Miami Herald*, May 25, Neighbors Section.

Coleman, James S. 1988. "Social Capital in the Creation of Human Capital." *American Journal of Sociology* 94 (supplement): S95–121.

Diaz-Briquets, Sergio, and Lisandro Perez. 1981. "Cuba: The Demography of Revolution." *Population Bulletin* 36: 2–41.

Dinnerstein, Leonard. 1977. "The East European Jewish Migration." In *Uncertain Americans: Readings in Ethnic History*, edited by Leonard Dinnerstein and Frederic C. Jaher. New York: Oxford University Press.

Durkheim, Émile. [1893] 1984. *The Division of Labor in Society*. New York: Free Press.

Forment, Carlos A. 1989. "Political Practice and the Rise of the Ethnic Enclave: The Cuban-American Case, 1959–1979." *Theory and Society* 18: 47–81.

Fratoe, Frank A., and Ronald L. Meeks. 1985. "Business Participation Rates of the 50 Largest U.S. Ancestry Groups: Preliminary Reports." Minority Business Development Agency, U.S. Department of Commerce. Unpublished report.

Geertz, Clifford. 1963. *Peddlers and Princes*. Chicago: University of Chicago Press.

Gold, Steve. 1988. "Refugees and Small Business: The Case of Soviet Jews and Vietnamese." *Ethnic and Racial Studies* (November): 411–38.

Gouldner, Alvin. 1960. "The Norm of Reciprocity: A Preliminary Statement." *American Sociological Review* 25: 161–79.

Granovetter, Mark. 1985. "Economic Action and Social Structure: The Problem of Embeddedness." *American Journal of Sociology* 91: 481–510.

———. 1990. "The Old and the New Economic Sociology: A History and an Agenda." In *Beyond the Marketplace*, edited by Roger Friedland and A.F. Robertson. New York: Aldine de Gruyter.

———. 1995. "The Economic Sociology of Firms and Entrepreneurs." In *The Economic Sociology of Immigration: Essays on Networks, Ethnicity and Entreprenurship*, edited by Alejandro Portes. New York: Russell Sage Foundation.

Guarnizo, Luis E. 1992. "One Country in Two: Dominican-owned Firms in New York and in the Dominican Republic." Ph.D. diss. The Johns Hopkins University.

Hechter, Michael. 1987. *Principles of Group Solidarity*. Berkeley, Calif.: University of California Press.

Howe, Irving. 1976. *The Immigrant Jews of New York: 1881 to the Present*. London, England: Routledge and Kegan Paul.

Kim, Illsoo. 1981. *New Urban Immigrants: The Korean Community in New York*. Princeton, N.J.: Princeton University Press.

Laumann, Edward O., and David Knoke. 1986. "Social Network Theory." In *Approaches to Social Theory*, edited by Siegwart Linderberg, James S. Coleman, and Stefan Nowak. New York: Russell Sage Foundation.

Leff, Nathanael. 1979. "Entrepreneurship and Economic Development: The Problem Revisited." *Journal of Economic Literature* 17: 46–64.

Light, Ivan H. 1972. *Ethnic Enterprise in America: Business and Welfare among Chinese, Japanese, and Blacks*. Berkeley, Calif.: University of California Press.

Light, Ivan H., and Edna Bonacich. 1988. *Immigrant Entrepreneurs: Koreans in Los Angeles 1965–1982*. Berkeley, Calif.: University of California Press.

Marks, Carole. 1989. *Farewell—We're Good and Gone: The Great Black Migration*. Bloomington, Ind.: Indiana University Press.

Marsden, Peter U. 1990. "Network and Data Measurement." *Annual Review of Sociology* 16: 435–63.

Marx, Karl. [1894] 1967. *Capital*. Vol. 3. New York: International Publishers.

Marx, Karl, and Friedrich Engels. [1846] 1947. *The German Ideology*. New York: International Publishers.

———. [1848] 1948. *The Communist Manifesto*. New York: International Publishers.

McCloskey, Donald, and Lars Sandberg. 1971. "From Damnation to Redemption: Judgments on the Late Victorian Entrepreneur." *Explorations in Economic History* 9: 89–108.

Miller, Jake C. 1984. *The Plight of Haitian Refugees*. New York: Praeger.

Mintz, Beth, and Michael Schwartz. 1985. *The Power Structure of American Business*. Chicago, Ill.: University of Chicago Press.

Nee, Victor and Brett de Bary Nee. 1973. *Longtime California: A Documentary Study of an American Chinatown*. New York: Pantheon Books.

148   The New Institutionalism in Sociology

Neison, Candace, and Marta Tienda. 1985. "The Structuring of Hispanic Ethnicity: Historical Contemporary Perspectives." *Ethnic and Racial Studies* 8: 49–74.

Olzak, Susan, and Elizabeth West. 1991. "Ethnic Conflict and the Rise and Fall of Ethnic Newspapers." *American Sociological Review* 56: 458–74.

Parsons, Talcott. 1937. *The Structure of Social Action.* New York: McGraw-Hill.

Parsons, Talcott, and Neil J. Smelser. 1956. *Economy and Society.* New York: Free Press.

Pedraza-Bailey, Silvia. 1985 "Cuba's Exiles: Portrait of a Refugee Migration." *International Migration Review* 19 (spring): 4–34.

Perez, Lisandro. 1986. "Immigrant Economic Adjustment and Family Orientation: The Cuban Success Story." *International Migration Review* 20: 4–20.

Polanyi, Karl, Conrad Arensberg, and Harry Pearson. 1957. *Trade and Markets in the Early Empires.* New York: Free Press.

Portes, Alejandro, and Luis E. Guarnizo. 1991. "Tropical Capitalists: U.S.-Bound Immigration and Small Enterprise Development in the Dominican Republic." In *Migration, Remittances, and Small Business Development: Mexico and Caribbean Basin Countries,* edited by Sergio Diaz-Briquets and Sidney Weintraub. Boulder, Col.: Westview Press.

Portes, Alejandro, and Rubén G. Rumbaut. 1990. *Immigrant America, A Portrait.* Berkeley, Calif.: University of California Press.

Portes, Alejandro, and Alex Stepick. 1993. *City on the Edge: The Transformation of Miami.* Berkeley, Calif.: University of California Press.

Portes, Alejandro, and Min Zhou. 1993. "The New Second Generation: Segmented Assimilation and Its Variants." *The Annals of the American Academy of Political and Social Sciences* 530: 74–96.

———. 1995. "Divergent Destinies: Immigration, Poverty, and Entrepreneurship in the United States." In *Poverty, Inequality, and the Future of Social Policy,* edited by Katherine McFate, Roger Lawson, and William J. Wilson, New York: Russell Sage Foundation.

Rischin, Moses. 1962. *The Promised City: New York Jews, 1870–1914.* Cambridge, Mass.: Harvard University Press.

Rumbaut, Rubén G. 1985. "Mental Health and the Refugee Experience." In *Southeast Asian Mental Health,* edited by Tom C. Owan. Rockville, Md.: National Institute of Mental Health.

Rumbaut, Rubén G., and Kenji Ima. 1988. *The Adaptation of Southeast Asian Refugee Youth: A Comparative Survey.* Washington, D.C.: U.S. Office of Refugee Resettlement.

Schumpeter, Joseph A. 1954. *History of Economic Analysis.* London, England: George Allen and Unwin.

Simmel, Georg. 1964. "The Metropolis and Mental Life." In *The Sociology of Georg Simmel,* edited and translated by Kurt H. Wolff. New York: Free Press.

———. [1908] 1955. *Conflict and the Web of Group Affiliations.* New York: Free Press.

Stepick, Alex. 1982. "Haitian Refugees in the U.S." *Minority Rights Group Report,* no. 52. London, England: Minority Rights Group.

Suarez-Orozco, Marcelo M. 1987. "Towards a Psychosocial Understanding of Hispanic Adaptation to American Schooling." In *Success or Failure? Learning and the Languages of Minority Students,* edited by Henry Torris Trueba. New York: Newbury House Publishers.

Swedberg, Richard. 1991. "Major Traditions of Economic Sociology." *Annual Review of Sociology* 17: 251–76.

Tan, Amy. 1989. *The Joy Luck Club.* New York: Putnam.

Thomas, William I., and Florian Znaniecki. 1984. *The Polish Peasant in Europe and America.* Edited and abridged by Eli Zaretsky. Chicago, Ill.: University of Illinois Press.

Tilly, Charles. 1990. "Transplanted Networks." In *Immigration Reconsidered: History, Sociology, and Politics,* edited by Virginia Yans-McLaughlin. New York: Oxford University Press.

U.S. Bureau of the Census. 1991. *Census of Minority-Owned Business Enterprises: Asians.* Washington, D.C.

Uehara, Edwina. 1990. "Dual Exchange Theory, Social Networks, and Informal Social Support." *American Journal of Sociology* 96: 521–57.

Veciana-Suarez, Ana. 1983. "Nicaraguan Exiles Begin to Climb the Ladder." *Miami Herald,* March 28, Business Section.

Wacquant, Loïc J.D., and William J. Wilson. 1989. "The Cost of Racial and Class Exclusion in the Inner City." *Annals of the American Academy of Political and Social Science* 501: 8–26.

Wall Street Journal. 1991. "Asian-Americans Take Lead in Starting U.S. Businesses," August 21, Enterprise Section.

Weber, Max. [1904] 1958. *The Protestant Ethic and the Spirit of Capitalism.* New York: Charles Scribner's Sons.

———. [1922] 1947. *The Theory of Social and Economic Organization.* New York: Free Press.

Wellman, Barry, and Scott Wortley. 1990. "Different Strokes from Different Folks: Community Ties and Social Support." *American Journal of Sociology* 96: 558–88.

White, Harrison. 1970. *Chains of Opportunity: System Models of Mobility in Organizations.* Cambridge, Mass.: Harvard University Press.

Wilson, Kenneth, and W. Allen Martin. 1982. "Ethnic Enclaves: A Comparison of the Cuban and Black Economies in Miami." *American Journal of Sociology* 88: 135–60.

Wilson, Kenneth, and Alejandro Portes. 1980. "Immigrant Enclaves: An Analysis of the Labor Market Experiences of Cubans in Miami." *American Journal of Sociology* 86: 295–319.

Wrong, Dennis. 1961. "The Oversocialized Conception of Man in Modern Sociology." *American Sociological Review* 26: 183–93.

Yancey, William, Eugene P. Ericksen, and Richard N. Juliani. 1976. "Emergent Ethnicity: A Review and Reformulation." *American Sociological Review* 41: 391–403.

Zhou, Min. 1992. *Chinatown: The Socioeconomic Potential of an Urban Enclave.* Philadelphia, Penn.: Temple University Press.

Part II

Institutional Embeddedness in Capitalist Economies

— 7 —

The Organization of Economies

Gary G. Hamilton and Robert Feenstra

M ost theories of economic organization, regardless of discipline, involve sleight of hand. Theorists begin by assuming the existence of decision-making individuals. Then they provide these actors with inner motivations: desire for gain, for power, or for social honor and reputation. Driven by these motivations, economic actors are set in motion. They plot strategy, they use guile, they take actions reflexively in the company of others. Whatever they do, however, shapes the calculations and subsequent actions of others. Assuming an inherent mutuality among individuals and their actions, economic theorists then posit an orderly, organized economy, such as a capitalist economy composed of vertically integrated, multidivisional corporations. Economic organization, when theorized in this fashion, is pulled, like a rabbit from a hat, out of aggregated individual decisions.

Attempts to induce societal-level structure from individual actions are common enough in every social science. In sociology, anthropology, and political science, theorists often similarly generate social and political structure from individual behavior. In these disciplines, however, the reverse trick is equally widespread: the inner motivation and actions of individuals are produced, as if by magic, from descriptions of the whole. Remember Karl Marx's famous line in the preface to *Das Kapital*: "Here individuals are dealt with only in so far as they are the personifications of economic categories, embodiments of particular class relations and class interests."

Although common in other social sciences, in economics the efforts to deduce individual actions from descriptions of collective wholes are less prevalent because of the influence of the classical and neoclassical paradigms, which are wedded to economic individualism. Indeed, the famous invisible hand of Adam Smith shows us that the outcomes of a perfectly competitive economy with millions of firms will be the same, theoretically, as that arising from a benevolent planner seeking to maximize the public interest. In this way, the outcomes of a entire economy are reduced to that of a single agent maximizing the appropriate measure of social welfare. This commonplace mental experiment explains why economic theorists are often satisfied with modeling the structure of entire economies by the stereotyped calculations of individual entrepreneurs, who are assumed to act with a collective consciousness. Without questioning the usefulness of these simplifying assumptions for modeling purposes, they certainly do not do justice to the wide array of economic organizations found in reality: from the vertically integrated, multidivisional corporations of the West, to the interconnections between firms within business groups found in Asia and elsewhere.

In this chapter, we argue that these various forms of economic organization

153

cannot be properly understood by using theories that generate economic organization from aggregated individual behavior. Instead, we suggest that economic organization always represents in some fashion the patterned interplay and connectedness of markets within and across economies. We will begin by summarizing the theories of economic organization that assume individual aggregation, particularly those developed by the new institutionalist economists and by their counterparts in economic sociology. Contributions in both these disciplines arose from a dissatisfaction with the minimalist conception of economic organization found in the economic paradigm that posits perfect competition. However, we argue that their respective explanations for the organization of economic activity have led away from the central feature that the competitive paradigm sought to explain, namely the interconnectedness of markets, as conceived conventionally through the price system. In our alternative explanation for the organization of economic activity, we argue that market participants are embedded in ongoing organized environments, the dynamics of which constrain and channel individual and firm-level economic processes. In such a setting, calculability, as introduced and generalized across firms and markets through a price system, plays an important role as a force in rationalizing an economy's existing or emerging economic organization, leading firms in some cases to coordinate their activities within a business group because the incentives exist for this, but in other cases to avoid coordination if the price incentives are not there. We suggest that such actions are, in effect, "system actions," those taken with reference to a specific ongoing pattern of economic organization. System actions are self-reinforcing in the sense that they are jointly constructed and mutually maintained. In other words, we argue that if market participants want to succeed in such a rationalized economic environment, for whatever reasons, they are drawn into playing by the rules of the organizational game, necessarily taking those rules for granted as a part of their decisionmaking environment. By conceptualizing this interdependence between the organizational choices made by different agents in the same economic environment, we can offer a set of propositions that we believe are better suited than those found in institutional economics to explaining the diverse forms of economic organization found in reality.

BOTTOM-UP THEORIES OF ECONOMIC ORGANIZATION

Until a few years ago, most economists would have agreed with George Stigler's aphorism (1968, 1): "There is no such subject as industrial organization." The meaning behind Stigler's punch line is that everything covered by the topic of industrial organization comes out of microeconomic theory, or what he calls "price or resource allocation theory."

Stigler, like most economists working on issues related to industrial organization, based his theoretical assumptions on a view of perfect competition most closely associated with Alfred Marshall. In contrast to Léon Walras's theory of general equilibrium, in which all markets in an economy are interrelated, Marshallian economics is founded on theories of partial equilibrium. Marshallian economists examine an economy market by market, industrial sector by industrial sector, and for each market or sector they conceptualize equilibrium models in which "the ensemble of all buyers and all sellers [in that market] determine price" (Stigler 1968, 9). For the purpose of equilibrium analysis, they view each market as being independent of all other markets. Hence, Marshallian economics is a theory of economies based on partial equilibria.

Given this narrowed focus, a Marshallian competitive market economy has three characteristics: large numbers of buyers and sellers for the same product, independence of action for all parties, and complete participant knowledge of all market activity (Stigler 1968, 5–6). In the ideal market situation that meets these criteria, firms have an optimum size, which is a function of two factors: the demand for a product and the economies of scale needed to produce it (Stigler 1968, 69). When for any reason markets are not fully competitive, firm size is also influenced by additional constraints being placed upon market interaction that go beyond the demand factors of production. Such constraints typically come from factors relating to the product, such as technological or capital barriers to entry, product differentiation, and advertising, and from noneconomic factors corrupting market competition, such as market collusion in the form of cartels and political intervention (Chamberlin 1933; Robinson 1933; Scherer and Ross 1990). When such constraints exist, a condition of imperfect competition gives rise to a given industrial organization (for example, monopoly or oligopoly), which in turn influences market conduct (for example, the pricing of goods) and market performance (for example, the fairness for consumers in the price or the quality of the goods). However, when markets are fully competitive, Marshallian economics predicts that firms are essentially "price-takers"; that is, they are passive reflections of market forces.

The New Institutional Economics

In the past two decades, economists have greatly revised the foundations of Marshallian economics. The economists most responsible for this revision have styled themselves as the "new institutionalists." Although not a cohesive theoretical group, these economists in general no longer see firms as passive receivers of economic signals. Instead, drawing their theoretical spirit from an early article by Ronald Coase (1937), they see firms as agents in actively setting prices, making markets for their products, and creating market organization. In his article, Ronald Coase (p. 388) triangulates Alfred Marshall's initial concern with organization as a factor of production, Joan Robinson's work on markets characterized by imperfect competition in a Marshallian sense, and Frank Knight's insights on market uncertainty and entrepreneurial risk-taking. Focusing on the costs of interfirm transactions, Coase makes firms the primary agents in establishing, in each market, an equilibrium between production and demand functions.

Coase's 1937 article stirred little interest until the early 1970s, when a number of economists began to question the neoclassical assumptions about competitive firms as simple price-takers. In raising these questions, they did not abandon a Marshallian partial equilibrium framework, but instead reworked this framework, correcting what they considered to be faulty assumptions and expanding the theoretical scope to take in topics that economists had never before addressed. Most theorists initially concentrated on the nature of firms in relation to markets (see, for example, Williamson 1975).

Agency theory and transaction cost theory were the two principal institutional perspectives that took shape in the 1970s and 1980s. Agency theorists reconceptualized the main actors in the economy: the firm and its decisionmaking parts, the shareholders, the boards of directors, and the salaried managers (Jensen and Meckling 1976; Alchian and Demsetz 1972). These theorists typically examined incentives that induce actors to behave in predictable ways, and they concluded that macro-level organizations are in reality incentive structures that various sets of actors have knowingly created. Transaction-cost theorists reconceptualized the interaction among participants in a market. These theorists primarily specified the conditions under which firms would prefer organizational over market solutions to their economic problems, and they concluded that macro-level economic organizations and societal institutions represent solutions to transaction cost inefficiencies (Williamson 1975; North and Thomas 1973).

Whatever their particular emphases, the new institutional economists concentrated their efforts on explaining the nature and economic roles of maximizing firms as well as of decisionmaking, risktaking entrepreneurs in creating and making markets work. As interest grew in institutional arguments, these theorists flipped the Marshallian paradigm. They increasingly theorized the nature of organization and underplayed the role of price systems in equilibrating markets (Putterman 1986; Williamson and Winter 1993). As Harold Demsetz (1993, 159), one of the first of the new institutional economists, put it, "the preoccupation of economists with the price system . . . undermines serious consideration of the firm as a problem solving institution."

Downplaying the assumption that markets represent price-setting equilibria, the new institutionalists began to expand their definition of markets beyond anything that Marshall would recognize as a competitive market. Reducing equilibrium to metaphor, they discovered maximizing, market-like behavior in households and family planning (Becker 1981, 1988), in public agencies, in race relations, in foreign relations (Olson 1982), in gift exchanges (Akerlof 1984), and in winner-take-all contests (see Frank in this volume). Without the discipline of a price structure, markets could be portrayed as any means-end rationality, so much so that game playing became the analog for market behavior. Most aspects of society were viewed as game-theoretic terrain, with firms, entrepreneurs, and individuals of all types as the principal players on that terrain—the *deus ex machina*—moving societal institutions to and fro, and thus creating the organizational structures that maximize individual goals. In this rather grand vision of the world, the Marshallian partial equilibrium frame served, and continues to serve metaphorically, as the institutionalist vehicle for generating interpretations of large-scale economic and social organizations, entire economies, and even global configurations.

A brief example of this line of thinking will help illustrate the leap that the new institutional economists take in going from a level of analysis that, as Williamson (1994, 92) notes, deals predominantly with "dyadic contractual relations" to the structure of an entire economy.[1] It is widely known that large business networks provide the organizational structure of the Japanese economy (Clark 1979; Dore 1987; Aoki 1990; Gerlach 1992; Imai 1992; Orrù, Hamilton, and Suzuki 1989). Among the many competing explanations for these networks (see, for example, Gerlach 1992; Hamilton and Biggart 1988; Granovetter 1994), the new institutional economists offer a typical bottom-up explanation that starts by stereotyping firm and interfirm behavior, and then aggregating the results to produce an overall economic structure. First, they argue that the Japanese case represents an imperfect market, a market in which monopolistic competition is the rule (Leff 1978; Chandler 1984; Jorgensen, Hafsi, and Kiggundu 1986). This classification allows them to treat Japanese business networks as the functional equivalents of Western corporations (see Chandler 1984, 22) and as organizations that arise from market inefficiencies. The usual explanation infers a causal link between the transactional problems that exist between firms and the organization of the overall economy. Akira Goto (1982, 69), one of the first to make this causal connection, argues that "the (Japanese) group is an institutional device designed to cope with market failure as well as internal organizational failure. Under certain circumstances, transactions within a group of firms are more efficient than transactions through the market or transactions through the internal organization of the firm." Accordingly, Goto maintains that the postwar Japanese economy and its principal engines, the business groups, have performed more efficiently than economies organized through "the market mode or internal organization mode of the carrying out of transactions." Imai (1992), Aoki (1984, 1988, 1990, 1992), and Williamson (1991 and 1994) have developed slightly different versions of a firm-centered explanation of Japanese business organization, each starting with assertions about the "nature" of the Japanese firm or the interfirm network and then generating a rationale for the organization of the entire economy.

Similar transaction cost and agency-centered explanations of societal-level economic organization have been offered for the industrial structures of South Korea and Taiwan (Levy 1991), for differences in industrial organization between countries (Caves 1989), for global networks of multinational firms (Caves 1995), for the organizations structuring international trade regimes (Yarbrough and Yarbrough 1987), for the organizations of trade in the Middle Ages (Greif, Milgrom, and Weingast 1994; Greif 1994), for "the rise of the Western world" (North and Thomas 1973), and for "the economic institutions of capitalism" (Williamson 1985). As we will discuss later, it is important to note that as the level of analysis moves from interfirm interaction to the organization of national and international economies, such theorists as North (1990 and in this volume) and Greif (in this volume) begin to posit the independent effects of institutions and culture on the organization of economies. This step brings them much closer to the theoretical perspective that we develop in this chapter.

Economic Sociology

Economic sociology, and particularly those works in the field based on the theoretical premises of Mark Granovetter's embeddedness perspective, presents a sociological version of the bottom-up theories of macro-level economic organization. As economists broadened the definition of market behavior to include all behavior, they ventured into intellectual territory that other social scientists had already claimed. This encroachment inspired a spirited reaction, with some in favor but with others very much against economic theorizing. Those in favor formed a rather substantial group of interdisciplinary scholars (Hechter 1987; Elster 1986; Coleman 1990; Cook and Levi 1990; Nee and Ingram in this volume) who promoted rational choice theory as the intellectual extension of institutional economics outside of economics. Those against this form of theorizing, however, were less unified, except in their attitude toward economists as intruders and economic models as totally inadequate (see Hirsch, Michaels, and Friedman 1990). One group of opponents working on economic development went to great lengths to argue that the state (via its functionaries), not the market, was the principal actor creating capitalist development (Evans, Rueschemeyer, and Skocpol 1985; Amsden 1989; Wade 1990; Haggard 1990; Evans 1995). Another interdisciplinary group gathered around Amitai Etzioni's Durkheimian vision (1988) of a new economics based on "the moral dimension." Yet another interdisciplinary group identified with Karl Polanyi's critique of economic universalism (Dalton 1969; Block and Somers 1984; Block 1990; Halperin 1994). However, the largest and arguably the most influential group of scholars (see Friedland and Robertson 1990; Swedberg 1993) aligned themselves theoretically with Mark Granovetter's work on embeddedness.

In the decade since its publication, Granovetter's seminal article, "Economic Action and Social Structure: The Problem of Embeddedness" (1985), has become the central theoretical statement of economic sociology.[2] Granovetter attacked the institutional economists' notion of actor agency. He maintains that economic theories, epitomized by Oliver Williamson's transaction cost theory, rest on the false assumptions that each actor is independent from all others and that each attempts to maximize his or her gains, often at the expense of others. Such a Hobbesian view of the economy, according to Granovetter, is simply wrong. He argues that the opposite point of view, that societal roles determine individual actions, is also incorrect.

The most accurate conception, he says, lies between these two extremes. In this "middle-of-the-road" conception, people's real-life activities provide a sociological foundation for economic action. To Granovetter, that is what embeddedness means. Out of people's real-life activities, out of their "concrete personal relations and structure (or 'networks') of such relations," comes the "production of trust in economic life" (1985, 400–401). These social relations, "rather than institutional arrangements or generalized morality" (p. 401; see also Granovetter 1994) generate order in the economy, an order represented by patterns of small firms, vertical integration of big firms, and the structure of business groups, in other words, macro-level economic organization.

Although Granovetter inveighs against Williamson's economistic conception of agency, it is important to note that both Williamson and Granovetter generate macro-level economic organization from the bottom-up interaction of economic participants in the economy. The crucial difference between the two points of view rests on the nature of the interactions between economic actors. Williamson argues that the nature of the transaction itself suggests a course of action that "rational" participants should follow. In this regard, transaction cost theory employs game-theoretic or rational choice models. The exchange situation generates its own logic, which induces participants to respond to the situation and to the possible actions of others. In calculating how to respond to exchange situations, entrepreneurs continually adjust the transactional context, including changing the organization of their firms, in order to maximize their economic advantages and minimize their disadvantages. As Williamson (1981, 568) stated, "There are so many kinds of organization because transactions differ so greatly and efficiency is realized only if governance structures are tailored to the specific needs of each type of transaction."

Firm-level economic organization, therefore, represents the rational responses of transacting actors at any one point in time. The organization of transacting firms generated at this point in time will in turn have effects on actor calculation at a later point. Industrial organization (the organization of a sector or even of an entire economy) therefore comprises rational economic decisions aggregated and reaggregated over time. Characterized in this way, industrial organization and the accompanying institutional environment serve as constraints that influence but do not determine each subsequent transaction decision. Because each transaction represents a move or a countermove in a fluid economic context, each transactional set has the potential for altering the organization of the economic sector. For transaction cost theory, the transaction remains the key focus of analysis.

Granovetter, on the other hand, argues that the organization of an industry or an economy reflects the social organization of participants. In making this claim for social embeddedness, Granovetter is very careful to focus on the ongoing interaction among economic participants. He wants to portray economic actors as being neither mindless game players who only respond to a narrow economic frame (which he calls an "under-socialized conception of human action") nor equally mindless social actors who represent only social roles (which he calls an "over-socialized conception of human action"). Arguing for the realism of the middle way, Granovetter wants his economic actors to be rationally acting individuals whose objective thinking is socially and historically bounded.

So long as Granovetter remains locked in debate with Williamson, serving as a proxy for other economists as well, his embeddedness theory constitutes a sociological version of a bottom-up theory: interaction among "properly" socialized individuals creates the social organization that defines trust in an economy and leads to macro-level economic organization. Thus Granovetter, like Williamson, views economic organization as an outcome produced by the interactions of economic actors, with the crucial difference between his and Williamson's theories being the nature of human nature. Williamson, in fact, has recognized the similarities between the embeddedness approach and transaction cost theory and has incorporated elements of the embeddedness approach into his own work. Granovetter's "entire argument," says Williamson (1994, 85), "is consistent with, and much of it has been anticipated by, transaction cost reasoning. Transaction cost economics and embeddedness reasoning are evidently complementary in many respects."

As Granovetter (1993) himself recognizes, however, there is another side to embeddedness theory that has no affinity with the conceptual terrain of the new institutional economists. This is the side to embeddedness theory that we employ in this chapter. Insofar as the objectivities of economic actors are socially, historically, and situationally constructed, the interaction between actors in an economy involves not merely exchange situations and their aggregated effects but also socially constructed realities that structure the exchange and the exchange process, that create identities for the subjects involved in the exchange, and that create a subjectively meaningful social context in which the exchange takes place. In other words, economic activity always involves socially defined participants acting in organized environments. We argue that the actual organization of such environments, what we here call the organization of economies, has independent and emergent effects on individual and firm-level action. Because this level of organization dynamically constitutes intra- and interfirm interactions, it needs to be theorized and conceptually distinguished from bottom-up theories of economic organization.

MACRO-LEVEL ECONOMIC ORGANIZATION AS THE INTEGRATION OF MARKETS

In 1954, Kenneth Arrow and Gerard Debreu presented a formal theory proving the "existence of an equilibrium for a competitive economy" (1954, 265). Many regard this proof as the culmination of the general equilibrium theories that were initially formulated by Léon Walras in the 1870s. A few years ago, in an interview with Richard Swedberg, Arrow (1990, 149) said he believed that "general equilibrium theory will not be the site of a cooperation between economics and sociology; rather microscopic analysis, or game theory, provides a better avenue." This prediction has proven true: such compatibility as exists between economics and sociology usually occurs at a microscopic level, because it is at this level that analysts can bracket the phenomena they wish to study, invoke the ceteris paribus clause, and then analyze and argue about the effects of firms, entrepreneurs, and networks on their topic of choice. In this kind of Marshallian analysis, questions about agency, particularly questions about the nature of human nature and the rationality of the human actor, become very important aspects of explanations.

Although they are useful within a narrow framework, such bottom-up theories of economic organization offer distorted views of the ways entire economies actually work. One of the problems of the new institutional economics is that it equates economic organization with a theory of the firm. In this role, the theory of the firm is a theory of agency without a corresponding theory of the *economic* environment in which agency occurs that is analytically independent of agents.[3] Economic organization disappears into the firm; outside the firm is the world of impersonal market transactions. As Samuel Bowles (1986, 352) describes it, this view of economic organization, what he calls the Coasian view, depicts "the capitalist economy as a multiplicity of mini-command economies operating in a sea of market exchanges." This view, he continues, is "radically different from the Walrasian [view]."

It is our belief that a very important area for economists and sociologists to work together is precisely in the analysis of entire economies, which is the Walrasian framework. The Walrasian view conceptualizes an economy as a set of interconnected markets. Here, we first describe the Walrasian view as it is represented in general equilibrium theory and then suggest that if the formal mathematical constraints imposed by general equilibrium theory are loosened, thereby making it more amenable to empirical applications in the real world, a Walrasian view of how economies work also contains a useful characterization of societal-level economic organization. Within the Walrasian view, economic organization becomes the patterned integration of firms across markets and sectors.

General Equilibrium Theory

General equilibrium theory assumes that the analyst must step outside the narrow framework of self-interested actors and their intentions. This necessity can be described mathematically as an "overdetermined set of simultaneous equations," in the sense that "the existence of n partial equilibria does not in any way guarantee general equilibrium for the whole economy made up of n markets" (Blaug 1985, 571). In other words, the assumption that an equilibrium exists in each of n markets (a conclusion reached by Marshallian economics) neither acknowledges nor works out the consequences of the interconnectedness of all markets. Thus, as Arrow (1968, 376) notes, underlying general equilibrium theory is the "notion that through the workings of an entire system effects may be very different from, and even opposed to, [human] intentions."

Walrasian economics therefore attempts to specify how buyers and sellers in all markets simultaneously influence each other. Walras believed that such simultaneity, when one conceives of the economy as a static system, would move toward, but not instantly result in, a general equilibrium. Markets in an economy are composed of overlapping sets of buyers and sellers. People are simultaneously producers of goods (through their wage labor) and consumers of goods. Markets must continuously adjust price and wage structures according to what is happening in other markets. A change in the price of raw commodities will change the price of final goods. A change in the wage of labor will change the demand for goods, which will also change their price. This process of mutual adjustment across markets, Walras believed, pushes the entire economy, by gradual steps, toward a equilibrated price structure. Walras called this step-wise movement toward equilibrium *tâtonnement* or "groping." Walras's theory of *tâtonnement* was his way of describing the process of trial and error by which buyers and sellers across all markets groped their way toward a price structure without anyone knowing in advance what the final outcome would be (Blaug 1985, 578). Very early on, Walras realized that there was no one equilibrium solution, rather that multiple equilibria were possible. The final equilibrium solution would always be contingent on earlier conditions.

The assumptions underlying Walrasian economics led economists toward an increasingly mathematical conception of general equilibrium theory and away from Walras's original desire to explain how economies actually worked. Walras's theory of *tâtonnement* was especially ridiculed on the grounds that the process of mutual adjustment seemed more metaphysical than scientific; some likened Walras's idea of groping to an economy's having a fictitious auctioneer who mysteriously adjudicated prices for sellers in response to the calls from buyers. Later proponents of general equilibrium theory abandoned the gradualism of *tâtonnement* by assuming perfect knowledge in the present of future production and consumption possibilities (Debreu 1959, xi). Such simplifying assumptions permitted a mathematical solution to the simultaneous equations (Arrow and Debreu 1954; Debreu 1959) but further removed general equilibrium theory from being useful in empirical assessments of markets, except in the most general ways (Blaug 1985, 580). Equally important, this formalized version of general equilibrium theory has only a rudimentary theory of the firm.[4]

Reconceptualizing Producers and Consumers

The assumptions that permitted Arrow and Debreu's solution for general equilibrium undermined any consideration of diversity in the organization of firms across markets. Their solution was mathematical, formal, and entirely generalized. In the idealized Walrasian world they constructed, producers and consumers form two internally undifferentiated classes of agents, each planning for the "right" prices but neither possessing the agency to alter price systems independent of their joint actions. The Walrasian world, however, even for the purpose of constructing models, does not have to be configured this way.

There are two obvious as well as theoretically significant changes to make in this characterization of a Walrasian economy, the first having to do with the organization of production and the second with the organization of ownership and control of economic assets, neither of which is discussed within Walrasian economics. The first change is to distinguish, within each class of producer and consumer, whether the exchange between a buyer and a seller represents a final or an intermediate step in the production and distribution of a good. It is well-known that most buying and selling occurs at intermediate stages in the production of products, rather than at the point of final sale and use. For example, the purchase of an automobile by a final user is but one transaction in a vast number of transactions of innumerable goods and services that lead to the final sale of the automobile. Most exchanges occur before the final sale of a good. We can also conceptualize these intermediate exchanges as occurring between producers and consumers of goods and services, but with a very important distinction. Most intermediate exchanges occur between firms, and hence in this context interfirm organization—for instance in the form of business groups (Hamilton and Feenstra 1995)—is an important component of intermarket integration.

Making this distinction between intermediate producers and consumers, on the one hand, and final consumers, on the other, allows us to incorporate economic organization as a feature of cross-market integration and of price systems in an economy. Gary Gereffi's work on commodity chains provides a way to conceptualize this type of economic organization. In ideal terms, commodity chains represent the organization of all steps in the production and distribution of a product before final consumption. Gereffi (1994, 219) conceptualizes commodity chains in terms of three main dimensions: "(1) an input-out structure (that is, a set of products and services linked together in a sequence of value-adding economic activities); (2) a territoriality (that is, spatial dispersion or concentration of production and marketing networks, comprised of enterprises of different sizes and types); and (3) [coordination procedures] that determine how financial, material, and human resources are allocated and flow within a chain."[5] Using these three dimensions in his empirical examination of many commodity chains in different product areas, he observes that the interfirm transactions in commodity chains seldom represent simple "arm's-length" market exchanges but are "organized" exchanges in that they are repetitive, coordinated, or even aggressively controlled by firms occupying key locations in a chain (Gereffi 1994; Gereffi and Hamilton 1996).

Based on this observation, Gereffi and Hamilton (1996) argue that the sequencing of intermediate producers and consumers in commodity chains typically are structured around critical barriers to entry. They distinguish, in ideal terms, between barriers to entry that result in very different configurations. For goods that are difficult to produce (for example, capital or technology-intensive products such as automobiles, aircraft, electrical machinery), the most economically powerful firms in the chain are those closest to the final assembly of the product. For example, in the airline industry the aircraft assembly firms, such as Boeing, and the manufacturers of jet engines, such as Rolls-Royce, control or attempt to control the entire chain, backward to the suppliers of initial inputs and components, and forward to the final consumers (the airline companies). Gereffi (1994) calls these "producer-driven" chains. For standardized products that are relatively easy to make, such as clothes, footware, household electronics, the critical point of control in the chain is not the manufacture but the design and marketing of the product. Gereffi calls these "buyer-driven" chains because they are controlled by "big buyers" (brand-name companies such as The Gap and Nike, and mass retailers such as Wal-Mart, Circuit City, and Home Depot) that merchandise products but do not actually make them.

The second change that we make in this Walrasian frame is the characterization of the organization of ownership and control of economic assets. This change is crucial to the entire Walrasian vision of the economy as the interconnectedness of markets. The change is also crucial to the empirical analysis of interfirm networks, such as the vast Asian business groups composed of firms that share some forms of ownership, management, and asset control. Some of these business groups (for example, the Korean *chaebol* and the Japanese *keiretsu*) are vertically integrated. In other business groups, however, such as in the Chinese family-owned conglomerates found in Taiwan, Hong Kong, and Southeast Asia, there is relatively little integration among the firms in a group.

Contrasting the degree of overlap between the intermarket organization of production and the organization of ownership in different economies forces one to reconsider the conventional distinction between markets and hierarchies. Transaction cost theory assumes that the organization of production (market transactions) and the organization of ownership and control (hierarchy) are co-determined, as being causally linked, the latter being an efficient outcome of the former. This theoretical specification makes economic organization in the form of hierarchies a dependent variable, with variation in market transactions being the independent variable. Vertical integration, says Williamson (1991) is the "paradigm problem" for transaction cost theory.

As we have discussed elsewhere (Hamilton and Feenstra 1995), however, it is the *duality* of hierarchy and market, each conceived of as independent variables, that constitutes capitalist economies. Whereas transaction cost theorists conceive of hierarchy as being coterminous with the firm, we argue that authority relations within capitalist economies differ qualitatively from economy to economy, and in most economies such authority relations reach beyond the firm to form complex interfirm networks that relate to each other, for instance, in terms of shared ownership and asset control. We argue that the origins of these interfirm networks, which we call "embedded networks" (Gereffi and Hamilton 1996), cannot be explained by a bottom-up theory of economic organization.

There is no reason to theorize, a priori, as does transaction cost theory, that interfirm authority-bearing networks necessarily overlap with the set of firms linked together in a commodity chain. In fact, it is obvious from Gereffi's two ideal types that the degree of overlap between the organization of ownership and asset control and the organization of production is an empirical question and will vary by the nature of the commodity chain. For example, in a producer-driven chain, the main producing firms would exert their formal control, often in the form of shared ownership, and informal controls, in the form of market power, over their intermediate suppliers in order to coordinate the output, quality, and price of their intermediate goods. In buyer-driven chains, however, big buyers do not formally control their subcontractors. In fact, the cost structure of producing less expensive and technologically more standardized products than those pro-duced in producer-driven chains creates an incentive in the opposite direction, away from formal ownership and formal managerial controls. In producer-driven chains, we would predict that coordination procedures would overlap with formal ownership and other procedures of asset control. In buyer-driven chains, we would predict that formal ownership and asset-control procedures would be much less likely to overlap with the organization of production. In the latter case, we would predict that profits generated from one line of business would be diver-sified across other markets. Our limited tests contrasting South Korean and Tai-wanese business networks support these hypotheses (Hamilton and Feenstra 1995; Feenstra, Huang, and Hamilton 1996). The same studies also show that the network configurations in South Korea and Taiwan have origins, analytically speaking, that are anchored in noneconomic institutions. Crucial variations be-tween South Korea and Taiwan in kinship institutions and inheritance practices differentially shape the ability of entrepreneurs to create and control large inter-firm networks. These differences in turn create an affinity with certain types of commodities and manufacturing procedures (see also Orrù, Biggart, and Ham-ilton 1997).

In sum, we propose that a Walrasian framework is, in principal, the best perspective from which to conceptualize the organization of economies. Interfirm networks are not simply bottom-up creations of market forces but more accu-rately represent an emergent system of interaction among firms once a capitalist economy is a going concern. In the next section we work out a few of the theo-retical implications of viewing an economy in a Walrasian way as consisting of interconnected markets.

NETWORKED EQUILIBRIA: CAPITALIST ECONOMIES AS PRICE-RESPONSIVE ORGANIZATIONAL SYSTEMS

Once we begin systematically to specify the economic relationships among pro-ducers and consumers, we overlay a Walrasian vision of an economy with a Weberian perspective. In fact, the Walrasian and Weberian perspectives are com-patible and complementary. Although Weber's economic writings had an indirect influence on the new institutional economists, Weber's concern with economic and political organization has largely been overlooked by both economists and sociologists alike (Swedberg forthcoming; Hamilton 1997). The great dividing line in Weber's magnum opus, *Wirtschaft und Gesellschaft* (*Economy and Society*), is the same line that so concerned Williamson in his book *Markets and Hierarchies*, the distinction between market transactions and economic organization (Hamilton and Feenstra 1995, 57–63). For Weber, however, economic action always represents organized action in some respects, regardless of the form of the economy. In advanced capitalist economies, where rational action involves explicit means-end calculations, economic organization is necessarily complex, involving layered levels of control (for example, within and between firms), regulation (for example, from the state and from such economic regulatory agencies as securities exchanges, federal reserve systems, and financial accounting systems), and sanction (for example, as defined through law or custom or as enacted through the market in the form of boycotts). Hence, it is essential, argues Weber ([1921–1922] 1978, 67–68) "to include the criterion of power of control and disposal [that is, the ability to buy and sell property, labor, and capital] in the sociological concept of economic action, if for no other reason than that at least a modern market economy essentially consists in a complete network of exchange contracts, that is, in deliberate planned acquisitions of powers of control and disposal."

Once Weber introduces the notion of power and control in the economy, however, he makes the crucial distinction between economic power (that is, power by virtue of a constellation of interests) and authority (that is, power by virtue of the legitimacy of command). Economic power is based on a calculation of utilities, whereas authority is based on established principles and institutions of legitimate domination. In Western market economies, historically developed legal systems provide an independent foundation for authority within economic organizations. In other societies, other principles may also have legitimacy, such as authority within the family (as, patriarchalism), and may take precedent over Western-style legal systems, even if the laws are instituted in some fashion.

From a Weberian perspective, therefore, economic organization is defined by the span of effective authority, which would include "not only business corporations, co-operative associations, cartels, partnerships, and so on, but all permanent economic establishments which involve the activities of a plurality of persons, all the way from a workshop run by two artisans to a conceivable communistic organization of the whole world" (Weber [1921–1922] 1978, 74). The specific content of authority, as well as the organizational structure that derives from this content, originates not from economic processes but from historical, developmental conditions. Nonetheless, economic organizations in a capitalist economy must respond to the economic conditions imposed by capitalism itself. Among the conditions imposed by capitalism, says Weber, is a system of "capital accounting."

A system of capital accounting pushes all enterprises into the practice of rational calculations that are "oriented to expectations of prices and their changes as they are determined by the conflicts of interests in bargaining and competition and the resolution of these conflicts" (Weber [1921–1922] 1978, 92) According to Weber (161–74), the resulting price structure fosters systemic linkages that create an ongoing structure of interdependent connections among enterprises in an economy and provides a continuous force compelling the rationalization of economic organizations and of other organizations that regulate the economy (that is, "economically regulative organizations" such as the modern state [74]).

This very brief overview of Weber's economic sociology shows that the Weberian and the Walrasian visions of an economy share a number of features. They both stress the importance of the rational calculation of producers and consumers, the interconnectedness of markets, the importance of price structures in the creation of an capitalist economy, and the process of step-by-step systemization (rationalization to Weber and *tâtonnement* to Walras). The Weberian perspective, however, provides three crucial correctives to the Walrasian vision that allow us to incorporate economic organization as an independent feature of the system. First, conceptualizing economic organizations as configurations whose historical origins can be traced to noneconomic institutional foundations, ranging from state structures to inheritance practices, provides a way to theorize the independent effects that economic organizations have on the development of a complex economy. For instance, the American corporation, a product of the legal order that arose in the aftermath of the Civil War, had a tremendous effect on reordering the American economy at the turn of the century. Similarly, Asian business networks, a historical product of strongly normative family institutions in Asia, have completely reordered Asian economies (Biggart and Hamilton 1992; Hamilton 1996).

Second, by assuming that different institutional conditions have independent effects on the emergence of capitalist economic organizations, a Weberian approach predicts that different capitalist configurations would emerge and become systematically oriented to the prevailing conditions of capitalist production and exchange in quite different ways. With the spread of global capitalism, this approach further predicts the existence of many distinct types of stable, systematically interconnected capitalist economies. For instance, Weberian economics interprets Japanese capitalism as organizationally and economically distinct from capitalism in the United States.

Third, Weberian analysis would logically suggest that economies with different types of interconnected markets should have different price structures. Although this was implied by his analysis, Weber did not follow the logical conclusions of his economic sociology in this regard because in the second decade of the twentieth century, Weber saw only one instance of capitalism, that which developed in Western Europe and the United States. Moreover, he did not work out even for that capitalist economy the implications of how price structures rationalize economic organizations. It is our desire here to take a step in this direction.

Walrasian Equilibrium Models as Weberian Ideal Types

It is at this point, in conceptualizing price systems, that Walrasian economics provides a way to convert Weberian economic sociology into more formal economic theory. Walrasian general equilibrium models are highly stylized versions of how economies work. It was Weber's methodological views that logically consistent, highly stylized models of action—what he called ideal types—should be used to disentangle the complexity of the real world. At one point, he (1949, 103) suggested that formal economic models of action could serve as ideal types if they were not confused with the real world. The logic of analysis is to contrast the ideal and hence an unreal conceptualization with the empirical world, thereby pinpointing real causal connections leading to distinctive outcomes. Thus the use of formal economic models synthesizing and stylizing crucial features of economic action allows us to combine Weberian methodology with formal economic theory in order to understand the interrelationship between economic organizations and price structures.

How can the distinction between exchanges among firms and exchanges among producers and consumers be used to develop a formal theory of economic organization? To answer this question, it is useful to consider a stylized model in which we abstract from the complexity of actual economies but at the same time include structural features not usually incorporated into the Walrasian framework.[6] In this stylized setting, let us divide the economy into two sectors: an upstream sector producing intermediate inputs from some primary factor and a downstream sector using these intermediate inputs (and other primary factors) to produce a final consumer good. Suppose that both sectors are characterized by product differentiation, so that each firm retains some limited monopoly power by virtue of the uniqueness of its product and therefore charges a price that is above its marginal cost of production. As usual under monopolistic competition, we will allow for the free entry of firms in both the upstream and downstream sectors, to the point where economic profits are driven to zero. That is, the profits earned by firms through charging prices above marginal cost simply go to cover their fixed costs of production, where these fixed costs can represent that research, development, marketing, or any other lump-sum costs associated with having a differentiated product.

In contrast to conventional treatments of monopolistic competition, we will also allow firms to align themselves, authoritatively, with other firms when this is advantageous. In particular, there will be an incentive for upstream and downstream firms to align themselves, because in the absence of any such integration the market prices for intermediate inputs are above marginal cost, which is a sure sign that agents could do better by internalizing the sale and pricing the input at exactly its marginal cost of production. By internalizing the sale in this manner, the upstream and downstream firms will be obtaining higher joint profits than if the input was just traded at its market price, and we take this to be the definition of a business group: an authoritatively organized set of firms that maximize their joint profits. In the same way that we allow for the free entry of individual firms, we will also allow for the free entry of business groups. We are, of course, abstracting for the moment from the many political and social factors that will influence the configuration of business groups in any setting. Here we simply ask what outcomes we might expect from pure economics, focusing on the pricing decisions of the firms in general equilibrium.

A business group producing N final goods and M intermediate inputs is more efficient than a set of independent firms selling the same number of products, because the business group prices its intermediate inputs internally at their true marginal cost.[7] It follows, then, that a zero-profit equilibrium involving business groups, upstream independent firms, and downstream independent firms cannot occur: either the upstream or the downstream independent firms will be driven out of existence by the free entry of business groups. Thus, an equilibrium orga-

nization of this stylized economy can have at least three possible configurations:
(1) business groups dominate in the upstream sector and are vertically integrated
downstream but also compete with some independent downstream firms; (2)
business groups dominate in the downstream sector, while purchasing some inputs internally and others from independent upstream firms; (3) business groups
drive out independent producers in both the upstream and downstream sectors,
while competing with each other.

From this line of reasoning, we see that the price system itself, abstractly
considered, imposes some structure on the organization of the economy but,
equally important, does not necessarily determine which of these equilibria will
arise: in principle, an economy with the same underlying conditions (such as
factor endowments and consumer tastes) could give rise to more than one possible equilibrium organization. Each of these configurations would be locally stable, meaning that once they are established there is no reason for them to
change, even though the economy experienced some degree of change in underlying conditions. We will refer to this situation where there is more than one
type of equilibrium organization as multiple equilibria.

To explore the possibility of multiple equilibria more closely, we need to consider what the incentives are for firms to vertically integrate within a business
group. As we have already argued, the gain from integration is that intermediate
inputs can be sold at their most efficient price, equal to marginal cost. It follows,
therefore, that the incentive to integrate will depend on how far the market price
differs from marginal cost or, to put it simply, on the markup charged by independent upstream producers. This incentive will, in turn, depend on the degree
of horizontal concentration in the upstream sector. But now there is a circularity
in the argument: the incentives to integrate vertically are strongest when there is
a high degree of concentration in the upstream sector, but this concentration
could simply reflect the presence of a small number of business groups dominat-
ing a market. Conversely, if there were a large number of business groups and
independent firms selling in the upstream market, then the markups would be
correspondingly lower, as would be the incentive to integrate vertically. This kind
of circular reasoning is precisely what gives rise to multiple equilibria in any
economic model, and in our stylized economy we therefore expect to observe
equilibria both in a small number of business groups that are highly concen-
trated/integrated and in a large number of groups (and independent firms) that
are less concentrated/integrated. The economics of the situation does not select
further between these possible organizational outcomes: both can arise, and both
would be locally stable.

In sum, our stylized model shows that, even in the absence of other conditions, the price structure among competing, organizationally linked sets of firms
is a sufficient condition to push the cross-market organization of an economy in
one of several directions. This suggests that more than one kind of cross-market
economic organization not only is possible but would be economically rational
and internally coherent, other things begin equal. Nothing in the theory itself
would suggest that economic factors alone predispose an economy to any one
type of economic organization or another. The model simply suggests that given
the assumption, for a capitalist economy, that enterprises, however organized, are
subject to the logic of capital accounting, firms must relate to other firms in the

same economy reflexively—in a systemic, calculating way. Therefore, price structures and the interconnectedness of markets—both in terms of the organization of production and the organization of ownership and control—are interdependent aspects of any capitalist economy.

It is therefore obvious that the degree of vertical integration in an economy is variously encouraged or discouraged by the dynamics of cross-market economic organization. If this Walrasian view of economic organization is correct, then the presence or absence of vertical integration in an economy is not the outcome of transaction cost efficiencies, as the new institutional economists would argue. Rather, as we discuss in the next section, economic considerations other than transaction costs are important in determining the organization of economies.

Combining Walrasian economics with Weberian sociology, we can now discuss these considerations in the form of three sets of propositions about the organization of capitalist, economies. The first set of propositions concerns multiple equilibria, the second, economic reflexivity, and the third, path dependence.

Multiple Equilibria and the Stability of Alternative Forms of Capitalism

As our stylized model shows, nothing inherent in the theoretical assumption of rational calculation leads an economy toward any one of the relatively small number of internally stable cross-market organizational configurations. We therefore propose that economics alone does not determine the organization of capitalist economies. What factors, then, do account for differences in the organization of such economies?

Drawing on Weberian economic sociology, we would argue that the manner in which authority relationships are articulated in a society directly influences the types of organizations that people in that society routinely put together. The ability to create and, subsequently, to control large, complex organizations (for example, firms as well as interfirm networks) varies from place to place and rests on such institutional factors as kinship and inheritance practices, the centrality of an autonomous legal system, and enforceable political policies. Our examination of Asian economies (Orrù, Biggart, and Hamilton 1997; Hamilton and Feenstra 1995) shows that, despite cultural similarities, different Asian societies vary on crucial dimensions having to do with the integration of households, including the control of personal property, into other social spheres, and that these small differences have large impacts on the creation of all types of socially organized groups, including groups having economic goals. The formation of groups and interpersonal networks, in other words, is a sociological process not reducible to rational economic calculation.[8]

We therefore propose that the initial conditions influencing the subsequent organization of capitalist economies should not be theorized as being the result of random processes or simple historical accidents. Instead, we would argue that the organizational parameters of developing economies reflect significant underlying sociological realities in those societies.[9] This proposition is, of course, a statement that macro-level economic organizations are ultimately embedded in the social organization of society. This statement, however, differs from Granovetter's original formulation of embeddedness, in that he wanted to include "concrete personal relations" and interpersonal networks and to exclude "institutional arrangements" from his notion of embeddedness. Granovetter's later formulations of embeddedness (1993), however, would include both levels. We will have more to say about embeddedness in our next set of propositions.

Given that different societies have different affinities with the types of groups they organize, we propose that these differences will influence, but not determine, the organization of capitalist economic development. At the outset, these affinities, in combination with the specific historical situation, set the organizational parameters of early capitalist development—the range of organizational alternatives and the social recipes for putting groups together. Once an economy is oriented toward capitalist production, however, then economic factors relating to the prevailing conditions of market capitalism, such as the technology of production, capital accounting practices, and globalized price systems, all of which have local, regional, and global dimensions, create a systemic interdependence among firms and among other economic institutions supporting those firms (for example, banks, insurance companies, state economic agencies, and the like), the sum of which Richard Whitley (1992) calls a business system. The price responsiveness of business systems moves the organizational structure of the entire economy, step by step, toward conditions where the organizational configuration of firms across markets becomes increasingly interrelated or rationalized.[10] The step-by-step adjustment, which we refer to in the next section as economic reflexivity, might be seen as an organizational version of Walras's concept of *tâtonnement*.

As the ideal typical model suggests, in terms of pure economics there are only a limited number of cross-market economic organizations that will approach these conditions of equilibrated stability. In the real world, of course, many noneconomic factors, such as state policy, will influence the organization of economies. Furthermore, no economy rooted in global capitalism will ever approach general equilibrium. Nonetheless, insofar as global capitalism has become a major factor in the spread of uniform price structures and uniform capital accounting systems, and insofar as governments have become supporters of similar institutions of global capitalism, such as banking, insurance and equity systems, we propose that the formation of distinct business systems approximating our model's predictions of multiple equilibria should be a empirical feature of world economy today. In other words, *the uniform practices underlying the development of global capitalism should not lead to a convergence of the world's economies but rather should be a significant causal factor in the development of diverse business systems.*

Our own research suggests that the economies of South Korea and Taiwan (Hamilton and Feenstra 1995) represent two very different dynamic, yet at least in the short term, integrated economic systems. Economic development in both countries is led by export trade in the global economy, but the organization and performance of each economy is very different (Feenstra, Yang, and Hamilton 1996). Even more suggestive in revealing possible multiple equilibria is the research of the late Marco Orrù (Orrù, Biggart, and Hamilton 1997). Orrù describes in great detail the striking similarities in the cross-market economic organizations of Japan and German, on the one hand, and of Taiwan and Italy, on the other. Although these matched pairs of economies are different in almost every cultural and social respect, they each shared initial structural conditions that pushed the system of firms toward similar systemic solutions in their attempts to integrate into the global economy, thereby producing an organizational multiple equilibria.

Economic Reflexivity: Embeddedness and Isomorphism

Once a specific configuration of firms starts to be a going concern, we propose that the interrelationships of people and firms in the economy begin to nurture what we call a "self-reflexive" economic system. Economic reflexivity is organizationally induced in modern economies through the development of standards by which enterprises can be compared with one another, including financial accounting systems, and the formation of a considerable range of what Weber calls "economically regulative organizations" (*wirtschaftsregulierender Verband*), such as banks, government agencies (for example, in the United States, the Department of Commerce, the Federal Reserve Board, the Internal Revenue Service), stock markets, investor service firms, insurance companies, and so forth. In such an organizational environment, economic actors of all types monitor themselves and evaluate others in terms of how they perceive the economic system to be constituted and how they see themselves and others fitting into that generalized system. In constantly looking at others—in scrutinizing suppliers, consumers, bankers, credit rankings, stock prices, competitors—economic actors learn to see themselves in light of how they view others and how others view them, and they learn to use this self-knowledge to develop strategies of action.[11] This self-reflexive behavior is empirically substantiated and given greater importance by the presence of monetary systems creating relative values within the system—relative market shares, relative stock prices, relative credit ratings and, of course, relative prices for produced goods and services. Therefore, it is this economic reflexivity that pulls economic actors into a system of mutually determined action. In principle, the presence of such a system does not depend on a structure of authority to enforce the rules of behavior underlying the economic activity, but in reality regulative agencies of all types are present and sanction rule breakers (Abulafia 1997). Reflexive economic systems, therefore, consist of mutually created status orders of economic actors (Podolny 1993; Abulafia 1997), the dynamics of which rest on institutionalized economic power in the Weberian sense: "domination by virtue of a constellation of interests" (Weber [1921–1922] 1978, 943).

We propose that reflexivity in an economic environment encourages two closely related processes. First, reflexivity encourages the social embeddedness of economic action. At this point, we need to make an analytic distinction between the embeddedness of the initial conditions that formed the organizational parameters for capitalist development and the social organization of the economy that develops once economic reflexivity is fully in place. In the early period of capitalist development, the institutional patterning of a society creates the organizational backdrop for early capitalist development. Early development is embedded in such features as the household's patriarchal control of assets in Chinese societies or the lineage's patrimonial control of assets in Korean society. These very same features, however, are no less important in the modern capitalist economies of Taiwan and South Korea, but in the process of industrialization they have been thoroughly reconstructed to become integral parts of the economic system.

For instance, patrimonial control of the *chaebol* (business group) is a standard feature of the Korean economy (Orrù, Biggart, and Hamilton 1997). Although such patrimonial controls have demonstrable historical origins, their presence in a modern capitalist economy is not anachronistic but rather an enacted solution to problems of how to build large enterprise groups in an increasingly capitalist economy. Equally, intrafamily control and interfamily networks form the organizational rules to the game by which Taiwanese capitalism operates (Orrù, Biggart, and Hamilton 1997). In other words, while socially embedded factors may influence capitalist development, the capitalist system itself will induce, and perhaps even intensify, social features of economic activity that have particular relevance to the interpersonal dynamics that characterize a specific economy. We therefore propose that embeddedness in developed capitalist economies needs to be conceptualized as an ongoing process of construction and reconstruction, the basic features of which are maintained through the interrelatedness and reflexivity of economic actors.

Second, economic reflexivity encourages what DiMaggio and Powell (1991) have called "organizational isomorphism." DiMaggio and Powell have argued that organizations in the same institutionalized environment tend to develop similar types of organizational forms. Organizations do this, they suggest, for a variety of reasons, including coercion based on regulations, imitation of successful models in risk-averse contexts, and conformity to professional norms.[12] Although DiMaggio and Powell do not theorize the organizational setting in this way, it is clear that self-reflexive monitoring, as described above, is a necessary feature of all three types of isomorphism that they discuss, and following their line of reasoning we also hypothesize that economic organizations in the same economies will also exhibit isomorphism.

Our research on East Asian business groups (Orrù, Biggart, and Hamilton 1997; Hamilton and Feenstra 1995) strongly supports this hypothesis. Our empirical measures of isomorphism demonstrate that the business groups in the three most advanced capitalist economies in East Asia—Japan, South Korea, and Taiwan—are strongly isomorphic within each economy but are very dissimilar among economies. This research substantiates the systemic nature of capitalist economic organization in each economy and the qualitative differences in macro-level organization among economies.

Path Dependence and the Trajectories of Economic Development

Most theorists of economic development do not distinguish between the initial conditions of capitalist development and changes in economies that are already industrialized in large part. Our perspective suggests that these two types of economic development are analytically very different and should be analyzed accordingly. The initial period of development amounts to an economic transformation. A huge reorientation occurs when an economy changes from agrarian production for local and regional markets to manufacturing and service industries linked to global commodity chains. This reorientation needs to be analyzed in its own right. As we have proposed, social organization at the time of development provides the structural underpinnings for and shapes the subsequent organization of capitalist development.

Once economies have become at least partially incorporated into widely integrated systems of economic production and distribution, as did the countries of East Asia in the last half of the nineteenth century, the initial conditions of success fuel subsequent changes (Hamilton 1996). We can identify this recurring effect as a property of economic reflexivity, as we have described in the previous section. Once economic actors become embedded in a mutually coordinated economy, then changes in that economy have systemic effects, in the sense that changes in one area of economic life will likely ripple through the entire economy. Weber called this kind of change "rationalization," meaning that the direction of change is toward greater systemization of existing structures. He argued that the process of rationalization in capitalist economies works at two levels: at the level of the authoritative economic organization (for example, the enterprise) and at the level of the entire economy. Enterprises attempt to increase their control of the economic environment, often in competition with other firms, in order to secure, for instance, monopoly positions vis-à-vis buyers or sellers. While enterprises attempt to increase their economic power in relation to others, organizations that regulate the economy in some respect attempt, on a formal basis, to spread their system of control logically and consistently throughout their prescribed domains. The reflexive actions of both sets of economic actors increasingly channel and standardize the actions of all economically active participants.

The concept of path dependence, insightfully used by evolutionary economists (Nelson and Winter 1982) to describe the continuity between initial conditions and subsequent trajectories, is similar in some respects to Weber's theory of economic rationalization. Once a reflexive economy is in place, the process of economic change is in part also an organizational process. Entrepreneurial strategy is necessarily embedded in an array of existing economic interactions and organizations. In such a context, competitive enterprises would use their existing organizational repertoires to chase efficiencies, that is to rationalize, so as to reduce transaction costs, to upgrade technology, to relocate manufacturing to another site. State agencies, for instance, would use their regulative powers to promote firms in one sector or another. In both cases, economic change is incremental change that leads economic actors, and hence the whole economy, reflexively toward greater systemic integration. Greater systemic integration, however, does not necessarily lead to higher profits for firms or to the greater accomplishment of individual or collective goals. As many organizational studies, including those by Weber, show, rationalization often undermines the very goals that are sought.

CONCLUSION

In this chapter, we have presented a theoretical argument for rethinking how economies are organized. Most such theories have a microeconomic focus that so privileges firms as the crucial economic actor that they become "free floaters" in a sea of economic activity. Quoting Joan Robinson's analogy, Coase (1937, 388) makes this point very clear when he likens firms to "islands of conscious power in this ocean of unconscious co-operation like lumps of butter coagulating in a pail of butter milk." Sociological critiques of this rational choice conception of firms as economic actors assert that firms are not autonomous actors but rather are embedded in networks of ongoing relationships that provide the crucial framework for market activity. Both sets of theories, we argue, generate large-scale economic organizations (that is, the organization of entire economies) from micro-level interactions.

In contrast to such bottom-up theories, we offer a neo-Walrasian conception of economies as the organized interconnections across markets. In this conception, firms are not free-floating actors but rather one of several types of economically active agents that, through their reflexive monitoring of their own activity in relation to others, create system-like patterns of large-scale economic organization. We also suggest that in globalizing capitalist economies two of the principal factors forcing all types of agents to adopt reflexive orientations to their own activities are price structures and capital accounting systems. In this chapter, we develop a very simple model based on pricing decisions among firms producing, variously, intermediate and final goods to demonstrate that interfirm reflexivity based on the price structure alone can result in multiple equilibria. These multiple stable solutions to pricing decisions suggest in ideal terms that advanced capitalist economies can be organized in radically different ways and still be economically viable. In other words, our neo-Walrasian view would suggest that with capitalist development convergence is not destiny but potentially a source of economic diversity.

Reflexively based economic organization at both the firm and economy-wide levels therefore represent emergent phenomenon. The trajectory of this emergence is an outcome that is neither based on pure economics nor predetermined in advance of the interaction among economically active agents. Instead, large-scale economic organization emerges from the reflexive interaction of these agents in their respective competitive efforts to gain economic advantage in a globalizing economy. A historically determined lineup of agents, including the activities of state officials, and the institutional environment in which they operate, exert a powerful influence on these emergent outcomes, but global product worlds and pricing structures also matter a great deal. We maintain that it is the combination of historical and institutional factors, on one hand, and global product and price structures, on the other, that foster organizational integration across markets and that push different economies in different directions.

To clarify this point in closing, it is useful to contrast our theoretical position with that taken by North and Greif in this volume. Both North and Greif move well beyond a conception of economies as free-floating firms in oceans of market activity. North's point—"it is the interaction between institutions and organizations that shapes the institutional evolution of an economy. If institutions are the rules of the game, organizations and their entrepreneurs are the players"—is essentially the same argument that we make in this chapter. The main difference between North's theory and ours is that the "incentive structure embodied in institutions" for North is something that precedes and provides "the underlying determinants of economic performance," whereas for us the incentive structure is not outside the economy but is an emergent and essential element of economic activity itself, the organization of which is rationalized through price structures as well as through historically constructed rules to the game.

Greif's theory is also very close to our own position. Greif suggests that since economic activity is closely linked to culture and institutional structure there should be a range of stable ways for different societies to organize in their economic activities. Like us, he conceptualizes these different organizations as multiple equilibria. The factors underlying and inducing equilibria are, however, different in Greif's theory than in our own. In our depiction, equilibria are generated from a price system that is internal to the model of economic activity. In Greifs chapter, however, equilibria are introduced as a feature of different social structures, a factor that is outside his models of economic activity.

In these characterizations, both North and Greif move the focus of their analysis from a bottom-up to a top-down theory of economic organization, in which external social and political structures determine the organization of economies. Our view, much closer to Granovetter's middle way (1985), is that the organization of economies represents an emergent process that is generated reflexively from the interaction of knowing participants.

The authors gratefully achnowledge the following people who read and commented on an earlier draft of this chapter: Nicole Biggart, Mark Granovetter, John R. Hall, Michael Hechter, Edgar Kiser, James Rauch, and especially Mary Brinton and Victor Nee. Of course, they bear no responsibility for any errors or shortcomings in the text, which is ours alone.

NOTES

1. As Williamson (1994, 92–93) states, "Transaction cost economics deals predominantly with dyadic contractual relations. Viewing the firms as a nexus of contracts, the object is to prescribe the best transaction/governance structure between the firm and its intermediate product market suppliers, between the firms and its workers, between the firm and finance, etc. Japanese economic organization appears to be more complicated." But, Williamson continues, "transaction cost economics can help to explicate the complementaries [between Japanese and U.S. economic organization]."

2. This subfield has developed so quickly that a compendium, *The Handbook of Economic Sociology* (1994) was recently published to summarize its recent advances and to advertise its promise for the future.

3. The new institutionalists, of course, posit the importance of noneconomic institutions, such as the state and the legal system, which provide an incentive structure within which economic actors operate.

4. All firms are price takers, so the number and size of firms make no difference in final outcomes.

5. Gereffi uses the term "governance structure" instead of "coordination procedures." We, however, want to theorize authority and power relationships in a more complex way. Therefore, we incorporate the meaning of governance structure in our discussion of the organization of ownership and control, leaving coordination procedures as an essential aspect of commodity chains without, however, predefining the exact nature of those procedures.

6. For a full discussion of this model and substantiating evidence, see Feenstra, Huang, and Hamilton (1996), and Feenstra, Yang, and Hamilton (1996).

7. Offsetting these marginal costs are any "governance costs" within a group. These governance costs are introduced in our formal model but ignored here. See Feenstra, Huang, and Hamilton (1996).

8. "This point is a rather obvious one for sociologists, but less so for economists. Kenneth Arrow (1990, 138–39), however, makes the same point in a way that would appeal to the members of his discipline:

> In a rational type of analysis it will be said that it is profitable to be trustworthy. So I will be trustworthy because it is profitable to me. But you can't very easily establish trust on a basis like that. If your basis is rational decision and your underlying motive is self-interest, then you can betray your trust at any point when it is profitable and in your interest to do so. Therefore, other people can't trust you. For there to be trust, there has to be a social structure which is based on motives different from immediate opportunism. Or perhaps based on something for which your social status is a guarantee and which functions as a kind of commitment. How all this works is not explainable in Becker-type terms. . . . One of the aspects [of economic analysis] is the fact that the transactions, which are modeled in ordinary economic theory, depend for their validation in several senses on a larger social system. By "social system" I mean a shared set of symbols, a shared set of social norms, and a set of institutions for the enforcement of the norms.

9. The way to think about this underlying reality is very much in the same way as Tocqueville (1971, 78) once described the causes of the French Revolution:

> For my part I hate all those absolute systems that make all the events of history depend on great first causes linked together by the chain of fate and thus succeed, so to speak, in banishing men from the history of the human race. Their boasted breadth seems to me narrow, and their mathematical exactness false. I believe, *pace* the writers who find these sublime theories to feed their vanity and lighten their labours, that many important historical facts can be explained only by accidental circumstances, while many others are inexplicable. Finally, that chance, or rather the concatenation of secondary causes, which we call by that name because we can't sort them all out, is a very important element in all that we see taking place in the world's theatre. But I am firmly convinced that chance can do nothing unless the ground has been prepared in advance. Antecedent facts, the nature of institutions, turns of mind and the state of mores are the materials from which chance composes those impromptu events that surprise and terrify us.

10. We should note that Richard Whitley does not include the price system in his notion of the business system.

11. Harrison White (1981, 543–44), one of the first to recognize this reflexivity, states that "markets are tangible cliques of producers observing each other. Pressure from the buyer creates a mirror in which producers see themselves, not consumers."

12. However, DiMaggio and Powell (1991), argue that private business organizations, in contrast with publicly funded organizations such as schools, would be less likely to become isomorphic because of economic competition. We, however, believe the same processes of standardization and isomorphism also operate in capitalist economies (Orrù, Biggart, and Hamilton 1997).

REFERENCES

Abulafia, Mitchell. 1997. *Making Markets*. Cambridge, Mass.: Harvard University Press.

Akerlof, George A. 1984. "Gift Exchanges and Efficiency-Wage Theory: Four Views." *American Economic Review* 74: 708–20.

Alchian, Armen, and Harold Demsetz. 1972. "Production, Information Costs, and Economic Organization," *American Economic Review* 62: 777–95.

Amsden, Alice H. 1989. *Asia's Next Giant: South Korea and Late Industrialization*. New York: Oxford University Press.

Anderson, Philip W., Kenneth J. Arrow, and David Pines, eds. 1988. *The Economy as an Evolving Complex System*. Reading, Mass.: Addison-Wesley.

Aoki, Masahiko, ed. 1984. *The Economic Analysis of the Japanese Firm*. Amsterdam: North-Holland.

———. 1988. *Information, Incentive, and Bargaining in the Japanese Economy*. Cambridge, England: Cambridge University Press.

———. 1990. "Toward an Economic Model of the Japanese Firm." *Journal of Economic Literature* 28 (March): 1–27.

———. 1992. "Decentralization-Centralization in Japanese Organization: A Duality Principle." In *The Political Economy of Japan. Volume Three: Cultural and Social Dynamics*, edited by Shumpei Kumon and Henry Rosovsky. Stanford, Calif.: Stanford University Press

Arrow, Kenneth. 1968. "Economic Equilibrium." In *International Encyclopedia of the Social Sciences*. New York: Macmillan.

———. 1990. "Kenneth J. Arrow." In *Economics and Sociology*, edited by Richard Swedberg. Princeton, N.J.: Princeton University Press.

Arrow, Kenneth J., and Gerard Debreu. 1954. "Existence of an Equilibrium for a Competitive Economy." *Economietrica* 22(3): 265–90.

Becker, Gary. 1981. *A Treatise on the Family*. Cambridge, Mass.: Harvard University Press.

———. 1988. "Family Economics and Macro Behavior." *American Economic Review* 78: 1–13.

Biggart, Nicole Woolsey, and Gary G. Hamilton. 1992. "On the Limits of a Firm-based Theory to Explain Business Networks: The Western Bias of Neoclassical Economics." In *Networks and Organizations: Structure, Form, and Action*, edited by Nitin Nohria and Robert G. Eccles. Boston: Harvard Business School Press.

Blaug, Mark. 1985. *Economic Theory in Retrospect*. 4th ed. Cambridge, England: Cambridge University Press.

Block, Fred. 1990. *Postindustrial Possibilities: A Critique of Economic Discourse*. Berkeley, Calif.: University of California Press.

Block, Fred, and Margaret R. Somers. 1984. "Beyond the Economistic Fallacy: The Holistic Social Science of Karl Polanyi." In *Vision and Method in Historical Sociology*, edited by Theda Skocpol. Cambridge, England: Cambridge University Press.

Bowles, Samuel. 1986. "The Production Process in a Competitive Economy: Walrasian, Neo-Hobbesian, and Marxian Models." In *The Economic Nature of the Firm, A Reader*, edited by Louis Putterman. Cambridge, England: Cambridge University Press.

Caves, Richard E. 1989. "International Differences in Industrial Organization." In *Handbook of Industrial Organization*, Vol. 2, edited by Richard Schmalensee and Robert. D. Willig. Amsterdam, Holland: Elsevier Science.

———. 1995. "Growth and Decline in Multinational Enterprises: From Equilibrium Models to Turnover Process." In *Corporate Links and Foreign Direct Investment in Asia and the Pacific*, edited by Edward K.Y. Chen and Peter Drysdale. Pymble, Australia: HarperEducational.

Chamberlin, Edward. 1933. *Theory of Monopolistic Competition*. Cambridge, Mass.: Harvard University Press.

Chandler, Alfred D. 1984. "The Emergence of Managerial Capitalism." *Business History Review* 58: 473–502.

Clark, Rodney. 1979. *The Japanese Company*. New Haven, Conn.: Yale University Press.

Coase, Ronald. 1937. "The Nature of the Firm." *Economica* 4: 386–405.

Coleman, James S. 1990. *Foundations of Social Theory*. Cambridge, Mass.: Harvard University Press.

Cook, Karen Schweers, and Margaret Levi. 1990. *The Limits of Rationality*. Chicago, Ill.: Chicago University Press.

Dalton, George. 1969. "Theoretical Issues in Economic Anthropology." *Current Anthropology* 10 (February): 63–80.

Debreu, Gerard. 1959. *Theory of Value: An Axiomatic Analysis of Economic Equilibrium*. New Haven, Conn.: Yale University Press.

Demsetz, Harold. 1993. "The Theory of the Firm Revisited." In *The Nature of the Firm: Origins, Evolution, and Development*, edited by Oliver E. Williamson and Sidney G. Winter. New York: Oxford University Press.

DiMaggio, Paul J., and Walter W. Powell. 1991. "The Iron Cage Revisited: Institutional Isomorphism and Collective Rationality in Organization Fields." In *The New Institutionalism in Organizational Analysis*, edited by Walter W. Powell and Paul J. DiMaggio. Chicago, Ill.: Chicago University Press.

Dore, Ronald P. 1987. *Taking Japan Seriously*. Stanford, Calif.: Stanford University Press.

Elster, Jon, ed. 1986. *Rational Choice*. Oxford, England: Basil Blackwell.

Etzioni, Amitai. 1988. *The Moral Dimension: Toward a New Economics*. New York: Free Press.

Evans, Peter B. 1995. *Embedded Autonomy: States and Industrial Transformation*. Princeton, N.J.: Princeton University Press.

Evans, Peter B., Dietrich Rueschemeyer, and Theda Skocpol. 1985. *Bringing the State Back In*. Cambridge, England: Cambridge University Press.

Feenstra, Robert C. 1994. "New Product Varieties and the Measurement of International Prices." *American Economic Review* 84: 157–77.

Feenstra, Robert C., Deng-shing Huang, and Gary G. Hamilton. 1996. "Business Groups and Trade in East Asia: Part 1, Networked Equilibria." Working Paper 5886. Cambridge, Mass.: National Bureau of Economic Research.

Feenstra, Robert C., Tzu-han Yang, and Gary G. Hamilton. 1996. "Business Groups and Trade in East Asia: Part 2, Product Variety." Working Paper 5887. Cambridge, Mass.: National Bureau of Economic Research.

Friedland, Roger, and A. F. Robertson. 1990. *Beyond the Marketplace, Rethinking Economy and Society*. New York: Aldine de Gruyter.

Fukuyama, Francis. 1995. *Trust: The Social Virtues and the Creation of Prosperity*. New York: Free Press.

Gereffi, Gary. 1994. "The Organization of Buyer-Driven Global Commodity Chains: How U.S. Retail Networks Shape Overseas Production Networks." In *Commodity Chains and Global Capitalism*, edited by Gary Gereffi and Miguel Korzeniewicz. Westport, Conn.: Greenwood Press.

Gereffi, Gary, and Gary G. Hamilton. 1996. "Commodity Chains and Embedded Networks: The Economic Organization of Global Capitalism." Unpublished paper presented at the Annual Meeting of the American Sociological Association.

Gerlach, Michael. 1992. *Alliance Capitalism: The Strategic Organization of Japanese Business*. Berkeley, Calif.: University of California Press.

Goto, Akira. 1982. "Business Groups in a Market Economy." *European Economic Review* 19: 53–70.

Granovetter, Mark. 1985. "Economic Action and Social Structure: The Problem of Embeddedness." *American Journal of Sociology* 91: 481–510.

———. 1993. "The Nature of Economic Relationships." In *Explorations in Economic Sociology*, edited by Richard Swedberg. New York: Russell Sage Foundation.

———. 1994. "Business Groups." In *Handbook of Economic Sociology*, edited by Neil Smelser and Richard Swedberg. Princeton, N.J.: Princeton University Press.

Greif, Avner. 1994. "Cultural Beliefs and the Organization of Society: A Historical and Theoretical Reflection on Collectivist and Individualist Societies." *Journal of Political Economy* 102: 912–50.

Greif, Avner, Paul Milgrom, and Barry Weingast. 1994. "Coordination, Commitment, and Enforcement: The Case of the Merchant Guild." *Journal of Political Economy* 102: 732–45.

Haggard, Stephan. 1990. *Pathways from the Periphery: The Politics of Growth in the Newly Industrializing Countries*. Ithaca, N.Y.: Cornell University Press.

Halperin, Rhoda H. 1994. *Cultural Economies, Past and Present*. Austin, Tex.: University of Texas Press.

Hamilton, Gary G. 1996. "Overseas Chinese Capitalism." In *The Confucian Dimensions of Industrial East Asia*, edited by Tu Wei-ming. Cambridge, Mass.: Harvard University Press.

———. 1997. "The Structure of Business Networks in Taiwan." In Marco Orrù, Nicole Woolsey Biggart, and Gary G. Hamilton. *The Economic Organization of Capitalism in East Asia*. Thousand Hills, Calif.: Sage Publications.

Hamilton, Gary G., and Nicole Woolsey Biggart. 1988. "Market, Culture, and Authority: A Comparative Analysis of Management and Organization in the Far East." *American Journal of Sociology* 94 (Supplement): S52–94.

Hamilton, Gary G., and Robert Feenstra. 1995. "Varieties of Hierarchies and Markets." *Industrial and Corporate Change* 4(1): 93–130.

Hechter, Michael. 1987. *The Principles of Group Solidarity*. Berkeley, Calif.: University of California Press.

Hirsch, Paul, Stuart Michaels, and Ray Friedman. 1990. "Clean Models Vs. Dirty Hands: Why

Economics Is Different from Sociology." In *Structures of Capital: The Social Organization of the Economy*, edited by Sharon Zukin and Paul DiMaggio. Cambridge, England: Cambridge University Press.

Imai, Ken-ichi. 1992. "Japan's Corporate Networks." In *The Political Economy of Japan*. Vol. 2, *Cultural and Social Dynamics*, edited by Shumpei Kumon and Henry Rosovsky. Stanford, Calif.: Stanford University Press.

Jensen, Michael C., and William H. Meckling. 1976. "Theory of the Firm: Managerial Behavior, Agency Costs, and Ownership Structure." *Journal of Financial Economics* 3: 305–60.

Jorgensen, Jan. J., Taieb Hafsi, and Moses N. Kiggundu. 1986. "Towards a Market Imperfections Theory of Organizational Structure in Developing Countries." *Journal of Management Studies* 24(4): 419–42.

Leff, Nathaniel. 1978. "Industrial Organization and Entrepreneurship in the Developing Countries: The Economic Groups." *Economic Development and Cultural Change* 26(4): 661–75.

Levy, Brian. 1991. "Transactions Costs, the Size of Firms, and Industrial Policy: Lessons from a Comparative Case Study of the Footwear Industry in Korea and Taiwan." *Journal of Development Economics* 34: 151–78.

Nelson, Richard, and Sidney Winter. 1982. *An Evolutionary Theory of Economic Change*. Cambridge, Mass.: Harvard University Press.

North, Douglass C. 1990. *Institutions, Institutional Change, and Economic Performance*. Cambridge, England: Cambridge University Press.

North, Douglass C., and Robert P. Thomas. 1973. *The Rise of the Western World: A New Economic History*. Cambridge, England: Cambridge University Press.

Olson, Mancur. 1982. *The Rise and Decline of Nations: Economic Growth, Stagflation, and Social Rigidities*. New Haven, Conn.: Yale University Press.

Orrù, Marco, Gary G. Hamilton, and Mariko Suzuki. 1989. "Patterns of Inter-Firm Control in Japanese Business." *Organization Studies* 10(4): 549–74.

Orrù, Marco, Nicole Woolsey Biggart, and Gary G. Hamilton. 1997. *The Economic Organization of Capitalism in East Asia*. Thousand Hills, Calif.: Sage Publications.

Podolny, Joel. 1993. "A Status-based Model of Market Competition." *American Journal of Sociology* 98: 829–72.

Putterman, Louis, ed. 1986. *The Economic Nature of the Firm: A Reader*. Cambridge, England: Cambridge University Press.

Robinson, Joan. 1933. *Economics of Imperfect Competition*. London, England: Macmillan

Scherer. R. M., and David Ross. 1990. *Industrial Market Structure and Economic Performance*. 3d ed. Boston, Mass.: Houghton Mifflin Company.

Solow, Robert. 1996. Review of *Trust: The Social Virtues and the Creation of Prosperity*, by Francis Fukuyama. *The New Republic*, September 11, 1995, 37.

Stigle, George J. 1968. *The Organization of Industry*. Chicago, Ill.: University of Chicago Press.

Swedberg, Richard, ed. 1993. *Explorations in Economic Sociology*. New York: Russell Sage Foundation.

———. Forthcoming. *Max Weber's Economic Sociology*. Princeton, N.J.: Princeton University Press.

Tocqueville, Alexis de. [1893] 1971. *Recollections*. Garden City, N.Y.: Anchor Books.

Wade, Robert. 1990. *Governing the Market: Economic Theory and the Role of Government in East Asian Industrialization*. Princeton, N.J.: Princeton University Press.

Weber, Max. [1921–1922] 1978. *Economy and Society*. 3 vols. Translated and edited by Guenther Roth and Claus Wittich. Berkeley: University of California Press.

———. 1949. *The Methodology of the Social Sciences*. Glencoe, Ill.: Free Press.

White, Harrison, C. 1981. "Where Do Markets Come From?" *American Journal of Sociology* 87: 517–47.

Whitley, Richard. 1992. *Business Systems in East Asia*. London, England: Sage.

Williamson, Oliver E. 1975. *Markets and Hierarchies: Analysis and Antitrust Implications*. New York: Free Press.

———. 1981. "The Economics of Organization." *American Journal of Sociology* 87: 548–77.

———. 1985. *The Economic Institutions of Capitalism*. New York: Free Press.

———. 1991. "Comparative Economic Organization: The Analysis of Discrete Structural Alternatives." *Administrative Science Quarterly* 36 (June): 269–96.

———. 1994. "Transaction Cost Economics and Organization Theory." In *The Handbook of Economic Sociology*, edited by Neil J. Smelser and Richard Swedberg. Princeton, N.J.: Princeton University Press.

Williamson Oliver E., and Sidney G. Winter. 1993. *The Nature of the Firm: Origins, Evolution, and Development*. New York: Oxford University Press.

Yarbrough, Beth V., and Robert M. Yarbrough. 1987. "Institutions for the Governance of Opportunism in International Trade." *Journal of Law, Economics, and Organization* 3 (1): 129–39.

8

Institutional Embeddedness in Japanese Labor Markets

Mary C. Brinton and Takehiko Kariya

R ecent sociological arguments about labor markets have emphasized the embeddedness of labor market transactions in social relations (Granovetter 1985; Granovetter and Swedberg 1992). One such transaction is the matching of people to jobs. An extensive literature addresses the question of whether the social status and income of the jobs people enter is affected by who helped them find those jobs. Sociologists have paid particular attention to whether the type of social tie ("strong" or "weak") between a job-searcher and a contact person affects the sort of job a person obtains (Boxman, DeGraaf, and Flap 1991; Lin, Ensel, and Vaughn 1981; Lin 1990; Marsden and Hurlbert 1988).

Despite the utility of this sociological emphasis on how an individual's *interpersonal* context affects his or her job search, the approach has serious limitations. First, perhaps reflecting the individualistic legacy of early status attainment research in the United States, social institutions are not much in evidence in the sociological job-search literature. This spawns two unfortunate consequences. For one thing, little attention is paid to how individuals get jobs through the institutions, such as schools, labor unions, and apprenticeship programs, with which they are affiliated. As we will argue in this chapter, ties between employers and these types of institutions deserve to be placed in theoretical juxtaposition with the social ties between individuals. Moreover, the converse of individual job-search strategies—employers' recruitment strategies—are too often overlooked in sociological studies. If job-movers' actions are affected by their interpersonal and institutional contexts, then certainly employers' actions are as well. The interests and resources of both job-seekers and employers must be taken into account theoretically because individuals are *matched* into jobs (Granovetter 1981).[1]

The second limitation of the sociological emphasis on labor market outcomes for an individual who does or does not use interpersonal ties to find a job is that the use of such ties is not typically seen as a variable that is dependent on cultural and historical circumstances. In this chapter, we argue for a broader research agenda that asks the macrosociological question of what gives rise to an environment where interpersonal ties predominate over institutional ties, or vice versa. Alternatively, one might ask what determines an environment in which either of these ties predominates over a more atomistic job market in which people search on their own without the benefit of ties. What kind of embeddedness is dominant for which individuals and in what kinds of labor markets? How and why does the prevalence of one type of embeddedness in an economy wane in favor of another type?

It is unfortunate that there has been so little research focusing on variations in types of embeddedness over time or across different cultural contexts, for such an effort promises to be of considerable theoretical and practical importance. Answers to such questions as we have posed can facilitate the understanding of the implications of various types of embeddedness for social inequality, particularly among ascriptive groups such as those demarcated by socioeconomic background, ethnicity, or gender.[2] There are also implications for our assessment of how efficiently or inefficiently labor is allocated among employers in a given society.

In this chapter, we limit ourselves to the labor market for youth who are standing at the brink of leaving one institutional setting—school—to enter another—the labor market. Recent educational debates in the United States have raised the issue of whether cooperation between high schools and employers can facilitate the transition to work and thereby lower youth unemployment and job turnover rates (Rosenbaum and Kariya 1989a, 1989b). While these debates have not phrased the issue in such terms, this is a prime example of what we here term "institutional embeddedness." Understanding the circumstances under which institutional ties between schools and firms can be fostered and maintained, and understanding who benefits and who loses, is important for both theoretical and policy reasons.

We first specify several ideal-typical job-search patterns and then generate some initial hypotheses about where and when they may predominate. Then we turn to an analysis of a specific cultural setting. While we recognize that a more complete treatment of the subject would involve comparative research on labor markets over time and across cultures, such an empirical endeavor is beyond the scope of a single chapter. We have chosen instead to look at the case of one country: Japan.

Japan is a particularly important case because it exhibits a high degree of embeddedness of various types of markets in social and institutional relations (Dore 1983, 1986, 1987; Gerlach 1992; Murakami and Rohlen 1992). The labor market is no exception. Job-search processes in some labor markets in Japan (notably the labor market for new graduates) exhibit a high degree of institutional embeddedness, which makes the choice of Japanese society particularly relevant for our purpose of bringing institutions back into the analysis of job-search processes. Labor economists and sociologists have carried out extensive analyses of Japanese labor markets and of aspects of Japan's so-called permanent employment system, and they frequently mention the traditional preference of large firms in particular for hiring graduates straight out of school (Clark 1979; Cole 1979; Dore 1976; Inui 1993; Koike 1984, 1987a). But there has been little analysis of how the recruitment of new graduates occurs and how schools and firms coordinate their placement and recruitment activities to create an orderly and highly embedded youth labor market.[3]

We use cohort data to look at embeddedness patterns for different Japanese youth labor markets (university graduates and high school graduates) both at present and historically. We then turn to historical and contemporary qualitative data to explore in more detail how and why what we term institutional embeddedness and its successor, semi-institutional embeddedness, has evolved. This gives rise to some concluding thoughts on the stability or fragility of institutional embeddedness.

TYPES OF EMBEDDEDNESS AND THEIR OCCURRENCE

One can think of three ideal-typical job-search (or labor recruitment) patterns:

Atomistic Job Search

In this case, individual buyers and sellers (employers and job applicants) conduct their search based on information provided in the market at large. This includes newspaper advertisements and other mechanisms of distributing and acquiring information about job opportunities that do not involve an intermediary, whether a person or an organization. Individuals apply directly to employers, sending out their résumés or making "cold calls." As Granovetter and others have shown, this is a highly reified conception of job searching, even in the United States where one might expect greater atomism than in many other countries.

Social Embeddedness, or Job Search Through Interpersonal Ties

Here, the transaction between individual buyers and sellers of labor is mediated by a third party (an individual).[4] The intermediary may provide information about available jobs or an introduction to his or her employer. There are two variants of social embeddedness, strong and weak ties, that is, friends or kin, and "friends of friends," respectively (Granovetter 1973, 1995). When the individual's match with an employer is contingent on either a strong or a weak tie it is said to be socially embedded. In other words, "who you know" is important.

Institutional Embeddedness, or Job Search
Through Institutional Ties

Here, individual buyers and sellers of labor are introduced through organizations to which they belong. This type of embeddedness diverges from the social embeddedness in that it is not "who you know" but "*how* you know who you know." The individual's job match is contingent upon his or her being part of a particular organization (a labor union or an apprenticeship program, for example), therefore the reputation of that organization as a supplier of good-quality labor is important. In the case of Japan, for new graduates initially entering the labor market, the institution of the school often plays an important role. For instance, linkages between high schools and employers in Japan are salient for workbound graduates; if a school has links with local employers, it can recommend or in effect "sponsor" students looking for their first full-time jobs (Rosenbaum and Kariya 1989a, 1989b; Rosenbaum et al. 1990).

Both social and institutional embeddedness involve an intermediary between the job searcher and the employer. In the case of social embeddedness, the intermediary is a person who knows or is connected to both the searcher and the employer. In the case of institutional embeddedness, the job searcher belongs to an organization that has a tie with an employer.[5] We use the term "institutional ties" rather than "organizational ties" because we mean to signify ties between two different types of social institutions, between schools and firms, for example, or between labor unions and firms, or apprenticeship programs and firms. Within the category of "school" as an institution, different schools may be called different organizations, just as within the category of "firm," different businesses are called different organizations. But our concern here is with the flow of individuals (job-seekers) between different types of social institutions with different purposes. Our fundamental question is: Under what circumstances are social embeddedness or institutional embeddedness likely to predominate as a recruitment pattern?

Employers' and Schools' Interests

Let us first consider the demand side of the labor market. Both social and institutional embeddedness increase the information available to employers about job candidates above and beyond what individuals themselves offer in an "atomistic" job market, where individuals reply directly to job advertisements without using an intermediary (Arrow 1973; Granovetter 1995; Rees 1966). It is therefore easy to see why embeddedness per se would be useful to employers. Information should be particularly valuable to employers who: a) are going to make sizable investments in employees (by paying high starting wages or by placing them in firm-internal labor markets, starting them out at low initial wages and offering on-the-job training and job security), and/or b) are entrusting employees with valuable information or materials. Such employers should be more motivated to pay attention to signals than employers who are hiring workers for unskilled or low-skilled jobs, or for jobs in which there is little necessity for trust and few opportunities for serious and costly malfeasance. The latter type of employer should be less concerned about carefully screening employees since the costs incurred by a hiring mistake are lower than for the former type of employer.

We can hypothesize, then, that employers who are hiring for high-skill or high-trust jobs can benefit from the information or informal guarantee provided by an intermediary, whether through social or institutional embeddedness. (See the paper by Frank in this volume for a discussion of highly leveraged jobs in advanced capitalist economies.) Of course, employers at the other end of the spectrum who are hiring for unskilled or low-skilled jobs with short or nonexistent promotional ladders can also benefit from as much information as they can get about potential employees. But because their investment in employees is not very high we can hypothesize that they will be less willing to incur the transaction costs, if any, of establishing a relationship with a school (as a supplier of labor) and will therefore rely more on recommendations derived from personal ties (for example, from friends or kin of a current employee) than on ties with schools or vocational programs.[6]

In terms of labor supply, why should friends, family, or institutions such as schools get involved in trying to help people find jobs? Individuals may have a variety of motives, ranging from the altruistic to the more instrumental tit for tat. But why should educational institutions care where their students land jobs? Obviously, some schools do not; their reputation does not rest on it. If a school principally bases its reputation on the somewhat intangible offer of a "good education," it is unlikely that it will seek either a formal or informal commitment from firms to hire its graduates, who will be left to their own devices in the labor market. But whenever a school bases its reputation at least in part on its ability to place graduates in good jobs, we should be more likely to see the emergence of explicit or implicit agreements to engage in labor market transactions with specific firms. The reputational factor will be strongest for schools that must actively recruit applicants, that is, in settings where potential students and their parents can weigh the advantages of choosing one school over another. As we discuss later, this condition is met by Japanese high schools and universities.

The impetus for institutional ties could come from the employer side as well, with school placement officers cooperating with the employers to the degree that they see such cooperation reflecting well on their own reputations or that of their school. But the thrust of our argument about institutional embeddedness is that both sides—employers and schools—must gain more than they lose from such arrangements in order for them to persist. For employers, the main currency is quality of labor; for schools, the main currency is reputation. To the extent that neither of these matters, we should expect to see little evidence of institutional ties between schools and firms.

We can summarize our hypotheses about labor market variation in the prevalence of atomistic labor transactions, social embeddedness, and institutional embeddedness as follows: 1) Social embeddedness will be more common in most labor markets than atomistic labor transactions. This is so because on the labor-supply side there are various reasons for individuals to try to help each other, and on the labor-demand side employers can gain extra information and save on screening costs by following up on personal introductions. 2) Institutional embeddedness will be more common in contexts where employers seek high-quality labor in which they will make a significant future investment *and* where schools' reputations are based on placing graduates into good jobs. It will be less common in contexts where these conditions are not met. In those contexts, social embeddedness will be more common.

Ideology and Legitimacy: The Public's Interest in Meritocracy

The previously stated hypotheses are based on the perceived interests of schools and employers; to get this far, a rational action perspective is sufficient theoretically. But this does not mean that theoretical considerations concerning ideology and legitimacy play no role. Employers' and schools' interests are not the only ones that matter in job-search and recruitment processes; the public's interest is also a factor. Here, the contributions of the new institutionalist perspective on organizations come into play as well, for issues of legitimacy are central (Meyer and Rowan 1977). In countries that are democratic and have a strong meritocratic ideology, complaints about social embeddedness and institutional embeddedness are likely to arise. Nepotism is the most obvious form of social embeddedness, but institutional embeddedness may also be visible and perceived as unfair if schools openly admit students on criteria that are considered non-meritocratic—on the basis of nepotism, social class, ability to pay, and so forth. In such cases, connections between schools and employers may be seen as reinforcing social inequalities that are reproduced by the nature of school admissions requirements. Of course, for nonmeritocratic criteria to be criticized they must indeed be highly visible to the public and there must be a dominant ideology of meritocracy in the society. Where social or institutional embeddedness is evident to members of society who have no presence in powerful social networks, and where popular and political pressure can be brought to construct legal rules or informal norms to monitor particularism in recruitment, then social and institutional embeddedness are at risk of becoming extinct.

As an example, the near-eradication of social embeddedness in the form of "old-boy" networks has occurred in some professional and elite labor markets in the United States. These labor markets arguably changed as a result of the legal environment, including affirmative action rules, equal employment opportunity guidelines, and requirements that jobs be widely posted and advertised. Successful sanctions against such old-boy networks may lead to one of two outcomes: a more atomistic labor market or institutional embeddedness that is perceived to be meritocratic.

Institutional embeddedness, such as an implicit contract between schools and employers, is subject to much less criticism than social ties *if* school entrance requirements are meritocratic (or are at least judged by the public to be so). Therefore, institutional embeddedness is likely to be more acceptable than social embeddedness in a social and political environment where meritocratic standards are highly valued, and where such standards are institutionalized in school entrance requirements. But empirically, we can still predict that institutional embeddedness is quite rare because of the necessary alignment of schools' and employers' interests that is required to support it.

To summarize, social and political pressures for meritocracy lead to the following predictions about temporal change in embeddedness patterns in a given society: 3) To the extent that a) social and institutional embeddedness patterns are visible to nonbeneficiaries of them and b) an ideology of meritocracy is so strong that attempts to monitor these forms of particularism receive legal or normative support, they will tend to decline over time (with the caveat in proposition 4, below). The decline of social embeddedness should be particularly evident at the higher, "elite" end of the labor market (again, if it is visible to nonparticipants) where the potential rewards at stake (such as social status and salary) are high and are visibly contested. 4) Institutional embeddedness will be perceived as less onerous by the public to the extent that schools are considered to be meritocratic in their admissions standards. In this case, institutional embeddedness may persist and even increase (*ceteris paribus*) at the high end of the labor market, where employers strongly desire the information provided by embeddedness.

We now turn to the Japanese case to test the predictions we have drawn. Japan provides a good setting in which to explore patterns of embeddedness because previous research has shown that many types of transactions tend to be highly embedded in the Japanese context (Dore 1983, 1986, 1987; Gerlach 1992; Murakami and Rohlen 1992; Sako 1991, 1992). The use of intermediaries is common, and Japan is considered by many scholars to be a strong instance of a "network society," in which there are more extensive ties of obligation among individuals and among organizations than in most Western societies. It is therefore a rich environment for testing predictions about what gives rise to different types of embeddedness. Moreover, by examining whether there are variations among different labor markets in Japan, we can begin to separate out the driving forces of culture and structure. In other words, in response to our arguments about embeddedness based on the interests of employers, schools, and the public, one might counter that cultural values are a more important determinant of embeddedness patterns. For instance, a simple counterargument could be framed to the effect that American society has a combination of atomistic and social embeddedness patterns because of its emphasis on individualism, and Japanese society has a combination of social and institutional embeddedness patterns because of its collectivistic emphasis. This predicted contrast springs to mind quite naturally from the *nihonjinron* (or "Japanese uniqueness") literature (see Nakane 1980). If culture supersedes structure as the dominant explanation, then the variations among different types of labor markets within Japan should be minimal.

We approach the analysis of the embeddedness of job-search and recruitment processes in Japan employing three methodologies. First, we use data on the educational and work histories of a large sample of Japanese men aged twenty-five to sixty-nine to test our predictions of how graduates were recruited into different types of jobs as they left school. Second, we use historical materials on the development of the educational system and the labor market in twentieth-century Japan to examine how job-search/recruitment patterns have changed over time. Third, we use qualitative data to consider recent changes in the recruitment of university graduates. The latter two strategies allow us to consider the importance of meritocracy and school reputation, both of which are impossible to study through analysis of individual-level survey data.

EMBEDDEDNESS IN JAPANESE LABOR MARKETS: AN EXAMINATION WITH COHORT DATA

To look at historical changes in embeddedness patterns as well as differences across labor markets we use data from the "1981 Survey on Occupational Mobility and History" conducted by the Japan Institute of Labor. The survey asked 4,255 Japanese males aged twenty-five to sixty-nine about their work history, including how they found their first job out of school. This question was worded, "Through what path did you enter your first workplace?" We report on the 3,244 men who specified the job-search method that was successful, excluding those who were self-employed in their first job (the latter were not asked by the survey to specify their job-search method). We define social embeddedness as finding one's first job through family, friends, or acquaintances. Institutional embeddedness is equivalent to finding one's first job through an introduction from one's school. We classify other routes (such as using an employment agency or responding to an advertisement) as nonembedded or atomistic modes of job search because they involve neither social nor institutional ties.

We use the respondents' educational attainment as a proxy for high-quality labor. A second indicator of the high end of the job market is the size of the firm. Large Japanese firms are more able financially than small firms to offer "permanent employment" to a select number of male high school and university graduates, placing them in entry-level jobs in internal labor markets and investing heavily in them through on-the-job training and job rotation (Brinton 1991, 1993; Clark 1979; Cole 1979; Koike 1984, 1987a, 1987b). Because these generally have been considered by graduates to be the most desirable jobs in the economy, high schools and universities that are able to place a high percentage of their graduates into large firms can use this as a successful advertising strategy to lure talented prospective students into applying to them. This creates a self-reinforcing cycle in which good students apply to those schools that are able to place their graduates in the "best" jobs. This phenomenon is not unlike what happens with elite universities in the United States (again, see Frank in this volume). But for reasons we examine in the historical section of this chapter, this tendency is much more exaggerated in Japan.

Variation in Embeddedness Across Time

Figure 8.1 shows the distribution of successful job search methods for nine cohorts of Japanese male school-leavers (irrespective of level of schooling). Members of the oldest cohort, born between 1912 and 1916, entered the labor market in the late 1920s and early 1930s. Members of the youngest cohort entered the labor market forty-five years later. As predicted by our first hypothesis, for every cohort social embeddedness is more common than the atomistic (nonembedded) pattern. In fact, the proportion of graduates who found their first job through neither social nor institutional ties is amazingly low and stable across the nine cohorts, ranging only from 15 percent to 19 percent. This shows how consistently *uncommon* atomistic job search patterns have been and continue to be in Japan.

Institutional embeddedness has become more prevalent over time, while social embeddedness has declined, the latter having been the method used by 67 per-

Figure 8.1   Job Search Method by Cohort

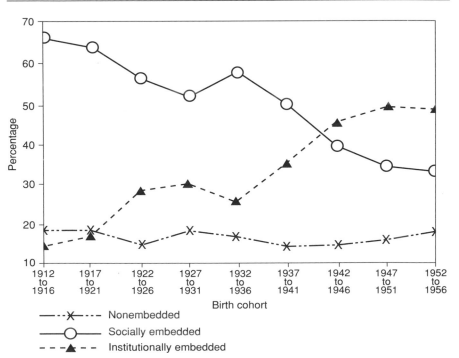

cent of the oldest cohort and by only 33 percent of the youngest cohort. In contrast, while only about 15 percent of the oldest cohort were introduced into their first job by their school, this figure rose to 49 percent for the most recent cohort. This is consistent with our hypothesis that social embeddedness will decline and institutional embeddedness will increase with the drive toward a meritocratic society.

We also argued that the waning of social embeddedness should be especially noticeable at the highest end of the labor market, where it may be replaced by institutional embeddedness if school admissions criteria are perceived by the public to be fair and there are thus no sanctions against institutional embeddedness. Table 8.1 reveals the change in job-search patterns across cohorts at each educational level. (We combined five-year birth cohorts into three groups: men born in 1912 to 1926, 1927 to 1941, and 1942 to 1956. We also combined elementary and junior high school in one category, compulsory education. Elementary education was compulsory prior to the end of World War II, and Japanese postwar educational reforms extended the period of compulsory education to junior high school.) The use of social ties to get a first job generally declined through successive cohorts. Interestingly, the decline was least pronounced at the highest educational level. This is not consistent with our expectation that the decline of social embeddedness should be the most pronounced at this level, presuming that the general public objects to the use of particularistic ties in high-status circles and that legal or informal norms are created to combat them. This is an important point to which we will return later in this chapter when we examine the history of the labor market for Japanese university graduates.

The use of institutional ties increased over time for graduates at all levels of schooling, but this was not as pronounced for graduates with university degrees as we predicted it would be. Here again, our historical examination of higher education later in the paper will elucidate why this is the case.

Variations in Embeddedness Across Labor Markets

We hypothesized that with all other factors held constant, social embeddedness will be more prevalent than an atomistic job-search pattern because the informa-

Table 8.1 New Male Graduates' Job Search Methods by Birth Date

| | Educational Level | | | | | | | | |
| | Compulsory % | | | High School % | | | University % | | |
	S	I	NE	S	I	NE	S	I	NE
1912–1926 (N=651)	71.5	10.5	18.0	52.0	35.3	12.7	33.7	42.7	23.6
1927–1941 (N=1,229)	64.2	22.7	13.3	53.0	31.7	15.3	26.8	45.6	27.6
1942–1956 (N=1,412)	46.8	42.1	11.2	33.0	51.9	15.0	31.4	47.4	21.2

Note: S = Social; I = Institutional; NE = Nonembedded.

tion provided by social embeddedness helps employers in their hiring decisions. We also hypothesized that in labor markets where employers need high-quality or highly trustworthy employees to fill starting positions in internal labor markets and/or schools base their reputation partly on how well they place their graduates into jobs, the prevalence of institutional embeddedness will be high.

Figure 8.2 shows that during the forty-five-year period covered by our data, male educational attainment rose rapidly in Japan. Whereas only 2 percent of the oldest cohort attained a four-year university degree, 34 percent of the youngest cohort did so. Figure 8.3 illustrates the strong relationship between educational attainment and type of job-search method in the sample. The least-educated workers (elementary and junior high school graduates) are more likely than high school and university graduates to have gotten their first job through social ties, whereas the use of institutional ties is more common in the latter two groups than among the least-educated. Supporting our hypothesis about employer demands and school reputation, both high school and university graduates are more likely to be hired through institutional means (recruitment from their school by the firm) than through social ties. (Note that Japanese high schools and universities require applications from potential students, meaning that school reputation is important for schools at these levels but not at the mandatory elementary and junior high school levels.)

Figure 8.2   Educational Attainment by Cohort

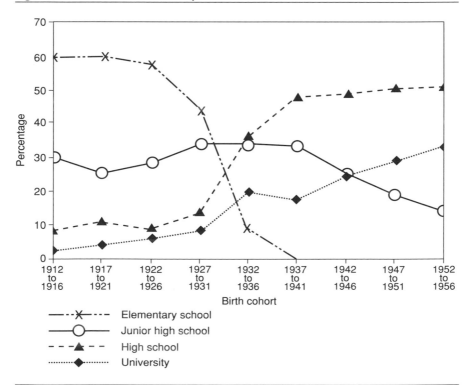

Figure 8.3   Job-Search Method by Educational Attainment

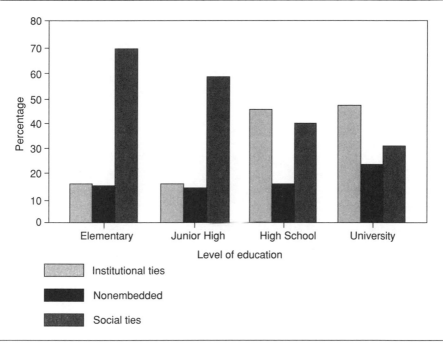

To look more closely at the significance of the relationship between educational level and the use of institutional ties, controlling for the cohort composition of the sample, we employ multinomial logit methods and compare the effects of the independent variables on the probability of individuals finding their first job through institutional (school) versus social ties, and the probability of using atomistic methods (nonembeddedness) versus social ties (table 8.2). The results are similar whether we use education as an ordinal variable or as a series of dummy variables. We opted for the latter so that we could also test for interactions between cohorts and educational levels.

Even when cohort and education are entered simultaneously into the equation, both exert a statistically significant positive effect on the probability of Japanese men getting their first job through institutional versus social ties. Men born earlier in the century were significantly less likely than men born more recently to have used school ties rather than social ties when they entered the labor market. Compared to high school graduates (the reference category), elementary and junior high school graduates are significantly less likely to have used school ties than social ties, and university graduates are significantly more likely to have done so, although there is not as strong a contrast between the latter as between graduates at the lower levels of schooling and high school graduates.

The comparison of determinants of nonembeddedness versus social ties shows that cohort is not a strong factor, but that education is. Elementary and junior high school graduates are significantly less likely than high school graduates to have used atomistic methods rather than social ties, and university graduates are

Table 8.2   Determinants of New Graduates' Job-Search Methods

	Institutional Versus Social Ties	Unstructured Versus Social Ties
Constant	4.771***	−.630
	(.790)	(1.045)
Logged age	−1.281***	−.008
	(.218)	(.286)
Education		
Elementary	−1.064***	−.506*
	(.164)	(.189)
Junior high	−.627***	−.466**
	(.106)	(.142)
High school	—	—
University	3.649*	.214
	(1.715)	(2.078)
Maximum likelihood $\chi^2 = 6185.88$		
df = 3188		

*Statistically significant at the .05 level.
**Statistically significant at the .01 level.
***Statistically significant at the .001 level.

not statistically distinct from high school graduates. Tests for interaction effects (not shown here) between cohort and education also indicate that *recent* university graduates are significantly more likely than earlier graduates to use institutional rather than social ties. (As seen in table 8.1, 8 percent more university graduates in the earliest cohort used institutional ties than social ties, compared to a spread of 16 percentage points in the most recent cohort.)

Table 8.3 shows the relationship between entry into a large firm (logged firm size) and job-search methods, controlling for cohort and education. As we predicted, institutional ties are the most likely way in which graduates enter large firms; employers who are going to invest significantly in the "lifetime employment" of workers appear the most apt to recruit in this fashion. Social ties are the least likely channel into large firms, with nonembedded or atomistic channels falling between the two.

In sum, our hypothesis concerning the greater general prevalence of embedded over nonembedded, atomistic methods of job search is accurate. Moreover, successive cohorts have become ever more likely to use institutional rather than social ties. Institutional ties are more prevalent at the high school and university levels than at lower educational levels, where social ties remain the most important. Institutional channels are also the most prevalent mode of entry for school-leavers into large firms.

But a number of puzzles also are raised by the findings from these individual-level data. Perhaps the most interesting are those that concern higher education. This level shows less change than we predicted in our hypotheses. Even though more university graduates report institutional ties as their path into a first job rather than social ties or atomistic search patterns, their use of institutional ties has gone up only slightly over time, and their use of social ties has shown only a slight decline (table 8.1). While the use of institutional ties was considerably more prevalent for university than other graduates in early cohorts, the gaps in

Table 8.3   Determinants of Entry into a Large Firm

Constant	1.466**
	(.536)
Logged age	.956***
	(.138)
Education	
Less than high school	—
High school	1.122***
	(.082)
University	1.456***
	(.098)
Job-search method	
Social	−1.371***
	(.097)
Institutional	.218*
	(.100)
Atomistic (nonembedded)	—
Adjusted $R^2 = .215$	
N = 3207	

*Statistically significant at the .05 level.
**Statistically significant at the .01 level.
***Statistically significant at the .001 level.

the use of institutional ties among graduates of different educational levels have become narrower over time. In short, the use of institutional ties appears to have extended from the university level to lower levels of schooling, especially the high school level, and the use of social ties has retained moderate significance at the university level. An understanding of these patterns requires a more textured account of the development of educational institutions and the labor market and the links between them in twentieth-century Japan.

A HISTORICAL VIEW OF INSTITUTIONAL EMBEDDEDNESS IN JAPANESE LABOR MARKETS
Early Industrialization

Institutional embeddedness developed at the upper end of the educational system during the period of Japan's early industrialization. The establishment of compulsory universal education through the elementary level dates back to 1872, four years after the Meiji Restoration abolished the hereditary status system. The university system was initiated with the establishment of the Imperial University in 1886 (from the former Tokyo University, set up in 1877).[7] The university had an entrance examination, but its graduates were exempt from taking the government examination to become bureaucrats, so that institutional embeddedness characterized the government's recruitment of its graduates. According to the "Examination Regulations for Probationary Officers and Apprentices" enacted in 1887, "graduates of the Faculties of Law and Letters, and those earlier schools which had been merged into the Imperial University were allowed to join the government on a probationary basis without the exam" (Amano 1990). This strong institutional embeddedness was eventually criticized by newly developing private colleges, and the regulations were changed to stipulate that Imperial University graduates were exempt from the "preliminary" parts of the government examination but were required to take the main part. But Tokyo University graduates have continued to be the most heavily recruited into the government, a fact documented in numerous studies by Japanese and Western scholars (see, for example, Azumi 1969; Ishida 1993; James and Benjamin 1988; Koh 1991).

The educational ladder leading to Tokyo Imperial was clearly established by the early twentieth century, with school-specific entrance exams at each level above the compulsory elementary level. Quality differentiation among schools at the same horizontal level developed and crystallized because of the sorting of students by these school-specific entrance exams. James and Benjamin (1988, 15), in describing the system encountered by reformers during the postwar occupation, note that "the chief characteristic of these high schools and universities was that they were selective, career-oriented in conception, and highly differentiated into different tracks and different curricula."

In sum, the school system was the result of educational reforms that began in the late nineteenth century and that institutionalized an ideology of merit-based selection for specialized schools geared to particular parts of the labor market. The utilitarian view that an educational credential from a specific school provides a ticket to a job with a good employer appears to have been firmly established early in the twentieth century. Scholars generally agree that Japanese educational expansion and the competition to enter prestigious schools, especially at the university level, has historically been closely tied to the development of the labor market and the demand for qualified workers (Brinton 1993; James and Benjamin 1988; Nakata and Mosk 1987). That is, the public has been keenly aware that the probability of getting a "good job" increases if one gains admission to a top university.

Institutional embeddedness appears not only to have characterized the recruitment relationship between Tokyo Imperial University and the civil service in the early twentieth century but to have developed between other universities and the private sector and to have existed at the secondary vocational level as well. With the growth of private industry, relationships between universities and employers began to be established by the end of the century's second decade. From 1917 on, many firms and banks adopted "regular hiring practices" (*teiki saiyō*) for college graduates, meaning that employers hired new graduates on a regularly scheduled, yearly basis (Ozaki 1980). Based on these hiring practices, colleges began recommending graduates to employers and relationships between employers and colleges became closer. Connections between vocational secondary schools and local employers also developed, with vocational schools feeding graduates to certain employers in local labor markets on a regular basis.

Postwar Japan

Post–World War II educational reforms consolidated the Japanese school system into a 6–3–3–4 pattern in the American mold, with compulsory education extending through the junior high school level. It was originally intended that high schools would be comprehensive and provide both vocational and academic tracks, but in practice high schools have become highly differentiated to the point where each school district has several high schools and each school represents a particular track, accepting students of a specified academic ranking (Rohlen 1984). This is a significant departure from the American system. Reputational factors are highly significant in such an "educational marketplace," where high schools essentially compete for student applicants, who are admitted or rejected on the basis of their junior high school grades and their score on the standardized prefectural high school entrance examination.

Recent research indicates that the recruitment of Japanese high school graduates into the labor market is typified by institutional embeddedness (Rosenbaum and Kariya 1989a). Some high schools and employers create and maintain long-term relationships that involve the school's recommendation of job candidates to specific employers and the employers' probable acceptance of these candidates. In this implicitly contractual situation, schools essentially pay for part of employers' hiring costs by screening and choosing applicants, and these employers provide a market for the school's top graduates. Labor allocation and job matching is therefore accomplished in a manner different from either the "pure" atomized market mechanism of individual job search or the highly socially embedded mechanism of introductions through friends or "friends of friends." Job turnover and unemployment rates among Japanese youth are low relative to the rates in most industrialized nations, suggesting the efficiency of these job-matching processes (Rosenbaum and Kariya 1989a).

More research is required to understand the nature and extensiveness of the institutional relationships between Japanese high schools and employers and the origins of this pattern. The newly established general high schools in the postwar period that had a large number of workbound students appear to have adopted the prewar vocational school practice of providing placement services to help students find jobs and to have developed their own placement offices. Moreover, the Ministry of Labor encouraged the strong involvement by junior high schools and high schools in job placement, both as a means of efficient labor allocation and as a way of protecting teenagers from exploitation by labor brokers, which had been a common problem in industrializing Japan in the early part of the twentieth century.[8] Many schools also developed ties with particular employers; Rosenbaum and Kariya (1989a) report that nearly one-half of all graduating workbound seniors in their sample of high schools in the early 1980s took jobs with "contract employers," employers with whom their schools had an implicit contract to supply good graduates every year. Higher-ranked schools show a larger percentage of their graduates employed by contract employers than lower-ranked ones. This is consistent with our supposition of a relationship between school reputation and the use of institutional ties.[9] The increased use of institutional ties by recent cohorts of Japanese high school graduates (as shown in table 8.1) is consistent with the fact that to our knowledge, the Japanese public has not voiced criticism of high school–employer linkages. The high school application procedure is highly structured in Japan, with third-year junior high school students taking practice tests and receiving extensive guidance as to which high school to apply to (LeTendre 1996). The public's belief in the meritocratic nature of high school admissions practices appears to be high. But public evaluation of university-firm connections is somewhat different, and the recent history of firms' recruitment practices among university graduates sheds light on why institutional embeddedness has shown only a moderate historical increase there.

Institutional Embeddedness in the Labor Market for University Graduates

Throughout most of the postwar period up until the late 1970s, Japanese universities were heavily involved in selecting and recommending their graduates to employers. Most large Japanese companies formally restricted the "port of entry" into white-collar positions—the assumed stepping-stones to future managerial positions—to graduates from a handful of elite universities. They did this by sending job application forms *only* to their preferred institutions and requiring those institutions to recommend particular graduating seniors.[10] Job-seekers from other universities could not even apply to these large companies because the companies accepted only those application forms with certain universities' recommendations attached. This practice, called *shitei kōsei* (system of reserved schools), was similar to the current practice Japanese employers follow in recruiting from high schools; it is truly institutional embeddedness. As Azumi (1969, 56) observed in a detailed study published in the late 1960s that looked at higher education and recruitment in Japan:

> There is relatively little the Japanese applicant can do on his own in the recruitment process. Even when his university is designated by a desirable company, he himself is not automatically assured of consideration. It is the university that decides whether he deserves to be allowed to apply, for the student, in a sense, represents the university, and the university must make sure that he is a worthy representative.

A survey carried out by the Nihon Keieisha Dantai Renmei in 1957 found that 84 percent of firms recruited students by recommendations from a subset of universities. Of these, fully 90 percent relied on school placement office recommendations, either alone or in conjunction with recommendations from individual professors. A similar 1968 survey found that 62 percent of all firms reported hiring only from "restricted" universities; this figure climbed to 91 percent for firms with over 5,000 employees (Tokyo Shoko Kaigisho 1968, cited in Ogata 1975). And in a 1975 study, 35 percent of firms sampled from the first rank of companies listed on the Tokyo stock exchange used a "closed door" policy for managerial and clerical jobs for university graduates, and 47 percent did so for engineering and technical jobs (Keizai Doyukai 1975). As a student from a "second class" university reported in 1976: "I telephoned the personnel office of a firm I was interested in. But as soon as I told the person the name of my university, he hung up suddenly on me without listening to anything I had to say" (*Nobi Nobi*, January 1976: 19).

By the late 1970s, the "closed door" system of hiring university graduates came under harsh attack by Japanese social critics and the mass media. Some people felt that it was unfair for students to be "rejected at the front door" (*monzen barai*) and prevented from even applying for a job simply because they had attended less prestigious universities (Ogata 1975). Critics also charged that institutional embeddedness reinforced the "examination hell" (*jūken jigoku*) endured by Japanese high school students in their struggle to enter top universities. With top firms recruiting only from certain universities and refusing to cast a wider net, the pressure on male high school seniors to pass the exam to gain admittance to a top university was excruciating. Finally, the criticism arose that academic performance, as measured by university entrance exams, did not necessarily reflect the skills needed in the workplace. The charge that entrance examinations did not measure skills relevant to job productivity constitutes a challenge to the university admissions criteria, which is similar to the condition we mentioned in proposition 4 that could lead to sanctions against institutional embeddedness.

The Japanese Labor Ministry responded to these criticisms in 1979 by establishing the Supervising Committee on Recruitment to monitor school and employer compliance with the *shūshoku kyōtei* (recruitment contract) put forward by the ministry in 1953 to govern recruitment practices. Members of this committee are drawn from large firms and are generally members of Nikkeiren, one of the main employers' associations in Japan. The *shūshoku kyōtei* specifies a date before which in any given year employers are not allowed to make contact with graduating students seeking a job. It is a gentlemen's agreement that does not involve legal sanctions for offenders, but both companies and universities promise not to begin recruitment activities prior to the agreed-upon date. It was established to level the playing field for recruitment. (See Roth and Xing 1994 for a discussion of such agreements in American labor markets.) The supervising committee established in the late 1970s threatened firms with a normative sanction—to announce their names in public if they violated the *shūshoku kyōtei* by initiating recruitment activities too early.[11]

Firms responded to the criticisms by accepting applications from students from any university after the mandated date marking the start of the recruitment season. An analysis of reports from graduates of one private university in Tokyo (which we later refer to as University D) about their job-hunting experiences suggests that universities had indeed become less formally involved in the recruitment process by the early 1980s (Kariya et al. 1993).[12] In 1975, about one-third of the graduates mentioned the necessity or importance of a recommendation from the university, but the percentage dropped to zero by 1980 and then fluctuated between zero and 5 percent through 1990. Thus, as reflected in the students' own reports, school recommendations no longer play an important role in acquiring a first job.

Based on this brief historical review, can we say that the labor market for university graduates in Japan is a case where institutional embeddedness has been subjected to sanctions and has given way to a more atomistic recruitment pattern? The transparent answer would seem to be yes, which would mean that public criticism and government-promoted sanctions brought an end to a seemingly deeply embedded recruitment pattern. But as was demonstrated earlier, institutionally-based recruitment remains more prevalent than other types of labor recruitment at the university level and has even increased slightly over the mid- to late twentieth century. At the same time, university graduates' use of social ties to get their first job has decreased only slightly. What is going on? Why have these patterns persisted and why has there not been a shift toward the more positively sanctioned atomistic recruitment pattern? What happened once firms' explicit closed-door policy apparently succumbed to their critics? Did universities continue to send their graduates to certain firms? If so, how did this occur?

Patterns of Hiring University Graduates, 1975 to 1990

To see whether there was indeed continuity in employers' recruitment of graduates from certain universities even after sanctions against explicit institutional ties were introduced, we used published information from the annual "Survey on Entry into Firms from Universities and Colleges" (*Daigakubetsu shūshokusaki shirabe*) conducted by the private research organization Recruit, to construct a data set that enabled us to trace the placement of university graduates over the years 1975 to 1990.[13] We selected four prestigious private universities and two national universities (the latter are by definition prestigious) in the Tokyo metropolitan area,[14] and traced the placement of their alumni who had majored in business-related fields (economics, commerce, and management) for the sixteen-year period beginning in 1975.[15] Having restricted the labor-supplying institutions to a manageable number, we restricted the demand-side to companies in the financial sector (banks, leasing and credit companies, and securities firms), where a high proportion of business-related majors are hired each year. We then counted the number of graduates from the selected universities hired each year by every company in the financial sector. We also identified several firms as being particularly sought after or desirable employers and considered them separately.[16]

To measure the continuity of recruitment by financial institutions from our sampled universities we constructed five measures for each university: 1) the average number of graduates hired per firm; 2) this figure calculated only for those firms that hired at least one graduate from that university for more than half of the sixteen years under study ("continuous firms"); 3) this figure calculated for all firms not included in the continuous set ("discontinuous firms"); 4) this figure calculated for those firms in the subsample of highly desirable firms that qualify as continuous ones; and 5) this figure calculated for those firms in the subsample of highly desirable employers that are discontinuous firms.

Our results show that in nearly every year during the 1975 to 1990 period the average number of graduates from a given university hired by a continuous firm was greater than the average number of hires per firm across all firms or the average number per discontinuous firm. (The lowest figure was for discontinuous firms.) In other words, employers who hire year after year from a university are hiring larger numbers of its graduates than are other employers.[17] There is therefore considerable continuity in the recruiting relationship between particular prestigious universities and employers. Moreover, the difference between the number of graduates hired yearly from each university by continuous and discontinuous firms did not decline in the 1980s, as we would have expected following the demise of the restrictive closed-door policy. The number of students hired from continuous firms appears to have declined at the end of the 1970s and then recovered by the early to mid-1980s.

If firms' recruitment of students from particular Japanese universities had become a "one-shot transaction" and neither universities nor firms cared whether firms were repeatedly hiring from the same universities, it is unlikely (though not impossible) that we would have observed a significant difference between the behavior of continuous and discontinuous firms, nor a difference between these firms within the most desirable subset. Since the prestige rankings of the six universities are very close, it is difficult to explain the observed university-firm pairings solely on the basis of the greater desirability of one university's graduates over another. Given that explicit institutional ties declined, what mechanisms produced the patterns we found?

Obviously, the mere numbers of graduates hired by particular firms cannot give us information about the mechanisms behind the phenomenon. There is continuity over time, but this could conceivably be produced by any of the job-search/recruitment patterns discussed in this chapter: atomistic, social tie, or institutional tie. Yet the cohort data examined earlier demonstrates that the use of social ties by university graduates has declined only slightly, while the use of institutional ties has shown a slight increase. We turn now to the qualitative evidence that suggests that a hybrid pattern somewhere *between* social and institutional embeddedness has emerged. While we cannot definitively prove that this explains the cohort job-search patterns among university graduates, it is highly consistent with them, as well as with our theoretical arguments concerning the increased negative sanctions on university-employer relationships.

Alumni-Student Relations as Semi-Institutional Networks: Qualitative Evidence

In response to the criticism against the closed-door policy of hiring graduates only from certain universities, Japanese universities and employers appear to have devised an alternative that functions like the system of mandatory and exclusive university recommendation letters. We designate this reassertion of an institutional embeddedness pattern in new garb as a "semi-institutional" pattern.

Our qualitative evidence consists of university graduates' reports of their initial job-search experiences. These reports were collected each year by the placement offices of our six sampled universities. What the reports show is that *alumni-student relations* have taken on new significance since the late 1970s and have created bridges between universities and employers. Information from the student placement office at University D, for example, indicates that the proportion of graduates who discussed in their job-search report the necessity of a school recommendation decreased from 35 percent in 1975 to zero in 1980 (figure 8.4). Instead, students in the late 1970s and early 1980s increasingly mention the importance of contacts with alumni. In 1975, about 40 percent of graduates referred to their relations with alumni in their reports, but this number had increased to over 60 percent by 1980 and reached a remarkable 80 percent in 1981.

Documents from university placement offices also indicate that in the early 1980s visits to alumni became an integral part of students' job-hunting activities. It is not unusual, of course, for alumni to convey information about jobs and firms to current students. In many countries, alumni networks play a role in transmitting information about jobs and/or job-seekers (Dina 1988) and may

Figure 8.4   Frequencies of Graduates' Reports Mentioning Alumni Visits, Grades, and School Recommendations (University D)

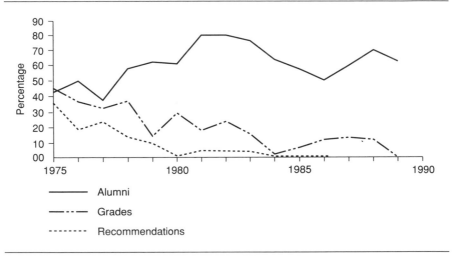

have some influence on hiring decisions.[18] Old-boy networks exist not only in Japan but in the United States, the United Kingdom, and other industrial societies. But while old-boy networks are viewed negatively and are often hidden from view in the United States, Japanese universities are actively involved in maintaining and publicizing such networks. University placement offices keep lists of the current positions, firms, addresses, and phone numbers of alumni for the use of job-seeking seniors. Thus, while meeting alumni is partly informal, it has a semi-institutional aspect because university placement offices are actively involved. As a male graduate from University D reported in the early 1980s, "In September, the placement office becomes crowded with seniors who struggle to get a list of alumni in order to make contact with them."

Firms are also actively involved in using alumni-student relations for recruitment. With the establishment of the Supervising Committee on Recruitment in 1979, it became risky for companies' personnel offices to formally approach university students before the set date. In order to get around this restriction, companies began to use employees who were alumni of certain universities as contact persons for job-seeking seniors from those universities. In this way, both universities and employers distorted the intention of the *shūshoku kyōtei* by shifting to a recruitment style that was superficially based on personal networks but was in essence semi-institutional, involving young alumni as informal recruitment agents for the firm.[19]

A distinctive feature of the Japanese use of alumni in job-search and recruitment is that many large firms choose young employees with less than ten years of work experience in the firm to act as *rikuruuta* (recruiters). While these employees are not personnel officers per se, they are expected to make contact with job-seeking seniors from their universities. This differs from an old-boy network in that these young alumni derive their power from the company rather than from their own personal prestige or status. It is this characteristic, plus the university placement office's involvement, that leads us to think of this system as semi-institutional embeddedness rather than as social (personal) embeddedness, for it represents an active attempt by schools and firms to remain informally linked to each other. According to a survey of about one thousand Japanese university seniors, 76 percent of the alumni students met during their 1993 job search had five or fewer years of experience in their firms (Kariya et al. 1994). Seventy-two percent of the survey respondents met at least one alumnus during their job search; on average, each student met 11.2 alumni. Among students whose meeting with an alumnus led to a job offer, about 30 percent reported that the meeting seemed to be the first stage of screening, and over 70 percent said that they talked "extensively" about jobs at that meeting.

Young informal recruiters are generally required to report their impressions or evaluations of job-seekers to their firm's personnel office, and some firms actually give them authority to screen candidates. Graduates frequently mention this alumni role in the selection process: One 1980 male graduate said, "I was told by a personnel officer in a company to meet some of the younger employees, so I did. Afterwards, I realized that they evaluated me and reported it to the personnel office." Another male graduate that year reported, "Visiting alumni was somehow advantageous. One of the young alumni I met turned out to be an interviewer during my job interview at the company." According to a 1981 male graduate, "It is not unusual that a *rikuruuta's* [recruiter's] evaluation leads to hiring." And a 1983 male graduate advised, "You should visit OBs [old boys].[20] Those visits will qualify you to go forward to official job interviews."

Meetings between young employees and job-seeking students are usually initiated by students' phone calls, but in the case of top-ranking universities, alumni visit the campus to initiate contact. Students meet alumni whom they have not met before but whose names they may have seen in the university's placement office list. In general, meetings occur outside the firm, in a coffee shop or restaurant. According to our analyses of graduates' reports, alumni sometimes give hints about hiring practices to students and provide information about their firms' shortcomings and problems. Thus, alumni play an informal role that personnel offices are unlikely to do.

In sum, alumni-student relationships in the Japanese university case can be termed "semi-institutional" because university alumni are explicitly acting as agents for their firms. This activity is formalized to the extent that universities actively maintain alumni lists and that these alumni come to campus to meet students. Yet it is an informal process, one imbued with ambiguity in the sense that it is not always clear to students what role these alumni play in screening prospective employees or in making hiring decisions and in the sense that alumni may occasionally offer a frank assessment of their companys' problems to potential applicants. We believe that the subtle changes in the job-search patterns at the university level that we observed in the individual-level data—a gradual increase in institutional embeddedness and only a slight decrease in social embeddedness—reflect the complexity of the underlying shifts over time between explicit, formal institutional methods of recruitment and less formal, semi-institutional ones.

CONCLUSION

In this chapter, we have raised the macrosociological question of why patterns of job-search embeddedness may vary across labor markets and across time. We specified institutional embeddedness (ties between institutions, such as between schools and firms) in addition to the often-analyzed social embeddedness (ties between individuals) and the reified atomistic labor market. Referrals received by employers from social ties or institutions are useful in making hiring decisions because they provide additional information about job applicants. But such ties can also be publicly criticized if they are perceived to lead to decisions that unfairly privilege some applicants over others. We argue that this criticism is most likely to occur at the upper end of the labor market, where particularism matters most in terms of unfairly allocating prestige and income to those who are "well-connected." For this reason, there are counterpressures that affect social and institutional embeddedness. While their benefit to employers suggests that they will be a dominant feature of labor markets, their susceptibility to attack by proponents of fairness suggests that they will decline over time. Complicating the picture, institutional embeddedness requires that both participating institutions benefit from an arrangement or it will cease to exist. In the case of the labor market for entry-level graduates, the employer's supply-side counterpart is the school. We argue that institutional ties between schools and employers are only feasible when school reputation depends heavily on the successful placement of its graduates and when employers are hiring for jobs for which they need all the help they can get in screening for good applicants. Otherwise, schools and employers presumably have little incentive to cooperate with each other, either in an aboveboard (institutional) or other (what we have called a semi-institutional) fashion.

Japanese society served as the setting for testing our hypotheses. We looked at the micro level—graduates' job-search patterns—and the macro historical level—the development of the secondary and higher educational system and its relationship to employers. A range of data sources indicate that institutional embeddedness is important at both the high school and university levels in Japan; educational institutions at these levels have established and maintained relationships with specific employers, and substantial proportions of graduates report that they found their first job through a school introduction. We argue that these institutional connections are beneficial to Japanese employers. Entrance examinations to high schools and universities mean that the student population is differentiated across schools, and schools therefore perform a significant screening function for employers. Early on in the development of the Japanese higher educational system, schools established their reputation based on where they placed their students in the job market. Institutional embeddedness thereby benefits schools as well, as it ensures that they can consistently send their graduates to certain employers.

At the high school level, institutional embeddedness developed and has been maintained throughout the postwar period, whereas institutional embeddedness has a longer history in the upper end of the labor market—the market for university graduates—and has recently given way to what we term a semi-institutional pattern. Institutional embeddedness is highly visible and may be open to criticism if people question the fairness of school entrance requirements or the relationship between what is learned at a specific school and the skills necessary in the workplace. That is, it is open to criticism if people perceive that it is functioning mainly as a mechanism of elite reproduction, in the manner of social embeddedness. We note that while institutional embeddedness has been criticized at the university level in Japan, it has not received such criticism at the high school level. It is probable that social attacks are less likely here because it does not involve the elite segment of the labor market.

We find two implications of our analysis sobering. First, what is curious about efforts at the reform of institutional embeddedness is that so long as repeated recruitment from a school by an employer continues to benefit both parties, it is doubtful that the recruitment relationship will be eradicated. The Japanese university case suggests that it will simply go underground. Once a sanctioning mechanism against restrictive recruitment was established, it was relatively easy for universities and employers to begin to use alumni-student relationships more systematically than previously. This semi-institutional embeddedness continues to provide benefits (in the form of information to employers and reputation to schools) while at the same time being partially hidden from public view. This may be well and good if the admissions requirements to universities are truly meritocratic, so that the semi-institutional ties are not excluding otherwise talented students who for some reason could not enter top universities. Unfortunately, there is considerable scholarly evidence for Japan as well as the United States that the distribution of students' socioeconomic backgrounds at elite universities is skewed to the right (Ishida 1993; Kingston and Lewis 1989). Thus, the efficiency of institutional and semi-institutional ties for schools and employers needs to be evaluated in the context of how—and which—students are admitted into the school side of school-employer cooperative arrangements.

Second, we argue that whatever the merits and demerits of institutional embeddedness, it is likely to be common only under certain conditions. Schools and firms need to have substantial and overlapping incentives in order for institutional embeddedness to emerge. One of the strong incentives for a school is that the labor market access afforded its graduates by ties with firms enhances its reputation. Institutional embeddedness at the upper end of the labor market can also easily become subject to public criticism as a form of particularism. These aspects of institutional embeddedness bear witness to its complexity and fragility, and merit serious consideration in the United States as scholars and policymakers examine Japanese and European models of forging school-employer linkages.

We gratefully acknowledge the assistance of Yuki Okitsu, Keiko Yoshihara, Takayasu Nakamura, and Hisashi Kondo of the University of Tokyo. We thank Mark Granovetter, David Hachen, Satoshi Kanazawa, Victor Nee, William Parish, participants of the East Asia Workshop at the University of Chicago, and the late James S. Coleman for helpful comments on an earlier draft of this chapter. Brinton expresses her gratitude to the Japan Institute of Labor and Kariya thanks the Recruit organization for allowing us to use their respective data.

NOTES

This chapter is a revised version of a paper prepared for presentation at the annual meeting of the American Sociological Association in Miami Beach, Florida, August 1993.

1. Except in the case of self-employment, of course.

2. Roos and Reskin (1984), for example, discuss a range of recruitment practices that implicitly discriminate against women.

3. Koya Azumi's study (1969) is an exception to this and is discussed later in this chapter.

4. We use the terms social embeddedness, social ties, and interpersonal ties interchangeably throughout this chapter. We also use the terms institutional embeddedness and institutional ties interchangeably.

5. The extent to which mutual ties of obligation exist between Japanese schools and employers is an empirical question that deserves much more attention than we can give it in this chapter. For the present we assume that such ties of obligation do exist, although we recognize that their strength varies from case to case. This is explored in greater detail in Brinton (forthcoming).

6. We do not go into the issue of start-up costs or continuing transaction costs entailed by school-employer recruitment relationships. As with the ties of obligation mentioned in note 5, we assume that there are some costs but that they will vary across empirical cases of school-employer dyads. Qualitative treatment of twenty urban Japanese public high schools can be found in Brinton (forthcoming).

7. The name changed to Tokyo Imperial University in 1897 to distinguish it from Kyoto Imperial University which was established in that year. "Imperial" was dropped from the names of both universities after World War II.

8. See Brinton (forthcoming) for a discussion of the postwar legal context governing labor advertising and recruitment as well as the historical involvement by the Ministry of Labor in the allocation of new graduates to jobs.

9. However, Japanese teachers in the job placement and guidance section of urban public general high schools interviewed by Brinton state that the most important factor affecting a school's reputation is the percentage of students entering university, not the job destination of its work-bound students. The reputation of vocational high schools is based more strongly on job placements for graduates (Brinton 1997).

10. A similar practice is followed by some prestigious firms in South Korea. Brinton thanks Yong-Hak Kim for pointing this out to her.

11. See Upham (1987) for an excellent discussion of Japanese law and the use of informal sanctions rather than monetary penalties.

12. These reports from graduating students were collected yearly by the placement office of this university.

13. Both male and female graduates' placements are included in the published data, with no disaggregation by sex.

14. We measured prestige or quality on the basis of published *hensachi*, a standardized score for indicating the difficulty of a university's entrance examination.

15. We focused on these graduates in order to control for field of specialization. Business-related majors are a large group, making up close to half of all humanities and social science majors who enter the labor market each year.

16. These include the six government banks, the thirteen large city banks, and seven large trust banks. The large city banks have branches nationwide and are more prestigious than local banks. Of these twenty-six government, city, and trust banks, twelve were among the "top one hundred" firms selected as the most desirable job destination by humanities and business majors (Recruit Research 1991). The others (especially the government banks) are also considered to be very prestigious workplaces by virtue of their nationwide scope.

17. It could be that continuous employers in our sample hire a higher average number of graduates per university because they are larger firms than the discontinuous employers. We controlled for this possible size effect by comparing figures for continuous and discontinuous firms in the subset of government banks, large city banks, and large trust banks. Even in this group, the figure for continuous firms is nearly always higher than the figure for discontinuous firms.

18. Some elite American universities currently appear to be investing more resources in creating job information networks among alumni.

19. The costs of maintaining this system seem to be limited to the costs of communication between universities and firms, that is, in constructing lists and contact information for alumni employed at various firms. Implicit contract costs, that is, costs in terms of a firm's obligation to recruit from a specific school or a university's obligation to recommend to a student that he or she apply to a specific firm, are not in evidence. Sakakibara and Westney (1985, 6) discuss engineers as an interesting exception to this: "If a company rejects top university students who have recommendations, it will become difficult in the future for that company to hire students from that university. Therefore, Japanese corporations tend to hire a fixed number of students from selected major universities every year."

20. The term *OB* carries a slightly different connotation in Japan than in the United States, often referring to one's *senpai* or predecessors, who could be as little as one or two years older.

REFERENCES

Amano, Ikuo. 1990. *Education and Examination in Modern Japan.* Translated by William K. Cummings and Fumiko Cummings. Tokyo: Tokyo University Press.

Arrow, Kenneth. 1973. "Higher Education as a Filter." *Journal of Public Economics* 2: 193–216.

Azumi, Koya. 1969. *Higher Education and Business Recruitment in Japan.* New York: Teachers College Press.

Boxman, Ed, Paul DeGraaf, and Hendrik Flap. 1991. "The Impact of Social and Human Capital on the Income Attainment of Dutch Managers." *Social Networks* 13(1): 51–73.

Brinton, Mary C. 1991. "Sex Differences in On-the-Job Training and Job Rotation in Japanese Firms." *Research in Social Stratification and Mobility* 10: 3–25.

———. 1993. *Women and the Economic Miracle: Gender and Work in Postwar Japan.* Berkeley: University of California Press.

———. 1997. "Harvesting the Green Shoot: Japanese Firms' Recruitment of New Graduates." University of Chicago. Working paper.

———. Forthcoming. *Manufacturing Class: High Schools, Jobs, and Inequality in Japan.*

Clark, Rodney. 1979. *The Japanese Company.* New Haven: Yale University Press.

Cole, Robert. 1979. *Work, Mobility, and Participation: A Comparative Study of Japanese and American Industry.* Berkeley: University of California Press.

Dore, Ronald P. 1976. *British Factory, Japanese Factory.* Berkeley: University of California Press.

———. 1983. "Goodwill and the Spirit of Market Capitalism." *British Journal of Sociology* 34(4): 459–82.

———. 1986. *Flexible Rigidities: Industrial Policy and Structural Adjustment in the Japanese Economy.* London: Athlone.

———. 1987. *Taking Japan Seriously.* Stanford: Stanford University Press.

Gerlach, Michael L. 1992. *Alliance Capitalism: The Social Organization of Japanese Business.* Berkeley: University of California Press.

Granovetter, Mark. 1973. "The Strength of Weak Ties." *American Journal of Sociology* 78(6): 1360–80.

———. 1981. "Toward a Sociological Theory of Income Differences." In *Sociological Perspectives on Labor Markets*, edited by Ivar Berg. New York: Academic Press.

———. 1985. "Economic Action and Social Structure: The Problem of Embeddedness." *American Journal of Sociology* 91(3): 481–510.

———. 1995. *Getting a Job.* 2d ed. Chicago: University of Chicago Press.

Granovetter, Mark, and Richard Swedberg, eds. 1992. *The Sociology of Economic Life.* Boulder: Westview.

Inui, Akio. 1993. "The Competitive Structure of School and the Labour Market: Japan and Britain." *British Journal of Sociology of Education* 14(3): 301–13.

Ishida, Hiroshi. 1993. *Social Mobility in Contemporary Japan.* Stanford: Stanford University Press.

James, Estelle, and Gail Benjamin. 1988. *Public Policy and Private Education in Japan.* New York: St. Martin's.

Kariya, Takehiko, Yuki Okitsu, Keiko Yoshihara, Marayasu Nakamura, and Hisashi Kondo. 1993. "The Embeddedness of College to Work Transitions in Alumni-Student Relations" (in Japanese). *Bulletin of the Faculty of Education* (University of Tokyo) 32: 89–118.

Kariya, Takehiko, ed. 1995. *From College to Work: A Survey Report of College Students' Job Search Activities* (in Japanese). Research Institute for Higher Education, Hiroshima University.

Keizai Doyukai. 1975. "Kigyōnai shūshokusha no gakureki tou ni kansuru jittai chōsa" (in Japanese). (Survey report on the educational background of new employees). Tokyo, Japan.

Kingston, Paul, and Lionel S. Lewis. 1989. "Studying Elite Schools in America." In *The High-Status Track*, edited by Paul Kingston and Lionel S. Lewis. New York: State University of New York Press.

Koh, B. C. 1991. *Japan's Administrative Elite.* Berkeley, Calif.: University of California Press.

Koike, Kazuo. 1984. "Skill Formation Systems in the U.S. and Japan: A Comparative Study." In *The Economic Analysis of the Japanese Firm*, edited by Masahiko Aoki. New York: Elsevier.

———. 1987a. "Human Resource Development and Labor-Management Relations." In *The Political Economy of Japan.* Vol. 1, *The Domestic Transformation*, edited by Kozo Yamamura and Yasukichi Yasuba. Stanford, Calif.: Stanford University Press.

———. 1987b. "Skill Formation Systems: A Thai-Japan Comparison." *Journal of the Japanese and International Economies* 1(1): 408–40.

LeTendre, Gerald K. 1996. "Constructed Aspirations: Decision-Making Processes in Japanese Educational Selection." *Sociology of Education* 69(3): 193–216.

Lin, Nan. 1990. "Social Resources and Social Mobility: A Structural Theory of Status Attainment." In *Social Mobility and Social Structure*, edited by Ronald Breiger. New York: Cambridge University Press.

Lin, Nan, Walter Ensel, and John Vaughn. 1981. "Social Resources and Strength of Ties: Structural Factors in Occupational Status Attainment." *American Sociological Review* 46(4): 393–405.

Lindquist, Dina A. 1988. "Working with Alumni." *Journal of Career Planning and Employment* (summer): 37–39.

Marsden, Peter, and Jeanne Hurlbert. 1988. "Social Resources and Mobility Outcomes: A Replication and Extension." *Social Forces* 66(4): 1038–59.

Meyer, John W., and Brian Rowan. 1977. "Institutionalized Organizations: Formal Structure as Myth and Ceremony." *American Journal of Sociology* 83(2): 340–63.

Murakami, Yasusuke, and Thomas P. Rohlen. 1992. "Social-Exchange Aspects of the Japanese Political Economy: Culture, Efficiency, and Change." In *The Political Economy of Japan.* Vol. 3, *Cultural and Social Dynamics*, edited by Shumpei Kumon and Henry Rosovsky. Stanford, Calif.: Stanford University Press.

Nakane, Chie. 1980. *Japanese Society.* Berkeley, Calif.: University of California Press.

Nakata, Yoshifumi, and Carl Mosk. 1987. "The Demand for College Education in Postwar Japan." *The Journal of Human Resources* 22(3): 377–404.

Ogata, Ken. 1975. *Gakureki shinkō shakai* (The society that believes in diplomas) (in Japanese). Tokyo: Jiji Tshushin-sha.

Ozaki, Morimitsu. 1980. "Gakureki shakai seiritsu ni kansuru ichi kōsatsu" (An inquiry into the "educational credential" society) (in Japanese). *Daigaku Ronshū* (Hiroshima Daigaku, Daigaku Kyoiku Kenkyu Center) 8: 143–54.

Recruit Research. 1991. *Daigukusei no ninki kigyō chōsa* (in Japanese). Tokyo: Recruit Research.

Rees, Albert. 1966. "Information Networks in Labor Markets." *American Economic Review*: 559–66.

Rohlen, Thomas. 1984. *Japan's High Schools.* Berkeley: University of California Press.

Roos, Patricia A., and Barbara F. Reskin. 1984. "Institutional Factors Contributing to Sex Segregation in the Workplace." In *Sex Segregation in the Workplace: Trends, Explanations, Remedies*, edited by Barbara F. Reskin. Washington, D.C.: National Academy Press.

Rosenbaum, James E., and Takehiko Kariya. 1989a. "From High School to Work: Market and Institutional Mechanisms in Japan." *American Journal of Sociology* 94, 6: 1334–65.

———. 1989b. "Japan Offers Way to Link School, Jobs." *Forum for Applied Research and Public Policy* 4.

Rosenbaum, James E., Takehiko Kariya, Rick Settersten, and Tony Maier. 1990. "Market and Network Theories of the Transition from High School to Work: Their Application to Industrialized Societies." *Annual Review of Sociology* 16: 263–99.

Roth, Alvin E., and Xiaolin Xing. 1994. "Jumping the Gun: Imperfections and Institutions Related to the Timing of Market Transactions." *American Economic Review* 84(4): 992–1044.

Sakakibara, Kiyonori, and D. Eleanor Westney. 1985. "Comparative Study of the Training, Careers, and Organization of Engineers in the Computer Industry in the United States and Japan." *Hitotsubashi Journal of Commerce and Management* 20: 1–20.

Sako, Mari. 1991. "The Role of 'Trust' in Japanese Buyer-Supplier Relationships." *Richerche Economiche* 45: 449–74.

———. 1992. *Prices, Quality, and Trust: Inter-firm Relations in Britain and Japan.* Cambridge, England: Cambridge University Press.

Upham, Frank. 1987. *Law and Social Change in Postwar Japan.* Cambridge, Mass.: Harvard University Press.

$$—— 9 ——$$

Winner-Take-All Markets and Wage Discrimination

Robert H. Frank

Women and minorities continue to receive lower wages, on average, than white males with similar levels of education, training, experience, and other measures of human capital. This pattern poses a profound challenge to standard theories of competitive labor markets, which hold that workers with equal amounts of human capital will be paid the same. Defenders of standard theories attribute the wage gap to unmeasured differences in human capital. Critics of these theories, who reject the idea that labor markets are effectively competitive, attribute the gap to discrimination by employers.

The data pose awkward questions for both camps. Whereas available evidence supports the belief of traditional theorists that labor markets are, for the most part, highly competitive, a significant earnings gap has survived several decades of determined efforts by traditional theorists to explain it away.

In this chapter I will describe an alternative theoretical view of the labor market, one that is consistent with both patterns in the data. Like standard theories, mine begins with the assumption that labor markets are highly competitive. I go on to describe forces, however, whereby even minimal employer discrimination might result in two equally talented workers earning dramatically different wages.

My account derives from recent work in collaboration with Philip Cook in which we argue that the reward structure common in sports and entertainment—where literally thousands compete for a handful of big prizes at the top—has now spread widely to other sectors of the economy. In a growing number of winner-take-all markets in law, consulting, finance, management, publishing, and other fields, small differences in effort or ability give rise to enormous differences in incomes.

The winner-take-all perspective suggests that individual wage differences are the result less of differences in people than of differences in the degree to which jobs provide leverage for their skills (Frank and Cook 1995). A truly gifted salesman, for example, is worth little if her task is to sell children's shoes, but she is worth millions if her job is to sell securities to the world's largest pension funds. The opportunity to occupy a highly leveraged (and correspondingly well-paid) position is, in effect, the prize for having survived an intensely competitive series of elimination tournaments.

Employers who fail to hire the best available candidates for these positions cannot hope to survive under competitive market conditions. Yet competitive pressures often do little to assure that the finalists for these positions constitute a representative sample of the initial population of qualified contenders. To become a finalist, one must have survived the early rounds, and in these rounds the penalties to the employer for failing to hire the most able candidates are often too small to matter. Small, unobservable differences in ability, or a small degree of employer discrimination, at the early stages of the tournament process may thus translate over time into large differences in final reward.

The chapter is organized in five parts. I begin with a description of the standard competitive model and why it appears to rule out employer discrimination as an explanation of persistent differences in wages. Next I survey some of the empirical attempts to explain why wages differ among groups, noting that although these studies have narrowed the unexplained gaps, significant differentials remain. I then describe the winner-take-all perspective of the labor market and explain why, in this framework, large wage differentials grounded in employer discrimination might persist even when there is intense competition among employers. In the next section, I describe some testable hypotheses generated by the winner-take-all model. I conclude by describing an indirect test of one of these hypotheses.

WAGE DISCRIMINATION IN PERFECTLY COMPETITIVE LABOR MARKETS

Employer discrimination is the term used to describe wage differentials that arise from an arbitrary preference by the employer for one group of workers over another. Suppose that there are two labor force groups, the Ms and the Fs, and that, although there are no productivity differences between them, some employers ("discriminators") prefer hiring Ms while others ("nondiscriminators") hire on the basis of ability alone. Since the Ms and Fs have equal productivity by assumption, this means that the wage rate will be higher for Ms, owing to the asymmetrically higher demands for them by discriminators.

Apart from the isolated cases in which customer discrimination might be a relevant factor, a consumer will be unwilling to pay more for a product produced by an M than for an identical one produced by an F. If product price is unaffected by the composition of the workforce that produces the product, a firm's profit will be smaller the more Ms it employs. The most profitable firm will be one that employs only Fs.

The initial wage differential provides an opportunity for employers who hire mostly Fs to grow at the expense of their rivals. Indeed, because such firms make an economic profit on the sale of each unit of output, their incentive is to expand as rapidly as they possibly can. And to do that, they will naturally want to continue hiring only the cheaper Fs.

But as profit-seeking firms continue to pursue this strategy, the supply of Fs at the lower wage rate will not be adequate for further expansion. The short-run solution is to offer the Fs a slightly higher wage. But this strategy works only if other firms do not pursue it. Once they also start offering a higher wage, the Fs will again be in short supply. In the end, of course, the only solution is for the wage of the Fs to be bid up to equality with the wage of the Ms, thereby eliminating further opportunities for profitable expansion by hiring additional Fs. The wage for both Ms and Fs will thus settle at the common value of their marginal product (VMP).

Any employer who wants to voice a preference for hiring Ms must now do so by paying Ms a wage in excess of VMP. Employers can discriminate against Fs if they want to, but only if they are willing to pay premium wages to the Ms out of their own profits. Suppose the discriminating firm hired only Ms and paid them 10 percent more than VMP. How would such a firm's profits compare with those of a nondiscriminating firm? In an illustrative case in which labor costs are 70 percent of a nondiscriminating firm's total costs, the interest rate is 10 percent, and firms own half their capital, a firm that hires only Ms and pays them 10 percent more than VMP will earn almost 50 percent less than the competitive return on its invested capital.[1] Few firms could continue to attract capital for long at profit rates that much below normal.

The competitive labor market model thus suggests that the persistence of significant employer discrimination requires the owners of a firm to supply capital at a rate of return substantially below what they could earn by investing their money elsewhere. Even the harshest critics of the competitive model have difficulty imputing such behavior to the owners of capitalist enterprises.

EMPIRICAL ATTEMPTS TO EXPLAIN THE WAGE GAP

Standard attempts to explain individual wage differences rest on the human capital model developed by Gary Becker (1975), Jacob Mincer and Solomon Polachek (1974), and others. Work in this tradition sees individual workers as embodying a host of personal characteristics that account for differences in their productivity, and hence for differences in their market-determined rates of pay.

Empirical studies in this literature typically regress the log of individual wage rates against such individual human capital measures as education, training, experience, and age. Other control variables, such as occupation, industry, and union status, are also typically included in these regressions. Not surprisingly, such crude proxies for productivity can explain only a small proportion of individual variations in wages.

Residual wage differentials among groups—those not explained by available human capital variables—may then be decomposed into two parts, one representing unmeasured individual differences in productivity, the other attributable to employer discrimination. The ongoing enterprise of neoclassical economists who study wage differentials has been to come up with more and better measures of productivity differences in an attempt to reduce the unexplained wage gap to zero.

Noting that productivity is influenced not only by the quantity of education an individual has but also its quality, some researchers (Juhn, Murphy, and Pierce 1991; Card and Krueger 1992) have suggested that part of the black-white differential in wages may be due to the fact that schools in black neighborhoods have not been as good, on the average, as those in white neighborhoods. Differences in the courses people take in college appear to have similar implications for differences in productivity. For instance, students in math, engineering, or business—male or female—tend to earn significantly higher salaries than those who concentrate in the humanities. The fact that males are disproportionately represented in the former group gives rise to a male wage premium that is unrelated to employer discrimination.

A related tack in explaining wage differentials relies not on unmeasured differences in ability or training but on the consequences of behavioral choices that affect productivity. Scholars in this tradition focus on choices that stem from the fact that women are more likely than men to specialize in childrearing. Such commitments have historically implied more intermittent patterns of labor force participation for women than for men. Solomon Polachek (1975) showed that it is not just the total amount of experience that matters, but also the manner in which that experience accumulates. Individual histories—male or female—that are characterized by continuous labor force participation exhibit significantly higher wages than otherwise similar histories characterized by intermittent labor force participation. That part of the male-female wage differential that stems from this pattern cannot be attributed to employer discrimination.

In a similar vein, Gary Becker (1985) and Edward Lazear and Sherwin Rosen (1990) have argued that women's greater commitment to work in the home makes it less profitable for them to invest in the acquisition of skills that are valued in the marketplace. Some of any resulting skill deficits will show up as deficits in measured human capital. But many others will go unmeasured and will further widen the unexplained wage differential. Sex differences in occupational aspiration, whatever their source, can be expected to result in human capital differences, both measured and unmeasured, with similar consequences for unexplained wage differentials (see Marini and Fan 1997).

Employer behavior, and even misperceptions of employer behavior, can have similar influences on decisions to invest in human capital. Building on work on statistical discrimination by Aigner and Cain (1977), for example, Lundberg and Startz (1987) have argued that because employers have had less experience dealing with minorities and women than with white males they are less confident in their estimates of individual productivity differences for women and minorities than for white males. Competitive pressure in the labor market will still force employers to pay women and minority members in accord with the average productivity for those groups, but the relative imprecision of individual productivity estimates will cause wages to cluster more closely to the respective mean productivity values for women and minorities. Thus, the wage schedule for white males has a steeper slope around its mean than do the respective wage schedules for minorities and women.

The upshot is that individual efforts to boost productivity are more heavily rewarded for white males than for the other groups. The rational response to this incentive structure is for males to invest more heavily in human capital than the other groups. And again, since only part of any individual's human capital is captured by available statistical measures, this pattern of differential investment will contribute to the unexplained wage gap.

Customer discrimination is another possible explanation for differential patterns of investment in human capital (Kahn 1991). For example, if people believe that juries and clients are less likely to take the pronouncements of female or minority attorneys seriously, members of these groups will face diminished incentives to attend law school, even if law firms themselves care only about the amount of billable hours new associates will generate. Still another source of differential investment in human capital is premarket discrimination and socialization within the family. For example, families may provide fewer educational resources for their female children, or they may socialize them to believe that lofty career ambitions are not appropriate. Either or both would be likely to result in differential investments in human capital.

Of course, similar differential patterns of investment may occur in response to employer discrimination, suggesting that if such discrimination exists, it will tend to be self-reinforcing. More troubling still, even false perceptions that employer discrimination exists would cause differential investments in human capital, with the attendant effects on wage differentials. The irony here is that if employer discrimination is not, in fact, a significant explanation of wage differentials, falsely attributing these differentials to discrimination may well cause existing differentials to grow larger rather than smaller.

Family location constraints provide another possible explanation of wage differentials by sex. For two-career couples, it is unlikely that the best job opportunities for both spouses will happen to lie in the same local labor market. For spouses who wish to live together, this means that one or both must compromise and accept something less than the best available job offer. Because women, on average, marry men who are several years older and have more education and experience than they do, the burden of compromise in families whose goal is to maximize total family income will tend to fall disproportionately on wives (see Frank 1978; Mincer 1978; Bielby and Bielby 1992).

This explains the historical pattern in which family location was dictated by the location of the husband's best offer, and wives took the best job they could find in that particular labor market. Even within local markets, wives may be relatively more geographically constrained in their choice of jobs by their desire to be closer to home and to their children's schools. These constraints imply that part of the sex differential in wages is attributable to the fact that males are able to make fuller use of whatever human capital they have than are females.

Related to differential location constraints are differentials in preferences for other nonwage elements of the compensation package. Jobs that involve exposure to physical risk, for example, command higher wages, and if men are relatively more willing to accept such risks, we will see a difference in wages between males and females with otherwise identical stocks of human capital. (The same result would obtain if employers felt constrained by social forces not to assign female employees to risky jobs.) There is also evidence that women are more likely than males to choose jobs, such as those commonly seen in the nonprofit sector, that provide a measure of moral satisfaction in exchange for smaller monetary compensation (Frank 1996; Handy 1995). When males choose such jobs, they earn the same low wages that women do. But women are much more likely than males to choose such jobs, and this observation, too, helps reduce the previously unexplained sex-differential in wages.

Despite these efforts to explain sex and race differentials in wages, significant gaps remain. One recent survey (Blau and Ferber 1992, 193), for example, reported that 39.9 percent of the 31 percent wage gap between men and women with high school educations could not be explained by the usual human capital variables. The corresponding figures for college-educated men and women were 34.5 percent and 28.2 percent. Studies of wage differentials by race report similar findings.

LABOR MARKETS AS WINNER-TAKE-ALL TOURNAMENTS

The human capital model explains differences in wages by asserting that some workers are "better" than others, in the sense of having acquired more education, training, and whatever other attributes the market values. Taken together, these attributes make up an aggregate called human capital, which commands a price in the labor market, just as financial capital commands a price in the capital markets. Thus, a worker with twice as much human capital as another will earn twice the wage, just as someone with $10,000 in the bank will earn twice as much interest as someone with only $5,000.

The human capital model does not insist that the relationship between earnings and readily observed personal characteristics be linear. For example, someone with twice as much education as a coworker, or twice as much experience, will not necessarily earn twice the wage. Yet neither does the human capital model predict sharp discontinuities in the relationship between personal characteristics and wages. Thus, a 1 percent difference in intelligence or education would not be expected to give rise to, say, a hundredfold difference in wages.

Unlike the human capital model, which directs our attention to the worker, the winner-take-all model directs our attention to the job. A person who embodies a given level of human capital will realize its full value only if placed in a position with adequate scope and opportunity. For example, an automotive engineer with rare talents would add high value if employed to design the engine for Ford's new midsize car, yet would add relatively little if employed to design Kmart's float for the Orange Bowl Parade.

Organizations have hierarchies of positions, with pay scales that reflect the level of responsibility or scope of each position. High salaries are associated with positions where there is a great deal of leverage of the worker's efforts. In these positions, small differences in performance translate into large differences in the profitability of the venture. Corporations seek the ablest candidates for these highly leveraged positions and are willing to pay a hefty price for them.

An economist under the influence of the human capital metaphor might ask, Why not save money by hiring two mediocre people to fill that position instead of paying the exorbitant salary required to attract the best? Although that sort of substitution might work with physical capital, it does not necessarily work with human capital. Two average surgeons or CEOs or novelists or quarterbacks are often a poor substitute for a single gifted one.

For positions in which additional talent has great value to the employer or the marketplace, there is no reason to expect that the market will compensate individuals in proportion to their human capital. For these positions—ones that confer the greatest leverage or "amplification" of human talent (Rosen 1986)—small increments of talent have great value and may be greatly rewarded as a result of the normal competitive market process.

Given a choice, most workers naturally prefer jobs that provide high leverage for their talents. The high salaries that accompany these positions, after all, are a form of economic rent. But since leverage, like most other things, is a relative concept, the jobs that provide maximal leverage are inherently limited in number. Their lucrative nature assures that they will attract a surfeit of ostensibly well-qualified applicants.

If the characteristics that define individual productivity were observable at a glance, employers could simply choose the best applicants and be done. But ability and talent are of course not easily measured. The result is intense competition among the most talented and well-trained workers for the right to occupy the economy's most leveraged positions. Philip Cook and I use the term "winner-take-all markets" to describe the markets for these positions, including the entry-level and intermediate-level positions through which the candidates for highly leveraged positions must pass.

The winner-take-all model suggests that we view the labor market for the most leveraged positions as a tournament. The underlying rationale for this conceptualization, however, is different from the one described in the tournament literature in labor economics (Lazear and Rosen 1981; Rosen 1986). Authors of that literature see tournament payoff schemes as devices purposely constructed by employers to elicit additional effort under conditions in which standard incentives might otherwise lead employees to shirk. The winner-take-all model, by contrast, views the tournament payoff scheme as a natural consequence of competition to fill highly leveraged positions.

The contests for these positions typically involve a succession of trials. The aspiring major league baseball player, for example, starts with T-ball, moves on to Little League and then, if he shows enough talent and determination, to Babe Ruth League. Only the best from Babe Ruth League can hope to start for the most competitive high school teams and, among those, only a fraction go on to the minor leagues, where formidable hurdles remain before landing a shot at the majors. Even then, most players who make it onto a major league roster ultimately fail to land a starting berth, and only a small fraction of starters go on to become stars.

Competition for the most highly leveraged positions in other sectors of the economy is no less intense. For example, the multimillion-dollar salaries of Wall Street investment bankers have stimulated thousands of highly qualified young people to apply for each entry-level position in investment banking firms. These firms obviously cannot review each application in detail. Instead, they use a handful of salient characteristics—such as grades or the quality of the undergraduate institution—to screen out candidates who fail to meet certain thresholds.

According to one account, 40 percent of Yale's 1986 graduating class, many with top grades and clear records of achievement outside the classroom, interviewed for a position with First Boston (Lewis 1989, 24). Many outstanding graduates of lesser-ranked schools now fail even to land an interview with the elite firms that control access to the most highly leveraged positions. As Philip Cook and I have shown elsewhere, the contest for these positions has increasingly become a contest for admission to the nation's most prestigious colleges and universities (see Frank and Cook 1995, ch. 8; see also Brinton and Kariya, this volume).

Winning the lead in the high school play does not assure one of a career as a leading film star, any more than winning a first-round match at Wimbledon assures one of going on to become the champion. Similarly, being chosen for a high-profile entry-level position provides no guarantee of one going on to occupy one of the economy's most highly leveraged positions. As at Wimbledon, however, success in the early rounds of the tournament for these positions is *necessary* for success in the later rounds. It is almost certain, for example, that many of the applicants who failed to land associates' positions in the leading Wall Street law firms were just as well-qualified as those who did; and yet their very failure to land those positions all but assures that they will not go on to become partners in the leading firms.

To recapitulate briefly, the winner-take-all perspective envisions a limited number of highly leveraged positions atop the economic pyramid and an increasingly well-ordered hierarchy of jobs that lead to those top positions. The rents that accrue to incumbents in the top positions are often large and attract large numbers of highly qualified persons to the contests for entry-level and subsequent positions. At each stage of this tournament, employers must choose among large numbers of highly qualified candidates for promotion to the next round. Candidates passed over at any stage, even if they are just as qualified as those who were chosen, essentially *become* less qualified by virtue of not having been chosen, since eligibility for further promotion is contingent on the opportunities to learn and demonstrate competence at the next level.

Consider the implications of this process for the competitive viability of a firm that discriminates against members of a specific group in its selection and promotion criteria in the entry-level round. Suppose, for the sake of argument, that the hiring committees of most investment banks discriminate in favor of male applicants for their entry-level financial analysts' positions. Confronted with a female candidate with truly outstanding credentials, they will make her an offer. But when filling in the lower reaches of their entry-level class, they favor males over seemingly equally qualified females.

In the standard labor market model, such firms should end up with lower-quality workers, which in turn should compromise their ability to compete with rivals who hire on the basis of talent alone. Things are different, however, in markets for entry-level jobs on the career paths leading to highly leveraged positions. As we have seen, because the top positions to which they lead command such large rents, these entry-level jobs attract an abundance of highly qualified applicants. Even among "highly qualified" applicants, of course, some are clearly more qualified than others. At the head of the applicant queue are the obvious stars, those whose prospects for success are so clear that virtually all firms will actively recruit them, even to the point of offering generous signing bonuses. But given that all employers are actively recruiting the same pool of star applicants, no firm can expect to fill all its entry-level positions by making offers only to stars. It must also dip into the second tier of applicants, and here it is much more difficult to identify which individuals will succeed. As the firm works its way down its applicant pool, it typically reaches a point at which it has essentially no objective basis for believing one applicant more likely to succeed than another.

Having reached that point, an employer is then in a position to discriminate on the basis of characteristics that are not related to productivity. If the firm is hiring from that part of its applicant pool in which it is unable to rank individuals with respect to their respective probabilities of success, its performance will not be compromised if it arbitrarily chooses, say, only Irish applicants, or only male applicants, or only white applicants. Nor, by the same reasoning, would its performance be compromised if affirmative action guidelines led it to favor women and minorities at this stage of its hiring process.

In the worst case, even if discriminatory hiring did reduce the quality of entry-level workers slightly, the competitive penalty would be relatively small. The entry-level jobs themselves, after all, are not highly leveraged. The firm's competitive position might be threatened, of course, if quality were to fall in the more leveraged positions further up the career path. But since attrition rates at each promotion step are high, even a firm that arbitrarily passed over half its initial applicant pool would still have many qualified people it could promote to the second level.[2] Beyond the first level, then, not even a small quality deficit would persist.

Note, however, the implications of the assumed pattern for male-female earnings differentials. To the extent that they are hired into entry-level jobs leading to highly leveraged positions, females will tend to earn the same salaries as males. But the assumed pattern of discrimination translates into a reduced number of females being hired into entry-level jobs. Thus, even if promotion out of entry-level jobs in based strictly on merit, males will continue to be overrepresented at each successive level. Because salaries take a quantum jump each time a worker survives an additional round of the winner-take-all tournament, the average earnings premium for males will continue to grow as the tournament proceeds, even if promotion at every stage is completely meritocratic.

How does the assumed discrimination against females in entry-level hiring decisions affect the lifetime trajectory of earnings differentials between the sexes? If fewer females are accepted for entry-level jobs leading to the most highly leveraged jobs, relatively more females must seek employment elsewhere. In practical terms, this means that females who might have been hired in an entry-level job leading to one of the most highly leveraged positions will end up in an entry-level job leading to a less highly leveraged position. At each stage on the latter career path, the skills she acquires will be worth less than the skills she would have acquired on the former one. So in a proximate sense, much of the accumulating earnings deficit she will experience is the result of the fact that her human capital grows progressively less valuable relative to that of her male counterpart who was chosen for the favored entry-level job. Yet the entire earnings deficit might be more accurately attributed to the single act of employer discrimination she suffered at the entry level.

The winner-take-all model is thus compatible with persistent earnings differentials grounded in employer discrimination. Earlier we saw that the standard competitive model is not. What accounts for this difference? It does not lie with any assumed lack of competition in winner-take-all markets. Indeed, the result would not be changed even if employers could enter and leave winner-take-all markets costlessly and instantaneously. The driving force behind the difference is that highly leveraged positions command large rents, which means that employers confront excess demands for the entry-level jobs leading to these positions. And with so many highly qualified applicants to choose from at this stage, employers have latitude to discriminate if they choose to.

If employers confront excess demand for entry-level positions, why don't they simply lower the wage rates for these positions? For the same reason that Harvard doesn't reduce its tuition in response to the fact that it rejects four applicants for each one it accepts. When quality matters, the firm benefits from the existence of excess demand because this enables it to be more selective. Suppose, for example, that Morgan Stanley were to cut its entry-level salary by 10 percent relative to the other prestigious investment banks in New York. It would still attract many applicants, possibly even sufficiently many that it could still hire a highly qualified entry-level class. But the applicants with the strongest credentials—those who can be sure of drawing offers from many employers—would have no reason to accept a pay cut. And in many industries, especially management consulting and investment banking, employers want the candidates with the strongest credentials even if, in some objective sense, those with weaker credentials are equally talented. These employers, after all, depend on perceptions of quality, which in turn depend as much or more on credentials as on objective reality. The client has little objective basis for assessing whether the advice of a consultant is sound, especially in the short run. But it is easy to observe that the consultant has an honors degree from an elite institution of higher learning. And if the firms whose employees have the best credentials get the best contracts and hence acquire the most valuable experience, then the employees with the best credentials soon *become* the most qualified, even in strictly objective terms.

We should stress that our view of labor markets as winner-take-all tournaments does not, by itself, provide any motive for employers to discriminate in their hiring for entry-level positions. It merely suggests that they may have the opportunity to do so with only negligible risk to their competitive position.

Nor does our view imply that there are no forces that might penalize the firm that discriminated in its entry-level hiring decisions. As we saw earlier, even such firms have a powerful interest in recruiting the candidates with the strongest credentials, irrespective of race or sex. If discrimination is to be viable under competition it must be confined to the marginal members of the entering class. Yet social forces might militate against such a strategy. Thus, the candidates with the strongest credentials might be reluctant to join a firm that discriminated against relatively less-qualified women and minorities. The extent to which such social forces might constrain discrimination remains an empirical question.

SOME TESTABLE PREDICTIONS OF THE THEORY

The winner-take-all model offers a number of testable predictions about observable events in the labor market. For example, it implies that discrimination, if it exists, will tend to be concentrated on the marginal members of the entry-level class. This, in turn, suggests that those members of the less-favored groups who are hired will tend to be well above average in terms of their observable qualifications. And if observable qualifications are correlated with total qualifications, this suggests the following contrarian prediction: promotion rates for members of less-favored groups will tend to be higher than those for favored groups. Of course, any attempt to test this prediction empirically would have to grapple with other factors that might affect promotion rates. For example, the female associates of top law firms might, on average, be more talented than their male counterparts and yet be less likely to be promoted because family commitments make them less willing to put in eighty-hour workweeks.[3]

Another prediction of the model is that the earnings differential between favored groups and others will be larger along winner-take-all career paths than along the career paths envisioned in standard labor market models, where discrimination should be strongly constrained by competitive forces. It predicts as well that the earnings differential will be small or zero in entry-level jobs but will grow larger as career trajectories unfold.

The winner-take-all model also suggests that the ultimate size of discrimination-based earnings differentials will be positively related to the degree of leverage embodied in the top positions in the labor market. Elsewhere, Cook and I have argued that the information revolution and other changes have caused this leverage to grow sharply over the past several decades (Frank and Cook 1995). Just as the compact disc has enabled the world's best soprano to serve a broader market, similar developments in other areas have enabled top performers to extend their reach. Other things equal, these changes imply greater latitude for discrimination in entry-level jobs leading to the most highly leveraged positions. (But other things, of course, have not been equal during this period, which has also seen the implementation of affirmative action legislation and increased informal social pressure to achieve greater workforce diversity.)

A PRELIMINARY EMPIRICAL TEST

In this section, I report the results of a preliminary attempt to test the prediction that unexplained male-female earnings differentials will be small or zero in entry-level jobs. In this test I make use of data from an employment survey of late 1980s graduates of Cornell University's College of Arts and Sciences. This survey provides information on the current activities of respondents nine months after their graduation. For those who were gainfully employed, the survey recorded information on annual salary, job title, and the name and location of employer. Taking special steps to protect the anonymity of respondents, I was able to match the individual survey response forms with the college transcript of each respondent. Thus, unlike standard employment survey data sets, my data make it possible to control for the respondent's degree field as well as for a rich variety of other details related to academic performance. And since almost all of these data pertain to first jobs, I have access to almost as much information as did the employers who did the actual hiring. I am aware of no other data source that permits a detailed examination of the determinants of entry-level salaries for such a homogeneous sample.

My first step was to calculate the gross earnings differential between men and women in the sample who were employed full-time in the year following graduation. To do this, I regressed the natural logarithm of annual salary, measured in 1986 dollars, against a constant term and a dummy variable that took the value of 1 for male and 0 for female. As the coefficient for the male dummy in table 9.1 shows, men in the Cornell sample earned almost 14 percent more than women. For this sample, we can reject the null hypothesis that sex has no influence on earnings at conventional significance levels.

My next step was to control for as many factors other than gender as might reasonably be expected to influence earnings. The regression results shown in table 9.2 include the following control variables: the numbers of mathematics, science, economics, and business courses taken; cumulative undergraduate grade

Table 9.1   Gross Male-Female Earnings Differential in the Cornell Sample

Dependent Variable: Natural Logarithm of Salary
$R^2 = 2.4\%$ $R^2(\text{adjusted}) = 2.2\%$
$s = 0.4486$ with $680 - 2 = 678$ degrees of freedom

Source	Sum of Squares	df	Mean Square	F-ratio
Regression	3.29545	1	3.2955	16.4
Residual	136.444	678	0.201245	

Variable	Coefficient	s.e. of Coeff	t-ratio	
Constant	9.77481	0.0238	411	
Male	0.139384	0.0344	4.05	

Table 9.2   Net Male-Female Earnings Differential in the Cornell Sample

Dependent Variable: Natural Logarithm of Salary
$R^2 = 38.6\%$ $R^2(\text{adjusted}) = 37.2\%$
$s = 0.3596$ with $680 - 17 = 663$ degrees of freedom

Source	Sum of Squares	df	Mean Square	F-ratio
Regression	53.9990	16	3.375	26.1
Residual	85.7403	663	0.129322	

Variable	Coefficient	s.e. of Coeff	t-ratio
Constant	9.83066	0.1311	75.0
Male	0.035003	0.0290	1.21
Math	0.020190	0.0031	6.51
Science	−0.001513	0.0027	−0.558
Economics	0.009255	0.0046	2.03
Business	0.027121	0.0087	3.11
GPA	−0.012217	0.0359	−0.340
Profit	0.039890	0.0464	0.860
Government	0.00	—	—
Nonprofit	−0.282060	0.0504	−5.60
Occupational Social Responsibility			
OSR < −1	0.135668	0.0526	2.58
−1<OSR<−.5	−0.062383	0.0470	−1.33
−.5<OSR<.5	0.00	—	—
.5<OSR<1	−0.252458	0.0820	−3.08
OSR>1	−0.294529	0.0559	−5.27
Employer Social Responsibility			
ESR<−.5	0.120664	0.0492	2.45
−.5<ESR<.5	0.00	—	—
ESR>.5	−0.068348	0.0843	−0.810
Unmeasured OSR	−0.080600	0.0374	−2.15
Unmeasured ESR	−0.075870	0.0393	−1.93

point average; dummies for employment in the profit, nonprofit, and government sectors; and dummies indicating an outside panel's evaluation of the degree of social or moral satisfaction that accompanies work in specific occupations and for specific employers.[4]

As the regression coefficients in table 9.2 indicate, salaries are positively and significantly associated with the number of courses taken in business, economics, and mathematics. Business courses had the largest association, followed by economics and math. Surprisingly, the number of science courses taken was weakly negatively associated with starting salaries, but this effect was not statistically significant at conventional levels. Perhaps even more surprising, grade point average was also weakly negatively associated with starting salaries, but here too the effect was not statistically significant.[5]

Employment in the government sector is the reference category in table 9.2, which means that the coefficients for the profit and nonprofit variables represent deviations from that category. Thus, a person employed by a private, for-profit firm earns almost 4 percent more than she would if she were employed by government, whereas a person working for a nonprofit firm earns more than 28 percent less.

For both the occupational social responsibility (OSR) and employer social responsibility (ESR) variables, entries in the interval $(-.5,.5)$ were designated as the reference category. Coefficients on the remaining categories are interpreted as the fractional salary deviations from their respective reference categories. Thus, for example, employees in the occupations rated most socially responsible $(OSR>1)$ earned almost 30 percent less than did otherwise similar workers whose occupations were rated between $-.5$ and $.5$. Those in the occupations rated least socially responsible $(OSR<-1)$ earned almost 14 percent more than those in the reference category. The coefficients on the employer social responsibility (ESR) variables were less extreme, but here too the salary differential between categories at the opposite end of the spectrum was both large and statistically significant.

As the coefficient on the male dummy in table 9.2 indicates, the effect of controlling for these other factors is that males earn only 3.5 percent more than females in this sample. Given that this estimate is only slightly larger than its standard error, it seems fair to say that, for this sample, there is essentially no remaining earnings differential between the sexes.

The empirical results reported in table 9.2 are consistent with the hypothesis that there will be no male-female earnings differentials in entry-level jobs once we control for other relevant determinants of earnings. But these results are of course silent on whether the hypothesized effects of discrimination will be observed as the career paths of these workers unfold through time.

CONCLUSION

In traditional competitive labor markets, employer discrimination cannot be a source of persistent earnings differentials unless owners are willing to suffer large losses to support their taste for hiring favored groups. In winner-take-all markets, by contrast, differentials due to employer discrimination can persist, even under the most bitterly competitive conditions. This can happen because the large rents associated with highly leveraged positions attract a surfeit of highly qualified applicants for the entry-level jobs that lead to these positions. But even in winner-take-all markets, competition forces firms to hire on merit alone when dealing with candidates with the strongest credentials. The theory predicts that if discrimination does exist, it will be focused on the least well-qualified candidates among each entering cohort. Although the effects of discrimination are expected to be very small at the entry level, they may grow considerably larger as time passes.

Is the winner-take-all phenomenon confined to the upper reaches of the labor market? Cook and I have found that although it is strongest there, qualitatively similar forces appear to be at work further down the income ladder (see Frank and Cook 1995, ch. 5). Even among jobs that pay modestly, some have more leverage than others, and there often appear to be equilibrium queues of ostensibly qualified applicants for the relatively good jobs. Where such queues exist, firms have latitude to discriminate.

I thank Mary Brinton for helpful comments on an earlier draft.

NOTES

1. Consider the case of a nondiscriminating firm that hires labor in a competitive market at an annual wage rate w, and that can borrow at the annual interest rate r. If L denotes this firm's employment level, and K the size of its capital stock, and these are its only factors of production, then its total costs, TC, are given by

$$TC = wL + rK.$$

Suppose that $r = .10$ and that labor costs are 70 percent of total costs. Then

$$TC = 0.7\ TC + 0.1K,$$

from which it follows that $K = 3TC$.

   Now consider a firm identical to the one above except that it hires only Ms and pays them 110 percent of the competitive wage level. Let Π denote the economic loss it sustains as a result of its discrimination. To calculate Π, note first that the discriminator's total revenue (which will be the same as the nondiscriminator's total costs, TC) will equal its total costs minus its economic loss. Thus we solve

$$(1.1)(0.7)TC + (0.1)3TC + \Pi = TR = TC$$

for Π, which yields $\Pi = -0.07\ TC$. Suppose half of the firm's capital stock (1.5TC) is owned by stockholders, the other half financed by loans. Its rate of return will then be the sum of the competitive return on capital ($0.10 \times 1.5\ TC = 0.15\ TC$) and its negative economic profit ($-0.07\ TC$) divided by the capital it owns (1.5 TC), which yields 0.08 TC/1.5 TC $\approx$ 0.53, or 47 percent less than the competitive rate of return.

2. Many occupations have internal labor markets in which incumbent employees are more or less assured of an orderly sequence of promotions for as long as they remain with their employers. But in those occupations with the highest rewards at the top—elite consulting, law, investment banking, professional sports, entertainment, and others—the attrition rates between entry- and higher-level positions are almost invariably high.

3. See Landers, Rebitzer, and Taylor (1996) for a discussion of why law firms rely heavily on weekly hours in their promotion decisions.

4. See Frank (1996) for a detailed description of the social satisfaction evaluations.

5. Ashenfelter and Mooney (1968) found that academic performance also did little to explain earnings differentials among Woodrow Wilson Fellows from Princeton. These negative science and GPA coefficients almost certainly do not imply that taking an extra science course or having higher grades will actually cause a worker's starting salary to go down. A more plausible account is that people in the sample who took more science courses or earned higher grades were for some other reasons led to choose jobs with slightly lower starting salaries. In support of this interpretation, we observe that sample members who chose jobs in the nonprofit sector had an overall grade point average of 3.14, as compared with 3.09 for those who chose jobs in the for-profit sector. Similarly, those who chose jobs in the nonprofit sector had an average of 1.05 fewer math courses, 2.4 fewer economics courses, and 1.5 fewer business courses—but almost five more science courses—than did those who chose jobs in the for-profit sector. Another possible interpretation, supported by the findings of at least two other studies, is that a significant positive correlation between academic performance and earnings does not show up until several years after graduation (see, for example, Sharp 1970; Hauser and Daymont 1977).

REFERENCES

Aigner, Dennis, and Glen Cain. 1977. "Statistical Theories of Discrimination in Labor Markets." *Industrial and Labor Relations Review* 30 (January): 175–87.

Ashenfelter, Orley, and J. Mooney. 1968. "Graduate Education, Ability, and Earnings." *Review of Economics and Statistics* 50 (1): 78–86.

Becker, Gary S. 1985. "Human Capital, Effort, and the Sexual Division of Labor." *Journal of Labor Economics* 3 (January): S33–58.

———. 1975. *Human Capital*. 2d ed. Chicago, Ill.: University of Chicago Press.

Bielby, William T., and Denise D. Bielby. 1992. "I Will Follow Him: Family Ties, Gender Role Beliefs, and Reluctance to Relocate for a Better Job." *American Journal of Sociology* 97 (March): 1241–67.

Blau, Francine D., and Marianne Ferber. 1992. *The Economics of Women, Men, and Work*. 2d ed. Englewood Cliffs, N.J.: Prentice Hall.

Blau, Francine D., and Lawrence Kahn. 1992. "Race and Gender Pay Differentials." In David Lewin, Olivia S. Mitchell, and Peter D. Scherer, eds., *Research Frontiers in Industrial Relations and Human Resources*, Madison, Wis.: Industrial Relations Research Association.

Card, David, and Alan Krueger. 1992. "Does School Quality Matter? Returns to Education and the Characteristics of Public Schools in the United States." *Journal of Political Economy* 100 (February): 1–40.

Frank, Robert H. 1978. "Why Women Earn Less: The Theory and Estimation of Differential Overqualification." *American Economic Review* 68 (June): 360–73.

———. 1996. "What Price the Moral High Ground?" *Southern Economic Journal* 63 (July): 1–17.

Frank, Robert H., and Philip J. Cook. 1995. *The Winner-Take-All Society*. New York: Martin Kessler Books at the Free Press.

Handy, Femida. 1995. "Wage Differentials in the Nonprofit Sector: A Resolution of the Principal-Agent Problem." Department of Economics, York University. Mimeograph.

Hauser, Robert, and Thomas Daymont. 1977. "Schooling, Ability, and Earnings: Cross-Sectional Findings 8 to 14 Years After High School Graduation." *Sociology of Education* 50 (2): 182–205.

Juhn, Chinhui, Kevin M. Murphy, and Brooks Pierce. 1991. "Accounting for the Slowdown in Black-White Wage Convergence." In Marvin H. Kosters, ed., *Workers and Their Wages*, Washington, D.C.: AEI Press.

Kahn, Lawrence. 1991. "Customer Discrimination and Affirmative Action." *Economic Inquiry* 29 (July): 555–71.

Landers, Renee M., James B. Rebitzer, and Lowell J. Taylor. 1996. "Rat Race Redux: Adverse Selection in the Determination of Work Hours in Law Firms." *American Economic Review* 86 (3): 329–48.

Lazear, Edward, and Sherwin Rosen. 1981. "Rank-order Tournaments as Optimal Labor Contracts. *Journal of Political Economy* 89 (5): 841–64.

———. 1990. "Male-Female Wage Differentials in Job Ladders." *Journal of Labor Economics* 8 (January): S106–23.

Lewis, Michael. 1989. *Liar's Poker*. New York: W. W. Norton.

Lundberg, Shelly, and Richard Startz. 1983. "Private Discrimination and Social Intervention in Competitive Labor Markets." *American Economic Review* 73 (June): 340–47.

Marini, Margaret Mooney, and Pi-Ling Fan. 1997. "The Gender Gap in Earnings at Career Entry," *American Sociological Review* 62: 588–604.

Mincer, Jacob. 1978. "Family Migration Decisions." *Journal of Political Economy* 86: 749–75.

Mincer, Jacob, and Solomon Polachek. 1974. "Family Investments in Human Capital: Earnings of Women." *Journal of Political Economy* 82 (March): S76–108.

Polachek, S. W. 1975. "Discontinuous Labor Force Participation and Its Effects on Women's Market Earnings." In Cynthia B. Lloyd, ed., *Sex Discrimination and the Division of Labor*. New York: Columbia University Press.

Rosen, Sherwin B. "Prizes and Incentives in Elimination Tournaments." 1986. *American Economic Review* 76 (September): 701–16.

Sharp, L. M. 1970. *Education and Employment: The Early Years of College Graduates*. Baltimore, Md.: Johns Hopkins University Press.

10

Institutions and the Labor Market

Bruce Western

E conomic theories often take an ahistorical view of labor markets. In some analyses, labor is exchanged for wages in competitive markets much like other commodities. If unions are considered, imperfect competition models are applied just as they would be to other settings where the seller has monopoly power. The historical context of social conflict that attends empirical labor markets is neglected and the economic theories claim broad generality, independent of time and place.

In this chapter, I offer an alternative, institutional, approach to the labor market. In this approach, social conflict is a pervasive feature of the employment relationship. This conflict is crystallized in historically specific institutional arrangements that shape the offer of wages for labor. Highly abstracted metaphors, such as competitive markets or union monopoly, have little descriptive utility when it comes to this distinctive commodity. Instead of viewing labor markets as generic forums for wage-labor exchanges, I treat them as highly differentiated institutional settings. The employment relationship is secured in a wide variety of ways because its institutional surroundings show such great variation.

In sociology's rich tradition of labor market research, recent developments have focused on the role of nonmarket process (Kerckhoff 1995). Studies of social networks, firms, and discrimination point to sociological mechanisms that add realism to the abstracted labor markets of economic theory. In the network approach, labor market transactions flow through interpersonal connections rather than through atomized and anonymous market actors (Granovetter 1995). Organizational perspectives on the labor market emphasize how firms affect the distribution of jobs and pay (Baron 1984). Work on sex discrimination finds persistent differences in earnings and earnings growth between men and women even after accounting for characteristics of workers and their jobs (England 1992). Research in all these areas sees labor markets as embedded in a rich social context consisting of social ties, organizations, and disparities in social power.

The institutional approach to labor markets expands and encompasses other sociological analysis. It expands by identifying another group of nonmarket processes that significantly influence the allocation of jobs and pay. It encompasses other analyses by specifying the conditions under which networks, firms, employer bias, and the market conditions of economic theory allocate labor market rewards. Institutional analysis is fundamental in this way because it is, above all, contextual analysis. Institutional analysis identifies the background rules and norms that enable the markets to operate. A classical statement of this idea is given by Schumpeter (1954, 34) in describing his "sociology of economics": "The historical nature of the economic process unquestionably limits the scope of general concepts. . . ." Consequently our theories of economic processes "work out differently in different institutional conditions. . . ."

This institutional reasoning applied to the labor market runs as follows. Historically, labor markets grew out of political conflicts between emergent classes of owners and workers. These conflicts vitally affected relations of cooperation and conflict among workers. The resulting rules that regulated the exchange of wages for labor provided a durable expression of the balance of power in these struggles. In some countries, institutions emerged that provided broad, class-wide, representation of workers and owners. In others, rules for labor market representation encouraged fragmented organization. The impact of institutions on competitive relationships between labor market actors has consequences for the allocation of jobs and pay. Where principles of class-wide representation were only weakly inscribed on the labor market institutions, collective action among workers was costly, and intense labor market competition fueled inequality. Where the labor market was embedded in broad representative institutions for workers and owners, wages and employment were more equally distributed and collective action flourished.

I illustrate these ideas by focusing on the industrial relations of contemporary capitalism. In the advanced capitalist labor markets, institutional contexts differ in their degree of centralization. In some West European countries, the labor market is largely concentrated into a single transaction between national representatives of workers and employers. In the decentralized institutional contexts of North America, wage-labor exchanges are much more uncoordinated. Institutionalized variability in centralization is important for understanding labor market outcomes for three reasons. First, labor market institutions affect the size of the social pie and its distribution. Second, institutions filter the effects of exogenous conditions on wages and employment. The effects of these conditions thus depend on the institutional context. Third, institutions affect the formation of actors that negotiate the price of labor. To illustrate these arguments, I draw on research examining the performance of labor markets in the last two decades in the advanced capitalist countries.

These ideas about institutional effects suggest three general lessons that might apply to other topics in an institutional economic sociology. Research in the institutional approach is: (1) comparative, (2) contextual, and (3) focuses on collective action. Comparative research is necessary to observe institutional variation. Contextual research highlights how the microprocesses of markets depend on the institutional setting. Finally, because of the formative impact of institutions on collective actors, collective action itself becomes a key research problem. This last point suggests that the empirical range of labor market sociology can be expanded to include processes of unionization and strike action whose study has been traditionally dominated by labor economists and industrial relations specialists. While sociologists of the labor market have focused largely on status attainment and inequality, the institutionally conditional impact of economic forces on collective action is also drawn within the scope of economic sociology.

PROPERTY RIGHTS AND INSTITUTIONS

Labor markets are different from other sorts of markets. A distinctive structural feature of labor markets is the asymmetric dependency of sellers (workers) on buyers (employers). Workers' livelihoods are intimately connected to maintaining an employment relationship with their employer. Unemployment for a worker usually involves substantial loss of income, at least temporarily. The costs of finding a new job can also be high. Employers are not so dependent on any particular worker. If a worker leaves a firm, the employer's livelihood is not threatened to the same degree by the job loss. The firm will continue to generate revenue because of the contributions of the employer and other workers. If a worker leaves a firm, the employer may even substitute capital for the worker's labor. Unlike workers, employers can also hedge against the risk of lost employment by diversifying their investment. Because of the asymmetric dependence of workers on employers, the formal equality of buyers and sellers in exchange provides a poor description of the relative standing of the two parties to the employment contract. Instead, the employment relationship expresses a power relationship in which the costs to workers of lost employment are generally far higher than for employers.

Many theorists have observed that labor markets are unusual in this way. The distinctiveness of labor as a commodity is a building block of the Marxist understanding of the capitalist economy: labor is an unusual commodity because it is inseparable from its seller, the worker. Marx thus makes the classic distinction between labor (work done) and labor power (the capacity to do work). The same distinction drives neoclassical analysis of the agency problems of the firm (Alchian and Demsetz 1972). In this analysis, workers act as employers' agents and employers' property rights in labor cannot be completely specified. Employers cannot fully control workers by contract, so they adopt nonmarket strategies to extract work effort. For much Marxist and neoclassical research on labor markets, this is the central analytical insight. Capitalist labor markets share the invariant structural feature that labor is inseparable from its seller. Alienation and agency problems follow.

For the institutional approach to labor markets, this structural feature is the starting point for analysis. Because workers generally depend more on individual employers than employers depend on individual workers, and the employment contract thus expresses a power relationship, the labor market is a political as well as an economic forum. The terms under which wages are exchanged for labor has been the object of a relentless contest between more or less organized social groups. This contest is not just empirical noise added to the ideal type of labor market structure. Rather, the political conflict over the earliest exchange of wages for labor is a constitutive feature of capitalist labor markets rooted in the unusual characteristics of the labor commodity.

This is where institutions come in. From their formation in British crafts and agriculture in the sixteenth and seventeenth centuries, labor markets have been the focus of political struggles. At issue in these struggles was the regulatory framework that would govern how workers sold their labor. Historically, the outcomes of these struggles were highly variable, and this is reflected in the rich institutional variability of contemporary employment relations. Empirical labor markets can accordingly be understood as heterogeneous institutional forums—the current culmination of a long process of political struggle.

The link between political conflict and the institutional origins of labor markets can be seen in the Webbs' classic account (1920) of the emergence of the earliest capitalist labor markets in the craft industries of late medieval Britain. In Britain, Parliament assumed a broad responsibility for guaranteeing workers a "competent livelihood" as early as 1563 with the enactment of the Statute of Artificers. The statute regulated apprenticeships and set wage rates in crafts. Combinations of journeymen in clothing and textile industries asserted rights under the statute in petitions to the Crown and the House of Commons throughout the seventeenth and eighteenth centuries. In response to further petitions of operatives, other legislation was periodically passed in the House throughout the first half of the eighteenth century, adjusting wages and extending apprenticeship rules to other crafts. In the latter half of the eighteenth century, master craftsmen moved to force down wages, employ unskilled workers, and generally undo the regulations imposed by the legislation. This exposed the skilled craftsmen to the wage competition of unskilled workers. The beginnings of the factory movement introduced the earliest deregulation of wages and employment, in the Woollen Cloth Weavers' Act of 1756. The Weavers' Act was followed by the abandonment of wage rates in a variety of other textile industries and the progressive influx of unapprenticed laborers. The expansion of trade unions to include unskilled workers from the 1830s and 1840s onward initiated another wave of institutional change. This time, factory legislation renewed restrictions on the free allocation of labor by owners for the next forty years.

Polanyi ([1944] 1957, 145–50) tells a similar story in which the birth of the British labor market was marked by the Poor Law Reform of 1834 that repealed wage subsidies for the working poor. He likens the emergence of British labor markets and the subsequent protective legislation of the late 1800s to a "double movement." First came market creation with the Poor Law Reform; then came social protection in the Factory Acts and other social legislation. For the Webbs however, Polanyi's double movement did not unfold through the nineteenth century one stage after another. In the Webbs' account, the institutional emergence of the British labor market was incremental and uneven, propelled by the contingent outcomes of collective action. From this perspective, early British labor markets were fashioned in collective struggles between masters and journeymen over the institutional determination of wages.

The broad empirical claim of my institutional approach is that such organized social conflict not only describes the origins of labor markets but leaves a long-lasting institutional footprint. When it comes to labor markets, there is no pre-institutional state of nature, either theoretically or historically. Because institutions are analytically and empirically fundamental, ostensibly general theories can be understood to operate under specific, often unstated, institutional conditions. As we will see below, competitive models of the labor market that underpin neoclassical accounts of unemployment may only apply in a handful of the contemporary capitalist democracies. Many empirical employment regimes have few competitive features, and market mechanisms simply do not operate. A clear example is given by the strong collective bargaining systems of Western Europe. In these cases, theories of union monopoly may seem more appropriate, but even these explanations are wrong in their most basic predictions about the distribution of earnings and employment. Despite the importance of historical contingency in labor market analysis, the situation is not hopelessly ideographic. Institutional theories provide a systematic way of describing this contextual variability and explaining its effects on collective action and on the allocation of pay and jobs. The following section shows how labor markets depend on historically formed institutional settings.

LABOR MARKET INSTITUTIONS

As the preceding historical sketch suggests, a central dilemma for workers in the long historical development of capitalist labor markets involves whether to compete against each other to secure individual gains or to cooperate for collective gains. The resolution of this dilemma depends on prior institutional conditions and is expressed in subsequent institutional regulation. By structuring the relations of labor market competition and cooperation, institutions have far-reaching effects on labor market allocation and collective action.

What exactly are labor market institutions? *Labor market institutions are the enduring legal and normative frameworks that establish how the price of labor is determined.* Thus, the Elizabethan legislation was an important institutional feature of the early British labor markets that established a floor below which wages were prevented from falling. This institutional setting was progressively augmented by rules of collective bargaining and wage regulation throughout the nineteenth and twentieth centuries (Fox 1985).

In the contemporary capitalist societies of Western Europe and North America, sociologists, economists, and political scientists have described institutional variation in terms of the centralization of labor market regulation (Goldthorpe 1984; Calmfors and Driffill 1988; Cameron 1984). The U.S. institutional setting lies at one end of this continuum. In the United States, wage determination is decentralized and features the piecemeal negotiation of individual employment contracts largely in the absence of union representation or legislated wage setting. In the union sector of the economy, collective bargaining is chiefly conducted in individual plants and enterprises. At the other end of the continuum, wages in Scandinavia and Austria have been centrally determined in collective bargaining systems that involve national representatives of employers and unions. Under these institutional conditions, national or industry agreements shape pay rises and working conditions.

Institutional centralization of labor markets influences labor market outcomes by shaping the competitive relationships among workers. Institutions can pit workers against one another or facilitate mobilization in pursuit of collective goals. Through the central regulation of wages, highly regulated labor markets restrict price competition. Workers are institutionally precluded from bidding up wages beyond the centrally agreed level when the demand for labor is strong and constrained from underbidding when demand is weak. Decentralized institutional settings, on the other hand, provide the conditions for competition among workers. Wages in decentralized labor markets show greater variation in response to demand, reflecting variability in workers' productivity and employers' discrimination.

In the literature on corporatism, researchers have tried to quantify the institutional centralization of labor markets by grading the level of collective bargaining or by ranking the powers of central union confederations over union affiliates. Typically, focus on the level of collective bargaining yields some variant on a three-category scheme distinguishing countries with: (1) strong systems of national bargaining between union confederations and national employer associations, (2) industry bargaining between industrial unions and industry-level employer representatives, and (3) bargaining within enterprises between employers and local unions or individual workers. Examination of union confederation power distinguishes organizations with influence over collective bargaining and strikes from those that divest these powers to union affiliates. Table 10.1 shows a selection of these measures for a number of OECD (Organization for Economic Cooperation and Development) countries. The first two columns report measures of the levels of collective bargaining and the power of central union confederations. The third and fourth columns report more general measures of corporatism or labor market centralization. These measures, in columns (3) and (4), combine information about confederation power and bargaining level. Clearly, the level of collective bargaining and the power of the union confederation are closely related. This makes good organizational sense, as credible bargaining by union confederations depends on their capacity to commit union affiliates to central agreements.

The empirical importance of this variation in labor market institutions can be seen in light of the performance of the advanced capitalist labor markets over the

Table 10.1 A Summary of Rankings of Measures of Corporatist Bargaining in Eighteen Advanced Capitalist Countries

	Study			
Country	(1)	(2)	(3)	(4)
Austria	1	1	1	1
Norway	1	3	4	2
Sweden	1	3	5	3
Finland	1	6	8	5
Denmark	5	7	7	4
Belgium	6	3	9	8
Netherlands	6	2	3	7
Switzerland	6	8	6	16
Australia	9	8	15	10
Germany	9	8	2	6
Italy	9	12	14	13
United Kingdom	9	12	12	12
Canada	13	12	16	18
France	13	11	13	11
United States	13	12	17	17
New Zealand	—	12	11	9
Japan	16	—	10	15

Sources: Column headings are as follows: (1) scope of centralized bargaining (Cameron 1984); (2) union centralization (Stephens 1979); (3) corporatism index (Bruno and Sachs 1985); (4) labor market centralization (Calmfors and Driffill 1988).

last two decades. From 1973, wage and employment trends in the advanced capitalist countries became quite varied. In response to the two oil price shocks, economic growth widely declined through the 1970s and 1980s. Price shocks and declining growth had widely varying effects. Unemployment rose sharply in all but a handful of countries and. remained high through the 1980s (Layard, Nickell, and Jackman 1991) and into the 1990s. While just over 10 million workers were unemployed in the OECD countries in 1973, 35 million were jobless by 1994 (OECD 1994, 1). Growth in real earnings slowed in many West European countries and throughout North America. On average, real wage growth slowed from about 3 percent a year in the 1970s to less than 1 percent annually in the 1980s (Western 1996). In several countries, sluggish wage growth was associated with steep rises in inequality (Freeman and Katz 1994).

These trends in the allocation of jobs and pay were closely related to collective action in the labor market. Workers' representation has also widely, but not universally, eroded. The American disease of union membership decline had spread through continental Europe during the 1980s, as the most active constituency of organized labor shifted from manufacturing to the public sector. In the United States, unions lost over 3 million members between 1980 and 1989, while unionization rates fell even in Scandinavia by the end of the 1980s (Visser 1991). Strike action was similarly curtailed. The volume of strikes in manufacturing declined in nearly every OECD country in the 1980s compared to the 1970s, in several cases by 20 percent or more (Shalev 1992).

In sum, both labor market performance and collective action declined through the 1970s and 1980s. Unemployment rose, wage growth slowed, union membership fell and strikes became more uncommon. These general trends however mask significant cross-national variation. In some countries, high levels of employment and earnings equality were maintained and unions remained organizationally powerful. Much of this variation in labor market outcomes is rooted in the diverse institutional contexts of the advanced capitalist countries. Three types of institutional effects are important here: (1) institutions influence the size of the social product and its distribution, (2) institutions filter the impact of exogenous market conditions, and (3) institutions are constitutive of labor market actors.

Social Welfare and Distribution

Institutions affect earnings and employment by influencing the size of total output and its distribution. Institutions are redistributive in the fundamental sense that they provide an allocation of labor and wages that is different from the one that would obtain under fully competitive markets. They influence social welfare—the size of total output—by narrowing or expanding the interests of labor market representatives. Union leaders in centralized institutional settings take a broad view of social welfare, moderating current wage demands for continued investment and low unemployment. The theoretical significance of the institutional account can be seen in contrast to standard union monopoly models of labor markets in labor economics.

In the standard economic analysis, labor unions do two bad things. They contribute to economic inequality by raising wages in the union sector and depressing wages among the unorganized. As monopolists, unions also contribute to a general decline in social welfare resulting from the rent extracted in union wage claims (Farber 1986). This may be experienced as unemployment as the price of labor in the union sector of the economy is raised above market-clearing levels.

These arguments, however, are especially puzzling in light of the comparative performance of labor markets in the last two decades. While labor markets have generally fared poorly, full employment economic growth has been best approximated in several countries with strong union movements and centralized labor market institutions. These outcomes fueled research on corporatist institutions through the 1980s. Researchers argued that in centralized labor markets, national union confederations effectively represent all workers in the labor force. As a result, they cannot externalize the employment effects of their wage demands and consequently do not act as monopolists. Instead, class-wide representation— what Olson (1982) called "encompassing organization"—provides an incentive for union leaders to restrain wage growth, making more resources available for current investment and future employment. Consistent with these ideas, comparative research shows that countries with highly centralized collective bargaining experienced relatively fast economic growth during the recessionary 1970s (Bruno and Sachs 1985; Alvarez, Garrett, and Lange 1991).

This type of argument also has implications for the relationship between labor market centralization and unemployment. Calmfors and Driffill (1988) argued that the wage moderation characteristic of centralized labor markets restricted the growth of unemployment through the 1970s and 1980s. Thus, in Austria, Norway, and Sweden, where collective bargaining was conducted at the national level, unemployment was held below 5 percent while it climbed to double digits elsewhere in Europe. Calmfors and Driffill also argued that in the deregulated labor markets of North America and Japan, the absence of institutional protections allowed wages to fall to full-employment levels. Their institutional theory holds that the level of labor market centralization has a humped-shaped relationship to unemployment. There is low unemployment at high and low labor market centralization but high unemployment where collective bargaining is conducted at the intermediate—industry—level. From the perspective of Calmfors and Driffill, the competitive model of the labor market operates only under specific institutional conditions in a small number of countries. Soskice (1990) objected that the true success story of these decentralized countries, Japan, should really be counted as a centralized institutional setting because of the strong influence of pattern bargaining on Japanese wage movements. In Japan, collective bargaining within enterprises strongly follows the lead of a pattern-setting union. In sum, although the positive effects of labor market decentralization on unemployment remains in dispute, there is a strong consensus that labor market centralization is closely related to low unemployment.

The distributional effects of labor market institutions also appear clear. Instead of contributing to inequality as the union monopoly model predicts, unions— under the right institutional conditions—have contributed to equalizing the earnings distribution. In highly centralized institutional contexts, unions can secure collective agreements that extend beyond the unionized labor force. Collective agreements are generally extended to nonunion workers in one of two ways. Employers with nonunion labor pay union rates as an obligation of their membership in the employer association that signs a central agreement. Thus, in Germany, where about 40 percent of the workforce is unionized, over 80 percent of German workers are covered by collective agreements because employer association membership binds owners to pay the union wage (Markovits 1986, 40). Coverage is even more extensive where the scope of collective agreements is broadened by the state through executive order, as in Belgium and the Netherlands (Blanpain 1990; Rood 1993). Both institutional mechanisms extend the representative function of unions beyond their membership.

Through the 1980s, labor markets were widely deregulated as conservative governments and growing employer opposition to labor organizing reduced union membership (Western 1995). As a result of this labor market deregulation, earnings inequality increased rapidly in several countries (Freeman and Katz 1994). However, inequality remained virtually unchanged in centralized institutional contexts, where the terms of collective agreements were extended beyond the union sector. Evidence is provided in table 10.2, which reveals the relationship of the changes in earnings inequality in nine countries to institutional conditions facilitating the extension of collective agreements to unorganized workers.

Table 10.2   Changes in Earnings Inequality and Institutionalized Extension of Collective Agreements to Nonunion Workplaces, Selected OECD Countries, 1979 to 1990

Countries	Change in Earnings Inequality	Institutionalized Extension Provisions
United Kingdom	.28	No extension of collective agreements and moderate unionization
Canada	.21	No extension of collective agreements and low unionization (particularly in the private sector)
United States	.17	No extension of collective agreements and low unionization
Japan	.09	No extension of collective agreements and low unionization
France	.03	No extension of collective agreements, although compulsory bargaining in all private sector workplaces was introduced in 1982
Italy	−.01	Extension attempted by legislative reform in 1971 but was not effectively implemented
Netherlands	−.02	Minister for Social Affairs and Employment can extend collective agreements by executive order
Germany	−.03	Employers bound to collective agreements through membership in employers' association
Sweden	.06	Employers bound to collective agreements through membership in employers' association

Sources: Inequality data are from Freeman and Katz (1994); institutional information is taken from Blanpain (various years).

Notes: The change in wage inequality is measured as the change in the log of the ratio of wages of the ninetieth percentile earner to the tenth percentile earner. Earnings inequality was estimated for males for all countries except Sweden, where the sample was based on all wage-earners. Changes in earnings inequality are estimated for 1979 to 1987 in France, Italy, Germany, and Canada.

Large increases in earnings inequality can be found in the United States and Britain through the 1980s, where unions suffered large membership losses and nonunion workers have little institutionalized wage protection. Earnings inequality remained stable and the union monopoly model seems deficient where institutional extension of collective agreements is strongly developed.

Comparative case studies of earnings in the Scandinavian countries provide additional evidence. Hibbs (1991) has shown that centralized bargaining allowed the Swedish blue-collar confederation to successfully pursue a policy of wage compression from the mid-1960s. Wage inequality declined until the mid-1980s, when collective bargaining became more decentralized as national wage agreements were increasingly replaced by industry-level bargaining. Along similar lines, Colbjørnsen and Kalleberg (1988) find that the wage advantage of unionized workers over nonunion workers is much smaller in Norway than in the United States. The smaller wage premium persists in Norway even though the centrally organized Norwegian labor movement has superior organizational strength to the American. Not all these distributional effects are patterned along class lines. For instance, Rosenfeld (1991) finds that the gender gap in earnings narrows under centralized systems of collective bargaining with encompassing union representation. Women's earnings in the Nordic countries approach four-fifths of men's, while this ratio is around two-thirds in North America and Britain.

Filtering Economic Conditions

The direct effect of wage fixing institutions on labor market performance discussed in the previous section provides only a partial picture of how labor market processes are dependent on institutional context. The discussion so far has ignored how institutions responded to two economic shocks that reverberated throughout the world economy—the oil price shocks of 1973 to 1974 and 1979. In response to the OPEC (Organization of Petroleum Exporting Countries) oil embargo, the nominal price of crude oil jumped by 69 percent from 1973 to 1975. Following the Iranian revolution, oil prices skyrocketed again, this time by 53.5 percent from 1979 to 1981 (Bruno and Sachs 1985, 164). Both price shocks fueled inflation and dramatically constricted economic growth.

The idea that exogenous market conditions such as these are intimately linked to labor market outcomes dates from the origins of capitalist labor markets themselves. Thus, as Adam Smith ([1776] 1976, 78) observed, "It is not the actual greatness of national wealth, but its continual increase, which occasions a rise in the wages of labour." In the institutional approach to labor markets, exogenous changes in economic conditions affect labor market outcomes differently according to institutional context. Institutions can transmit market conditions or insulate wages and employment from their effects. This idea of institutional effects shares the flavor of that discussed by Hamilton and Feenstra (in this volume) who emphasize the impact of institutionalized connections among markets. The current emphasis on contextual explanation also shares a strong affinity with Szelényi and Kostello's analysis (in this volume) of inequality in the transitional societies of Central Europe.

A now-classic statement of how the effects of exogenous economic shocks are institutionally mediated is given by Bruno and Sachs (1985, 274, quoted in Alvarez, Garrett, and Lange 1991, 541):

> It would seem only natural that a theory for a country's (or several countries') response [to economic shocks] can only be formulated if one takes its specific institutional or structural features into consideration. However, macroeconomic theory, whether Keynesian or monetarist, has for a long time tended to consider one and the same basic model as applicable to all economies. . . . Our analysis highlights a third structural element—the importance of incorporating the structure of labor markets explicitly into macroeconomic theory that is applied across industrial economies.

This perspective generated a cottage industry of research among macroeconomists who studied how the impact of economic variables on wages and unemployment depended on the institutional context (see Flanagan, Soskice, and Ulman 1983; Layard, Nickell, and Jackman 1991; the Supplement of *Economica* 1986; Drèze and Bean 1991).

Institutional centralization of the labor market is of key importance here. In some countries, the centralized adjustment of wages to inflation is a major feature of labor market regulation. The sensitivity of Italian wages to inflation provides an extreme example. In Italy, the *scala mobile* wage indexation system provided quarterly economy-wide adjustment of wages to movements in consumer prices (Flanagan, Soskice, and Ulman 1983, 502). In the late 1970s, Italian wage movements in secondary industries actually overcompensated for increases in double-digit inflation. In other countries, like the United States, overlapping long-term contracts, combined with uncoordinated wage indexation, decouples wage movements from inflation in the unionized part of the economy (Bruno and Sachs 1985). Institutional links between wage movements and prices are partly offset by the wage moderation found in centralized systems. Labor market centralization can thus also decrease the responsiveness of wages to economic shocks (Layard, Nickell, and Jackman 1991, ch. 9). Given these offsetting tendencies, the relationship between labor market performance and labor market institutions in the presence of economic shocks remains an empirical question.

Comparativists have observed a positive relationship between corporatist bargaining and low unemployment under pressure of the oil shocks (Alvarez, Garrett, and Lange 1991; Layard, Nickell, and Jackman 1991; Crouch 1994). The comparative picture is illustrated by the analysis of Layard, Nickell, and Jackman (1991) in figure 10.1. This figure plots nominal wage rigidity against the increase in unemployment from 1973 to 1985 for eighteen OECD countries. Nominal wage rigidity measures the extent to which changes in inflation are passed on to changes in money wages. The scatterplot shows that increases in unemployment in response to the oil shocks are generally small when nominal wages are highly rigid in the face of mounting inflation. Corporatist countries, measured by a discrete version of Calmfors and Driffill's index (1988), are indicated by squares on the scatterplot. Nominal wage rigidity is generally low in the corporatist countries. In Denmark, where union contracts are of short duration, and the degree of indexation is high, inflation is associated with high unemployment. By 1985, Danish unemployment had increased by more than eight points

Figure 10.1   Nominal Wage Rigidity and Changes in Unemployment for Eighteen Corporatist and Noncorporatist OECD Countries, 1973 to 1985

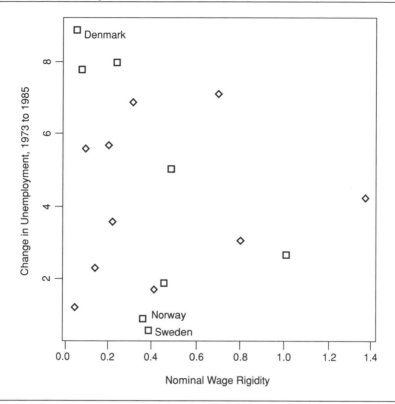

Source: Layard, Nickell, and Jackman (1991).
Note: Corporatist countries are indicated by squares, noncorporatist countries by diamonds.

from its full-employment level in the late 1960s. The two best employment performers through the 1970s and 1980s—Sweden and Norway—also feature highly centralized collective bargaining. In these countries however, central agreements are of longer duration than in Denmark, and wage indexation is not an automatic feature of union contracts (Bruno and Sachs 1985, 238). Centrally orchestrated wage restraint in these two countries contributed to very strong employment performance through the 1970s and early 1980s.

Representation and Collective Action

Actors and their preferences do not come fully formed to the market. Instead, labor market actors are constituted by the institutions in which labor markets are themselves embedded. Thus, the rules for centralized bargaining were formed in tandem with highly centralized union and employer organizations. Institutions constitute labor market actors in two ways, by establishing rules for representation and by influencing processes of collective action.

First, consider the way labor market institutions provide rules for representation. The agents of employers and workers vary greatly in the scope of their representation. Representative scope is established in wage-setting institutions through collective agreements. With corporatist bargaining, class becomes an important principle of representation, as leaders of unions and employer associations negotiate wage agreements that govern entire national labor markets. In Germany and the Netherlands, for example, less than half the workforce are union members, but collective agreements are broadly extended. In these settings, German and Dutch union leaders are institutionally constituted as class representatives. Such classwide representation is precluded in the United States, where union organization is legislatively restricted to "a unit appropriate for collective bargaining." Apart from a few, now largely historical, exceptions in the steel and coal industries, union representatives in the United States act for the blue-collar workers within individual enterprises or plants (Katz 1993).

The importance of institutions as a source of rules for representation underlines the analytical importance of class to an institutional approach to labor markets. Instead of describing a social structural location, class in the institutional approach refers to a principle of representation. From this perspective, there is one basic division in the labor market, between owners and workers. Institutions express the salience of this division in organizing the parties to wage-labor exchanges. Institutional rules that provide for the economy-wide representation of workers on one side and employers on the other contribute significantly to the development of classes as organized social forces. Corporatist institutions provide for the representation of classes—all workers or all employers—in economy-wide bargaining. Corporatist institutions thus make union and employer association officials into class representatives (Przeworksi and Sprague 1986, 78). This breadth of representation can be distinguished from narrower representative principles found in enterprise-level bargaining. In these decentralized settings, the class division is virtually invisible. Competition is ubiquitous and unity of interest among workers and among employers is weakly expressed in collective action. While many economic sociologists have rejected social structural conceptions of class, the institutional idea of class as a rule for representation seems to have obvious descriptive application.

Scope of representation also influences the likelihood of collective action in the labor market. Researchers have argued that the institutional extension of collective agreements beyond the unionized workforce lowers employer resistance to union organizing (Freeman 1989). With provisions for the extension of collective agreements, employers must pay the union wage regardless of whether their workplace is organized. Intense employer resistance to unionism in the United States can be explained by this argument. Without the institutional extension of collective agreements in the United States, the costs of unionization are narrowly focused on the firm. Accordingly, employer opposition is intense. Employers routinely contest union certification elections, frequently engaging management consultants to mount oppositional campaigns (Freeman and Medoff 1984, 230–42). As a result of employers' opposition to unionism and their institutional opportunity to advance this opposition in certification elections, unions in the United States are small compared to those in Western Europe. Where the costs of unionism are extended to all employers, as in most European countries, the right of workers to make collective wage claims is institutionally legitimated and largely uncontested.

On the labor side, labor market centralization establishes the entire labor force as the target constituency for unionization (Stephens 1991). Solidaristic organization of the labor movement also facilitates the redistribution of organizational resources. Thus, in highly centralized labor markets large payments from strong unions representing well-organized industries are made to central confederations (Headey 1970). The central confederations can then use these funds to take an active role in the unionizing of less-organized industries. Organizational competition among unions also tends to be weak in the centralized labor markets and jurisdictional disputes are rare (Western 1993). Consequently, unionization is high in the centralized labor markets of Scandinavia but low under the system of decentralized industrial relations of North America. The strong causal link between labor market centralization and unionization suggests that collective action develops along class lines where class is established as a rule for representation. The institutional reality of classes thus provides a mechanism for their organizational reality in trade unions.

GENERAL LESSONS

What general lessons can be drawn from an institutional approach to studying labor markets? Three points seem applicable to other institutionally-oriented work on labor markets or in economic sociology more generally. First, the institutional approach to studying labor markets is comparative, with researchers observing institutional effects by comparing different settings. Second, institutional research is contextual; researchers examine how market transactions are conditioned by their institutional environment. Third, the institutional approach defines collective action in the marketplace as a major research problem. These ideas can be illustrated by reference to other institutionally-oriented work in political and economic sociology.

Comparative Research

To observe the effects of institutions on social welfare and distribution in the labor market, researchers must observe variations in the institutions themselves. In an institutional sociology of the labor market, then, research is comparative in the specific sense of being cross-institutional. While this design may be cross-national, involving the comparison of countries, it might also be comparative in the sense of observing institutional variation within nation-states, or over time where there is institutional change.

These comparative research designs would share two other features. First, they must involve an explicit attempt to make measurements on the institutions. Some examples of institutional measurement in comparative sociology can be found in research on industrial relations, political representation, and the welfare state. In the industrial relations field we have already seen the indices of labor market centralization. Students of political democracy have developed indicators that incorporate information about elections, the selection of government officeholders, and political liberties (Bollen 1980). Welfare state researchers have constructed indexes that go beyond simple social spending figures, measuring the generosity of welfare eligibility criteria (Esping-Andersen 1990). These indices help pin down causal mechanisms, distinguishing institutional effects from rival sources of variation.

Second, like any good research design there must also be an explicit effort to address these rival sources of variation and somehow control them statistically or quasi-experimentally (Campbell and Stanley 1963). Successful application of a statistical design will depend on the abundance of information—the number of institutional settings available for comparison. The more cases there are, the more confidence one may have in estimates of institutional effects. The effectiveness of the quasi-experimental design will depend on how well cases can be selected to eliminate alternative institutional explanations as sources of variation in the outcome of interest. Here, Mill's methods of agreement and difference seem likely research tools. Statistical and comparative case study designs have strong research traditions, and the power of each approach is reflected in the healthy macrosociological debate on "small-N" studies (see Skocpol 1984; Lieberson 1992).

Contextual Research

If labor market institutions filter the impact of economic conditions and shape exchanges between employers and workers, institutional analysis should do more than focus on the direct effects of rules governing market exchange. It should also investigate how, in Schumpeter's phrase, economic laws work out differently in different institutional settings. Statistical analysis provides a useful vocabulary for specifying these ideas. Interaction effects, where the impact of one variable is written as conditional on the level of another, capture the simplest specification. The filtering effects of institutions could thus be modeled as interactions. For instance, we might think that rapid growth in the price of raw materials raises wages. From the institutional perspective, however, the impact of supply shocks on wages depends on the degree of labor market centralization.

The importance of contextual analysis has been proposed by Isaac and Griffin (1989) who call for historically sensitive analysis that involves investigating the stability of statistical relationships over time. Where relationships vary across historical periods, researchers should study contextual changes that might influence the relationship under study. In their application, Isaac and Griffin observe that the relationship between strikes and unionization in the United States was altered as a consequence of the Supreme Court's confirmation of the constitutionality of the National Labor Relations Act in 1937.

This picture of labor market institutions, as macro-level contexts for micro-level processes, is similar to Przeworski and Teune's classic description (1970) of comparative research, which for them was essentially contextual: "Comparative studies were defined as those in which the influence of larger systems upon the characteristics of units within them is examined at some stage of analysis" (74). Indeed, to identify the impact of the institutional context on labor market exchanges, it is necessary to follow the preceding recommendation to make observations of a number of institutional settings.

This contextual approach seems quite different from many large-scale regression analyses of institutional effects in comparative sociology. For example, economic conditions such as rates of unemployment and economic growth are commonly held to influence social welfare spending. Typically, the effects of these variables are specified to be identical across countries despite the acknowledged importance of the mediating effects of institutions (see, for example, Pampel and Williamson 1989, 45; Korpi 1989, 314). Following a contextual approach we could allow economic effects to differ across countries depending on the institutional surroundings.

Collective Action

If institutions modify competitive relations between labor market actors, collective action becomes a central research problem in an institutional sociology of the labor market. Strikes and unionization, typically topics for labor economists and industrial relations specialists, stimulate compelling sociological questions in the institutional approach. The labor economics tradition has narrowly focused on the American scene, neglecting institutional variation as a causal force in collective action. Where there is comparative economic research on strikes and unionization, it has tended to emphasize the generality of business cycle models. Thus the work of Ashenfelter and Pencavel (1969) on union growth and Ashenfelter and Johnson (1969) on strikes has been widely applied in diverse institutional contexts. In this research, statistical departures from the American regime are given ad hoc interpretations rather than systematic institutional explanations (Bain and Elsheikh 1976).

Although research on collective action in the labor market has been dominated by noninstitutional business cycle explanations, historical sociologists have brought a more contextual approach to these topics. For instance, Tilly's political sociology of the French working class (1986; Shorter and Tilly 1974) emphasizes how patterns of collective action vary with preexisting institutional contexts of working class organization. For Franzosi (1995), the Italian "Hot Autumn" of 1968 created an institutional turning point in the history of working-class collective action in Italy. The patterns of class-based collective action in Italy can thus be broken into two parts coinciding with the institutional change in Italian industrial relations. Cross-national variation in strikes has been studied by Korpi and Shalev (1980) and Snyder (1975). Korpi and Shalev found that corporatist countries had lower strike activity because unions could effectively advance their interests through the state, rather than through the extrainstitutional channel of industrial action. Snyder found that the impact of the business cycle on strikes was strongest in the postwar United States where collective bargaining is strongly institutionalized. In France and Italy, where the role of unions in industrial relations was more tenuous, business cycle effects on strike action were much weaker. In this sociological research, the history of social conflict congealed in the rules of the labor market exerts an important influence on collective action.

SUMMARY AND CONCLUSION

Sociological research on the labor market has a long and rich tradition. Recent work has examined the impact of social networks, gender relations, and the organizational characteristics of firms on labor market outcomes. The institutional approach that I describe here, which views the market for labor as deeply embedded in social relations, can be understood as another effort to move labor market theories away from standard models of competitive markets and union monopoly. Social relations in this context refers to the pervasive social conflict that has attended capitalist labor markets since their formation. The residue of these conflicts—labor market institutions—shape subsequent labor market exchanges between workers and employers. Institutional explanation does more than add to the list of sociological explanations of labor market outcomes; it challenges us to specify the surrounding conditions that enable the operation of other sociological and economic mechanisms.

In this chapter, I have focused on the impact of the centralization of industrial relations in contemporary capitalist labor markets, although other types of institutions could be analyzed. Institutional centralization of the labor market is important for understanding labor markets for at least three reasons. First, centralization has aggregate-level consequences for social welfare and income distribution. Second, institutions operate as a screen, filtering the impact of exogenous economic conditions on labor market outcomes. Third, by establishing rules for representation and shaping competition among workers, labor market institutions are constitutive of collective actors. Class emerges as an important theoretical category in this context, describing the broad economy-wide representation of workers and employers. The empirical research I have reviewed suggests that where class is a well-developed institutional principle, that is, in corporatist settings, labor markets are better able to secure high levels of employment, equality, and security from exogenous economic shocks.

Each of these three institutional effects has a distinctive research implication. The aggregate impacts of institutions on welfare and distribution suggests research must be comparative to observe variation in institutional settings. To see how institutions filter exogenous economic conditions, research must also be contextual, examining how the effects of economic and other variables are institutionally dependent. The impact of institutions on collective action suggests the importance of explaining why and how workers and employers cooperate and compete in the labor market.

This last implication brings the analysis full circle. If institutions have their origins in organized social struggles, investigating processes of collective action suggests a causal analysis of the institutions themselves. The institutions that provide the conditions under which collective action emerges and is foiled, in turn have an impact on institutional change and continuity. Although a detailed account of institutional change is beyond the scope of this chapter, the institutional approach presented here suggests a way of thinking about labor markets in terms of their historical setting. The advantage of this type of analysis resides in its empirical nature, in that it enlists new types of labor market variation to be explained and specifies the institutional conditions under which particular labor market processes operate.

This chapter was presented at the Conference on New Institutionalism in Economic Sociology, Russell Sage Foundation, New York, April 1995. I gratefully acknowledge the helpful comments of Victor Nee and Mary Brinton.

REFERENCES

Alchian, Armen, and Harold Demsetz. 1972. "Production, Information Costs and Economic Organization." *American Economic Review* 62: 777–95.

Alvarez, R. Michael, Geoffrey Garrett, and Peter Lange. 1991. "Government Partisanship, Labor Organization, and Macroeconomic Performance." *American Political Science Review* 85: 539–56.

Ashenfelter, Orley, and George E. Johnson. 1969. "Bargaining Theory, Trade Unions, and Industrial Strike Activity." *American Economic Review* 59: 35–49.

Ashenfelter, Orley, and John H. Pencavel. 1969. "American Trade Union Growth: 1900–1960." *Quarterly Journal of Economics* 83: 434–48.

Bain, George Sayers, and Farouk Elsheikh. 1976. *Union Growth and Business Cycle*. Oxford, England: Blackwell.

Baron, James N. 1984. "Organizational Perspectives on Stratification." *Annual Review of Sociology* 10: 37–69.

Blanpain, Roger. 1990. "Belgium." In *International Encyclopaedia for Labour Law and Industrial Relations*. Deventer, the Netherlands: Kluwer Law and Taxation Publishers.

———, ed. Various years. *International Encyclopaedia for Labour Law and Industrial Relations*. Deventer, the Netherlands: Kluwer Law and Taxation Publishers.

Bollen, Kenneth A. 1980. "Issues in the Comparative Measurement of Democracy." *American Sociological Review* 45: 370–90.

Bruno, Michael, and Jeffrey Sachs. 1985. *The Economics of Worldwide Stagflation*. Oxford, England: Blackwell.

Calmfors, Lars, and John Driffill. 1988. "Bargaining Structure, Corporatism, and Macroeconomic Performance." *Economic Policy* 3: 14–61.

Cameron, David R. 1984. "Social Democracy, Corporatism, Labor Quiescence, and the Representation of Economic Interest in Advanced Capitalist Society." In *Order and Conflict in Contemporary Capitalism: Studies in the Political Economy of Western European Nations*, edited by John Goldthorpe. Oxford, England: Oxford University Press.

Campbell, Donald S., and Julian Stanley. 1963. *Experimental and Quasi-experimental Designs for Research*. New York: Houghton Mifflin.

Colbjørnsen, Tom, and Arne L. Kalleberg. 1988. "Spillover, Standardization and Stratification: Earnings Determination in the United States and Norway." *European Sociological Review* 4: 20–31.

Crouch, Colin. 1994. *Industrial Relations and European State Traditions*. Oxford, England: Oxford University Press.

Drèze, Jacques, A., and Charles R Bean, eds. 1990. *Europe's Unemployment Problem*. Cambridge, Mass.: MIT Press.

Economica. 1986. 53 (210, Supplement).

England, Paula. 1992. *Comparable Worth: Theories and Evidence*. New York: Aldine de Gruyter.

Esping-Andersen, Gøsta. 1990. *Three Worlds of Welfare Capitalism*. Cambridge, England: Polity.

Farber, Henry S. 1986. "The Analysis of Union Behavior." *Handbook of Labor Economics*, Vol. 2. Edited by O. Ashenfelter and R. Layard. Netherlands: Elsevier Science.

Flanagan, Robert J., David W. Soskice, and Lloyd Ulman. 1983. *Unionism, Economic Stabilization, and Incomes Policies: European Experience*. Washington, D.C.: Brookings.

Fox, Alan. 1985. *History and Heritage: The Social Origins of the British Industrial Relations System*. London, England: Allen and Unwin.

Franzosi, Roberto. 1995. *The Puzzle of Strikes: Class and States Strategies in Postwar Italy*. New York: Cambridge University Press.

Freeman, Richard B. 1989. "On the Divergence in Unionism in Developed Countries." Working Paper 2817. Washington, D.C.: National Bureau of Economic Research.

Freeman, Richard B., and Lawrence F. Katz. 1994. "Rising Wage Inequality: The United States versus Other Advanced Economies." In *Working Under Different Rules*, edited by Richard B. Freeman. New York: Russell Sage Foundation.

Freeman, Richard B., and James L. Medoff. 1984. *What Do Unions Do?* New York: Basic Books.

Goldthorpe, John H., ed. 1984. *Order and Conflict in Contemporary Capitalism: Studies in the Political Economy of Western European Nations*. Oxford, England: Oxford University Press.

Granovetter, Mark. 1995. *Getting a Job: A Study of Contacts and Careers.* 2d ed. Chicago, Ill. Chicago University Press.

Headey, Bruce. 1970. "Trade Unions and National Wages Policy." *Journal of Politics* 32: 407–39.

Hibbs, Douglas A. 1991. "Market Forces, Trade Union Ideology and Trends in Swedish Wage Dispersion." *Acta Sociologica* 34: 89–102.

Isaac, Larry, and Larry J. Griffin. 1989. "Ahistoricism in Time Series Analyses of Historical Process: Critique, Redirection, and Illustrations from U.S. Labor History." *American Sociological Review* 54: 873–90.

Katz, Harry C. 1993. "The Decentralization of Collective Bargaining: A Literature Review and Comparative Analysis." *Industrial and Labor Relations Review* 47: 3–22.

Kerckhoff, Alan C. 1995. "Institutional Arrangements and Stratification Processes in Industrial Societies." *Annual Review of Sociology* 21: 323–47.

Korpi, Walter. 1989. "Power, Politics and State Autonomy in the Development of Social Citizenship: Social Rights During Sickness in 18 OECD Countries Since 1930." *American Sociological Review* 54: 309–28.

Korpi, Walter, and Michael Shalev. 1980. "Strikes, Power, and Politics in the Western Nations." *Political Power and Social Theory* 1: 309–34.

Layard, Richard, Stephen Nickell, and Richard Jackman. 1991. *Unemployment: Macroeconomic Performance and the Labour Market.* Oxford, England: Oxford University Press.

Lieberson, Stanley. 1992. "Small *N*'s and Big Conclusions: An Examination of the Reasoning Based on a Small Number of Cases." In *What Is a Case? Exploring the Foundations of Social Inquiry,* edited by Charles C. Ragin and Howard S. Becker. Cambridge, England: Cambridge University Press.

Markovits, Andrei S. 1986. *The Politics of West German Trade Unions.* Cambridge: Cambridge University Press.

Olson, Mancur. 1982. *The Rise and Decline of Nations: Economic Growth, Stagflation, and Social Rigidities.* New Haven, Conn.: Yale University Press.

Organization for Economic Cooperation and Development (OECD). 1994. *The OECD Jobs Study: Labour Market Trends and Underlying Forces of Change.* Paris, France: OECD.

Pampel, Fred C., and John B. Williamson. 1989. *Age, Class, Politics and the Welfare State.* New York: Cambridge University Press.

Polanyi, Karl. ([1944] 1957). *The Great Transformation: The Political and Economic Origins of Our Time.* Boston, Mass.: Beacon.

Przeworski, Adam, and John Sprague. 1986. *Paper Stones: A History of Electoral Socialism.* Chicago, Ill.: University of Chicago Press.

Przeworski, Adam, and Henry S. Teune. 1970. *The Logic of Comparative Social Inquiry.* New York: Wiley.

Rood, Max Gustaf. 1993. "Netherlands." In *International Encyclopaedia for Labour Law and Industrial Relations,* edited by Roger Blanpain. Deventer, the Netherlands: Kluwer Law and Taxation Publishers.

Rosenfeld, Rachel A. 1991. "Gender Inequality in the Labor Market: A Cross-National Perspective." *Acta Sociologica* 34: 207–25.

Schumpeter, Joseph A. 1954. *History of Economic Analysis.* New York: Oxford University Press.

Shalev, Michael. 1992. "The Resurgence of Labour Quiescence." In *The Future of Labour Movements,* edited by M. Regini. London, England: Sage.

Shorter, Edward, and Charles Tilly. 1974. *Strikes in France, 1830–1868.* Cambridge, England: Cambridge University Press.

Skocpol, Theda. 1984. "Emerging Agendas and Recurrent Strategies in Historical Sociology." In *Vision and Method in Historical Sociology,* edited by Theda Skocpol. Cambridge, England: Cambridge University Press.

Smith, Adam. ([1776] 1976). *An Inquiry into the Nature and Causes of The Wealth of Nations.* Chicago, Ill.: University of Chicago Press.

Snyder, David. 1975. "Institutional Setting and Industrial Conflict: Comparative Analyses of France, Italy, and the United States." *American Sociological Review* 40: 259–78.

Soskice, David. 1990. "Wage Determination: The Changing Role of Institutions in Advanced Industrialized Countries." *Oxford Review of Economic Policy* 6: 1–23.

Stephens, John D. 1979. *The Transition from Capitalism to Socialism*. Urbana, Ill.: University of Illinois Press.

———. 1991. "Industrial Concentration, Country Size and Trade Union Membership." *American Political Science Review* 85: 941–49.

Tilly, Charles. 1986. *The Contentious French: Four Centuries of Popular Struggle*. Cambridge, Mass.: Belknap.

Visser, Jelle. 1991. "Trends in Trade Union Membership." *OECD Employment Outlook*. Paris: Organization for Economic Cooperation and Development.

Webb, Sidney, and Beatrice Webb. 1920. *The History of Trade Unionism*. New York: Longman's Green.

Western, Bruce. 1993. "Postwar Unionization in 18 Advanced Capitalist Countries." *American Sociological Review* 58: 266–82.

———. 1995. "A Comparative Study of Working Class Disorganization: Union Decline in 18 Advanced Capitalist Countries." *American Sociological Review* 60: 179–201.

———. 1996. "Recent Wage Trends in 14 OECD Countries." Paper presented at the meetings of Research Committee 28 of the International Sociological Association, Ann Arbor, Mich.

Part III

Institutional Change and Economic Performance

— 11 —

Economic Performance Through Time

Douglass C. North

E conomic history is about the performance of economies through time. The objective of research in the field is not only to shed new light on the economic past but also to contribute to economic theory by providing an analytical framework that will enable us to understand economic change. A theory of economic dynamics comparable in precision to general equilibrium theory would be the ideal tool of analysis. In the absence of such a theory we can describe the characteristics of past economies, examine the performance of economies at various times, and engage in comparative static analysis; but missing is an analytical understanding of the way economies evolve through time.

A theory of economic dynamics is also crucial for the field of economic development. There is no mystery why the field of development has failed to develop during the five decades since the end of World War II. Neoclassical theory is simply an inappropriate tool to analyze and prescribe policies that will induce development. It is concerned with the operation of markets, not with how markets develop. How can one prescribe policies when one does not understand how economies develop? The very methods employed by neoclassical economists have dictated the subject matter and militated against such a development. That theory in the pristine form that gave it mathematical precision and elegance modeled a frictionless and static world. When applied to economic history and development it focused on technological development and more recently on human-capital investment but ignored the incentive structure embodied in institutions that determined the extent of societal investment in those factors. In the analysis of economic performance through time it contained two erroneous assumptions: (1) that institutions do not matter and (2) that time does not matter.

This essay is about institutions and time. It does not provide a theory of economic dynamics comparable to general equilibrium theory. We do not have such a theory.[1] Rather, it provides the initial scaffolding of an analytical framework capable of increasing our understanding of the historical evolution of economies and a necessarily crude guide to policy in the ongoing task of improving the economic performance of economies. The analytical framework is a modification of neoclassical theory. What it retains is the fundamental assumption of scarcity and hence competition and the analytical tools of microeconomic theory. What it modifies is the rationality assumption. What it adds is the dimension of time.

Institutions form the incentive structure of a society, and the political and economic institutions, in consequence, are the underlying determinants of economic performance. Time as it relates to economic and societal change is the dimension in which the learning process of human beings shapes the way institutions evolve. That is, the beliefs that individuals, groups, and societies hold which determine choices are a consequence of learning through time—not just the span of an individual's life or of a generation of a society, but the learning embodied in individuals, groups, and societies that is cumulative through time and passed on intergenerationally by the culture of a society.

The next two sections of this essay summarize the work I, and others, have done on the nature of institutions and the way they affect economic performance and then characterize the nature of institutional change.[2] The remainder of the chapter describes a cognitive-science approach to human learning; provides an institutional/cognitive approach to economic history; indicates the implications of this approach for improving our understanding of the past; and finally suggests implications for current development policies.

THE NATURE OF INSTITUTIONS

Institutions are the humanly devised constraints that structure human interaction. They are made up of formal constraints (for example, rules, laws, constitutions), informal constraints (for example, norms of behavior, conventions, self-imposed codes of conduct), and their enforcement characteristics. Together they define the incentive structure of societies and, specifically, economies.

Institutions and the technology employed determine the transaction and transformation costs that add up to the costs of production. It was Ronald Coase (1960) who made the crucial connection between institutions, transaction costs, and neoclassical theory. The neoclassical result of efficient markets only obtains when it is costless to transact. Only under the conditions of costless bargaining will the actors reach the solution that maximizes aggregate income regardless of the institutional arrangements. When it is costly to transact, then institutions matter. And it is costly to transact. John J. Wallis and I demonstrated in an empirical study (1986) that 45 percent of U.S. GNP was devoted to the transaction sector in 1970. Efficient markets are created in the real world when competition is strong enough via arbitrage and efficient information feedback to approximate the Coase zero-transaction-cost conditions and the parties can realize the gains from trade inherent in the neoclassical argument.

But the informational and institutional requirements necessary to achieve such efficient markets are stringent. Players must not only have objectives but know the correct way to achieve them. But how do the players know the correct way to achieve their objectives? The instrumental rationality answer is that, even though the actors may initially have diverse and erroneous models, the informational feedback process and arbitraging actors will correct initially incorrect models, punish deviant behavior, and lead surviving players to correct models.

An even more stringent implicit requirement of the discipline-of-the-competitive-market model is that, when there are significant transaction costs, the consequent institutions of the market will be designed to induce the actors to acquire the essential information that will lead them to correct their models. The implication is not only that institutions are designed to achieve efficient outcomes but that they can be ignored in economic analysis because they play no independent role in economic performance.

These are stringent requirements that are realized only very exceptionally. Individuals typically act on incomplete information and with subjectively derived models that are frequently erroneous; the information feedback is typically insufficient to correct these subjective models. Institutions are not necessarily or even usually created to be socially efficient; rather they, or at least the formal rules, are created to serve the interests of those with the bargaining power to create new rules. In a world of zero transaction costs, bargaining strength does not affect the efficiency of outcomes; but in a world of positive transaction costs it does.

It is exceptional to find economic markets that approximate the conditions necessary for efficiency. It is impossible to find political markets that do. The reason is straightforward. Transaction costs are the costs of specifying what is being exchanged and of enforcing the consequent agreements. In economic markets what is being specified (measured) is the valuable attributes—the physical and property-rights dimensions—of goods and services or the performance of agents. While measurement can frequently be costly, there are some standard criteria: the physical dimensions have objective characteristics (size, weight, color, and the like), and the property-rights dimensions are defined in legal terms. Competition also plays a critical role in reducing enforcement costs. The judicial system provides coercive enforcement. Still, economic markets in the past and present are typically imperfect and beset by high transaction costs.

Measuring and enforcing agreements in political markets is far more difficult. What is being exchanged (between constituents and legislators in a democracy) is promises for votes. The voter has little incentive to become informed because the likelihood that one's vote matters is infinitesimal; further, the complexity of the issues produces genuine uncertainty. Enforcement of political agreements is beset by difficulties. Competition is far less effective than in economic markets. For a variety of simple, easy-to-measure, and important-to-constituent-well-being policies, constituents may be well informed, but beyond such straightforward policy issues ideological stereotyping takes over and (as I shall argue later in this chapter) shapes the consequent performance of economies.[3] It is the polity that defines and enforces property rights, and in consequence it is not surprising that efficient economic markets are so exceptional.

INSTITUTIONAL CHANGE

It is the interaction between institutions and organizations that shapes the institutional evolution of an economy. If institutions are the rules of the game, organizations and their entrepreneurs are the players.

Organizations are made up of groups of individuals bound together by some common purpose to achieve certain objectives. Organizations include political bodies (political parties, the Senate, a city council, regulatory bodies), economic bodies (firms, trade unions, family farms, cooperatives), social bodies (churches, clubs, athletic associations), and educational bodies (schools, universities, vocational training centers).

The organizations that come into existence will reflect the opportunities provided by the institutional matrix. That is, if the institutional framework rewards piracy then piratical organizations will come into existence; and if the institutional framework rewards productive activities then organizations—firms—will come into existence to engage in productive activities.

Economic change is a ubiquitous, ongoing, incremental process that is a consequence of the choices individual actors and entrepreneurs of organizations are making every day. While the vast majority of these decisions are routine (Nelson and Winter 1982), some involve altering existing "contracts" between individuals and organizations. Sometimes that recontracting can be accomplished within the existing structure of property rights and political rules; but sometimes new contracting forms require an alteration in the rules. Equally, norms of behavior that guide exchanges will gradually be modified or wither away. In both instances, institutions are being altered.

Modifications occur because individuals perceive that they could do better by restructuring exchanges (political or economic). The source of the changed perceptions may be exogenous to the economy—for instance a change in the price or quality of a competitive product in another economy that alters perceptions of entrepreneurs in the given economy about profitable opportunities. But the most fundamental long-run source of change is learning by individuals and entrepreneurs of organizations.

While idle curiosity will result in learning, the rate of learning will reflect the intensity of competition among organizations. Competition, reflecting ubiquitous scarcity, induces organizations to engage in learning to survive. The degree of competition can and does vary. The greater the degree of monopoly power, the lower is the incentive to learn.

The speed of economic change is a function of the rate of learning, but the direction of that change is a function of the expected payoffs for acquiring different kinds of knowledge. The mental models that the players develop shape perceptions about the payoffs.

COGNITIVE SCIENCE AND HUMAN LEARNING

It is necessary to dismantle the rationality assumption underlying economic theory in order to approach constructively the nature of human learning. History demonstrates that ideas, ideologies, myths, dogmas, and prejudices matter; and an understanding of the way they evolve is necessary for further progress in developing a framework to understand societal change. The rational choice framework assumes that individuals know what is in their self-interest and act accordingly. That may be correct for individuals making choices in the highly developed markets of modern economies,[4] but it is patently false in making choices under conditions of uncertainty—the conditions that have characterized the political and economic choices that shaped (and continue to shape) historical change.

Herbert Simon (1986, S210–11) has stated the issues succinctly:

If . . . we accept the proposition that both the knowledge and the computational power of the decisionmaker are severely limited, then we must distinguish between the real world and the actor's perception of it and reasoning about it. That is to say we must construct a theory (and test it empirically) of the process of decision. Our theory must include not only the reasoning processes but also the processes that generated the actor's subjective representation of the decision problem, his or her frame.

The analytical framework we must build must originate in an understanding of how human learning takes place. We have a way to go before we can construct such a theory, but cognitive science has made immense strides in recent years—enough strides to suggest a tentative approach that can help us understand decisionmaking under uncertainty.[5]

Learning entails developing a structure by which to interpret the varied signals received by the senses. The initial architecture of the structure is genetic, but the subsequent scaffolding is a result of the experiences of the individual. The experiences can be classified into two kinds—those from the physical environment and those from the socio-cultural linguistic environment. The structures consist of categories—classifications that gradually evolve from earliest childhood to organize our perceptions and keep track of our memory of analytic results and experiences. Building on these classifications, we form mental models to explain and interpret the environment—typically in ways relevant to some goal. Both the categories and the mental models will evolve, reflecting the feedback derived from new experiences: feedback that sometimes strengthens our initial categories and models or may lead to modifications—in short, learning. Thus the mental models may be continually redefined with new experiences, including contact with others' ideas.

At this juncture the learning process of human beings diverges from that of other animals (such as the sea slug—a favorite research subject of cognitive scientists) and particularly diverges from the computer analogy that dominated early studies of artificial intelligence. The mind appears to order and reorder the mental models from their special-purpose origins to successively more abstract forms so that they become available to process other information. The term used by Andy Clark and Annette Karmiloff-Smith (1993) is "representational redescription." The capacity to generalize from the particular to the general and to use analogy is a part of this redescription process. It is this capacity that is the source not only of creative thinking but also of the ideologies and belief systems that underlie the choices humans make.[6]

A common cultural heritage provides a means of reducing the divergence in the mental models that people in a society have and constitutes the means for the intergenerational transfer of unifying perceptions. In pre-modern societies cultural learning provided a means of internal communication; it also provided shared explanations for phenomena outside the immediate experiences of the members of society in the form of religions, myths, and dogmas. Such belief structures are not, however, confined to primitive societies but are an essential part of modern societies as well.

Belief structures get transformed into societal and economic structures by institutions—both formal rules and informal norms of behavior. The relationship between mental models and institutions is an intimate one. Mental models are the internal representations that individual cognitive systems create to interpret the environment; institutions are the external (to the mind) mechanisms individuals create to structure and order the environment.

ECONOMIC HISTORY

There is no guarantee that the beliefs and institutions that evolve through time will produce economic growth. Let me pose the issue that time presents us by a brief institutional/cognitive story of long-run economic/political change.

As tribes evolved in different physical environments, they developed different languages and, with different experiences, different mental models to explain the world around them. The languages and mental models formed the informal constraints that defined the institutional framework of the tribe and were passed down intergenerationally as customs, taboos, and myths that provided cultural continuity.[7]

With growing specialization and division of labor, the tribes evolved into polities and economies; the diversity of experience and learning produced increasingly different societies and civilizations with different degrees of success in solving the fundamental economic problems of scarcity. The reason is that as the complexity of the environment increased as human beings became increasingly interdependent, more complex institutional structures were necessary to capture the potential gains from trade. Such evolution requires that the society develop institutions that will permit anonymous, impersonal exchange across time and space. To the extent that the culture and local experiences had produced diverse institutions and belief systems with respect to the gains from such cooperation, the likelihood of creating the necessary institutions to capture the gains from trade of more complex contracting varied. In fact, most societies throughout history got "stuck" in an institutional matrix that did not evolve into the impersonal exchange essential to capturing the productivity gains that came from the specialization and division of labor that have produced the Wealth of Nations.

The key to the foregoing story is the kind of learning that the individuals in a society acquired through time. Time in this context entails not only current experiences and learning but also the cumulative experience of past generations that is embodied in culture. Collective learning—a term used by Friedrich A. Hayek—consists of those experiences that have passed the slow test of time and are embodied in our language, institutions, technology, and ways of doing things. It is "the transmission in time of our accumulated stock of knowledge" (Hayek 1960, 27). It is culture that provides the key to path dependence—a term used to describe the powerful influence of the past on the present and future. The current learning of any generation takes place within the context of the perceptions derived from collective learning. Learning then is an incremental process filtered by the culture of a society which determines the perceived payoffs, but there is no guarantee that the cumulative past experience of a society will necessarily fit them to solve new problems. Societies that get "stuck" embody belief systems and institutions that fail to confront and solve new problems of societal complexity.

We need to understand a great deal more about the cumulative learning of a society. The learning process appears to be a function of (1) the way in which a given belief structure filters the information derived from experiences and (2) the different experiences confronting individuals and societies at different times. The perceived rate of return (private) may be high to military technology (in medieval Europe), to the pursuit and refinement of religious dogma (Rome during and after Constantine), or to the research for an accurate chronometer to determine longitude at sea (for which a substantial reward was offered during the Age of Exploration).

The incentives to acquire pure knowledge, the essential underpinning of modern economic growth, are affected by monetary rewards and punishments; they are also fundamentally influenced by a society's tolerance of creative developments, as a long list of creative individuals from Galileo to Darwin could attest. While there is a substantial literature on the origins and development of science, very little of it deals with the links between institutional structure, belief systems, and the incentives and disincentives to acquire pure knowledge. A major factor in the development of Western Europe was the gradual perception of the utility of research in pure science.

Incentives embodied in belief systems as expressed in institutions determine economic performance through time, and however we wish to define economic performance the historical record is clear. Throughout most of history and for most societies in the past and present, economic performance has been anything but satisfactory. Human beings have, by trial and error, learned how to make economies perform better; but not only has this learning taken ten millennia (since the first economic revolution), it has still escaped the grasp of almost half of the world's population. Moreover the radical improvement in economic performance, even when narrowly defined as material well-being, is a modern phenomenon of the last few centuries and confined until the last few decades to a small part of the world. Explaining the pace and direction of economic change throughout history presents a major puzzle.

Let us represent the human experience to date as a 24-hour clock in which the beginning consists of the time (apparently in Africa between 4 and 5 million years ago) when humans became separate from other primates. Then the beginning of so-called civilization occurs with the development of agriculture and permanent settlement in about 8000 B.C. in the Fertile Crescent—in the last three or four minutes of the clock. For the other twenty-three hours and fifty-six or fifty-seven minutes, humans remained hunters and gatherers, and while population grew, it did so at a very slow pace.

Now if we make a new 24-hour clock for the time of civilization—the ten thousand years from development of agriculture to the present—the pace of change appears to be very slow for the first twelve hours, although our archeological knowledge is very limited. Historical demographers speculate that the rate of population growth may have doubled as compared to the previous era but still was very slow. The pace of change accelerates in the past five thousand years with the rise and then decline of economies and civilizations. Population may have grown from about 300 million at the time of Christ to about 800 million by 1750—a substantial acceleration as compared to earlier rates of growth. The last 250 years—just 35 minutes on our new 24-hour clock—are the era of modern economic growth, accompanied by a population explosion that now puts world population in excess of 5 billion.

If we focus now on the last two hundred fifty years, we see that growth was largely restricted to Western Europe and the overseas extensions of Britain for two hundred of those two hundred fifty years.

Not only has the pace varied over the ages; the change has not been unidirectional. That is not simply a consequence of the decline of individual civilizations;

there have been periods of apparent secular stagnation—the most recent being the long hiatus between the end of the Roman Empire in the West and the revival of Western Europe approximately five hundred years later.

UNDERSTANDING THE PAST

What can an institutional/cognitive approach contribute to improving our understanding of the economic past? First of all it should make sense out of the very uneven pattern of economic performance described in the previous section. There is nothing automatic about the evolving of conditions that will permit low-cost transacting in the impersonal markets that are essential to productive economies. Game theory characterizes the issue. Individuals will usually find it worthwhile cooperating with others in exchange when the play is repeated, when they possess complete information about the other players' past performance, and when there are small numbers of players. Cooperation is difficult to sustain when the game is not repeated (or there is an endgame), when information about the other players is lacking, and when there are large numbers of players. Creating the institutions that will alter the benefit/cost ratios in favor of cooperation in impersonal exchange is a complex process, because it not only entails the creation of economic institutions but requires that they be undergirded by appropriate political institutions.

We are just beginning to explore the nature of this historical process. The remarkable development of Western Europe from relative backwardness in the tenth century to world economic hegemony by the eighteenth century is a story of a gradually evolving belief system in the context of competition among fragmented political/economic units producing economic institutions and political structures that produced modern economic growth.[8] And even within Western Europe there were successes (the Netherlands and England) and failures (Spain and Portugal) reflecting diverse external environmental experiences.[9]

Second, institutional/cognitive analysis should explain path dependence, one of the remarkable regularities of history. Why do economies once on a path of growth or stagnation tend to persist? Pioneering work on this subject is beginning to give us insights into the sources of path dependence (Arthur 1989; David 1985). But there is much that we still do not know. The rationality assumption of neoclassical theory would suggest that political entrepreneurs of stagnating economies could simply alter the rules and change the direction of failed economies. It is not that rulers have been unaware of poor performance. Rather, the difficulty of turning economies around is a function of the nature of political markets and, underlying that, the belief systems of the actors. The long decline of Spain, for example, from the glories of the Hapsburg Empire of the sixteenth century to its sorry state under Francisco Franco in the twentieth century was characterized by endless self-appraisals and frequently bizarre proposed solutions.[10]

Third, this approach will contribute to our understanding of the complex interplay between institutions, technology, and demography in the overall process of economic change. A complete theory of economic performance would entail such an integrated approach to economic history. We certainly have not put all the pieces together yet. For example, Robert Fogel's pathbreaking work on demographic theory[11] and its historical implications for reevaluating past economic performance have yet to be integrated fully with institutional analysis. The same is true for technological change. The important contributions of Nathan Rosenberg (1976) and Joel Mokyr (1990) exploring the impetus for and consequences of technological change have ongoing implications, which need to be integrated with institutional analysis. An essay by Wallis and North (1994) is a beginning at integrating technological and institutional analysis. But a major task of economic history is to integrate these separate strands of research.

IMPLICATIONS FOR CURRENT DEVELOPMENT POLICIES

We cannot account for the rise and decline of the Soviet Union and world communism with the tools of neoclassical analysis, but we should be able to with an institutional/cognitive approach to contemporary problems of development. To do so—and to provide an analytical framework to understand economic change—we must take into account the following implications of this approach:

1. It is the admixture of formal rules, informal norms, and enforcement characteristics that shapes economic performance. While the rules may be changed overnight, the informal norms usually change only gradually. Since it is the norms that provide "legitimacy" to a set of rules, revolutionary change is never as revolutionary as its supporters desire, and performance will be different than anticipated. And economies that adopt the formal rules of another economy will have very different performance characteristics than the first economy because of different informal norms and enforcement. The implication is that transferring the formal political and economic rules of successful Western market economies to Third World and Eastern European economies is not a sufficient condition for good economic performance. Privatization is not a panacea for solving poor economic performance.

2. Polities significantly shape economic performance because they define and enforce the economic rules. Therefore an essential part of development policy is the creation of polities that will create and enforce efficient property rights. However, we know very little about how to create such polities because the new political economy (the new institutional economics applied to politics) has been largely focused on the United States and developed polities. A pressing research need is to model Third World and Eastern European polities. However the foregoing analysis does have some implications: (a) Political institutions will be stable only if undergirded by organizations with a stake in their perpetuation. (b) Both institutions and belief systems must change for successful reform since it is the mental models of the actors that will shape choices. (c) Developing norms of behavior that will support and legitimize new rules is a lengthy process, and in the absence of such reinforcing mechanisms polities will tend to be unstable. (d) While economic growth can occur in the short run with autocratic regimes, long-run economic growth entails the development of the rule of law. (e) Informal constraints (norms, conventions, and codes of conduct) favorable to growth can sometimes produce eco-

nomic growth even with unstable or adverse political rules. The key is the degree to which such adverse rules are enforced.

3. It is adaptive rather than allocative efficiency, which is the key to long-run growth. Successful political/economic systems have evolved flexible institutional structures that can survive the shocks and changes that are a part of successful evolution. But these systems have been a product of long gestation. We do not know how to create adaptive efficiency in the short run.

We have just set out on the long road to achieving an understanding of economic performance through time. The ongoing research embodying new hypotheses confronting historical evidence will not only create an analytical framework enabling us to understand economic change through time; in the process it will enrich economic theory, enabling it to deal effectively with a wide range of contemporary issues currently beyond its ken. The promise is there. The recognition of that promise by the Nobel Committee should be the essential spur to move us on down that road.

I am indebted to Robert Bates, Lee and Alexandra Benham, Avner Greif, Margaret Levi, Randy Nielsen, John Nye, Jean-Laurent Rosenthal, Norman Schofield, and Barry Weingast for their comments on an earlier draft and to Elisabeth Case for editing this essay.

NOTES

This article is the lecture Douglass C. North delivered in Stockholm, Sweden, December 9, 1993, when he received the Alfred Nobel Memorial Prize in Economic Sciences. The article is copyright © The Nobel Foundation 1993 and is published here with the permission of the Nobel Foundation.

1. In fact such a theory is unlikely. I refer the reader to Frank Hahn's prediction (1991) about the future of economic theory.

2. These two sections briefly summarize material contained in North (1990a).

3. See the author's "A Transaction Cost Theory of Politics" for a transaction-cost approach to the relative inefficiency of political markets (North 1990b).

4. However, see the anomalies even here in the studies by Amos Tversky and Daniel Kahneman (1986) and others (Hogarth and Reder 1986).

5. See John H. Holland et al. (1986) for an excellent introduction to the cognitive-science literature.

6. Ideologies are shared frameworks of mental models that groups of individuals possess that provide both an interpretation of the environment and a prescription as to how that environment should be ordered.

7. Ronald Heiner (1983), in a pathbreaking article, not only made the connection between the mental capacities of humans and the external environment but suggested the implications for arresting economic progress.

8. See North and Thomas (1973), Jones (1981), and Rosenberg and Birdzell (1986) for accounts of this growth.

9. See part III of North (1990a) for a brief discussion of the contrasting paths of the Netherlands and England on the one hand and Spain on the other.

10. DeVries (1976, 28) has a description of the bizarre remedies proposed by a royal commission to reverse Spain's decline.

11. See Fogel's Nobel lecture (1994).

References

Arthur, Brian. 1989. "Competing Technologies, Increasing Returns, and Lock-In by Historical Events." *Economic Journal* 99(394): 116–31.

Clark, Andy, and Annette Karmiloff-Smith. 1993. "The Cognizer's Innards: A Psychological and Philosophical Perspective on the Development of Thought." *Mind and Language* 8(4): 487–519.

Coase, Ronald. 1960. "The Problem of Social Cost." *Journal of Law and Economics* 3(1): 1–44.

David, Paul A. 1985. "Clio and the Economics of QWERTY." *American Economic Review* 75 (2): 332–37.

DeVries, Jan. 1976. *The Economy of Europe in an Age of Crises, 1600–1750*. Cambridge, England: Cambridge University Press.

Fogel, Robert W. 1994. "Economic Growth, Population Theory, and Physiology: The Bearing of Long-Term Processes on the Making of Economic Policy." *Americun Economic Review* 84(3): 369–95.

Hahn, Frank. 1991. "The Next Hundred Years." *Economic Journal* 101(404): 47–50.

Hayek, Friedrich A. 1960. *The Constitution of Liberty*. Chicago, Ill.: Chicago University Press.

Heiner, Ronald. 1983. "The Origin of Predictable Behavior." *American Economic Review* 73(4): 560–95.

Hogarth, Robin M., and Melvin W. Reder, eds. 1986. *Rational Choice: The Contrast between Economics and Psychology*. Chicago, Ill.: University of Chicago Press.

Holland, John H., Keith J. Holyoak, Richard E. Nisbett, and Paul R. Thagard. 1986. *Induction: Processes of Inference, Learning, and Discovery*. Cambridge, Mass.: MIT Press.

Jones, E. L. 1981. *The European Miracle*. Cambridge, England: Cambridge University Press.

Mokyr, Joel. 1990. *The Lever of Riches*. New York: Oxford University Press.

Nelson, Richard, and Sidney G. Winter. 1982. *An Evolutionary Theory of Economic Change*. Cambridge, Mass.: Harvard University Press.

North, Douglass C. 1990a. *Institutions, Institutional Change, and Economic Performance*. New York: Cambridge University Press.

———. 1990b. "A Transactions Cost Theory of Politics." *Journal of Theoretical Politics*. 2(4): 355–67.

North, Douglass C., and Robert P. Thomas. 1973. *The Rise of the Western World: A New Economic History*. Cambridge, England: Cambridge University Press.

Rosenberg, Nathan. 1976. *Perspectives on Technology*. Cambridge: Cambridge University Press.

Rosenberg, Nathan, and L. E. Birdzell. 1986. *How the West Grew Rich: The Economic Transformation of the Industrial World*. New York: Basic Books.

Simon, Herbert. 1986. "Rationality in Psychology and Economics." In *Rational Choice: The Contrast between Economics and Psychology*, edited by Robin M. Hogarth and Melvin W. Reder. Chicago, Ill.: University of Chicago Press.

Tversky, Amos, and Daniel Kahneman. 1986. "Rational Choice and the Framing of Decisions." In *Rational Choice: The Contrast between Economics and Psychology*, edited by Robin M. Hogarth and Melvin W. Reder. Chicago, Ill.: University of Chicago Press.

Wallis, John J., and Douglass C. North. 1986. "Measuring the Transaction Sector in the American Economy." In *Long-term Factors in American Economic Growth*, edited by Stanley L. Engerman and Robert E. Gallman. Chicago, Ill.: University of Chicago Press.

———. 1994. "Integrating Institutional Change and Technical Change in Economic History: A Transactions Costs Approach." *Journal of Institutional and Theoretical Economics* 150 (4): 609–24.

12

Changing the Rules: Interests, Organizations, and Institutional Change in the U.S. Hospitality Industry

Paul Ingram

North (1990, 3) defines institutions as "the rules of the game in a society or, more formally, the humanly devised constraints that shape human interaction." Nee and Ingram argue (in this volume) that this view of institutions is a promising base for building the new economic sociology. Combined with the simple and powerful behavioral assumption of rationality, the institutions-as-constraints position can explain a wide range of phenomena ranging from honesty in eleventh-century long-distance trade (Greif 1993), to modern business-government relationships (Hillman and Keim 1995).

As the number of demonstrations of institutional influence on action grows in sociology and other fields, the importance of explaining the creation and change of institutions increases. Complete institutional explanations require understanding not only the effect of institutions but also the origin of institutions (Brint and Karabel 1991; Alt and Shepsle 1990). Since institutions define the opportunities and incentives that determine outcomes for actors, and because institutions are humanly devised, we should expect actors to try to influence institutions. If institutions are the rules of the game that structure interaction, we should consider also a "supergame," where the rules themselves are the object of competition.

In this chapter, I examine the influence of organizations on institutional change. I argue that institutional dynamics and organizational dynamics are closely related and, in particular, that new organizational forms are an important source of institutional change. To illustrate this idea, I consider how hotel organizations affected change in the institutions in the United States related to training and education in the hospitality industry. There were a number of alternatives for the training and education of employees in this industry. The biggest question was whether such training should be provided by trade schools to low-level employees, such as clerks and waitstaff, or by universities to managers. The first alternative was favored by the traditional independent hotel and the second by the emerging hotel chains. Ultimately, university training prevailed.

ORGANIZATIONS AND INSTITUTIONAL CHANGE

Individuals, organizations, and other social groups are all affected by institutions and therefore have an interest in changing institutions in their favor. However, as Hannan and Freeman (1989, 3) observe, "almost all modern collective action takes place in *organizational* contexts; and organizations are the main vehicles for action in modern society" (emphasis in original). Therefore, organizations are a likely place to begin an explanation of institutional change.

North (1990, ch 9; 1993) also identifies organizations as the principal agents of institutional change. According to North (1993, 1), the key to institutional change is the generation and diffusion of skills and knowledge by competing organizations. "Competition in the overall economic setting of scarcity induces entrepreneurs and the members of their organizations to invest in skills and knowledge. Whether it is learning by doing on the job or the acquisition of formal knowledge, the key to survival is improving the efficiency of the organization relative to that of rivals" (3–4). Since the stock of knowledge in a society is the "deep underlying determinant of the performance of economies and societies . . . learning by individuals and organizations is the major influence on the evolution of institutions" (8).

North's basic assertion, that economic competition leads to investments in knowledge and that the advancement of knowledge leads to institutional change, is persuasive. However, there is a serious problem with this learning-based explanation of institutional change: it is grounded in a flawed micro theory. North's view of organizations, based on the economic theory of the firm, mischaracterizes the process by which organizations learn and generate knowledge. The root of the problem is that North, like most economists who talk about organizations, overestimates the capacity of organizations to change. North like other organizational and evolutionary economists holds a Lamarckian view of organizational change, that organizations can adapt to changes in their environment and respond to opportunities presented by new knowledge (Nelson and Winter 1982).

However, organizational sociologists have shown that the assumption of Lamarckian change is not supportable. Both internal and external factors make it difficult for organizations to change in substantial ways—organizations are inertial. Thus, change at the macro level often occurs when an organizational form replaces another, rather than through the transformation of existing organizations (Hannan and Freeman 1977). This Darwinian selection of organizations has implications for North's theory of institutional change. The process of institutional change begins, according to North (1990, 86), when an innovation through learning (or some other change in relative prices) causes one or more parties to an exchange to perceive that they can do better by altering their agreement or contract. Yet, if existing organizations cannot reliably change, they are unlikely to be the actors that exploit new knowledge and drive institutional change. Existing organizations cannot reliably benefit from a new institutional arrangement that facilitates the utilization of new knowledge because they cannot reliably reorganize themselves to incorporate this new knowledge or to fit into the new institutional arrangement. Rather than existing organizations, I argue, it is new organizations representing new organizational forms that exploit new knowledge and become the agents of institutional change.

Organizational Inertia

It is obvious that organizations are inertial to some degree at least. If they were perfectly adaptable, we would never see existing organizations fail or new ones founded. Still, the myth of perfectly adaptable organizations persists, so it is necessary to outline the argument for inertia. Hannan and Freeman (1984, 149) summarize the causes of inertia:

Some of the factors that generate structural inertia are internal to organizations: these include sunk costs in plant, equipment, and personnel, the dynamics of political coalitions, and the tendency for precedents to become normative standards. Others are external. There are legal and other barriers to entry and exit from realms of activity. Exchange relations with other organizations constitute an investment that is not written off lightly. Finally, attempting radical structural change often threatens legitimacy; the loss of institutional support may be devastating.

The following example illustrates the concept of inertia. Floating Point Systems, which, prior to 1980, was the dominant firm in the array processor industry (array processors enhance the computational speed of mini- and mainframe computers), discovered a new architecture that would represent a quantum improvement in the computational speed of its products. North, and others who believe in the capacity of organizations to change in order to utilize discoveries, would have predicted that Floating Point would successfully introduce a product based on the new technology. But Floating Point did not adopt the new technology it had discovered. One former Floating Point executive explained his company's failure to exploit its discovery with an observation that supports Hannan and Freeman's identification of intraorganizational political dynamics as a source of inertia: "There was a lot of interest in preserving personal wealth and less interest in taking risks" (Neal 1984). Another explanation for a failure of this type might be that investments in old technology result in a cognitive commitment on the part of executives to that technology, distorting their evaluation of the new technology. Still another explanation is that markets and technologies are so complex that executives cannot reliably predict what will be effective, so they simply stay with the old familiar technologies.

Importantly, the behavioral assumption at the heart of the inertia argument, bounded rationality, is the same one used by North and other so-called new institutional economists. Cognitive biases account, for example, for the failure to disregard sunk costs (Kahneman, Slovic, and Tversky 1982). The legitimacy attached to organizational structures may result from attempts to make sense of a complex world with limited cognitive capacity. Moreover, if individuals were perfectly rational, any organizational change that would improve the aggregate level of utility of affected actors (any change worth making) would generate a surplus that could be divided in such a way that all parties would benefit from the change, thus eliminating resistance from political coalitions and exchange partners. So, differing views on organizational change do not result because new institutional economists and organizational sociologists assume different things about individuals—both recognize that individuals are boundedly rational. However, sociologists have gone much further in considering the implications of this recognition for complex forms of social organization.

Evidence that change puts organizations at risk of failure supports the inertia argument. In a study of organizational change among Finnish newspapers, Amburgey, Kelly, and Barnett (1993) found that changes in a newspaper's content and frequency of publication caused an immediate increase in the likelihood that the organization would fail, although the effect decreased with time. Moreover, there is important evidence in support of the inertia argument in the work on the age dependence of organizational mortality. It is often argued that selection pressures that force failure apply mostly to young, small organizations but that large, powerful (and by implication, important) organizations adapt to their environment (Scott 1981, 204). Therefore, it is argued, organizations become less likely to fail as they grow older (Dosi 1995). The organizations subject to inertia are quickly weeded out, while those that "get it right" and avoid inertia grow larger, more powerful, and more robust as they age. This prediction is in direct conflict with the inertia argument—if inertia holds, organizations should become more antiquated and therefore more likely to fail as they age. The age dependence of organizational mortality has as a result been the subject of a vigorous empirical debate. The best recent evidence indicates that organizations are more likely to fail as they age, supporting the inertia position (Barron, West, and Hannan 1994).

Organizational Learning and Institutional Change in the Face of Inertia

If institutional change occurs because of advances in knowledge, then we must consider the effect of organizational inertia on the type of knowledge that organizations will seek. Since inertia makes it difficult for organizations to incorporate the new technologies and modes of exchange that drive institutional change, existing organizations are threatened rather than benefited by such advances in knowledge. We should therefore expect existing organizations to work to improve their efficiency through marginal improvements in existing modes of operation, rather than through more radical innovations that threaten their technical competencies and established organizational processes. This bias in organizational learning toward marginal improvements on old ways of doing things causes an organization's interests to be most closely aligned with existing institutions, which results in support for the status quo. Having been founded to exploit a given institutional framework, and with a limited capacity to change, existing organizations are favored by the stability of institutions. Therefore, existing organizations are a source of resistance to institutional change. Radical institutional change would render organizations designed to exploit an existing institutional framework obsolete. If such organizations are constrained from changing to conform with the new institutions, they will resist institutional change. Indeed, because existing organizations have an interest in institutional stability, they are an important source of the path dependence of institutions that North (1990) observes.

March (1991, 73) categorizes organizational learning efforts in a way that is applicable to this discussion of institutional change. He notes that organizations may engage in "exploitation" of existing knowledge and competencies or in "exploration" for new knowledge and competencies. The inertia argument suggests that organizations should favor exploitation over exploration, and March in fact argues that organizations favor exploitation, without explicitly considering inertia. He points out that "compared to returns from exploitation, returns from exploration are systematically less certain, more remote in time, and organizationally more distant from the locus of action and adaption." The implications of exploitation described by March support my argument that most organizational learning leads to path dependence and stability rather than to institutional change: "Each increase in competence at an activity increases the likelihood of rewards for engaging in that activity, thereby further increasing the competence and the likelihood."

If it is true that learning by existing organizations is generally limited to improving their existing activities, and therefore has minor implications for institutional change, what is the source of the new knowledge that generates significant institutional change? I argue that *new* (or even gestating) organizations are the source of this knowledge. New organizations are relatively free of the constraints that prevent existing organizations from benefiting from new knowledge. Until it is founded, an organization does not have a set organizational structure, a system of incentives, a network of relationships between employees, or political coalitions. Its founders are free to design all of these things to be congruent with the most attractive technological and operational activities. The managers of a new organization do not have investment histories in that organization that might lead them to fail to recognize or be biased against new opportunities. Thus, new organizations are relatively free of inertia. Some former Floating Point executives, for example, frustrated with Floating Point's failure to utilize the promising new technology it had developed, started a new company called Star Technologies. Since the executives of the new company did not have to rely on the old architecture to protect their positions, the new company could be designed to facilitate the introduction of the new array processor architecture. Star Technologies introduced the new architecture and within a few years, captured more than half the array processor market.

Because a new process or product that is an improvement over what existed before is valuable to a new organization designed to utilize it, the new organization is a likely source of pressure to change institutions to facilitate the new process or product. For example, such a new organization as Star Technologies might attempt to change U.S. government purchasing policies or the curricula of computer science schools to facilitate the market penetration of the new array processor architecture. Organizations that predate the new process or product may not be able to change to incorporate it due to inertia and will resist institutional changes that facilitate its use because such changes help new competitors and probably make it more difficult for existing organizations to use the processes and market the products they rely on. So, Floating Point Systems could be expected to resist attempts by Star Technologies to change U.S. government purchasing policies and the curricula of computer science schools because such changes would inhibit the marketability of the old array processor architecture that Floating Point relies on.[1]

INSTITUTIONAL CHANGE IN THE EDUCATIONAL SYSTEM OF THE U.S. HOSPITALITY INDUSTRY

The rest of this chapter focuses on a historical case to illustrate the idea that significant institutional change is championed by new organizations and resisted by existing organizations. I follow recent sociological works on institutional change in combining structural and historical analysis (Starr 1982; DiMaggio 1991; Brint and Karabel 1991). DiMaggio (1988) suggested that explaining in-

stitutional change requires attention to interest and agency, an idea consistent
with the rationality assumption of the new institutionalism as expressed by North
and others. Analysis of the organizational and institutional structure of industries, economies, and societies permits the identification of the institutional interests of actors and the power they have to pursue those interests. Historical analysis facilitates the connecting of directed human action to structural outcomes
(Starr 1982, 8), a connection that must be made to support an account of institutional change based on rationality.

In presenting the case of institutional change in the educational system of the
U.S. hospitality industry, I hope to illustrate the process by which new organizations cause institutional change. The new organizations in this case are hotel
chains, which were a fledgling organizational form in the first quarter of this
century. (There were three hotel chains in 1896, and twenty-five in 1918. In
1996, there were more than five hundred.) If new organizations do account for
institutional change, they must somehow overcome the entrenched interests of
older organizations, so I will also analyze the case so as to generate grounded
theory about what makes actors effective in attempts to change institutions.

The Labor Problem in the U.S. Hospitality Industry

Complaints of a shortage of labor were one of the most common topics of discussion at gatherings of hoteliers in the early part of the twentieth century
(AHMA Archives). The rapid growth of the industry combined with the lack of
a training system for hotel employees created the problem (Inman 1993). With
the outbreak of World War I, it became a critical problem. Previous to that, the
largest hotel organizations had relied on employees trained in European hotel
schools and in the apprenticeship system of the European hospitality industry to
fill minor executive roles. These employees provided training for subordinates
(AHMA Archives, IV 70). In 1914, many of these employees returned to Europe, and the supply of well-trained immigrants dried up.

After the war, the crisis continued. New U.S. immigration policies made it
much more difficult for Europeans to enter the country. The labor problem was
so severe that there were calls for the Hotel Association of New York City to use
its influence to get the immigration restrictions eased (AHMA Archives, VI 27).
The few European employees who could be acquired were no longer as valuable
because the "Red Scare" caused the public they served to view them with suspicion. At least one hotel chain (the Boomer-Dupont System in New York City)
went so far as to require foreign employees to study "Americanism" and to wear
red, white, and blue ribbons to disassociate themselves from "Bolsheviks" and
other "undesirable aliens" (AHMA Archives, VI 29).

The whole hospitality industry suffered from this shortage of labor, but the
problem faced by the early hotel chains was even more notable. These organizations needed not only the traditional hotel employees but also a new type of
hotel employee: the professional manager. Chandler (1977, 1) notes that management by a hierarchy of salaried executives is one of the defining characteristics of
the modern multiunit business enterprise, of which hotel chains are an example.
Hotel chains rely heavily on salaried executives or professional managers, and are
(typically) larger and more geographically dispersed than independent hotels.

Therefore, training and personnel practices, planning and coordination, and control of employees are important to the success of a hotel chain, which must be "managed," as opposed to merely operated.

Alternative Solutions to the Labor Problem

There are four groups that might reasonably be expected to pay for the training of employees in an industry: the state, the industry, individual organizations, and the employees themselves. The U.S. hotel industry ultimately pursued a centralized training system. After failed attempts to convince federal and state governments to support this system, the industry itself provided the necessary financial support. While this chapter focuses on this system and its creation, we turn first to a brief discussion of why two alternative systems, in-house training and apprenticeship, were not adopted by the industry.

Hotel organizations could have responded to the shortage of labor by assuming the costs of training. They could have established in-house training programs, and some hotel chains did. The Fred Harvey System had such a program dating back to the late nineteenth century. The product of this system, the Harvey Girl, became a part of American folklore and was immortalized in a mid-1940s MGM movie (Moon 1980). United Hotels and Statler Hotels also attempted in-house training (Inman 1993). The reason that in-house training did not become institutionalized throughout the industry is probably because of the high mobility of labor among hospitality organizations. If employees were likely to change employers frequently, then any hotel organization that incurred the cost of their training would end up paying to train someone else's workers. A 1926 advertisement for the Holman Hotel in Athens, Georgia, with its boast that the hotel's manager was "Statler Trained," illustrated this risk (*Hotel Red Book* 1926, 124).

It might also have been possible to put the cost of training on the employee, through some form of apprenticeship system. After all, such a system was used with great success in Europe. The evidence, while not conclusive, seems to indicate that the apprentice system was a victim of the isolationist sentiment that seized the United States after World War I. In a February 29, 1936, letter to a European hospitality educator, Dean Howard Meek of Cornell's hotel school claimed that apprenticeships were not "the American way." He claimed that the apprentice system had been tried but that very few hotels would take students on an apprenticeship basis (CUA, 28/1/1803, 1–6). It is not obvious why apprenticeships should be thought (then and now) to be "un-American" but it is interesting to note that while many industries in Europe use apprenticeship systems, this is not the case in the United States.

Another reason why apprenticeships were not adopted is also suggested in Meek's letter. He asserted that Cornell was "trying to lay the groundwork for the production of well-qualified, well-rounded, real executives" and that European executives trained in the apprenticeship system were found to be too "domestic and service," as opposed to business, oriented. So, it may be that apprenticeship was capable of producing the traditional hotel executive but incapable of producing the professional manager that U.S. hotel chains were demanding in increasing quantities. This argument makes sense when the demands on traditional hotel executives are contrasted with those on hotel chain managers. An apprentice in a hotel may learn about service, manners, and patchwork furnace repair but cannot reasonably be expected to absorb the operational and strategic demands of a multiunit chain. Further, the proprietary information that a chain would have to disclose to an apprentice manager would discourage the use of an apprenticeship system.

The remaining alternative for training hotel employees was some kind of centralized system, but this raised two questions: Who would pay for it? and What type of training would be provided? Hoteliers were united in their hope that government would foot the bill. However, there was a critical disagreement about what type of training should be provided. The vast majority of hoteliers in the United States immediately after World War I operated small, independent hotels. These hoteliers wanted practical training at a level below college for clerks, waitstaff, and housekeepers. The small number of hotel chain operators favored university degree programs that would produce professional managers. This conflict between new and existing organizations with respect to institutional preference supports my theory in that (the new) hotel chains were championing a radical change in the industry's system of education to train a new type of worker, while (the existing) independent hoteliers wanted marginal improvements in the educational system, to train more of the workers hotels had traditionally relied on. The resolution of this conflict is the story of institutional change in this industry.

The History of the Educational Project

The earliest specific suggestions for an industry-supported educational system for hotel employees began just after the turn of the century. *Hotel Monthly* for October 1903 noted that a proposal had been made at the recent International Stewards Association (ISA) convention to establish a chair of hotel education at the Tuskegee Institute in Alabama. That same year, the editor of *Hotel Monthly*, John Willy, began campaigning for technical schools for hotel workers, suggesting that "perhaps a society of hotel employers may be formed covering all America, to contribute, say, one-tenth of one percent of their payroll" (Willy 1903).

In 1907, the ISA announced plans to build a hotel training school near Indianapolis. This plan was widely endorsed by hotel associations, but attempts to raise funds were unsuccessful (AHMA Archives, II 27). Also in 1907, John McFarlane Howie, proprietor of the Touraine Hotel in Buffalo, claimed to have conceived the idea of establishing chairs of gastronomy at state universities.

Between 1911 and 1916, state hotel associations gave increasingly more attention to the labor problem, and their members became convinced that "the best solution lay in an educational program which should be handled on the national level" (AHMA Archives, IV 68). In 1911, both Columbia University and New York University offered courses in home economics and accounting that were promoted as being appropriate for hotel employees. The private Lewis Hotel Training School, which is still in existence, was established as a correspondence school in 1916, later becoming a residential school in Washington, D.C.

The labor shortage that crippled hotels in the period after World War I also affected other industries, and in response, the federal government engaged in some postwar retraining efforts. Specifically, the Smith-Hughes Act provided federal funds for vocational training. This caught the attention of hoteliers, and there were a number of proposals for the hospitality industry to acquire a share of these funds by establishing training programs in high schools.

The various proposals for hotel education were presented at the 1920 meeting of the American Hotel Association (AHA). Professor Flora Rose, codirector (with Martha Van Rensselaer) of the School of Home Economics in the College of Agriculture at Cornell, made the case for a degree program at Cornell. John Howie then took up the cause, claiming that there was no reason for the AHA to raise a million dollars to finance a training institute when public universities could produce hotel executives capable of training their own workers. Those favoring nonuniversity programs also made their case:

> H.J. Bohn [the editor of *Hotel World*] . . . took the floor to plead for AHA support for some sort of lower level training school. Gilbert Cowan, President of the ACA [American Caterers Association], urged that the hotelmen help the caterers establish a school, especially for cooks and bakers, in the old Calumet Club in Chicago. Edwin Piper, of the Lewis School, sought official recognition for a school already flourishing, boasting of its fifty textbooks on hotel subjects, of the thousand students enrolled in its correspondence courses, and of the residential part of the school, opening in Washington, D.C. (AHMA Archives, VI 8).

The response of the convention was to adopt a resolution stating that since the labor situation had grown increasingly worse since 1914, and since the use of Smith-Hughes funds for vocational training in other fields was already leading bright young people away from hotel careers, the AHA approved and endorsed the proposition to found a National Hotel Institute. The form of this institute was left undetermined, with a committee of twenty-one created and empowered to investigate and act on behalf of the AHA on the matter.

The membership of this committee of twenty-one is one of the important determinants of the outcome of the education debate. On the committee were the presidents of the largest hotel chains in the country, including John Bowman (Bowman Hotels), Lucious Boomer (Boomer-Dupont Properties), Frank Dudley (United Hotels), Eugene Eppley (Eppley Hotels), Ford Harvey (Fred Harvey Co.), and E. M. Statler (Statler Hotels). In fact, ten out of twenty hoteliers on the committee, including the chairman, were the heads of hotel chains (the twenty-first member was from the hotel press). This was impressive, given the fact that there were only twenty-eight hotel chains in 1920, while there were more than twenty thousand independently owned hotels. This meant that a hotel chain was more than seven hundred times as likely to be represented on the committee that would determine the form of education in the hotel industry than an independent hotel.

Without officially disregarding alternative options, the education committee immediately concentrated its efforts on establishing a university degree program for hotel managers at Cornell University. The connection with Cornell grew out of a friendship between John Howie and Flora Rose and Martha Van Rensselaer of Cornell's Home Economics Department. By 1921, that department was already offering some institutional management courses that seemed appropriate as building blocks for a hotel management program. Frank Dudley, the head of United Hotels (at that time the largest chain in the country), led the negotiations with Cornell. Albert Mann, the dean of Cornell's School of Agriculture, within which the hotel program would be operated, was most concerned that the money to operate the program should come from sources outside the university. Mann also wanted to establish a curriculum that minimized the number both of new courses and of courses outside the School of Agriculture that would be needed to satisfy hotel degree requirements.

For the AHA representatives, the issues were the curriculum and the association of the hotel program with home economics. Chain operators such as Lucious Boomer were adamant that the program should have a heavy emphasis on business courses. The curriculum first proposed by Cornell included three credit hours of accounting. When the program began in the fall of 1922, nine credit hours of accounting were offered, and six more hours were added in 1924 (CUA, 1/28/1803, 1–1). The concern over having hotel students under the control of the home economics department appears to have been the result of sexism. The hospitality industry was a pioneer in opening up job opportunities to women, but some hoteliers were averse to having the best and brightest young hotel managers study courses designed for women in a department operated by women (Inman 1993). Cornell did not respond to requests to establish the hotel program in another department, but it did agree to hire the strong-minded hotelier, Howard B. Meek, the AHA representatives recommended to head the program. From the beginning, Meek disregarded the vision of home economists and liberal educators and instead worked to establish the completely specialized, practical curriculum favored by chain operators such as Boomer.

The AHA originally hoped that the Cornell program would be financed by the New York state government. One reason for expecting such an outcome was that Frank Dudley, a member of the AHA committee, was a former state legislator, and his Ten Eyck hotel in Albany was a political center. AHA representatives and Dean Mann traveled to Albany in January 1922 to lobby the legislators, but their efforts were unsuccessful. The program nevertheless began that fall, with money put up by Dudley, Statler, and other chain owners.

From the beginning, Cornell's program had close ties with hotel chains. Even before the program accepted students, relationships with five hotel chains were established for training tours (CUA, 1/28/1803, 1–1). The chains also supported Cornell's program by paying for students to attend AHA annual meetings, lending executives to give lectures, and providing equipment (CUA, 1/28/1803, 1–6). Ninety percent of the summer placements of the first class were with hotel chains. Illustrative of the relationship of Cornell's program to the hotel chains is the June 17, 1924, letter from Professor Meek to United Hotels, in which he stated that he "wanted particularly to let [United] have the pick of our class" (CUA, 1/28/1803, 1–3). A February 24, 1936, letter from Meek to Walter I. Hamilton, an executive with Boomer-Dupont Properties, describes the careers of nine Cornell graduates, five of whom were executives with hotel chains. The January 4, 1935, issue of *Hotel and Catering Weekly* refers to the 232 living graduates of Cornell's program, 109 of whom held executive positions in hotel organizations. Today, the top executives of many hotel chains, including Holiday Inn, are graduates of Cornell's hotel school.

Other schools were also considered for hotel programs. At the 1922 AHA meetings, Dudley told those present that negotiations were "pending" with Harvard, Stanford, the University of Pennsylvania, and the state universities of Illinois, Iowa, and California (CUA, 1/28/1803, 1–1). Another group within the AHA had made a serious effort to establish a hotel school at the University of California, Berkeley, at the same time the Cornell program was being established, and Berkeley actually offered courses designed specifically for hotel students in the fall of 1921, a whole year before Cornell, making it the first university to do so. The first major hotel program established after Cornell's was at Michigan State University, and it is even now considered second only to Cornell's in the field. There are now more than one hundred four-year degree programs in hospitality management. Since 1922, these programs have been producing the type of manager that hotel chains require, but for which independent hotels have no use.

THE INGREDIENTS OF A SUCCESSFUL INSTITUTIONALIZATION PROJECT

The preceding account reveals the conflict of interest that existed between the new hotel chains and the older independent hotels. The question of how the hotel chains were able to change the institutions of the hospitality industry in their favor is central to my argument about institutional change—how do new organizations change institutions at the expense of older organizations that are more established, have greater legitimacy, and are more plentiful? One historian, amazed by the success of the hotel chain operators in establishing their educational program, wondered incredulously whether the authorities were "moved by the opinion that AHA educational policy should be determined by the heads of large groups of hotels located in large cities, despite the fact that most member hotels were then, and would continue for decades to be, small houses located far from the roaring streets of Manhattan" (AHMA Archives, VI 232–33).

Institutionalization projects are attempts by institutional entrepreneurs (actors who actively pursue their interests through institutional change) and their allies to establish the public theory that serves their interests (DiMaggio 1988, 14–15). In this instance, the chain operators engaged in a successful institutionalization project in the battle over education. Theirs was largely a political effort, requiring them to persuade hoteliers, governments, and universities that degree programs for hotel managers should be created and supported. By looking at this particular institutionalization project as an instance of collective action and by examining the conditions that allowed the upstart chains to overcome the interests of the much larger group of independent hotels, we can learn something about the nature of institutional change more generally.

Institutional Change as Collective Action

The reason that studies of institutional change often use the organizational form as a unit of analysis (as in this chapter, or as in DiMaggio 1991 on art museums, and Brint and Karabel 1991 on community colleges) is that an organizational form, that is, organizations with similar structures and strategies, represents a group of actors with the same interests with respect to the institutional framework. If an institution favors one organization, it favors other organizations of the same type. Thus, the organizational form represents a nexus of interests and is therefore a useful means of categorizing the actors subject to (and affecting) the institutional framework.

An institutional change that favors an organizational form favors all organizations of that form regardless of their contribution to the change and is therefore a public good (an asset that is not exclusive to those who contribute to its creation). Organizations of the same type can benefit from cooperation to change institutions in ways that favor them over other organizational forms with which they compete—hotel chains may cooperate to establish an educational system that favors them over independent hotels, and lumber producers in Washington State may cooperate to win import restrictions that favor them over Canadian lumber producers. However, since the products of such cooperation (the institutional change) benefit all hotel chains and all Washington lumber producers, it is not clear why any individual organization should contribute to the institutionalization project. This is the problem of collective action (Olson 1965).

Education of managers is certainly a public good for the hospitality industry. The stock of managers is a resource upon which all organizations in the industry may draw. However, some organizations benefit more directly than others. Hotel chains require professional managers but small, independently owned hotels do not. The process by which support for university hotel schools was mustered despite the apparent lack of interest on the part of independent hoteliers and the temptation for chain operators to free ride must be considered to understand why this instance of collective action was successful.

In order for university hotel schools such as Cornell's to become the institutionalized form of education in this industry, they needed two things: First, they needed the sanction of hoteliers, as expressed by the AHA. Why would independent hoteliers sanction university education for managers when their interests were served by a much more practical level of training? Probably because they were convinced that the university project would bring them something they desired more strongly than competent employees: the status of belonging to a profession. (The profession-building imagery used by those who tried to establish university hotel schools will be discussed in detail in the analysis of power and coalition building that appears later in this chapter.)

Second, they needed money. The problem of collective action with respect to gaining financial support for the education of managers is even more compelling. Hotel organizations would have the opportunity to hire university-educated managers even if they did not make a financial contribution to establish the educational program. It would seem rational for every hotel organization to have withheld financial support for the education of managers, in the hope of being able to free ride on the contributions of others. One solution to this free-rider problem might have been for a corporate body, such as the AHA, to coerce contributions from its members (Coleman 1990). But the AHA was not in a position to do this. Motions supporting the educational project made at the AHA annual meetings were supported by the membership, but always with the stipulation that the AHA make no financial commitment (AHMA Archives, VI 9). The problem was that the AHA had a heterogeneous membership, and there were rifts not only between chain hotels and independently owned hotels but also between geographical regions. Its existence was tenuous enough that a demand that members support a university educational project, especially one that was to start in the Northeast, would probably have destroyed the AHA.[2]

Since coercion was not feasible, the champions of university hotel schools had to find other means of financing. There were a number of campaigns to raise the necessary monies. As early as March 1906, a letter to the editor of the *Hotel Monthly* appealed to hoteliers to put up "a hundred dollars each toward establishing and maintaining a school for educating young men and women for hotel work." In 1909, the International Stewards Association established a committee to raise the $250,000 necessary to establish a school of cookery and food service (AHMA Archives, II 27). In November 1921, Frank Dudley, then chairman of the AHA's education committee, launched "a historic education fund-raising campaign, the like of which the hotel world had never seen and may never see again" (AHMA Archives, VI 111).

These campaigns were designed to solicit funds from a broad cross section of hotel organizations. Considering the free-rider problem mentioned earlier, it is not surprising that while these campaigns received many promises of contributions, they ultimately raised very little money (AHMA Archives, II 27). Many hoteliers liked the idea of an educational program but wanted someone else to pay for it. When efforts to raise money from the general hotel community failed, the chains had a simple choice: to finance the program themselves (and allow smaller organizations to free ride) or to give up the idea of university education for hotel managers. The eventual solution to the financing problem reflected the fact that university hotel education programs promised to benefit the large hotel chains much more than other hotel organizations. Thus, the large chains apparently thought it was worthwhile to incur the entire cost of establishing the Cornell program. The significant contributions to the educational fund were made by John Bowman, Lucious Boomer, Eugene Eppley, E. M. Statler and Frank Dudley—all presidents of large hotel chains (CUA, 28/1/1803, 1–44).

Interests, Coalitions, and Other Sources of Power

DiMaggio (1988) has argued that institutional change often requires coalitions of actors. Corresponding interests are a good basis for building coalitions if free-rider problems such as the one discussed in the preceding section can be overcome. Building coalitions is also facilitated by the ability of actors to present their interests as altruistic and by the consistency of proposed institutions with a society's basic values. An important reason for both of these coalition-building advantages is that they increase the likelihood of finding actors who share interests. For instance, if an institutional entrepreneur were organizing a coalition to establish an institution that defended a nationalistic sentiment (an example of an interest that is both altruistic and consistent with basic values in society), it should be easier for that person to find sympathetic others than if the institution promised only to make the institutional entrepreneur wealthier. Further, institutional entrepreneurs who champion altruistic interests and interests consistent with societal values have rhetorical advantages. Alexander and Smith (1993) suggest that there is a discursive structure of civil society, a democratic (and counter-democratic) code that can be used to legitimate political activity—although in an important difference from the argument made here, they do not see the classifications of actors and actions according to such discourse as subject to debate and strategic maneuvering.

Applying these ideas about coalitions to the institutionalization of education in the hospitality industry begins with the recognition that the hotel organizations were divided into two (homogenous) groups. The hotel chains shared an interest in a university-level program to produce professional managers. Independent hotels had no use for professional managers but shared an interest in a program that would produce lower-level employees such as clerks, waitstaff, and housekeeping staff. So, it is not surprising that the owners of the early hotel chains cooperated to bring about university education for hotel managers. What has to be explained is how they were able to overcome the competing interest of the more than twenty thousand independent hoteliers.

The most direct determinant of the ability of chain owners to influence the institutionalization of an educational program was their domination of the AHA's education committees. As noted earlier, half the twenty-one members of the original committee were chain executives. Subsequent committees, which likewise were appointed by the AHA's president were smaller (nine and seven members), but chain executives always had about half of the seats. Further, the chairman and the most active members were in every case chain executives. One reason for this overrepresentation of chain executives may have been that since they employed professionals to manage their chains, they were less involved in the day-to-day operation of their organizations and therefore had more time to participate in political and professional affairs than the proprietors of independent hotels. It may also be that it was easier for the smaller group of chain operators to recognize and act upon their shared interest in professional education. It is surely easier to manage a coalition of twenty-eight actors (the number of hotel chains in 1921) as opposed to one of twenty thousand (the number of independent hotels). And although independent hotels were homogenous in terms of their need for lower-level employees, they were heterogenous in a number of other ways. Their different geographic locations affected what they wanted from an educational program. The independent hotels were different in terms of size, age, and quality. These differences may have inhibited their ability to cooperate to establish an educational program for lower-level employees.

However, the success of the chain operators was not simply a result of the failure of independent hotel owners to organize around their interests. It can be argued that independent hoteliers were co-opted: they were enticed to support the university-level educational program by its promise to provide them with status. One of the most effective strategies employed by the chain operators was their emphasis on this promise. By arguing that professional status was the purpose of the university-level educational program, chain operators could seem unselfish and supportive of the interests of all hoteliers. Status was a widely shared interest around which it was possible to rally the diverse actors in this industry.

Evidence of the growing importance of professional status to hoteliers was the election of E. M. Tierney to the AHA presidency in 1921. As an industry observer noted: "Coming to the AHA Presidency just when hotelmen began to dream of college degrees as a means of lifting their occupation to professional status, Tierney's supporters could recall dozens of his well publicized speeches in which he begged hotelmen to think and act as proud professional men, and he was reportedly the first college graduate to preside over that organization" (AHMA Archives, VI 83). Tierney recognized that the educational program being pushed by the chain operators was the surest means of raising the status of hoteliers. He gave Frank Dudley extensive powers over the establishment of the educational program when he put him in charge of a nine-member education committee, recognizing at the time that this appointment might be the most important decision of his administration (AHMA Archives, IV 93).

The dreams of independent hoteliers regarding increased professional status are illustrated in the vision of John McF. Howie, the only independent hotelier who was active in establishing the hotel school at Cornell and the man credited with the idea for hotel education at the university level. Howie disagreed with Lucious Boomer and other chain operators on what Cornell's curriculum should be. Howie (himself capable of quoting Shakespeare "by the yard") favored a liberal arts curriculum for the hotel students. He felt they should be educated in a manner likely to add polish (and thereby presumably raise the status of all hoteliers) rather than to increase their business acumen. In later years, Howie was extremely bitter about what the school had become at the hands of the chain operators. In 1945, shortly before his death, he observed, "It is sad that a great educational institution can prostitute itself for a million dollars" (CUA, 28/1/1803, 1–46).

There were of course other factors that helped the chain operators establish the institutional framework that favored themselves. Perhaps most important was the fact that they were richer than other actors. When alternatives for financing Cornell's hotel school failed to come to fruition, they contributed the necessary money themselves. Influential chain owners such as Dudley and Eppley each gave $25,000 in 1922, and other chain owners made similar contributions. E. M. Statler's will provided one million dollars to be used in "research work for the benefit of the hotel industry of the United States" (CUA, 28/1/1801, 5–14). Chain operators also had social networks that increased their power (Granovetter 1991). Frank Dudley was a former state legislator in New York, and the perception that this increased his ability to obtain state funding for the Cornell project was one reason he was given authority. In 1937, F. A. McKowne, then president of Statler Hotels, was able to convince National Cash Register (NCR) to donate equipment to Cornell for use in teaching accounting to hotel students.

CONCLUSION

This chapter enriches North's ideas (1990; 1993) about how organizations affect institutional change. I do not differ from North in the identification of the increase of knowledge as the engine of institutional change, but I place greater emphasis on *which* actors affect institutional change and how they do so. I have argued that new organizations are the actors that change institutions. Existing organizations are prohibited by inertia from implementing the kind of organizational change that creates the impetus for institutional change. Existing organizations protect their entrenched interests in old ways of operating by resisting institutional change.

The case of institutional change in the educational system of U.S. hospitality supports this view. Around the turn of the century, a new organizational form, hotel chains, was introduced. This organizational form had different requirements of the institutional framework than the long-established independent hotels—in particular, hotel chains required educated professional managers. A political contest for institutional control between chain entrepreneurs and independent hoteliers ensued. The chain entrepreneurs were favored by a decision-making structure that relied on committees they dominated, giving them greater influence in the industry association than their numbers warranted, and they were also able to appeal to the dreams of professional status held by both chain and independent hoteliers. Ultimately, the institutions that favored hotel chains were established.

There are other examples in the literature of the role of new organizations in changing institutions. DiMaggio (1991) found that the champions of a new form of art museum were instrumental in changing institutions surrounding museums, and Brint and Karabel (1991) analyzed the significant role that those who favored a new type of community college had on the institutions of U.S. higher education. The importance of this type of radical, political institutional change in relation to the incremental change resulting from learning by doing that North describes is still to be determined. Perhaps the two views could be incorporated in a dynamic model of the coevolution of institutions and organizational forms. Empirical studies testing generalizations from case studies about what makes for successful institutionalization projects would be useful. Certainly, there must be many instances where new organizational forms fail to change institutions, and these failures should be compared to the successes.

The conflict between new and existing organizational forms over institutions may be a specific case of a more general explanation for institutional change: that conflict over institutional change is rooted in the implication of institutions for the distribution of resources. North's attention to the distributional consequences of institutions is consistent with this general explanation, which is developed in more detail by Knight (1992). Even if this is true, however, I think that the conflict in interests between new and existing organizational forms has a central role in a more general theory of conflict and institutional change. Organizational forms are representative of the congealed distributional interests of individuals and therefore provide a systematic, a priori way to approach conflict over institutions.

Finally, besides offering a more realistic view of organizational action to North's theory of institutional change, the arguments in this chapter also inform North's important discussion of "adaptive efficiency" (1990), which is "concerned with the kinds of rules that shape the way an economy evolves through time" (80). North recognizes that the advance of knowledge is furthered by rules that encourage "trials, experiments and innovations." I would add that for new knowledge to be exploited, it is important to encourage trials and experiments in organization. As Hannan and Freeman (1989) observe, the set of solutions to society's challenges is largely a function of the diversity of existing organizations. To the extent that it can be made cheaper to create innovative organizations—and to disband them if they fail—adaptive efficiency will be improved.

Ultimately, institutional dynamics cannot be separated from organizational dynamics. Explaining institutional change therefore requires an understanding both of the effect of institutions on interests and capabilities, and of the complexities of the organizations through which most utility-seeking behavior occurs. This chapter succeeds if it illustrates not only the promise but also the necessity of a joint venture between economics and sociology to address the problem of institutional change.

The history on institutional change in the U.S. hospitality industry presented here is from my dissertation and benefited from the comments of my dissertation committee, John Freeman, Bob Gibbons, and Victor Nee. Mary Brinton and Bruce Western provided helpful comments on a draft of this paper. The theory presented here benefited from my work with Joel Baum, Crist Inman, and Victor Nee.

NOTES

1. This view of institutional dynamics parallels the "competency destroying" technological innovations studied by Tushman and Anderson (1986) and Anderson and Tushman (1990). Competency destroying technological innovations threaten organizations that predate them and are typically championed by new organizations. However, Tushman and Anderson also identify "competency enhancing" technological innovations, which are marginal improvements on existing technologies and favor the existing organizations that use those technologies. Certainly, there are institutional innovations that, like competency enhancing technological innovations, represent marginal changes of the preexisting order and favor existing organizations. North's learning arguments explain marginal institutional changes such as these, and to the extent that such changes accumulate to account for substantial change in the institutional framework, attention to the competitive learning pursuits of existing organizations has value. The relative importance of marginal and more radical institutional changes is an empirical question. It is at least interesting that the greatest increases in technological efficiency come not from the marginal competency enhancing innovations but from competency destroying innovations and the competition between technological regimes that competency destroying innovations induce (Anderson and Tushman 1990). The relative importance of marginal and radical change in technological evolution, and the institutional histories of industries such as the U.S. hospitality industry suggest that whatever the importance of marginal institutional change, radical institutional change is important enough to be theorized about and studied.

2. Probably the most divisive issue for associations of hoteliers in the first quarter of the twentieth century was the dominance of operators from the Northeast, who were mostly from New York City. Westerners were most vocal about the lack of attention to their interests. Sam Dutton, a Colorado hotelier (trained in the Fred Harvey System) championed a "See America First" campaign that at times threatened to divide the AHA. Dutton and others felt that Eastern hoteliers ignored the necessity of promoting domestic travel. The rallying cry for Dutton's movement was "See Europe if you must, but see America first."

   Ultimately, the only way the AHA was able to establish itself as a stable, national association was with the adoption, in 1921, of the "Pellow Plan" (Robert Pellow was the San Antonio, Texas, hotelier who first proposed the plan). This reorganization gave increased voting privileges to state hotel associations. Eventually, the AHA (later the AHMA) would become a federation of state hotel associations.

REFERENCES

Alexander, Jeffrey C., and Philip Smith. 1993. "The Discourse of American Civil Society: A New Proposal for Cultural Studies." *Theory and Society* 22: 151–208.

Alt, James E., and Kenneth A. Shepsle. 1990. "Introduction." In *Perspectives on Positive Political*

Economy, edited by James E. Alt and Kenneth A. Shepsle. New York: Cambridge University Press.

Amburgey, Terry L., Dawn Kelly, and William P. Barnett. 1993. "Resetting the Clock: The Dynamics of Organizational Change and Failure." *Administrative Science Quarterly* 38: 51–73.

American Hotel and Motel Association (AHMA) Archives, Washington, D.C.

Anderson, Philip, and Michael L. Tushman. 1990. "Technological Discontinuities and Dominant Designs: A Cyclical Model of Technological Change." *Administrative Science Quarterly* 35: 604–33.

Barron, David N., Elizabeth West, and Michael T. Hannan. 1994. "A Time to Grow and a Time to Die: Growth and Mortality of Credit Unions in New York City, 1914–1990." *American Journal of Sociology* 100: 381–421.

Brint, Steven, and Jerome Karabel. 1991. "Institutional Origins and Transformations: The Case of American Community Colleges." In *The New Institutionalism in Organizational Analysis*, edited by Walter W. Powell and Paul J. DiMaggio. Chicago, Ill.: University of Chicago Press.

Chandler, Alfred D. 1977. *The Visible Hand*. Cambridge, Mass.: Belknap Press.

Coleman, James S. 1990. *Foundations of Social Theory*. Cambridge, Mass.: Belknap Press.

Cornell University Archives (CUA). Ithaca, N.Y. 28/1/1801.

———. Ithaca, N.Y. 28/1/1803.

DiMaggio, Paul J. 1988. "Interest and Agency in Institutional Theory." In *Institutional Patterns and Organizations: Culture and Environment*, edited by Lynne G. Zucker. Cambridge, Mass.: Ballinger.

———. 1991. "Constructing an Organizational Field as a Professional Project: U.S. Art Museums, 1920–1940." In *The New Institutionalism in Organizational Analysis*, edited by Walter W. Powell and Paul J. DiMaggio. Chicago, Ill.: University of Chicago Press.

Dosi, Giovanni. 1995. Lecture given at the Summer School in Economic Theory, Centre for Advanced Study, Hebrew University. Jerusalem, Israel (June 12, 1995).

Granovetter, Mark. 1991. "Economic Institutions as Social Constructions: A Framework for Analyses." Paper presented at the CREA Conference on the Economics of Conventions. Paris, France (March 27–28, 1991).

Greif, Avner. 1993. "Contract Enforceability and Economic Institutions in Early Trade: The Maghribi Traders' Coalition." *American Economic Review* 83: 525–48.

Hannan, Michael T., and John Freeman. 1977. "The Population Ecology of Organizations." *American Journal of Sociology* 82: 929–64.

———. 1984. "Structural Inertia and Organizational Change." *American Sociological Review* 49: 149–64.

———. 1989. *Organizational Ecology*. Cambridge, Mass.: Harvard University Press.

Hillman, Amy, and Gerald Keim. 1995. "International Variation in the Business-Government Interface: Institutional and Organizational Considerations." *Academy of Management Review* 20: 193–214.

Hotel Redbook. 1926. *Hotel Redbook*. New York: Official Hotel Redbook and Directory Co.

Inman, Crist. 1993. "Shifting Patterns of Social Order: The Creation of Current Rules and Roles Governing Hospitality." Cornell University. Unpublished paper.

Kahneman, D., P. Slovic, and A. Tversky. 1982. *Judgement Under Uncertainty: Heuristics and Biases*. Cambridge, England: Cambridge University Press.

Knight, Jack. 1992. *Institutions and Social Conflict*. New York: Cambridge University Press.

March, James G. 1991. "Exploration and Exploitation in Organizational Learning." *Organization Science* 2: 71–87.

Moon, Germaine L. Ramounachou. 1980. *Barstow Depots and Harvey Houses*. Barstow, Calif.: Mohave River Valley Museum Association.

Neal, Roger. 1984. "Rising Star." *Forbes*, June 18, 103–4.

Nelson, Richard R., and Sidney G. Winter. 1982. *An Evolutionary Theory of Economic Change*. Cambridge, Mass.: Belknap.

North, Douglass C. 1990. *Institutions, Institutional Change and Economic Performance*. New York: Cambridge University Press.

———. 1993. "Five Propositions about Institutional Change." St. Louis: Washington University. Unpublished paper.

Olson, Mancur. 1965. *The Logic of Collective Action*. Cambridge, Mass.: Harvard University Press.

Scott, W. Richard. 1981. Organizations: Rational, Natural, and Open Systems. Englewood Cliffs, N.J.: Prentice Hall.

Starr, Paul. 1982. *The Transformation of American Medicine*. New York: Basic Books.

Tushman, Michael L., and Philip Anderson. 1986. "Technological Discontinuities and Organizational Environments." *Administrative Science Quarterly* 31: 439–65.

Willy, John. 1903. "Editorial." *Hotel Monthly*. July 18.

13

The Importance of the Local: Rural Institutions and Economic Change in Preindustrial England

Rosemary L. Hopcroft

That men act in a social frame of reference yielded by the groups of which they are a part is a notion undoubtedly ancient and probably sound.
—Robert Merton and Alice Rossi, *Social Theory and Social Structure*

When we describe rights of ownership, or of use, or of tenancy, we are talking about relationships between people. Rights imply duties and liabilities, and these must attach to people. A hectare cannot be sued at law, nor is a boundary dispute a quarrel with a boundary.
—John Davis, *Land and Family in Pisticci*

In the application of the new institutional economics to the question of economic development, analytic primacy is typically given to economic institutions created by the state. That is, the focus usually is on the state's role in the creation and maintenance of a variety of economic institutions such as property rights and taxation systems (Barzel 1989; de Soto 1993; Campbell and Lindberg 1990; Bates 1990; North 1990b), and their implications for development. Other economic approaches share this bias, for example, work examining the state's role in rent seeking and its effect on development (Buchanan, Tollison, and Tullock 1980; Jones 1988; Tullock 1990).[1] In all these analyses it is often assumed that if the state creates the right sort of institutions, and does not do too much rent seeking, sooner or later development is inevitable. This is the theme of North and Thomas's account (1973) of economic development in early modern Europe.

In this chapter, I too use the historical Western experience to show how this focus on the state is not always adequate. The case of agricultural and economic development in late medieval and early modern England shows that an analysis of state economic policies and institutions is *not* always sufficient to explain economic development. Specifically, important regional differences arose in agricultural and economic development in late medieval and early modern England, despite common state policies and institutions throughout England. These regional differences are best explained by the nature of *local* economic institutions, and not by state policies and institutions, which we may assume affected all areas of England more or less equally.[2] In some regions, local institutions promoted agrarian change, in other areas they inhibited it. These local institutions may be regarded as the rural, preindustrial equivalent to the organizations described by Nee and Ingram (this volume). However, given their importance in shaping local affairs during an era when the influence of the central state was relatively weak and because the twentieth-century connotations of the term "organization" are inappropriate to the preindustrial time period,[3] I will continue to refer to them as "local institutions" here.

Regional differences in development in preindustrial England should not be dismissed as just historical detail, because there is reason to believe that development would *not have occurred*, and certainly would not have occurred as it did, had not certain regions led the way. The more innovative and productive areas of England served to catalyze change in other areas. In this chapter I show how in agriculture, the most important economic sector at the time, more advanced areas promoted change in other areas in several ways. First, they demonstrated which methods and approaches worked to raise agricultural productivity given the technology of the time. Second, the prosperity of farmers in more advanced regions provided incentives for farmers in other regions to make changes in their own farms and farming techniques. Third, representatives from the advanced regions pushed for state-level political changes favorable to both agriculture and trade (in a role not dissimilar to those of entrepreneurs championing institutional change in the twentieth century—see Ingram, this volume). The result was widespread agrarian change and rising rural prosperity throughout England, culminating in the "agricultural revolution" of the late seventeenth and eighteenth centuries. This in turn was an important precondition for further industrial development.

I do not suggest replacing an emphasis on state institutions with an exclusive emphasis on local institutions, nor even that the local is somehow more important than the national. This would not make sense. There is ample evidence that state institutions were and are vital in determining the course of economic development. In the case I examine here, for instance, I show how state policies, particularly state-supplied justice and protection of property rights, were of central importance in promoting development in more innovative areas of England. Yet, such state policies and institutions *alone* were not enough, as the more backward areas of England attest. Thus, I provide a reminder that local institutions play an important role in development in the same way state institutions do, by shaping costs and choices for individual producers, and that the effects of such local institutions can be of great importance for ultimate outcomes. In addition, I suggest that local institutions may also be an important source of ideologies or cultural value systems.[4] If ideology is an important factor influencing development, and there is reason to believe it is (Merton [1938] 1970; Chirot 1985; North 1990b, this volume; Greif, this volume), we have yet another reason not to forget about the local.

This chapter is organized as follows. First, I briefly outline the new institutional approach to economic development and show how this approach has been used to explain historical development in England, using North and Thomas's account in *The Rise of the Western World* (1973). I use this now-classic work because it is the best-known and most complete application of the new institutional economics to the development of Western Europe. Second, I show how this account overlooks the role played by local economic institutions in agricultural and economic development in preindustrial England, and how this phenomenon itself may be incorporated into the new institutional economic theoretical framework. Last, I briefly discuss the role of local institutions in the development of ideology in preindustrial England.

THE NEW INSTITUTIONAL ECONOMICS AND THE RISE
OF THE WESTERN WORLD

The main contribution of the new institutional economics to the understanding of economic development is the introduction of the concept of transaction costs and the focus on how social institutions influence economic change in discussions of the issue. The new institutional economics builds on the neoclassical economic model of behavior. Thus, the standard version of the new institutional economics (Williamson 1975, 1985; North 1981, 1990b; see also Nee and Ingram, this volume, 30.) accepts the neoclassical premise that individuals in all societies, on average, prefer more wealth to less, all else being equal. It should be noted that suggesting that people tend to maximize wealth does not imply that all people in all societies maximize their wealth all the time. Nor does it imply that including wealth as an individual utility excludes the possibility that individuals also have other utilities, such as status, social acceptance, and the like. It does mean that enough people maximize wealth, enough of the time, to shape development outcomes in somewhat predictable ways. According to the neoclassical model, the total output of a society (which we may use as a proxy for level of development) may thus be conceived as maximization of some wealth-preferring function, subject to constraints imposed by current levels of technology, population, and resources (Cameron 1982; Ransom, Sutch, and Walton 1982).

The major contribution of the new institutional economics is to incorporate institutions into this model. It does this in the following way. In the neoclassical model, constraints imposed by levels of technology and resources may be considered "costs." For example, if resources are scarce, their costs are consequently high. This raises the total costs of production and thus inhibits development. The new institutional economics suggests that other costs also affect development, including *transaction costs*, which are *socially created* costs involved in production and exchange. They include *costs of defining and enforcing property rights, ("the right to use, to derive income from the use of; to exclude others, to exchange"); of measuring the valuable attributes of what is being exchanged, and of monitoring the exchange process itself* (Coase 1960; Williamson 1975; North 1981; North 1990b, 27, 1990a, 184).[5] Transaction costs exist because information is costly and because uncertainty is inherent in exchange.

This is how institutions are introduced into the neoclassical model, as institutions shape transaction costs. In social science, "institution" can have a wide variety of meanings, but more narrowly here, an institution is defined as a system of social rules accompanied by some sort of enforcement mechanism. Rules may be formal: constitutions, laws, the specification of property rights, and so on (Coase 1960; Barzel 1989; North 1982, 23); or informal: norms, customs, mores (North 1990a, 192; Knight 1992), although the two categories often overlap. According to the new institutional economics, institutions, by defining and enforcing property rights and rules of exchange, help determine levels of uncertainty, and hence the social costs involved in transactions—that is, transaction costs (Coase 1960). Institutions that maintain high levels of uncertainty increase transaction costs and hence inhibit development. These we may call *inefficient* institutions. Institutions that reduce levels of uncertainty decrease transaction costs and hence encourage development. These we may call *efficient* institutions.

Institutions themselves exist (in part) because of the existence of positive transaction costs (North 1990b). That is, because transacting is costly, social groups develop rules to try to lower those costs and enforce those rules. No transacting may occur in a state of total anarchy. However, rule systems and hence institutional forms differ, and some institutions do a better job of lowering transaction costs than others. Thus, according to the new institutional economics development outcomes are a product not just of individual maximization given existing levels of resources and technology but also of the efficiency of existing institutional arrangements. Furthermore, institutions become fixed as individual interests become aligned with particular institutional forms. This means that institutional change is often slow, difficult, and almost always follows a path-dependent course. That is, new institutions typically are determined in part by preexisting institutions (Ingram, this volume; Western, this volume; North, this volume; Greif, this volume).

While the role of informal normative institutions in development has been acknowledged and examined in some detail (North 1990b, 23; Knight 1992; Putnam 1993), *local* economic institutions continue to receive little attention. However, in this chapter I show how the characteristics of local economic institutions can play an important role in determining the path of economic development. I also show how they are related to informal *normative* institutions, which also have implications for development outcomes (Greif, this volume).[6]

The analytical primacy given to national and state institutions by those using the new institutionalist approach is best illustrated by North and Thomas's account (1973) of the rise of the Western world. In this work, North and Thomas use English national institutions to explain early economic development and the eventual Industrial Revolution in England.

North and Thomas's central argument in *The Rise of the Western World* may be summarized very briefly as follows. Population growth from the eleventh to the thirteenth centuries promoted the emergence of more efficient factor markets (in land and labor, but not necessarily in capital) all over Europe. That is, as the population grew, the market expanded and "efficiency required the substitution of money payments for labor dues in a new contractual arrangement. In the process serfdom died, labor became free to seek its best rewards, land received rent, and the basic feudal manorial relationship withered and died" (92). According to North and Thomas, this movement was Europe-wide. Product markets lagged behind factor markets in increasing efficiency, thus the national divergences that emerged after this time were largely differences between countries in which product markets became more efficient and countries in which they did not. This in turn depended on the state and the national market (115), as the state had largely replaced the feudal lord as supplier of justice and protection (87).

North and Thomas connect the development of England and the Netherlands to the emergence of more efficient economic institutions in the factor and product markets in both countries, particularly after about 1500 (115). In England, property rights in land had been given legal protection as early as the thirteenth century (64). Nowhere else, except in the Netherlands, did legal institutions recognize exclusive property rights in land. The state fiscal system that emerged in England did not tax producers excessively and later (particularly after 1600) provided institutional means to further minimize transaction costs, including a stable currency, the joint stock company, and a central bank.

North and Thomas suggest two reasons for the early developments in England. The first was trade. England had exported a great deal of wool since the thirteenth century. Since it was relatively easy to tax imports and exports of wool, the state chose to derive most of its revenues from excise taxes, rather than from direct taxes on producers (North and Thomas 1973, 68).[7] Taxes on the wool trade were the main source of royal income in the thirteenth century, and they continued to provide the majority of royal income in the late fifteenth century (North and Thomas 1973, 83; see also Brown 1989). In other countries, it was more difficult to tax trade, as most trade was local, so the state made money either by granting monopolies to various groups or by taxing the producers directly (North and Thomas 1973, 100). Whereas this strategy penalized most producers and retarded economic development, the English taxation strategy was more favorable to producers and thus promoted economic development.

The second reason for the more benign taxation strategy followed by the English state was the strength of the English Parliament. Parliament prevented the state from granting monopolies and regulating production to the same extent that other European states did. It also helped prevent overtaxation of producers (and others) and currency debasement, and worked to protect the property rights of free men. Particularly after its victory over the monarchy in 1640, Parliament also oversaw the invention of economic institutions (or the importation of them from Holland) that further facilitated England's economic development. All of these national institutional developments lowered transaction costs in markets and promoted rising prosperity throughout England, which eventually culminated in the emergence of an industrial economy.

Thus, the nature of trade, combined with the existence of a strong Parliament, led to the emergence of economic institutions in England by the seventeenth century that promoted further economic development. Similarly efficient economic institutions had emerged in the Netherlands at a somewhat earlier date. North and Thomas argue that in the Netherlands, as in England, it was the development of trade, in combination with the enlightened state policies of the Burgundian rulers, that was responsible for the development of efficient institutions in the early modern period. We can see that in North and Thomas's analysis of both the Netherlands and England, the prime mover behind establishment of efficient economic institutions is the *state*.

There are two problems with North and Thomas's argument as applied to England. First, throughout Europe the emergence of efficient organization in the agricultural sector differed greatly by region in the late medieval and early modern periods. Population cycles of the fourteenth to sixteenth centuries, which North and Thomas suggest had similar effects everywhere, cannot account for these regional differences. Regional differences were particularly notable in England in the late medieval period and beyond (Campbell 1991; Hopcroft 1994b). For example, the move to contractual labor relations, enclosure, the decline of common rights to land, and improvements in farm layout all occurred in the late medieval period in some regions of England but not in others, and long before most of the innovations in state policies mentioned earlier. This meant that by the early modern period some regions were much more productive agriculturally than others. These regional differences cannot be explained solely by material factors such as population, location, or ecology but can be explained by also taking into account local institutions (Campbell 1981; Homans 1987a, 1987b; Hopcroft 1994a, 1995a; Overton 1996, 57).[8]

Second, state policies had different effects by region within England. For example, it is true that the rights of freemen were protected by the state as early as the thirteenth century in England, but freemen were concentrated in some regions and not others. Thus, laws supporting freemen's rights had little effect in regions with few freemen. Moreover, in later centuries, there is much evidence that local authorities differentially enforced state policies by region. This was because unpaid justices of the peace were much more responsive to local conditions than to state policies (Brown 1989; Fryde 1991; Sayer 1992).[9] Regional differences in response to state legislation persisted in England right up through the eighteenth and nineteenth centuries. For example, enclosure by act of Parliament, which was aimed at eradicating the last of the inefficient agricultural systems in England, predominated in some counties and not in others (Leonard 1962; Wordie 1983; Grigg 1989).

These enduring regional differences were a product of regional differences in *local* institutions. In some regions of southern England, local institutions that provided less-communal property rights and did not inhibit innovation by farmers promoted agrarian change. This resulted in more productive agriculture and a more prosperous rural economy in those regions of England at a very early date. These regional developments in turn promoted agrarian change and development throughout England. In what follows I examine in greater detail the association between local institutions and agricultural development and agrarian change from the fourteenth through the sixteenth centuries in England and show how it may be incorporated into the new institutional economic theoretical framework.[10] I also examine change after this period and how change in the more productive regions stimulated similar changes in other regions.

LOCAL ECONOMIC INSTITUTIONS IN ENGLISH REGIONAL DEVELOPMENT

There exists a common assumption that rural organization under feudalism was much the same everywhere (see North and Thomas 1973, 27). However, there were important regional differences in local rural organization throughout Europe. These differences dated back to the Dark Ages, and cannot always be simply explained by such material factors as population or ecology.[11] Some have considered them to have had ethnic origins, among other things, although this is a topic for another discussion (see Campbell 1981; Homans 1987a, 1987b; Hopcroft 1994a, 1995a). Historiography provides us with the convenient term "field systems" to describe these differences in local rural organization, but the term is somewhat misleading, since field systems corresponded to much more than the layout of fields. They encompassed an entire social order, including class relations, rules of agricultural practice, land use, and the inheritance of land, as well as social norms. All of these things shaped the course of agrarian change and development in the various regions. The different field systems can be described in broad strokes as follows, although there was some variation within types (see Gray 1915; Douglas 1927; Homans 1941; Baker 1973; Hallam 1981; Campbell 1981; Smith 1984; Overton 1996, 46).

The *regular open field system* is the system most often associated with feudal Europe. It is also called the "champion" system (champion being the English version of the French "champagne" meaning open country). In England, it was found in the midland and central regions (that is, area extends beyond modern day midlands, see figure 13.1). Here the two or three great arable fields of the farming community surrounded a compact cluster of homes. Although villagers individually possessed the strips of land scattered through the great fields, their land was subject to communal regulation of cropping as well as communal grazing at certain times of year. Fields were also subject to a communal biennial (two-field) or triennial (three-field) crop rotation. A true commons existed in addition to the two or three open arable fields. This commons could include rough grazing land and wasteland as well as high-quality hay meadow. Use of the great arable fields and the commons was regulated by a central body called the "byelaw." This body was responsible for coordinating cropping, harvesting, and grazing on arable fields, as well as for appointing village shepherds and fence keepers. The byelaw, in conjunction with the manorial court, also enforced customs of primogeniture (inheritance of all land by the eldest son). This custom was widespread in champion regions and kept individual landholdings intact across generations (Homans 1941; King 1973, 170).

Champion regions tended to be heavily manorialized regions. Villages in champion regions in England typically only had one lord, and strips of land belonging to both lord and peasant were usually intermingled in the open fields. Most villagers were customary tenants who held their land by custom of the manor and were subject to the authority of the manorial court. Manorial rules often prescribed labor services, limited the mobility of customary tenants, specified wages, and otherwise controlled tenant behavior. Freeholders who owned their lands outright and were largely free of feudal rules were few. Domination of the village community by the lord of the manor in champion regions is perhaps one reason why the regular open field system similarly dominates our conception of medieval life in England, since manorial authorities kept detailed records of various aspects of manor and village. These records have survived to modern times and have been the basis of much scholarship on the medieval period. In areas where manorial lords were less strong, fewer written records were kept, and details of life in these areas are less well known.

While the regular open field system characterized the midland and central region of England, *irregular open field systems* and *enclosed field systems* characterized the eastern and southwestern regions. These systems embodied more individual property rights than the regular open field system, although there were usually also some common rights.

Irregular open field systems were often similar in appearance to champion

Figure 13.1   Field Systems in Britain

systems, but there was more land in enclosures and less communal regulation of
cropping and grazing. Crop rotations were typically not by field but by "shift," a
smaller section of land. Private grazing often was facilitated by the concentration
of the strips of each landholding in one part of the village land. These systems
were not regular open field systems in decay—there is no evidence that irregular
open field regions had ever been in a regular state (Gray 1915; Thirsk 1967;
Campbell 1981). In these regions, villages tended to be smaller and less compact
than in regular open field regions. Unlike in champion communities, the village
church often stood alone and isolated in some prominent natural location. Such
irregular open field systems were found in both East Anglia, Essex, and Kent in
the east, and in the southwestern counties. A modern-day traveler going from
Cambridge to Norwich can still observe the change from compact villages and
centrally located churches to more scattered habitation and isolated churches.

Areas of enclosures were areas where fields were fenced (with hedges, trees, or
stones) and little land was left open. They tended to be concentrated in mountainous areas in the west and north, although they also could be found in parts of
East Anglia, Essex, and Kent, as well as in other parts of England. In mountainous areas they usually were associated with a pastoral economy, although in

the east and later in the southwest enclosed fields were also used for arable agriculture (cf. Hopcroft 1995a; Overton 1996, 61). In regions of enclosures, homes were scattered across the landscape and most fields were entirely enclosed and private. Since many of the fences were live hedges or included many trees, this gave the landscape a wooded appearance. This earned such regions the name of "woodland." In the southwest, the line of division between open field regions of large open fields and woodland regions of smaller, hedged fields is clearly apparent to this day.

In both regions of enclosures and those of irregular open fields, the tyranny of the manor was somewhat less than in champion regions. Demesne land (the home farm of the manorial lord) was often separate from peasant holdings. Labor services were fewer and commuted to money payments at an early date. Much of the peasantry was entirely free of feudal obligations, as there was a large proportion of freeholding peasants. This was particularly true in the east, where Kent, Essex, and East Anglia had long histories of a free peasantry. In East Anglia, the free population (including the poorer freemen or "sokemen") in the late medieval period reached 80 percent in some areas. Kent was also characterized by a majority of freeholders (Gray 1915; Douglas 1927; Dodwell 1939; Britnell 1991, 618). In the east, even customary tenants were better off than their counterparts in the midland and central region. Manorial dues and services tended to be proportionately lighter and less onerous. Several manorial lords might be represented in a single village in these regions. They often contested territorial and other rights of lordship, a situation the peasants could turn to their own advantage. For example, customary tenants were frequently able to take their legal cases to their choice of several manorial courts (Campbell 1981). Perhaps for these reasons copyhold tenure was well established in eastern England by 1450 (Britnell 1991, 621), and true villeinage disappeared very early in most eastern counties (on Kent, for example, see Homans 1941, 414).

The New Institutional Economics and Regional Economic Change

In the language of the new institutional economics, we can see that regular open field systems were institutions that embodied higher transaction costs (as well as other types of costs) than other types of field systems.[12] This is primarily because the costs of protecting rights over property were higher. That is, "the right to use, to derive income from the use of, to exclude others, to exchange" both land and products of the land was less well-defined and less well-assured in regions of regular open fields than in other regions. This increased uncertainty and promoted inefficiency, which discouraged development. *The problem was not simply that communal rights are less efficient than private rights but rather that in the communal system, rights were not as well-defined or as easy to protect as in the less-communal systems.*

Why was this so? First, in communal systems of agriculture the individual right to use the land was carefully defined by village byelaws. However, in practice, rights were subject to great uncertainty due to problems of monitoring and enforcement in the communal system. For example, in a system where a farmer always had neighbors on each side of every strip of his land, and where there were rules forbidding fences, his neighbors could "free ride" on his agricultural efforts. This was what "Piers Plowman" was referring to in William Langland's fourteenth-century poem when he said:

> If I go to the plough I pinch so narrow
> That a foot of land or furrow fetch I would
> Of my next neighbour, take of his earth;
> And if I reap, overreach, or give him advice that reap
> To seize to me with their sickle what I never sowed.

There was always a temptation for farmers, sight unseen, to take a little of a neighbor's crop. Piers Plowman also mentions the temptation for "devourers of furrows" (see also Bloch 1966, 37). These were people who, by driving their plough a little over the boundaries of their own into their neighbors' furrows, could eventually appropriate additional land for themselves. Bloch notes that there is at least one instance of a parcel of land that was enlarged by more than a third of its original size in this manner in the course of sixty years (Bloch 1966, 38).[13]

Second, neighboring farms created externalities (difficult to prevent even when there were rules against the practices) that could thwart the efforts of individual farmers to improve their agricultural output or the quality of their stock animals (see Thornton 1991). For example, communal grazing meant that it was impossible for individual farmers to control either stock breeding or the spread of disease. This made it difficult for farmers to improve the quality of their livestock. The close proximity of farmers' strips of land meant that a neighbor's negligence in weeding or maintaining his land could bring all of a farmer's efforts to rid his own land of weeds and unwanted insects to nought. This also made it difficult for any farmer to improve the quality and productivity of his land. All of this served to discourage farmers from trying to increase the productivity of their land (Clay 1984, 115).

Third, communal regulation of cultivation and the land market increased transaction costs. The village community regulated the types of crops that could be planted in the common arable fields (see Biddick 1985), thus it was often difficult for cultivators to change their crops in response to market demands. Neither could cultivators change their agricultural techniques and methods easily, as these were specified by customs enforced by the village council. Because of restrictions on exchange of land, the scattered strips of land making up an individual farm could not be consolidated easily into a single unit. Thus, even if a farmer expanded his land holdings, he would not benefit from the economies of scale usually to be had in a large farm, given the difficulty of farming many different plots of land. This in turn served to discourage the accumulation of land by farmers and growth in the size of farms.

Cultivators could not withdraw their land from the communal system, as there were village rules against enclosure of land in the open arable fields. This was strictly enforced by the entire community and the manorial courts since, given the scattered nature of landholding, if one person enclosed his land the whole system of agriculture would be threatened. For this reason, enclosure in these regions was difficult. Nor could cultivators sell their land if they wished to, as there were strong customs prohibiting alienation of patrimony (King 1973, 170). Most farmers could not leave the land even if they wanted to because feudal restrictions limited the mobility of customary tenants. Thus, the community organization and the manorial court, actively opposing any change in the existing agricultural system, also raised transaction costs faced by those who might wish to change to more efficient agricultural practices.

Finally, there were other costs to the communal field system besides these transaction costs. Feudal dues and taxes tended to be heavy in regular open field regions. This meant that cultivators had little reason to produce a surplus on their own land, since it could be taxed away. Nor did they have any reason to produce a surplus on the lord's land.

Given all of this, it may seem astonishing that such a seemingly inefficient system of agriculture ever evolved in the first place. However, it must be remembered that the system ensured adequate pasture, and at least some harvest, every year for all in the village. It was a system that minimized subsistence risk (Clay 1984, 65; Robisheaux 1994, 82). Furthermore, the communal system, and a strong communitarian spirit, meant that the poor were always provided for so that none were completely without means of survival. For example, even the landless typically had gleaning rights and rights to the straw left in the common fields after harvest, or could send a few animals into the common flock. Last, common ownership and intermixed land tenure were not merely obstacles to individual initiative but also guarantees against conspicuous mismanagement (Østerud 1978, 147). In the early stages of the development of this system, these benefits may have more than outweighed any loss of efficiency. At later stages, particularly with a large increase in population density, the reverse may have become true. At this point, however, too many people had an interest in preserving the existing system for it to be dismantled without difficulty.

The communitarian ethic associated with the communal agricultural system itself may have deterred increases in agricultural production, as it discouraged the growth of economic inequality and the concentration of wealth in a few hands. Economic activities in regular open field communities were dominated by "what can only have been a desire to maintain the equality of the members of the community in economic opportunity" (Homans 1941, 337); and a desire for "ensuring that everyone got a share in the relatively scarce resources upon which they all depended for their living" (Clay 1984, 65).[14] One can surmise that such sentiments were often antithetical to the individual search for profit and the accumulation of private wealth. This may have deterred production for the market and thus efforts to increase agricultural productivity. The common custom of holding the richest in the village accountable for the debts of all also may have discouraged the accumulation of wealth (Homans 1941, 338).

In less-communal and enclosed field systems, the lack of village regulation of economic matters lowered transaction costs involved in rural production. There was little to hinder innovators or those who wished to adopt more productive methods. The village community was less able to prevent changes in the crops grown and in agricultural practices. The grouping of landholdings in one part of the village land, and sometimes the existence of fences, also reduced the uncertainty in defining and protecting property rights. Cultivators did not have to be concerned that communal agricultural practices would ruin the results of their hard work. Free riding by neighbors could still be a problem, especially in regions where farms were made up of scattered strips of land. However, if a neighbor's practices were infringing on a farmer's land, he could put up a fence, or even sell his land. This also made the consolidation of strips of land easier and thus facilitated the expansion of farms.

Other costs were also lower. Manorial exactions were proportionately lower than in other regions. In fact, rent seeking in general was harder in such regions. Scattered habitations and smaller villages meant enforcing taxation was often more difficult in regions of enclosures and less-communal open fields than in regions of communal open fields. It would have been much easier to tax farmers in nucleated villages than to tax farmers scattered across the countryside, if only for the simple reason that it would have been easier for the latter to avoid being found by the tax collectors. Farmers in nucleated villages were easily accessible and had few places to hide either themselves or their goods. Farmers in scattered habitations and small villages were less accessible and had more places to hide themselves and their goods. Tax collectors often would have to cover long distances to reach the latter, often for little or no gain. Thus, residents of these regions were able to avoid taxation to a greater degree than residents of regular open field regions. In addition, there were few other feudal restrictions on cultivators' activities. Farmers were not only relatively free of feudal dues and taxes but free to move around, to buy and sell land, and to bequeath it to whomever they wished.

Moreover, unlike in communal open field regions, there was no strong spirit of communitarianism to inhibit the pursuit of individual profit and wealth. Lack of a communitarian ethic may help explain why in these regions a wider division developed between rich and poor peasants than existed in communal open field regions. Common gleaning rights were often absent. Since common grazing was rare, it was difficult for the poor to find grazing land for any animals they might have. In addition, partible inheritance customs (common in these areas) resulted in both an active land market as well as the proliferation of many tiny farms and class differentiation within the peasantry. People who had to depend on very small pieces of land for their livelihood were often forced to look for ways to supplement their incomes. They became a source of wage labor for the larger farms of better-off peasants who began to emerge in these regions in the late medieval period. They were also an important source of labor for the textile industries that often flourished in these regions.[15]

Improved Agricultural Productivity in Nonchampion Regions

Recent historical scholarship has turned up considerable evidence of regional differences in agricultural productivity in late medieval and early modern England, including differences in yields (both per acre and per seed) and in the use of innovative techniques. Most of this evidence comes from large manorial estates, which kept detailed records, not from the farms of freeholders. As noted, the latter were quite numerous in the east. We can assume that they would have been in the main even more productive and innovative than the large estates, an assumption for which there is some evidence (see Allison 1957; Britnell 1991). Given this assumption, manorial evidence should be seen as providing a conservative picture of regional differences in agricultural productivity.

One measure of agricultural productivity is cereal yields. Studies of manors in the nonchampion regions of late medieval Kent and East Anglia on the eastern seaboard and of the southwest show relatively high yields in these areas. In the late thirteenth century, yields per acre in eastern and southeastern England were higher than in most other areas of the country, as high as twenty bushels per acre for wheat.[16] Seed yield ratios were also exceptionally high by medieval standards, reaching seven to one (and higher) for wheat (Campbell 1983, 1988, 1991; Stacey 1986; Mate 1986, 1991, 277; Britnell 1991, 206). In the southwest, yields per acre were less outstanding than in the east, but seed/yield ratios were good compared to other parts of the country (4 and 5 to 1 in the early fourteenth century, see Slicher van Bath 1963, 37).

Agricultural methods in these regions at this time were also quite sophisticated. High levels of agricultural productivity were accomplished by many of the same methods that in later centuries helped produce the agricultural revolution. They included extensive use of leguminous plants (mostly peas in the early period), multiple ploughings, use of the horse rather than the ox, intensive soil fertilization and liming, and complex crop rotation schemes that left a comparatively small proportion of land fallow each year. All were in evidence as early as the thirteenth century on manors in parts of East Anglia and Kent (Stone 1956, 347; Langdon 1986; Hallam 1981; Mate 1986, 1991; Stacey 1986; Britnell 1991). Many of these innovative methods went out of use in the demographic and economic depression of the late fourteenth century, yet most were revived in the same regions in the fifteenth century. Convertible husbandry, which involves many of these techniques, was in evidence in both the southwest and the east by the early fifteenth century (Finberg 1951; Fox 1991, 313).[17]

Other innovative methods were pioneered in these regions in later centuries. For example, turnips were first introduced into England in the eastern counties in the sixteenth century (Chambers and Mingay 1966; Overton 1991). Clover appeared there in the seventeenth century (Overton 1991, 320). Labor productivity also was high in East Anglia as early as the sixteenth century, where it was the custom for laborers and ploughman to work two "journees" (half days) per day rather than one as was customary elsewhere (Riches 1967). By the eighteenth century, Norfolk in East Anglia was renowned for agriculture and was described as the "model agricultural economy" in Diderot's *Encyclopedia* (Braudel 1982, 281; see also Turner 1982).

Rise of Large Farms in Nonchampion Regions

Farmers in nonchampion regions usually could sell their land as they wished. This fostered an active land market involving both small and large plots of land. Partible inheritance customs in these regions also stimulated the land market, since people who had inherited only a small piece of land could seek either to buy land to enlarge their property or to sell their land and enter some nonagricultural occupation. This active land market in turn made enlargement and consolidation of farms easy, a process that was particularly notable in both the east and the southwest after the demographic decline of the mid-fourteenth century made a considerable amount of land available. Since landholdings tended to be concentrated in one area of the village land, consolidation of farms into a single unit was relatively uncomplicated. This encouraged the enlargement of farms in these regions at this time.

Historical evidence (again culled from manorial records) shows the regional difference in farm expansion after 1350. For example, in nonchampion Devon and Cornwall in the southwest, tenant farms increased in size during the fifteenth century until more than half of all tenant holdings were over thirty-six acres. (Fifteen or thirty acres were common farm sizes in thirteenth-century England). Tenant farms of one hundred fifty to two hundred acres have been documented in the area by the mid-fifteenth century.[18] In addition, figures from various manors in Devon and Cornwall consistently show a decline in the number of holdings of fewer than fifteen acres to as little as 10 percent of all holdings, and very few holdings of fewer than five acres (Fox 1991, 724, 725). Likewise, tenant farms increased in size on manors in nonchampion Norfolk (Campbell 1984, 125) and Kent (Fourquin 1990). They could reach several hundred acres in size, although large numbers of very small farms of fewer than five acres remained in these areas.

Champion regions also saw an increase in the size of tenant farms in the late medieval period, but to a lesser extent. For example, tenant farms in the midlands and in central England often increased in size to thirty or sixty acres but rarely exceeded one hundred acres (Tawney 1912, 64–65; Kerridge 1968, 289; Miller 1991, 703, 706, 712). Within the confines of the regular open field system, it was difficult for them to become much larger. In these areas, neither enclosure nor the consolidation of farms into compact units was common.[19]

However, despite early development of large farms in the east and southwest, and the general tendency across England for farm sizes to increase over the early modern period, many small farms persisted in these areas (Britnell 1991, 617; Mate 1991, 702). There were proportionately more small farms (five to one hundred acres in size) in both the east and southwest than in other regions as late as 1850, at which date the first national census of farm sizes was conducted (Grigg 1989). In fact, there is evidence that the smaller farms in these regions played an important role in agricultural innovation. Many new techniques used on large estates originated on small farms (Allison 1957; Campbell 1983; Britnell 1991, 210; Overton 1996, 205). Small farms also provided experienced managers and tenant farmers for the large farms of the great estates (Du Boulay 1965). Thus, families such as the Townshends and the Knatchbulls in eastern England can be traced from their origins as tenant farmers in the fourteenth and fifteenth centuries to their position as the local nobility in the eighteenth century (Du Boulay 1965; Moreton 1992).

Many improvements in land and labor productivity in seventeenth and eighteenth century England have been attributed to the general expansion of farm sizes (Allen 1988). Since the time of the eighteenth century's traveling agronomist Arthur Young, it has been assumed that large farms benefited from economies of scale, hence were more efficient than small farms. However, the important role of small farmers in increasing agricultural productivity in the east and southwest serves to cast doubt on the importance of size in and of itself. Cross-national evidence also shows that large farms alone do not necessarily increase agricultural productivity (Bates 1988). It may be that it is the existence of many smaller farms, alongside large farms, that provided the necessary conditions for improved productivity on the large farms (see Cancian 1988; Overton 1996, 205).

Regional Differences in Enclosure

Early agronomists such as Arthur Young extolled not only the virtues of large farms but also the value of enclosure for increasing agricultural productivity. As with the emphasis placed on farm size, this is somewhat misleading. It was not so much enclosure itself that promoted agricultural productivity as private property rights, which did not necessarily entail enclosure. In many of the more prosperous regions of the east and the southwest there had long been private rights to land, yet few enclosures or fences. Fences only helped enforce property rights that had already been established in social custom. Fencing itself was made cheaper by the consolidation of land, or the putting together of many smaller pieces of land to create contiguous, compact farms. Since, as I have noted, consolidation was easier in the east and southwest, both enclosure and consolidation were more common in those regions.

Thus, enclosure (for both arable and pastoral purposes) in the nonchampion east and southwest occurred early and with little complaint (Leonard 1962, 251; Thirsk 1967; Britnell 1991, 613; Fox 1991, 152). This regional difference in enclosure was noticed by a writer in Tudor times (who also noted the relative prosperity of the enclosed areas): "We se that countries where most Inclosures be, are most wealthie, as essex, kent, devenshire and such" (Lamond [1581] 1929, 49). All of these areas of the east and southwest were little affected by the Parliamentary enclosures of later centuries (Leonard 1962; Wordie 1983), which mostly affected the champion areas of central England.

In contrast to the experience in the east and west, enclosure in the midland and central regions was a long, drawn-out, and difficult process. It occasioned much social upheaval, as it involved the destruction of an entire agricultural system and (often) the uprooting of many people who depended on it for their living. Enclosure, and the farm expansion and consolidation that accompanied it, provoked many peasant revolts in these regions, the largest being the Midland Revolt of 1607 (Martin 1983). Enclosure in this area finally had to be legislated by act of Parliament. Even so, resistance to enclosure was still pronounced in the nineteenth century. Writers from Tudor times onward have described this process, and it became an important element in Marx's interpretation of the rise of agrarian capitalism in England (Marx 1906, 794).

Rise of Contractual Labor Relations and Industry in Nonchampion Regions

Local institutions in the east and southwest also promoted the emergence and spread of (more efficient) contractual labor relations. The weaker manorialization and the presence of many freeholders in the east and southwest, in conjunction with early development of a market economy, promoted an early change to the use of wage labor. Wage labor was used on all great estates in the east by the thirteenth century, while in other areas the use of customary labor services persisted (Campbell 1983). Use of wage labor was also in evidence in the southwest by the fifteenth century (Fox 1991).

Copyhold tenure also was established early in both the east and southwest. The establishment of copyhold tenure, like use of wage labor, reflected a change toward a more contractual, rather than customary, relationship between a lord and his tenants. Copyhold tenure means that tenants possess a copy of the terms (as entered in the manorial court roll) under which their land is held from the lord of the manor. In earlier centuries, these terms usually included labor services as well as the usual customary dues and payments, although use of labor services had mostly vanished in the east and southwest by the thirteenth century. Copyholders had fewer rights than freeholders, as they were not considered to "own" their land. However, they could sue a landlord in common law courts for personal trespass if the landlord infringed on their land rights (Kerridge 1969, 71; Hoyle 1990). These rights of freeholders and copyholders contrast with those of customary tenants, who could take their cases only to the manorial court. This court was run by the manorial lord, and can be expected to have been biased in his favor. For tenants in the east, copyhold tenure was widespread by 1450 (Britnell 1991). It was not until later that most customary tenants in the midland and central regions became copyholders (Hoyle 1990, 6).

The regional pattern of the rise of contractual labor relations is paralleled by the regional pattern of the development of rural industry and nonagricultural occupations. The east and southwest were characterized by very prosperous nonagricultural economies by the fifteenth century. They had flourishing textile industries as well as a large variety of nonagricultural occupations: for example, brewing, salt making, fishing, shipping, tanning, baking, carpentry, and tiling (Campbell 1984; Mate 1991). There was also tin mining in the southwestern counties of Devon and Cornwall (Fox 1991).

The Importance of Regional Differences

In sum, from the late thirteenth century onward, nonchampion institutions in the east and southwest of England encouraged production for the market and changes in farm layout and size by lowering transaction costs for farmers. Farmers were more able to make changes and to receive a good return for their efforts. Weaker manorialization and a large free peasantry also encouraged the early emergence of more efficient contractual labor relations. A more efficient agriculture in turn facilitated the development of industry and led to generally rising prosperity. These nonchampion regions saw the highest rates of growth of lay wealth from the second third of the fourteenth century to the early sixteenth century, as figure 13.2 shows.

In the champion regions, on the other hand, local institutions discouraged production for the market and agrarian change by increasing transaction costs for farmers. Property rights were harder to protect, and farmers were prevented from

Figure 13.2   Rates of Growth of Lay Wealth, 1334 to 1515

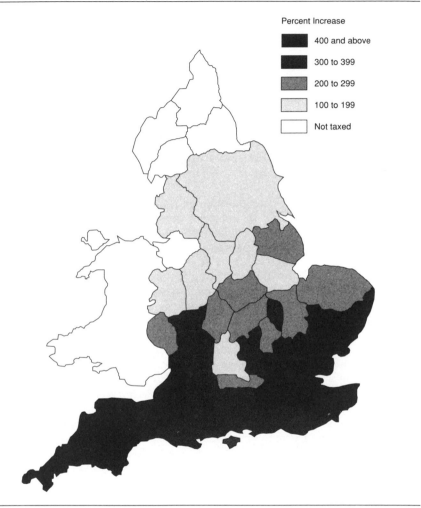

Percent Increase

- 400 and above
- 300 to 399
- 200 to 299
- 100 to 199
- Not taxed

Source: Adapted from Schofield (1965).

making major changes. The strength of manorial control also inhibited the emergence of contractual labor relations in these areas.

It is the eventual diffusion throughout England of the new agricultural techniques and ways of farming, pioneered in nonchampion regions, that is generally held to be responsible for the agricultural revolution of the seventeenth and eighteenth centuries (Overton 1996, 131). However, it was not just a question of developments occurring in the east and southwest that eventually would have occurred in all regions anyway, given the right state institutions, as North and Thomas suggest. The evidence suggests that these changes would *not have occurred* at all without the example of more innovative regions.

First, the prosperity of the east and southwest stimulated change in other areas. It prompted some farmers in champion out regions to adopt the new techniques that had proven so successful in raising outputs in the east and southwest. The diffusion of new agricultural techniques is difficult to document fully. However, techniques of convertible husbandry first developed in the east and southwest in earlier centuries were being adopted in champion regions by the seventeenth century (Kerridge 1968, 194). Likewise turnips, originally grown in East Anglia in the sixteenth century, began to be grown all over England in the seventeenth and eighteenth centuries (Overton 1996, 131). The productivity of the east and southwest also promoted change in other areas by encouraging regional specialization. For example, the comparative advantage of the east in producing cereals encouraged champion farmers to turn to pasture farming in the fifteenth century, and then again in the seventeenth century (Dyer 1991; Campbell 1991).

Moreover, people from the nonchampion regions of eastern and southwestern England spearheaded efforts to introduce more efficient economic institutions nationwide, the importance of which North and Thomas (1973) emphasize. As early as 1381, peasant rebels of eastern England took the opportunity to demand the abolition of serfdom, the lifting of restrictions on internal trade, and the abolition of the trading privileges of towns (Fryde and Fryde 1991, 774). Later it was the well-to-do from these same regions who ran the parliamentary campaigns to overturn privilege and monopoly in England. The best example is Edward Coke's seventeenth-century campaign against the granting of royal trading monopolies, which culminated in the Statute of Monopolies in 1624 (North and Thomas 1973, 148).[20] This statute effectively prohibited the hitherto common practice of granting royal trading monopolies. Elites (often Puritans) from these nonchampion regions were also important backers of the parliamentary cause in the Civil War of the 1640s. It was the victory of Parliament over the Royalists that assured the dominance of this trade-minded, market-oriented elite in Britain throughout the early modern period.

Under parliamentary prodding, the state began to provide a more favorable environment for economic development in England. Important changes included the elimination of all surviving feudal laws, the first patent law, the development of the joint stock company, the coffee house (a forerunner of organized insurance), and the bank note, stabilization of the currency, and the creation of a central bank in 1694 (Braudel 1982; North and Thomas 1973, 155). All of these developments helped provide an institutional framework in England that furthered economic growth. Finally, Parliament promoted change in local economic institutions by passing the Enclosure Acts, which finally eradicated the communal agricultural systems of central England, and paved the way for the further rise of agrarian capitalism in England.

Further confirmation of the importance of local rural institutions for long-term economic development is provided by that other paragon of economic development in the early modern period—the Netherlands. Rural organization in most of the Netherlands was, as in the east and southwest of England, characterized by irregular field systems, scarce common land, a large number of freemen, and weak manorialization. As in England, this rural organization provided the foundation for the emergence of a productive rural economy in the late medieval and early modern period (de Vries 1974), which in turn provided a domestic base for the subsequent economic growth and expansion of the Netherlands.

The Role of National Institutions

The importance of local institutions does not mean that national institutions, and especially the improvements in the institutions governing economic markets, were unimportant for the early economic development of England. But some were more important than others. In the early period (before 1600), governmental protection of freeholder's rights and a state taxation system that did not include a regular head tax or any kind of regular direct tax on the population were of particular importance (see Fryde 1991; Hopcroft 1995b). At a later date, the continued existence of Parliament was essential for continued development (as many analysts—including North and Thomas—emphasize).

As noted previously, the eastern counties of East Anglia, Essex, and Kent were regions of many freeholders and copyholders in the late medieval period. This was an important factor contributing to economic development in those regions. Yet, the status attached to "freeholder" or "copyholder" was only meaningful because the rights connected with these titles were enforced by law (Hoyle 1990; Sayer 1992, 1399). This enforcement was provided by the central state, which guaranteed the common law protections of freeholders' rights. This guarantee dates back to the twelfth century, at which time freeholders were granted substantial legal rights under English common law, including the right of appeal to the king's courts (Kerridge 1969; Hyams 1980). As North and Thomas (1973, 64) note, with the exception of the Netherlands, these developments were unique to England at the time. By the fifteenth century, the common law also guaranteed copyholders' rights against personal trespass. This meant that copyholders whose property was taken or misused unlawfully had some means of legal redress.[21]

The English state also mattered in terms of what it was *unable* to do at this time. Unlike many other continental states, during the late medieval period the English state was unable to establish a permanent head tax (or any other kind of regular direct tax) on the population (Fryde 1991; Hopcroft 1995b). Its strongest attempts at creating such a tax culminated in the Peasants' Revolt of 1381 (led, one should note, by the prosperous peasantry of the east). Although it was crushed, the revolt and others like it helped ensure that the state was not able to derive most of its revenues from direct taxes for several hundred years (Fryde 1991; Fryde and Fryde 1991). As North and Thomas note (1973, 83), reliance on indirect taxes rather than direct taxes helped to lessen the tax burden on producers. Indirect taxes were regularly levied on sales and exported commodities, but they were easier for producers to evade than a direct tax (see Bates and Lien 1985). Furthermore, the tax assessment of the early 1300s remained in effect, essentially unchanged, until the early seventeenth century (Fryde 1991). This meant that levels of taxation actually declined over the period. Low levels of taxes on producers preserved incentives for continued agricultural development and kept capital and investment flowing into the agricultural sector.[22] Reliance on indirect taxes also placed the primary tax burden on merchants, traders, and landlords whose representation in Parliament meant they could force the Crown to trade favors for revenue. Parliament subsequently was able to bring about the establishment of institutions favorable to trade and economic growth (North and Thomas 1973, 148), especially following the English Civil War. This role of Parliament demonstrates the importance of the continued existence of that body. That such a (nominally) representative government survived into the early modern period is itself extraordinary (Downing 1988; Tullock 1987). Why this occurred, however, is another discussion.

Local Economic Institutions and Ideology

I have suggested that local institutions were not only an important factor in shaping the economic development in preindustrial England but that without the existence of certain types of local institutional arrangements this development might never have occurred. However, local economic institutions may have promoted more than just *economic* change. Nonchampion economic institutions may have helped produce *normative* systems and ideologies important for later ideological change, just as they produced agricultural technologies important for later technological change.

As noted previously, in champion regions of regular open fields, communal regulation of agriculture and land use was accompanied by strong traditions of communitarianism (Overton 1996, 45). The church, centrally located within the village, was the center of the life of the community. As in regular open field communities in northeastern France, people in these regions, as Bloch (1966) puts it, "thought instinctively in terms of the community." Homans (1941, 308) also writes of the attitudes of champion villagers in England, who "felt that they were bound to help their neighbors and do what they could, each man in his office, to further the common good of their village." Wakes—large festivals through which a village celebrated its collective identity—were found only in champion regions (Homans 1941, 374). Communitarian attitudes were reflected in inheritance customs, which typically dictated that one child would inherit the family farm (King 1973). This kept the patrimony intact, prevented the proliferation of small holdings, and thus served to maintain the regular system of agriculture upon which the entire village depended.[23]

On the other hand, nonchampion regions of irregular field systems and enclosures tended to be regions where the village community was relatively weak and a more individualistic ethic reigned. Visitors remarked on the different cultures present in the different regions. In fact an individualist and often rationalist ethic prevailed over much of the east and parts of the southwest. This could be observed in East Anglia as early as the thirteenth century (see the examples given in Macfarlane 1978). This spirit of individualism was reflected in inheritance customs. In most areas of irregular open fields and enclosures the custom was for land to be divided among all heirs equally (Homans 1941; Dodwell 1967; Campbell 1980, 183), as every individual was considered to be entitled to an inheritance, however small.

This individualistic ethic in the east and southwest helped make these areas receptive to rationalist religious ideologies. Lollardy, followed by Lutheranism, and then Puritanism were concentrated here (Dickens 1964; Zaret 1985, Hopcroft 1997). Puritans from the east especially were important backers of the parliamentary cause in the English Civil War (Homans [1962] 1988, 182, 184).[24] The zeal with which the parliamentary cause was pursued (which helped ensure its eventual success) can be explained in part by the existence of this powerful shared religious ideology (Walzer 1965).

In turn, the victory of Parliamentarians and Puritans over the Royalists helped cement the victory not only of Parliament over king but also of a more individualistic over a communitarian ethic in England. England was henceforth dominated by a culture that may be described best as one of puritanical, civic-minded individualism, with all that entailed for national economic development (see Weber [1930] 1989; Merton [1938] 1970; Dickens 1964; Walzer 1965).

CONCLUSION

In this chapter, I have shown how less-communal economic institutions in certain regions of late medieval and early modern England promoted development, while communal economic institutions in other regions of England inhibited it. Local development in some regions, in turn, catalyzed change throughout England. The prosperity of more advanced regions helped provide incentives for other regions to imitate the economic organization and techniques that had proven so successful in those regions. Representatives of innovative areas also led political campaigns to establish more efficient economic institutions nationwide.

By pointing out the importance of local institutions to economic change in preindustrial England, this chapter seeks to broaden the new institutional economic approach to the study of development and change. The new institutional economics has shifted the focus of development studies from economic change itself to the individual motivations that fuel economic change and to the social institutions that influence those motivations. This has greatly improved our understanding of economic development. However, the approach can become yet more fruitful if institutional determinants of individual behavior are considered more broadly.

Scholars using the new institutional approach have tended to focus on economic institutions provided by the *state*. Yet this may not be adequate, as I have shown here with reference to the important case of economic development in late medieval and early modern England, and others have shown in other cases (see, for example, Szelényi 1988; Hamilton and Biggart 1988; Stark, Nee, and Kramer 1990; Putnam 1993). The development of particular institutions at the state level may not always be enough to promote (or hinder) general economic development, just as similar state forms do not inevitably result in uniform development outcomes. Interaction with local institutions/organizations and informal norms inevitably occurs, and thus outcomes may vary. In late medieval and early modern England, national institutions were constant, yet some regions developed much more rapidly than others.

This case study suggests that any analysis of economic development must consider the role of local economic institutions in *conjunction* with national or state institutions.[25] Local institutions, like state institutions, shape transaction costs and other costs individuals face, and hence shape individual behavior and choices. Local institutions also may play an important role in the formation of informal norms or ideological systems, which also have implications for economic development. For all these reasons, while a general retreat to community and local studies is not warranted, there is a need for a serious consideration of the nature and effects of local economic institutions in any analysis of long-term economic change.

The author appreciates the comments of the participants in the Conference on New Institutionalism in Economic Sociology, Cornell University, October 7–9, 1994, and at the Workshop on New Institutionalism in Economic Sociology, Russell Sage Foundation, New York, May 5–6, 1995, on earlier versions of this chapter. Particular thanks are due Jean Ensminger. This work was supported in part by funds provided by the Graduate School of the University of Washington, the London School of Economics, and the University of North Carolina at Charlotte.

NOTES

1. Putnam (1993) is a notable exception.

2. I have described and documented these regional differences in late medieval England more fully elsewhere (see Hopcroft 1994b).

3. For example, local institutions could not "go out of business" as modern organizations can.

4. This point is developed more fully in Hopcroft (1997). This is an example of the effect of organizations on informal norms (see Nee and Ingram, this volume, 33).

5. Note that information costs are also considered transaction costs.

6. Putnam (1993) demonstrates the same phenomenon in the contemporary world. He notes how social contexts in some regions of Italy create high uncertainty, low levels of trust, and high transaction costs, and thus inhibit economic development in those regions. He traces these regional differences to the historical development of norms of association and civil society in the different regions of Italy. In some respects this is the reverse of what I claim here. That is, I claim that local institutions produce regional norms and values, while Putnam shows how local norms and values influence the nature of local government and other institutions. There are no doubt reciprocal effects.

7. For a critique of this particular argument, see Hopcroft (1995b). It is not relevant to the present critique to repeat those arguments here.

8. This is not to say that ecological and geographical factors were unimportant in agrarian change in Europe or did not shape regional patterns. They did, but in conjunction with local institutional arrangements. Others have suggested that the local agricultural specialism, whether predominantly arable or pastoral, determined the regional differences in southern England (Thirsk 1967; Somers 1993). I have elaborated the many empirical problems with this explanation of regional differences in southern England in other discussions (see Hopcroft 1994a, 1995a; Overton 1996, 61). Space precludes a complete discussion of those arguments here. However, the evidence shows that 1) most regions of irregular open fields and enclosures in southern England cannot be described as primarily pastoral areas in the period under consideration here, or in later periods, and 2) agricultural specialism often changed in different regions depending on the prevailing market conditions. For example, there was a shift to a focus on pasture farming in many traditionally arable areas during the recessionary periods of the fifteenth and seventeenth centuries. While agricultural specialties fluctuated over time in various regions, however, the local institutions discussed here were much more unchanging.

9. There is also much evidence of this for European countries. For example, Root (1987) documents how French *intendants* of the seventeenth and eighteenth centuries modified various royal policies on agriculture to conform to realities of the local situation and thus to facilitate both stability and the successful collection of taxes.

10. The focus on agrarian change for the period in question is justified for several reasons. First, throughout the late medieval and early modern periods England was an agrarian society in which most economic activity *was* agricultural activity or else involved trade in agricultural products. Second, the regional pattern of agrarian change is generally duplicated in patterns of general economic growth. Third, agricultural development was a precondition for industrial development. Industrial workers, craftsmen, shopkeepers, and traders have to eat like everyone else, and there can be no trade or industry if agriculture is not productive enough to support workers in the nonagricultural sector or if food cannot be imported easily. This last situation does not apply to the English case, as imports of food were minimal in England until about 1800 (Beckett 1990; Campbell and Overton 1993, 39).

11. Although it is true that there was often some correlation. For example, mountainous areas were almost always areas of enclosures and individualistic agricultural practices. However, ecological differences provide an incomplete explanation of the regional differences.

12. Here, I refer to local economic organization as "local institutions." However, they may be regarded as the rural, preindustrial equivalent to the "organizations" described by Nee and Ingram, this volume.

13. Bloch [(1966a, 38)] also notes that this problem only occurred in champion (communal open field) regions.

14. This is an example of how organizations can shape informal norms (see Nee and Ingram, this volume).

15. This is seemingly the opposite of what Putnam (1993) claims for contemporary Italy, as he suggests that it is the more "individualistic" regions of southern Italy that are most economically backward, as opposed to the more communitarian north. Here I show that it was the more individualistic areas of southern England that developed the fastest. However, Putnam links the success of northern Italy more to the development of civil society than to "communitarianism" per se. In these respects, his findings do not contradict mine, as individualism does not preclude an active civil society. In many respects, civil society was *stronger* in the more *individualistic* regions of England than in other regions. This became even more true after the onset of the Reformation because of the impetus Protestantism gave to associational life. Yet underlying this active civil society were strong norms of individualism, just as there were in the America of Tocqueville's time.

16. Such high yields were not attained again in England until the early eighteenth century in East Anglia (Campbell 1991, 179).

17. Convertible husbandry (also called "up and down husbandry") is a flexible use of fields that involves "converting" fields from arable land to pasture and vice versa. Usually, legumes are grown on the field before it is converted to pasture, so both the nitrogen-fixing properties of legumes and the dung of animals serve to fertilize the ground (see Kerridge 1968).

18. Tenants might be free peasants or otherwise. These tenant farms should not be confused with the home farms—the demesnes—of the manorial lords. These tended to shrink in size after 1350.

19. After the late medieval period, the tendency for the very largest farms to be found in the east and southwest disappeared. In the midlands and central regions, the enclosure movement of the fifteenth and subsequent centuries threw many small peasant proprietors off their land and destroyed communal open field systems, making way for the rise of large, consolidated farms (Wordie 1983; Allen 1988; Grigg 1989). By 1850, very large farms (of over a hundred acres) predominated in these regions. By this date, all of England had become a nation of relatively large farms, and average farm sizes across England exceeded those of farms on the continent (as they do to this day).

20. The author of a biography of Thomas William Coke (a nineteenth-century descendent of Edward Coke who was both politician and agriculturalist) notes that Edward's father acquired land at Mileham (Norfolk) in 1554 and that "there is no doubt that Robert was resident at Mileham four years earlier, either as a tenant or upon land acquired in some other manner; for there in February, his illustrious son, Edward . . . was born" (Stirling 1912, 2). Coke may be thought of as an entrepreneur who promoted formal institutional change.

21. By the seventeenth century, almost all former customary tenants in England had become "copyholders" and received some protection under the common law (Kerridge 1969; Fryde and Fryde 1991, 819).

22. In addition, as I have argued in more detail elsewhere (Hopcroft 1995b), enforced reliance on indirect taxes may also have helped maintain the balance of power between crown and parliament in the years before the civil war.

23. It should be noted here that primogeniture in regular open field regions was not solely maintained by village custom. Manorial rules expressly forbade land division, as it was in the lord's interest that landholdings remain intact. This is because rents and dues were attached to landholdings, which became more difficult to collect when landholdings were broken up. Consequently, primogeniture was also enforced by the manorial court.

24. In the eighteenth century, these were the regions where the populace was most demanding of "citizenship rights," that is, equality with respect to the common law, equal participation in the lawmaking process, and social justice (Somers 1993, 594). Somers also notes the high development of civil society in these regions at that time.

25. The same theme emerges in recent studies of political change and state formation in preindustrial Europe (see Greengrass 1991, 7; Ertman 1997; Gustafsson 1994; Blockmans 1996, 244).

REFERENCES

Allen, Robert C. 1988. "The Growth of Labor Productivity in Early Modern English Agriculture." *Explorations in Economic History* 25:117–46.

Allison, K. J. 1957. "The Sheep-corn Husbandry of Norfolk in the Sixteenth and Seventeenth Centuries." *Agricultural History Review* 5(1): 12–30.

Baker, A. R. H. 1973. *Studies of Field Systems in the British Isles*. Cambridge, England: Cambridge University Press.

Barzel, Yoram. 1989. *Economic Analysis of Property Rights*. Cambridge, England: Cambridge University Press.

Bates, Robert. 1988. "Lessons from History, or the Perfidy of English Exceptionalism and the Significance of Historical France." *World Politics* 40(4): 498–516.

Bates. Robert H. 1990. "Macropolitical Economy in the Field of Development." In *Perspectives on Positive Political Economy*, edited by James E. Alt and Kenneth A. Shepsle. Cambridge, England: Cambridge University Press.

Bates, Robert H., and Da-Hsiang Donald Lien. 1985. "A Note on Taxation, Development, and Representative Government." *Politics and Society* 14(1): 53–70.

Beckett, J. V. 1990. *The Agricultural Revolution*. Oxford, England: Basil Blackwell.

Biddick, Kathleen. 1985. "Medieval Peasants and Market Involvement." *Journal of Economic History* 4: 823–31.

Bloch, Marc. 1966. *French Rural History*. Berkeley, Calif.: University of California Press.

Blockmans, W. P. 1996. "The Growth of Nations and States in Europe Before 1800." *European Review* 4: 241–51.

Braudel, Fernand. 1982. *The Wheels of Commerce*. New York: Harper and Row.

Britnell, R. H. 1991. "Eastern England." In *The Agrarian History of England and Wales*. Vol. 3, *1348–1500*, edited by Edward Miller. Cambridge, England: Cambridge University Press.

Brown, A. L. 1989. *The Governance of Late Medieval England 1272–1461*. London, England: Edward Arnold.

Buchanan, James M., Robert D. Tollison, and Gordon Tullock. 1980. *Toward a Theory of the Rent-Seeking Society*. College Station, Texas: Texas A&M University Press.

Cameron, Rondo. 1982. "Technology, Institutions and Long-Term Economic Change." In *Economics in the Long View: Essays in Honour of W. W. Rostow*, edited by Charles P. Kindleberger and Guido di Tella. New York: New York University Press.

Campbell, B. M. S. 1980. "Population Change and the Genesis of Commonfields on a Norfolk Manor." *Economic History Review*, 2d ser., 33: 174–92.

———. 1981. "Commonfield Origins: The Regional Dimension." In *The Origins of Open-Field Agriculture*, edited by Trevor Rowley. London, England: Barnes and Noble.

———. 1983. "Arable Productivity in Medieval England: Some Evidence from Norfolk." *Journal of Economic History* 43: 379–404.

———. 1984. "Population Pressure, Inheritance and the Land Market in a Fourteenth-Century Peasant Community." In *Land, Kinship and Life-cycle*, edited by R. M. Smith. Cambridge, England: Cambridge University Press.

———. 1988. "The Diffusion of Vetches in Medieval England." *Economic History Review*, 2d ser., 41(2): 193–208.

———. 1991. "English Seignorial Agriculture." In *Land, Labour and Livestock*, edited by B. M. S. Campbell and Mark Overton. Manchester, England: Manchester University Press.

Campbell, B. M. S., and Mark Overton. 1993. "A New Perspective on Medieval and Early Modern Agriculture: Six Centuries of Norfolk Farming c.1250–c.1850." *Past and Present* 141: 38–105.

Campbell, John L., and Leon N. Lindberg. 1990. "Property Rights and the Organization of Economic Activity by the State." *American Sociological Review* 55(5): 634–47.

Cancian, Frank. 1979. *The Innovator's Situation*. Palo Alto, Calif.: Stanford University Press.

Chambers, J. D., and G. E. Mingay. 1966. *The Agricultural Revolution 1750–1880*. London, England: B. T. Batsford.

Chirot, Daniel. 1985. "The Rise of the West." *American Sociological Review* 50(2): 181–94.

Clay, C. G. A. 1984. *Economic Expansion and Social Change: England 1500–1700*. Vol. I, *People, Land and Towns*. Cambridge, England: Cambridge University Press.

Coase, Ronald H. 1960. "The Problem of Social Cost." *Journal of Law and Economics* 3: 1–44.

Davis, John. 1973. *Land and Family in Pisticci*. New York: Humanities Press.

de Soto, Hernando. 1993. "The Missing Ingredient: What Poor Countries Need to Make Their Markets Work. *The Economist* (Sept. 11, 1993), 8–12.

de Vries, Jan. 1974. *The Dutch Rural Economy in the Golden Age 1500–1700*. New Haven, Conn.: Yale University Press.

Dickens, A. G. 1964. *The English Reformation*. New York: Schocken Books.

Dodwell, Barbara. 1939. "The Free Peasantry of East Anglia." *Norfolk Archaeology* 27: 145–57.

———. 1967. "Holdings and Inheritance in Medieval East Anglia." *Economic History Review*, 2d ser., 20: 53–66.

Douglas, David C. 1927. *The Social Structure of Medieval East Anglia*. Vol. 9. Oxford Studies in Social and Legal History. Oxford, England: Clarendon Press.

Downing, Brian M. 1988. "Constitutionalism, Warfare, and Political Change in Early Modern Europe." *Theory and Society* 17: 7–56.

Du Boulay, F. R. H. 1965. "Who Were Farming the English Demesnes at the End of the Middle Ages?" *Economic History Review*, 2d ser., 17(3): 443–55.

Dyer, C. C. 1991. "The West Midlands." In *The Agrarian History of England and Wales*. Vol. 3, *1348–1500*, edited by Edward Miller. Cambridge, England: Cambridge University Press.

Ertman, Thomas. 1997. *Birth of the Leviathan. Building States and Regimes in Medieval and Early Modern Europe*. Cambridge, England: Cambridge University Press.

Finberg, H. P. R. 1951. *Tavistock Abbey: A Study in the Social and Economic History of Devon*. Cambridge, England: Cambridge University Press.

Fourquin, Guy. 1990. *Histoire économique de l'Occident medieval*. Paris, France: Armand Colin.

Fox, H. S. A. 1991. "Devon and Cornwall." In *The Agrarian History of England and Wales*. Vol. 3, *1348–1500*, edited by Edward Miller. Cambridge, England: Cambridge University Press.

Fryde, E. B. 1991. "Royal Fiscal Systems and State Formation in France from the 13th to the 16th Century, With Some English Comparisons." *Journal of Historical Sociology* 4(3): 236–87.

Fryde, E. B., and Natalie Fryde. 1991. "Peasant Rebellion and Peasant Discontents." In *The Agrarian History of England and Wales*. Vol. 3, *1348–1500*, edited by Edward Miller. Cambridge, England: Cambridge University Press.

Gray, H. L. 1915. *English Field Systems*. Cambridge, Mass.: Harvard University Press.

Greengrass, Mark. 1991. "Conquest and Coalescence." In *Conquest and Coalescence: The Shaping of the State in Early Modern Europe*, edited by Mark Greengrass. London, England: Edward Arnold.

Grigg, David. 1989. *English Agriculture: An Historical Perspective*. Oxford, England: Basil Blackwell.

Gustafsson, Harald. 1994. *Political Interaction in the Old Regime. Central Power and Local Society in the Eighteenth-Century Nordic States.* Translated by Alan Crozier. Lund: Studentlitteratur.

Hallam, H. E. 1981. *Rural England 1066–1348.* Sussex, England: Harvester Press.

Hamilton, Gary, and Nicole Woolsey Biggart. 1988. "Market, Culture and Authority: A Comparative Analysis of Management and Organization in the Far East." *American Journal of Sociology* 94: S52–94.

Homans, G. C. 1941. *English Villagers of the Thirteenth Century.* Cambridge Mass.: Harvard University Press.

———. 1987a. "The Anglo-Saxon Invasions Reconsidered." In *Certainties and Doubts: Collected Papers 1962–1985.* New Brunswick, N.J.: Transaction Books.

———. 1987b. "The Explanation of English Regional Differences." In *Certainties and Doubts: Collected Papers 1962–1985.* New Brunswick, N.J.: Transaction Books.

———. [1962] 1988. "The Puritans and the Clothing Industry in England." In *Sentiments and Activities: Essays in Social Science.* New Brunswick, N.J.: Transaction Books.

Hopcroft, Rosemary L. 1994a. "The Origins of Regular Open Field Systems in Pre-Industrial Europe." *The Journal of European Economic History* 23(3): 563–80.

———. 1994b. "The Social Origins of Agrarian Change in Late Medieval England." *American Journal of Sociology* 99(6): 1559–95.

———. 1995. Comment: "Conceptualizing Regional Differences in Eighteenth Century England." *The American Sociological Review* 60(5): 791–96.

———. 1997. "Rural Organization and Receptivity to Protestantism in Sixteenth-Century Europe." *Journal for the Scientific Study of Religion* 36 (2): 158–81.

Hoyle, R. W. 1990. "Tenure and the Land Market in Early Modern England: Or a Late Contribution to the Brenner Debate." *Economic History Review,* 2d ser., 43(1): 1–20.

Hyams, P. R. 1980. *King, Lords and Peasants in Medieval England.* Oxford, England: Oxford University Press.

Jones, E. L. 1988. *Growth Recurring.* Oxford, England: Clarendon Press.

Kerridge, Eric. 1968. *The Agricultural Revolution.* New York: A. M. Kelley.

———. 1969. *Agrarian Problems in the Sixteenth Century and After.* New York: Barnes and Noble.

King, Edmund. 1973. *Peterborough Abbey 1086–1310.* Cambridge, England: Cambridge University Press.

Knight, Jack. 1992. *Institutions and Social Conflict.* Cambridge: Cambridge University Press.

Lamond, E., ed. [1581] 1929. *A Discourse of the Common Weal of this Realm of England.* Cambridge, England: Cambridge University Press.

Langdon, John. 1986. *Horses, Oxen and Technological Innovation.* Cambridge, England: Cambridge University Press.

Leonard, E. M. 1962. "The Inclosure of Common Fields in the Seventeenth Century." In *Essays in Economic History,* edited by E. M. Carus-Wilson. Vol. 2, London, England: Edward Arnold.

Macfarlane, Alan. 1978. *The Origins of English Individualism.* Oxford, England: Blackwell.

Martin, John E. 1983. *Feudalism to Capitalism: Peasant and Landlord in English Agrarian Development.* London, England: Macmillan.

Marx, Karl. 1906. *Capital.* New York: The Modern Library.

Mate, Mavis. 1986. "The Estates of Canterbury Cathedral Priory before the Black Death 1315–1348." *Studies in Medieval and Renaissance History* 8: 1–26.

———. 1991. "Kent and Sussex." In *The Agrarian History of England and Wales.* Vol. 3, *1348–1500,* edited by Edward Miller. Cambridge, England: Cambridge University Press.

Merton, Robert K. [1938] 1970. *Science, Technology and Society in Seventeenth Century England.* New York: Harper and Row.

Merton, Robert K., and Alice S. Rossi. 1957. "Contributions to the Theory of Reference Group Behavior" In *Social Theory and Social Structure* (revised and enlarged edition) by Robert K. Merton. Glencoe, Ill.: Free Press.

Miller, Edward. 1991. "The Southern Counties." In *The Agrarian History of England and Wales.* Vol. 3, *1348–1500,* edited by Edward Miller. Cambridge, England: Cambridge University Press.

Moreton, C. E. 1992. *The Townshends and Their World: Gentry, Law and Land in Norfolk c. 1450–1551.* Oxford, England: Clarendon Press.

North, Douglass C. 1981. *Structure and Change in Economic History.* New York: Norton.

———. 1982. "The Theoretical Tools of the Economic Historian." In *Economics in the Long View:*

Essays in Honour of W. W. Rostow, edited by Charles P. Kindleberger and Guido di Tella. New York: New York University Press.

————. 1990a. "Institutions and a Transaction-Cost Theory of Exchange." In *Perspectives on Positive Political Economy*, edited by James E. Alt and Kenneth A. Shepsle. Cambridge, England: Cambridge University Press.

————. 1990b. *Institutions, Institutional Change and Economic Performance*. Cambridge, England: Cambridge University Press.

North, Douglass C., and Robert Paul Thomas. 1973. *The Rise of the Western World*. Cambridge, England: Cambridge University Press.

Østerud, Øyvind. 1978. "Agrarian Structure of the Old Peasant Society." In *Agrarian Structure and Peasant Politics in Scandinavia: A Comparative Study of Rural Response to Economic Change*. Oslo, Norway: Universitetsforlaget.

Overton, Mark. 1991. "The Determinants of Crop Yields in Early Modern England." In *Land, Labour and Livestock: Historical Studies in European Agricultural Productivity*, edited by B. M. S. Campbell and Mark Overton. Manchester, England: Manchester University Press.

————. 1996. *Agricultural Revolution in England. The Transformation of the Agrarian Economy 1500–1850*. Cambridge, England: Cambridge University Press.

Putnam, Robert D. 1993. *Making Democracy Work: Civic Traditions in Modern Italy*. Princeton, N.J.: Princeton University Press.

Ransom, Roger, Richard Sutch, and Gary Walton. 1982. *Explorations in the New Economic History: Essays in Honor of Douglass C. North*. New York: Academic Press.

Riches, Naomi. 1967. *The Agricultural Revolution in Norfolk*. London, England: Frank Cass.

Robisheaux, Thomas. 1994. "The World of the Village." In *Handbook of European History 1400–1600*, edited by Thomas A. Brady, Jr., Heiko A. Oberman, and James D. Tracy. Vol. 1. Leiden, Netherlands: Brill.

Root, Hilton L. 1987. *Peasant and King in Burgundy: Agrarian Foundations of French Absolutism*. Berkeley, Calif.: University of California Press.

Sabean, David Warren. 1990. *Property, Production and Family in Neckarhausen, 1700–1870*. Cambridge, England: Cambridge University Press.

Sayer, Derek. 1992. "A Notable Administration: English State Formation and the Rise of Capitalism." *American Journal of Sociology* 97(5): 1382–1415.

Schofield, R. S. 1965. "The Geographical Distribution of Wealth in England 1334–1649." *Economic History Review* 2nd ser., 18(3): 483–510.

Slicher van Bath, B. H. 1963. *Yield Ratios 810–1820*. Wageningen, Netherlands: A. A. G. Bijdragen (10).

Smith, R. M. 1984. *Land, Kinship and Life-Cycle*. Cambridge, England: Cambridge University Press.

Somers, Margaret R. 1993. "Law, Community and Political Culture in the Transition to Democracy." *American Sociological Review* 58(5): 587–620.

Stacey, Robert C. 1986. "Agricultural Investment and the Management of the Royal Demesne Manors, 1236–1240." *Journal of Economic History* 46: 919–34.

Stark, David, Victor Nee, and Paulo Kramer. 1990. "Toward an Institutional Analysis of State Socialism." *Dados* 33(2): 181–209.

Stirling, A. M. W. 1912. *Coke of Norfolk and His Friends*. London, England: John Lane The Bodley Head.

Stone, E. 1956. "The Estates of Norwich Cathedral Priory, 1100–1300." Ph.D. diss., Oxford University.

Szelényi, Iván, in collaboration with Robert Manchin, Pal Juhasz, Balint Maqyar and Bill Martin. 1988. *Socialist Entrepreneurs: Embourgeoisement in Rural Hungary*. Madison, Wis.: University of Wisconsin Press.

Tawney, R. H. 1912. *The Agrarian Problem in the Sixteenth Century*. London, England: Longmans, Green.

Thirsk, J. 1967. "The Farming Regions of England." In *The Agrarian History of England and Wales*. Vol. 14, *1500–1640*, edited by Joan Thirsk. Cambridge, England: Cambridge University Press.

Thornton, Christopher. 1991. "The Determinants of Land Productivity on the Bishop of Winchester's Demesne of Rimpton, 1208–1403." In *Land, Labour and Livestock*, edited by Bruce M. S. Campbell and Mark Overton. Manchester, England: Manchester University Press.

Tullock, Gordon. 1987. *Autocracy*. Dordrecht, Netherlands: Kluwer Academic Publishers.

———. 1990. "The Costs of Special Privilege." In *Perspectives on Positive Political Economy*, edited by James E. Alt and Kenneth A. Shepsle. Cambridge, England: Cambridge University Press.

Turner, Michael. 1982. "Agricultural Productivity in England in the Eighteenth Century: Evidence from Crop Yields." *The Economic History Review*, 2d ser., 35: 489–505.

Walzer, Michael. 1965. *The Revolution of the Saints: A Study in the Origins of Radical Politics*. Cambridge, Mass.: Harvard University Press.

Weber, Max. [1930] 1989. *The Protestant Ethic and the Spirit of Capitalism*. Translated by Talcott Parsons. London, England: Unwin Hyman.

Williamson, Oliver E. 1975. *Markets and Hierarchies: Analysis and Anti-trust Implications*. New York: Free Press.

———. 1985. *The Economic Institutions of Capitalism. Firms, Markets, Relational Contracting*. New York: Free Press.

Wordie, J. R. 1983. "The Chronology of English Enclosure 1500–1914." *Economic History Review*, 2d ser., 36(4): 483–505.

Zaret, David. 1985. *The Heavenly Contract*. Chicago, Ill.: University of Chicago Press.

14

Outline of an Institutionalist Theory of Inequality: The Case of Socialist and Postcommunist Eastern Europe

Iván Szelényi and Eric Kostello

I n this chapter we develop an outline of an institutionalist theory to explain the recent history of inequality in state socialist and postcommunist countries. The theory does not assume that either market or redistributive institutions are inherently responsible for generating inequality. Instead, its premise is that inequality is a function of the types of market and redistributive institutions that operate at a given historical juncture and the specific property, social, and in particular class relations in which these economic institutions are embedded. Inequality is changing in the formerly state socialist countries, and while we do not offer a theory of transition from state socialism, we locate the dynamics of this change primarily in class relations. In its briefest possible form, our argument is that institutions explain inequality and that changes in institutions are explained by contention between and within classes. Yet, this formulation is too simple because it leaves out the interplay between institutions and the actors in an economy. Thus, we shall have to specify what we mean by institutions and by classes and show the relationship between them. We begin by reviewing briefly developments in institutionalist theory in both economics and sociology.

There have been two important developments in institutionalism over the past few decades. Both can be understood as responses to the "classical" institutionalism of Karl Polanyi (1957). The first is the new economic institutionalism of Oliver Williamson (1975, 1985). Williamson brought into institutionalism the analytical lucidity that—in their broadest possible interpretation—rational choice theory and neoclassical economics offered. He rejected, or at least did not apply in his analysis, Polanyi's notion of embeddedness—a concept that, for him, appeared to be of dubious analytical clarity. And he rejected Polanyi's ideologically driven implicit antimarket and pro-redistributive sympathies.

The second major development in institutionalism emerged in the sociological literature with Mark Granovetter's (1985) critique of Williamson. Granovetter's project is to bring embeddedness back into economic sociological analysis in a way that makes the concept more precise than it was in Polanyi's work and that avoids the pitfalls of the implicit antimarket ideology. Even more important, Granovetter seeks to do this in a way that defines a clear and powerful agenda for empirical research. He achieved this with great success by demonstrating that economic action is embedded in micro-level interpersonal networks (Granovetter 1985).

The book of which this chapter is a part—and the conference and workshop that produced it—aims to open a third chapter in the recent history of institutionalism. So far, the two innovations in institutionalism have been divided along disciplinary lines. As its name suggests, the new economic institutionalism of Williamson was mostly pursued by economists, while Granovetter's institutionalism mainly influenced sociologists.[1] While we admire Granovetter's contributions to sociology and do not dispute that networks matter, we believe that network-level understanding needs to be complemented by the macro perspective.

In attempting this we do not want to abandon Granovetter's important critique of Williamson. Our aim in this paper is to treat embeddedness as seriously as Granovetter does, but to do so from a *macro*sociological perspective and thereby to explore the macro social relations, in particular *class* relations, in which economic processes are embedded. We endeavor to show how class analysis can explain the dynamics of social inequality in reforming socialist and postcommunist societies. We do this by using the notion of class not in a narrow Marxist sense but rather in a more eclectic and broad sense. Our usage is perhaps closer to the Weberian than the Marxist perspective, although we are not embarrassed to use Marx when it seems insightful and appropriate. We want to take *agency* seriously and put it at the *center* of our analysis. We understand economic processes, and in particular the dynamics of social inequality, as a product of the historically contingent struggles of collective actors. Their behavior can indeed be formed by the rational economic considerations of the members of these collectives, but it is fatefully influenced as well by their socially formed sets of dispositions, which are malleable (but typically change only slowly) and which, at the macro level, are shaped by individuals at the same time that widely held dispositions shape individuals. (In this view, the subjective takes on a social character.) Finally, their behavior is influenced most immediately by the dynamics of the social struggles in which they are involved.

Our most ambitious aim is to contribute to what we call a *macroinstitutionalist new economic sociology*; to merge the macro orientation of the new economic institutionalism with the idea of embeddedness. We do not use embeddedness in Granovetter's microsociological way, but from a class-agency perspective—the macrosociological perspective so central to the institutionalism of Karl Polanyi. While what we offer here is in many respects a rather "old-fashioned" Polanyian institutionalism, we do not call simply for a return to Polanyi. He offered a one-sided critique of the market from a redistributive perspective. We aim to fundamentally reconstruct Polanyi (Szelényi 1991) by moving away from his anti-market, pro-redistribution perspective. His was an important achievement that should not be abandoned, but it should nevertheless be complemented by a critique of redistribution from the perspective of markets. Thus our macroinstitutionalist new economic sociology can be considered *neo-Polanyian*.

Since the concepts we have just introduced are either not in common use or are used differently by others, we will before proceeding spell out the meaning we attach to them and how we use them. As we said, we will try to develop a *neo-Polanyian macroinstitutionalist new economic sociology*. In what follows we try to answer three questions: (a) Why do we claim that our analysis is *institutionalist*? (b) In what sense do we adopt a *macro perspective*? (c) In what sense do we depart from Polanyi, and how is our analysis *neo*-Polanyian?

WHY IS OUR ANALYSIS INSTITUTIONALIST?

In order to explain what institutionalism is and in what sense our institutionalism derives from a macro perspective it is sufficient simply to return to Polanyi

(1957). In these two respects we are rather orthodox Polanyi "disciples." The key to understanding Polanyi's institutionalism can be found in his criticism of the "formal view of the economy" of classical economics. In his interpretation, classical economics holds that rational economic actors "economize"—that is, they try to achieve the highest possible return with the least possible effort. Polanyi argued that economizing is a far too narrow and ahistorical concept with which to understand what people do in different historical circumstances when they try to secure their livelihood. He showed that economic action is *instituted* in different ways in different historical circumstances. In studying economic systems of the world in different sites and at different points in history he identified three different types of institutions of economic integration: markets, redistribution, and reciprocity.[2] He characterized economies according to which of these is the dominant form of economic integration. Following Weber, Polanyi believed that it makes little sense for the analyst to declare a given form of economic integration rational or irrational. Instead, the task of an economic anthropologist or economic sociologist is to try to understand the varieties of ways in which economic action is instituted and the diverse *rationalities* that economic actors may pursue. Thus, when one studies the behavior of actors who operate in a redistributively integrated economy or in an economic system based on reciprocity, it makes little sense to try to explain their action in terms of the rationality of market actors. Polanyi's project was to identify three distinct sets of rules of the game, not to order them in an evolutionary sequence leading from reciprocity to redistribution and eventually culminating in markets. An economy that is predominantly redistributively integrated, or one that is based on reciprocity, is not less rational or less advanced than a market economy: it simply follows different rules and obeys a different logic. It was crucial to Polanyi's theory that the three forms of integration are likely to coexist rather than to replace or follow each other. After all, in *The Great Transformation* ([1944] 1957), his first statement on this subject, Polanyi aimed to show that (a) market integration in its pure form never existed, and (b) the closer an economy comes to the pure form of market integration the more likely market failures are. Since the different economic institutional arrangements cannot be ordered along some evolutionary line, or on a scale ranging from irrational to rational, Polanyi tried to demonstrate what kind of mixes of institutional arrangements one can find in history, implying that markets will also have to be complemented by other integrative mechanisms.

We attempt to offer an institutionalist theory of inequality along the lines of this tradition. We consider both socialist and postcommunist economies to be mixed systems in which redistribution, markets, and reciprocity coexist but in which markets and redistribution play qualitatively different roles. Our aim is to show that these different institutional arrangements will result in different systems of inequality: the degree of inequality is different, the role each institution plays in creating or counteracting inequality varies, and which actors are advantaged and which are disadvantaged is different as well.[3]

IN WHAT SENSE IS OUR APPROACH A MACRO ONE?

The macro/micro distinction is somewhat dated with respect to sociology and its usefulness limited. And while we do not wish to place too great an emphasis on the macrosociological nature of our analysis, the label does offer some help in distinguishing two concepts of embeddedness. The new economic sociology inspired by Granovetter emphasizes that economic action is embedded in interpersonal networks, and it has convincingly demonstrated that understanding social networks is important in explaining how people get jobs and, more generally, how business is conducted in modern capitalist societies. This line of research is valuable and has greatly enriched our understanding of the working of economic systems. We wish to complement this micro perspective with the macro-level concept of embeddedness in classical sociological institutionalism. In Polanyi's view, economic action is embedded in political processes. As demonstrated in his *The Great Transformation*, markets are not spontaneously arising institutions that spring from the workings of an economy which is an extension of human nature. Markets are created as a result of state action, and market institutions have to be created—and maintained—by political acts.

Analogously, our aim in this chapter is to explain how a certain balance in economic integrative mechanisms arise and what the social consequences of such institutional arrangements may be. We do this by looking at class formation and the struggle among classes and among other types of collective actors. For instance, Konrad and Szelényi (1979) argued that economic reform in the Soviet Union and in Eastern Europe during the 1960s was the result of the deepening legitimation crisis of the ruling Stalinist bureaucracy. After the death of the charismatic leader, the state bureaucracy searched for new ways to legitimate itself. On the one hand, it tried to pacify the working class by opening up opportunities in the service jobs and limited markets of the so called "second economy" so its members could improve their living conditions; on the other, it tried to bring the technocratic intelligentsia into a power-sharing arrangement by promising "rationalization" of the redistributive system. By the 1980s, it became obvious that no real power sharing could be achieved between the bureaucracy and the technocracy, and the technocratic intelligentsia gave up the project of rationalization of the redistributive system. Instead, it took the process of converting economic functions from the redistributive to the market sphere into its own hands and attempted to implement it for its own benefit. The marketization implemented by the late 1980s by the technocratic intelligentsia is rather different from the socialist petit bourgeoisification pursued earlier. Thus, around 1989 in Eastern Europe the technocratic fraction of the elite defeated the old-line bureaucracy (and its policy of promoting small-scale businesses) and put the privatization of public assets at the top of its reform agenda. With the dismantling of the redistributive sector of the economy, the second economy (which had existed in a close symbiotic relationship with the statist economy) also decayed, leading to the pauperization of some members of the petit bourgeois strata that had emerged during the period of late state socialism. Some elements of the technocracy tried to convert public property into private wealth, but in this they were confronted by a new political elite, which emerged from the ranks of former dissident intellectuals. This new elite tried to prevent the technocracy from converting its earlier positional power into private wealth. This should be sufficient to illustrate how our analysis follows a macro perspective. Our focus is on collective actors, such as classes, estates, and elites and their functions. We do not doubt that personal networks are eminently important too. If one wants to explain whether an actor will survive the shift toward markets, and benefit from it or will end up a loser, the interpersonal networks of that individual are of great importance. But beyond these networks we try to identify more macro phenomena and to explain the making of economic institutions and the social consequences of certain constellations of such institutions in terms of the historically contingent struggles of these collective actors.

WHAT IS NEO-POLANYIAN IN OUR ANALYSIS?

We are not the orthodox Polanyi disciples we may seem to be from the preceding discussion. In one very important respect we are not only different from Polanyi, but our analysis can be seen as the inverse of his. Polanyi was searching for a theory of redistribution and reciprocity in order to offer a criticism of the market. While at one level he argued that all three types of economic integration are rational and that all empirically observable economies can be seen as mixes of different mechanisms of integration, he nevertheless attributed destructive capacities to markets that he thought the other integrative mechanisms did not possess. Markets were destructive mechanisms in that, as they grew, they destroyed other mechanisms of economic integration. In this way, markets were also *self*-destructive. Polanyi believed that pure systems are unlikely to be able to reproduce themselves and, seeing powerful actors in market-integrated economies striving toward a purer market system, was therefore skeptical about the future of market capitalism. His political project was to stop markets from this self-destructive expansion. As a scholar, he never applied the theory of redistribution to modern economies, but we can say at the very least that he hoped that some redistributive mechanism would complement market forces in advanced capitalism. Occasionally, he may have considered the substitution of a modernized version of a redistributive economy for the market economy to be desirable, possible, and perhaps even necessary.

We shall try to bracket Polanyi's political project and formulate the problem analytically. Polanyi offered a critique of a market economy from the perspective of a redistributive economy. His aim was to show the temporariness of markets and an alternative means of running an economy. In our view, his critique was rather one-sided. Our aim here is to add to this criticism of the market from the standpoint of redistribution by offering a criticism of redistribution from the perspective of the market. Our focus in this chapter is on the question of inequality. While for those working within an orthodox Polanyian perspective the source of inequality is in markets and the way to counteract the effect of markets is through the redistributive intervention of the state, we claim that inequality is rooted in the dominant mechanism of economic integration. We define a *dominant* mechanism as that which regulates the allocation of the major factors of production, namely, land, labor, and capital. A *compensatory* mechanism exists when another mode of economic integration allocates other goods and services. (It is "compensatory" because it acts to reduce inequality by bringing the bottom up, rather than acting at both ends of the economic spectrum.) For example, in a social democratic welfare state the market is dominant since it allocates capital and labor, while redistribution is compensatory, since it provides the needy with housing and education and with other goods and services. The opposite is true for state socialism, where labor and capital are redistributed through central planning and the needy have to provide many other things for themselves by using markets. The dominant form of economic integration forms the basis of class power. If this is redistribution, then redistribution will be the major source of inequality and the underprivileged will use markets to fight back; if markets regulate the allocation of labor and capital then those who are powerless will have to rely on the redistributive intervention of the state to improve their lot. In this respect, our theory is a radical departure from Polanyi's position and a major reconstruction of the original theory. We may therefore call it neo-Polanyian.

DEFINING THE HISTORICAL CONTEXT: TYPES OF MARKET PENETRATION IN REFORMING SOCIALIST AND POSTCOMMUNIST SOCIETIES

To demonstrate our neo-Polanyian framework, we present a typology of market penetration and attempt to identify as concretely as possible the actors in each type of economic system in Eastern Europe over the past three decades, with particular reference to Hungary and Poland. We also try to show which *mechanism* of economic coordination is the source of social inequality. We develop this typology in an inductive way, from empirical observation of how economic institutions and social structure have changed over time in the countries under investigation. We *do not assume that the types we present are a necessary evolutionary* sequence and that progress from one stage to the next is inevitable. Indeed, much of our evidence shows that the movement between one type and another was the result of deliberate interventions or changes in policies or strategies. However, it is not unimaginable that our types *do* constitute an evolutionary sequence; we leave open the possibility that this may be established by further empirical research.

We distinguish three types of market penetration: (a) local markets in redistributively integrated economies, (b) socialist mixed economies, where the market and a redistributive system exist under the hegemony of redistribution, (c) and capitalist-oriented economies, where the aim is the establishment of market capitalism and the elimination of state socialism. In what follows, we elaborate on these types, show how markets in each type affect inequality, and identify the social actors who gain or lose under each type. We distinguish the three types of market penetration by describing the institutional characteristics of each type, paying particular attention to the market institutions in place in each type. In table 14.1, we offer hypotheses about the characteristics of three different market institutions in Eastern European countries.

Market reforms in Eastern Europe and, to the best of our knowledge, in China as well began with petty *commodity markets* where producers were allowed to sell products or services at prices regulated by supply and demand. Such commodification of consumer goods and services can proceed even though the allocation of the factors of production, labor and capital, remain redistributive. The greater the proportion of prices that are deregulated (that is, set by the mechanisms of supply and demand), the more highly developed commodity markets become. *Labor markets* exist when, in Marxist terms, people are legally free to sell their labor and are in addition compelled to enter the labor market by virtue of their separation from a means of subsistence. The more the price of labor is set

Table 14.1   Institutional Characteristics and Social Effects of Market Penetration in Reform-Socialist and Postcommunist Eastern Europe

	Type of Market Penetration		
	Local Markets in Redistributive Economies (1968–1980)	Socialist Mixed Economies (1980–1989)	Capitalist-Oriented Economies (1989–)
Institutional characteristics			
Commodity markets	+ +	+ + +	+ + + +
Labor market	–	+ +	+ + .+
Capital market	–	+	+ +
Social outcomes			
Dynamics of inequality	Some decline	Some increase	High increase
Source of inequality	Redistribution	Redistribution and market	Market
Return to human capital in labor or local markets	–	+	+ +
Equalizing mechanism	Markets	Some market	Redistribution
Winners	Peasants and peasant-workers	Petit bourgeois, technocrats and cadre children	Technocrats and new bourgeoisie
Losers	Redistributors	Old bureaucrats and no-hopers	Old bureaucats, most workers, and no-hopers

Note: A minus sign indicates "none," while plus signs indicate a range from minimal (+) to considerable (+ + + +).

by supply and demand the more developed the labor market becomes. In socialist redistributive economies there is trade for labor, but since labor's price typically is administratively set, this trade is nonmarket (in Polanyian language) and there is no labor market proper. *A capital market* refers to the allocation of capital goods. In a socialist redistributive economy, the surplus available to extend reproduction is typically appropriated first, then allocated by central planners through budgetary means. A reduction in the proportion of investment that is regulated by state agencies is an indicator of the making of a capital market. In capital markets, competitive investors allocate capital goods in expectation of higher returns on their capital investments. Following Polanyi (1957), we call an economy *market-integrated* or capitalist when labor and capital markets are the *dominant* mechanisms of the allocation of labor and capital. If labor and capital are primarily redistributively allocated and market exchange is generally restricted to the exchange of consumer goods, then there exist only what Polanyi calls *local markets*.

By the 1980s, the economic systems of Hungary and Poland were no longer simply redistributive systems coexisting with local markets. Petty private economic activities were by then legalized, and full-time private entrepreneurs had begun to operate and produce an increasing proportion of the gross national product (GNP). While most of the economy remained publicly or cooperatively owned, after decades of decay and stagnation a new private sector was in the making. Growing rapidly, it was beginning to be a site for capital accumulation. A new socialist petit bourgeoisie, a class of "socialist entrepreneurs" was emerging. Occasionally, these entrepreneurs employed other people.

Even after economic reforms began, Hungary and Poland were much more restrictive vis-à-vis private ownership than China has been during the past decade. Nonetheless, marketization progressed and by the early 1980s two-thirds of all prices were deregulated—a degree of marketization China reached in the mid-1990s—and there was very little bureaucratic control over the production of publicly owned firms. The point is that while China by the mid-1990s was much further along then Hungary and Poland in terms of changes in property rights, the reforming communist countries of Eastern Europe during the 1980s were much further along than China toward market reform. Unlike in China, in Hungary since the late 1960s there have been no production targets set for producers operating in publicly owned firms; they could produce whatever they wanted and sell to whomever they wanted. But while deregulation and marketization were well-established in the reforming economies of Eastern Europe, both of our examples were rather cautious about property reform until 1988 to 1989. The employment of wage labor and the accumulation of capital by private entrepreneurs remained a "gray area" of law, so that by the end of the 1980s even the most reform-oriented Eastern European countries were not quite fully mixed economies. In this respect, China today, though it may not have progressed as far in marketization as Hungary and Poland did during the 1980s, has created new spaces for private business and can be considered a more mature socialist mixed economy than these countries were then.

What happened in 1989 to 1990 in Eastern Europe represents a true system breakdown. Two events were extremely important: first, the elimination of the political authority of the Communist Party and the introduction of a multiparty democratic regime and, second, the decision to declare the publicly owned sector moribund and to adopt policies aimed at privatizing the public sector with the aim of completely removing the state from the sphere of production. While the Eastern European economies may not yet be capitalist—finding identifiable owners of the means of production, eliminating public ownership, and discontinuing the active role of the state in directing the economy proved to be more difficult than expected—these economies are undoubtedly capitalist-*oriented*. Not only have virtually all price regulations been eliminated, but the labor market is almost free. Thus, unemployment became legitimate and widespread, and the allocation of capital is to a large degree governed by the goal of profit maximization. Under these circumstances, enterprise managers have gained full autonomy from "redistributors." There is no class of redistributors or party apparatchiks any longer, and a propertied bourgeoisie is in the making.

Needless to say, such differences in market penetration are qualitative, not quantitative. The commodification of labor and the shift from redistributive to market allocation of capital goods are not only aspects of economic policy or of narrowly defined "economic" mechanisms. Rather, they correspond to processes of *class formation*; they depend on the transformation of property relations and the movement to a new and different type of allocation of authority and material privileges. This is another example of what we mean by the *macro perspective* of the embeddedness of economic processes.

The distinctions we draw between types of market penetration clarify which economic mechanism is dominant or compensatory. This is of central importance because it is our general hypothesis that it is neither the market nor redistribution but the dominant economic mechanism that is the main source of inequality. If secondary and compensatory mechanisms exist (as they do in most economic systems), they are generally likely to reduce the overall level of inequality, for the beneficiaries of secondary or compensatory mechanisms are typically those whose access to the dominant mechanism is restricted.

DYNAMICS OF SOCIAL INEQUALITY IN SOCIALIST AND POSTCOMMUNIST EASTERN EUROPE
Local Markets in Redistributively Integrated Economies

Hungary and Poland were countries with local markets in redistributively integrated economies from the mid-1960s until around 1980. The emergent local markets were typically for food or services and were peripheral to the economic system. Producers in these markets had little security; because their activities often bordered on the illegal, producers' participation was risky. The most typical actors were peasants and peasant-workers.

The expansion of local markets in Hungary began when the government began to tolerate family production in community-owned gardens or in household plots. Although family agricultural production was initially intended for subsistence production only, from the mid-1960s onward families began to be allowed to bring specialized products to urban markets. This generated extra, and eventually substantial, income for agricultural producers and led to a higher rural standard of living. This became visible in rural housing construction from as early as the late 1960s. Large, high-quality rural houses were being built with the extra income from the so-called second economy. Reciprocity, in addition to the key integrative mechanism of redistribution, played an important role in the rapid improvement of living and housing conditions of the rural working class. Future owners, as well as their kin, friends, and neighbors, often contributed their labor to the construction of new rural housing—which typically was larger and of higher quality than the housing the government could afford to build for its professional and political cadres in urban areas.

Local food and housing markets were matched early on by local markets for services. The second economy began to spread into cities and through service economy, initially in the form of moonlighting activities. Television repairmen, plumbers, car mechanics, and construction workers began to offer their services after hours and during weekends at prices set by supply and demand.

The Communist Party and the government were hesitant in their response to market activities that were either illegal or, at best, of dubious legality. While they saw the political benefits of improvements in the food supply and the provision of more efficient and better services, they were at the same time concerned about "creeping capitalism." Party members in positions of power, which we will refer to throughout this chapter as "cadres," were disturbed by the undermining of their capacity to control social processes. Before markets spread, workers were dependent on cadres for their livelihood. As the second economy opened up, workers gained more autonomy. Now they could take sick-leave to work at their moonlighting jobs, or they could report to work in the state enterprise. Some second economy actors also began to earn unexpectedly high incomes. The cadres were equally upset to see that while their own salaries stagnated or at best grew slowly, players in the second economy began to earn higher incomes, live in better housing, drive better-quality cars, and had greater access to desirable durable consumer goods than the cadres themselves. There were attempts to crack down on the expansion of the second economy. For instance, during the early 1970s in Hungary, it was illegal for private individuals to own trucks. Peasants adapted to this restriction by removing the back seats from their cars in order to transport goods to market. But this violated traffic law: cars with their back seats removed were "dysfunctional," and for a time police stopped them and fined their owners. Similarly, moonlighting workers were fined for engaging in a business without a license.

The case of the "sour cherry stone man" in the early 1970s in Budapest is illustrative. This man discovered that a state-owned firm disposed as garbage the stones of the sour cherries it used to make marmalade. However, the man knew that the stone of the the sour cherry was an important ingredient in a natural medication. He bought the stones from the marmalade-producing firm for virtually nothing, cleaned and dried them, and resold them at an astronomical price to a pharmaceutical company. He became one of the early millionaires in Hungary and built a luxurious villa for himself in the Buda hills. But his mistake was to show off his income. This led to a lawsuit and media campaign against him in which he was accused of running a business without a license. (While he had a market-gardening license, it was not supposed to be used for the resale of goods.) He was also accused of earning "unfair" income. This meant that the performance of such simple work as the cleaning and drying of cherry stones should not have been compensated at a higher rate than the work of persons who were better-educated than he was and performed more complex work. Principles of socialist meritocratic ideology were central to the arguments used against him.

While this case involved unusually large sums of money, it demonstrates the kind of production typical of these early markets: it was of the sort that required little skill and no credentials. Producers in such markets were typically unskilled or semiskilled industrial workers who had been forced out of full-time peasant existence. They had taken urban industrial jobs but had remained in their rural residences close to the sites of agricultural production.

Under these circumstances, local markets were likely to have equalizing effects (Szelényi and Konrad 1969; Szelényi 1978). Actors who produced for local markets were usually fairly low in the socioeconomic hierarchy but were rarely at the very bottom. They were not the "no-hopers," those who lacked the entrepreneurial spirit or resources required to take part in such productive activities.

These facts are consistent with most of the expectations of market transition theory as elaborated by Nee (1989): these direct producers and entrepreneurs in local markets in a redistributive economy did indeed have some "market powers" and "market opportunities." The expectation of market transition theory that "redistributors" were likely to experience a change in relative fortunes also seems to have been the case. Indeed, cadres were often resentful as they saw actors in the second economy, especially those with low levels of education, earning incomes that were sometimes substantially higher than their own. The case of the sour cherry man was only one instance where this resentment was translated into action against those not playing by the rules of the socialist redistributive system.

Socialist Mixed Economies

In socialist Hungary and Poland during the 1970s and 1980s a new type of market penetration began to emerge. With the crucial change that full-time private economic activities became legal (or nearly so), a low level of capital accumulation became possible as well. This early accumulation was the single most important characteristic of the socialist mixed economy. Nevertheless, on the whole, the still-dominant redistributive economy created disincentives for private accumulation; in fact, it oriented producers in the emergent private sector to consume rather than invest their incomes. (This led to substantial "overconsumption" during the late 1970s and early 1980s as many Poles and Hungarians began to live beyond their means.) Still, however unintentional, niches where "money begins to grow" were created. Probably the most important instance was in housing where there had been substantial capital gains on housing investments in both countries. While this capital was still not strictly productive, it was money that could be employed to obtain more money and might eventually become an important resource with which to start a business. We may call this process the "proto-accumulation of capital."

While full-time private businesses had never totally disappeared in most of Eastern Europe, they were typically run by marginal figures (they were often "stubborn" characters, people who would not acquiesce despite the message that private business was "out" and that success depended upon joining the state-bureaucratic sector), or occasionally by clients of political bosses. In Poland and Yugoslavia, where agriculture was never collectivized, private farming was important, although the authorities discriminated against private farmers, excessively regulating their activities and taxing them at very high rates. In other countries, only a few very marginal figures (to the extent that they were often regarded as village idiots) kept their private farms. The few artisans and shopkeepers who kept their businesses private were also marginal figures who were temperamentally able to live outside the mainstream, or else they served the more powerful cadres, who stopped the authorities from confiscating their private property in exchange for personal services they received.

Around 1980, this began to change in some countries in Eastern Europe. It became possible to obtain licenses and to start new businesses. This occurred in the tertiary sector, first in retail trade and with restaurants, then gas stations, car repair shops, television repair shops, and the like. One such important opening was the legalization of private taxicabs. The proportion of privately owned businesses and the full-time self-employed, after decades of gradual decline, began to increase slowly and by 1988 reached the 4–5 percent level in Poland and Hungary (Hanley and Szelényi 1997). Since many service activities required space, those individuals who had owned appropriate real estate were in an advantageous position with respect to opening a restaurant, small hotel, or car-repair shop. But the private taxi business was one where something that started out only as conspicuous consumption—owning a car—turned into a "means of production."

This change pointed toward the making of a socialist mixed economy, an economic system in which the dominant economic sector remained publicly or cooperatively owned, but small private businesses were allowed to come into existence. Private accumulation, while not yet encouraged, was at least tolerated. It is arguable that no fully developed socialist mixed economy existed in Eastern Europe before 1989. Nevertheless, the historic trend seems to have been pointing toward such a development in Hungary, Poland, and Yugoslavia.

Under the conditions of the socialist mixed economy (Stark and Nee 1989; Szelényi 1988) a new, more heterogeneous set of actors entered the marketplace. As economic behavior became more predictable and as some accumulation of capital became possible and indeed necessary, more-qualified people began to engage in business activities. Some professionals opted for self-employment and others entered markets on the margins of the economy. There were the engineers who quit state jobs to turn their cars into taxicabs in order to earn a higher income and, probably more important, gain greater autonomy over their work schedules. A young and able economist, who began his professional career in the Central Statistical Office and later became a close collaborator of the head of the Hungarian Price Bureau, quit his job and opened a tobacco shop during the late 1960s. He appeared to enjoy himself in his tiny shop where he had no bosses, no party secretaries, flexible working hours, and most likely a respectable income. After a few years he went on vacation to Switzerland and never returned. In retrospect, his career change from high official to tobacco shop operator may have signaled his own personal ideological revolution.

Others, engineers in particular, started new businesses in less marginal areas of the economic system with strong expectations of higher income. These new business opportunities ranged from private construction firms to software consulting companies.

During the early 1980s in Hungary, young, highly educated white-collar workers began to constitute a larger fraction of the top income earners. This trend extended to agriculture as well with the development of highly labor-intensive minifarms. As more qualified, younger professionals began to enter the second economy, some of the early pioneers, who tended to be less educated and socially marginal were pushed aside or wiped out altogether. As socialist local markets were transformed into a *socialist mixed economy* some of the peasant-workers were able to maintain their economic position, especially if they had inherited capital (whether cultural capital—such as a proper education and/or access to high culture in the form of a knowledge of foreign languages, or an appreciation of classical culture, music, art, theater—or economic capital) from their parents. Meanwhile, those who had come from the margins of society were likely to be relative losers. This was especially true for women who had come in from the margins: in Hungary, when we look at second economy participation between 1972 and 1982, we see that the proportion of women among the bigger private producers declined as men increasingly captured the newly attractive social and economic positions and became the new "socialist entrepreneurs" (Szelényi 1988).

Some cadres also oriented themselves to markets. Specifically, some members of the technocratic fraction of the cadre elite understood that the state socialist redistributive economy might disintegrate, and they began to build bridges to the newly emergent private economy (Manchin and Szelényi 1987). They "commodified" their bureaucratic privileges. For example, some early capital accumulation was possible in the new real estate markets, and in both Hungary and Poland leading cadres began building their own houses. Selling or leasing valuable state land to themselves at nominal prices, they built high-quality housing on it with the use of public resources. The very first experiments with "privatization" of existing assets occurred in housing. Leading cadres who had been assigned to luxurious upper-middle-class villas or condominiums during the 1950s or early 1960s offered themselves the option of purchasing their residences at low prices. Not surprisingly, most opted to buy this first-rate real estate in this manner. As discussed previously, the major form of capital accumulation in the early stages of the socialist mixed economy was in private housing rather than in productive investments. As a result, the increase in real estate values was phenomenal and those who entered the market early, used bureaucratic privileges to get good prices, and bought in primary housing markets accumulated substantial resources.

In addition to the young technocrats and self-interested cadres, the son and daughters of cadres also benefited from the emergent socialist mixed economy. Parents now used their connections to help their offspring to get into rapidly inflating private housing just as they had previously used their connections to get better-quality public housing for their children. Cadre offspring benefited in other ways from changes in the economic system as well. Some used the second economy as a way to revolt against their parents; ironically, they could do this because of parental political protection. In such families, some children entered private businesses in Hungary as early as the late 1970s. They started subcontracting businesses, or did manual work for private businesses. For instance, one of the daughters of a high-ranking official of the Hungarian banking industry went to work painting pieces of textiles. Not only did she make more money than she could have as a sociologist (the field in which she was trained), she simultaneously and with little risk expressed her disenchantment with the regime and with her father. A unique class emerged among the children of Communist foreign service bureaucrats. Many attended schools or colleges in the West, where they gained valuable language skills and were socialized into Western ways of business and social life. Many of these children established important interpersonal networks, became the earliest "liberals," were the most dedicated pro-capitalists. Some became compradores, professionals who helped foreign companies to invest in these countries after the fall of communism, in this way serving as "bridges" between foreign business and the domestic economy.

In sum, we can conclude from these admittedly unsystematic but nevertheless plentiful observations that in a socialist mixed economy, the market is far from a simple compensatory mechanism. Even though some individuals in relatively uneducated, low-income groups benefit from the secondary markets of what is still a predominately redistributive economy, a socialist mixed economy can more accurately be described as a *dual system of inequality* (Szelényi 1988; Walder 1995) in which advantages once gained from bureaucratic positions are now reinforced by privileges gained in the marketplace.

We believe that most of the recent literature on market transition in China accurately describes the characteristics of socialist mixed economies. Walder (1992, 1995), Oi (1992), Bian and Logan (1995) and Lin (1995) describe the coexistence of market and redistributive mechanisms and the resulting duality of the system of social inequalities. If we interpret his concept of partial reform in this way, Nee's contributions (1991, 1996; Nee and Lian 1994) can also be read as demonstrating the duality of inequality under hybrid property forms and in economic systems where both markets and redistribution operate. However, if Nee's theory of partial reform implies that further reform—meaning the ascendance of markets to the role of the dominant mechanism in allocating labor and capital—leads to gains for direct producers and losses (even if only relative ones) for cadres or former cadres, then he is likely to be wrong. Empirical evidence from postcommunist Eastern Europe suggests that extrapolating trends from local markets or from socialist mixed economies and projecting them onto capitalist-oriented economies is likely to be inaccurate and misleading. As the market becomes the dominant mechanism, the logic of marketization changes. At this point, the technocratic fraction of the former *nomenklatura*, which has the appropriate human capital and networks, will try to use the process of privatization of large public firms to push those who became petit bourgeois during the period of late state socialism to the side. As communism collapses, the big winners thus tend to be the former Communist technocrats, while those who made it into the late state socialist "middle class" often become downwardly mobile and are counted among the losers of the transition process.

Capitalist-Oriented Economies

After 1989 in Eastern Europe, a new type of market penetration emerged which is drastically different from that which occurred in China. The unique feature of Eastern European development since 1989 is that it has not simply *allowed* or encouraged the growth of a new private sector but that it has aimed at the privatization of the public sector. The single most important difference between China's and Eastern Europe's recent development can be found in their divergent policies toward the public sector: while after 1989 Eastern Europe has adopted the policy of privatization of public property, China maintains that the public sector should be sustained.

Stark's work on Hungary (1996) continues to undermine any assumptions that these changes will automatically bring about a market-coordinated society. Stark also demonstrates that Walder's (1994) distinction between property reform and privatization holds for Hungary as well as for China. However, without asserting that a newly emerging capitalist *orientation* will bring about capitalism, we contend that it qualitatively changes the dynamics of market penetration in postcommunist societies. The adoption of the state policy of privatization was the most fateful and far-reaching event in the recent history of Eastern Europe.

Around 1990, all Eastern European countries—where approximately 90 percent of the workforce was employed in the public sector—announced their intent to shut down the public sector and remove the state from the productive sphere. Even if the announced policy has not led to capitalism, it has had revolutionary and in many ways devastating implications throughout Eastern Europe. Overnight, it created major incentives for individuals to abandon the public sector. The result was one of the most massive disinvestments in modern economic history and the conversion of productive capital into means of consumption and assets in Swiss bank accounts, which led to one of the most dramatic declines ever in the productive capacities of modern economies.

It would be incorrect to think of the policy of privatization as simply a mistake. Far from it. It was a wise strategy for certain elements of the past elite for converting their political capital into economic capital and for the preservation of their social privileges in the transition from a one-party state. It is not a simple process however; how privatization plays out will depend to a significant degree on the ability of different class fractions to recognize and act upon their collective interests. In Hungary and Poland, the technocratic fraction of the *nomenklatura* has been quite powerful and has succeeded in establishing close ties with the emergent new postcommunist political elite, the former opposition to communist political rule. Hankiss noted as early as 1988 that spontaneous privatization is a strategy of the cadre elite to establish itself as the new "grand bourgeoisie" (Hankiss 1990; Staniszkis 1991). His observation proved to be largely correct (Róna-Tas 1994). We would only add that, in order to understand this process precisely, we need to make a distinction between the old and new elites of communism, between the bureaucracy and the technocracy. While it is quite true that the command positions of the new corporate sector in Poland and Hungary are held almost exclusively by members of the old technocratic elite (about 90 percent of the managers of the three thousand or so largest firms in these countries were in management positions in the earlier era), it is also true that many members of the old bureaucratic elite lost big. About half of those who managed the largest firms in 1988 in Hungary and Poland were by 1993 out of elite positions (Szelényi and Szelényi 1995). The significant downward mobility from the ranks of the bureaucratic fraction of the old communist ruling estate does not alter the fact that the big winner of 1989 was the technocratic-managerial fraction of the communist elites. While, according to all the data at our disposal, they did not turn themselves into the new grand bourgeoisie as Hankiss expected, they are nevertheless the ones who occupy the command positions in the curious "managerial capitalism" of Eastern Europe. Nineteen eighty-nine was the victorious revolution of the "socialist managers" against the redistributors, and they—not the "socialist entrepreneurs"—were the winners of this revolution (Eyal, Szelényi, and Townsley 1997).

We should add that in addition to the former cadres, clients of the new political elite benefited from "spontaneous privatization"—that is, from the policy that left to an enterprise's management the decision whether to privatize or not and permitted it to determine under what conditions the firm could be sold to private purchasers. The logic of patron-client relations not only preceded communism but survived it. The new political bosses frequently helped their relatives or protégés to get the best deals from privatization. This was not necessarily blatant corruption, for it may have been sufficient for them simply to share information. Access to information about business dealings is important for business transactions everywhere, but it has been particularly important under postcommunist privatization, where assessment of the real value of property has been notoriously poor.

So far, we have focused our attention on Hungary and Poland, but in many respects the Czech Republic is as interesting and instructive a case as these two countries. In the Czech Republic it appears that the "transition from redistribution to the market" took a rather different trajectory. In the postcommunist Czech Republic the old technocratic elite was less influential than in Poland and Hungary and as a result spontaneous privatization was not a realistic option. The Czech Republic instead moved toward what is called "voucher privatization," a version of worker ownership that is a more modest change in property relations than what occurred in Hungary or Poland. While many observers argue that the Czech Republic moved toward a private economy more rapidly than Hungary and Poland, we are skeptical. All three countries started with similarly outdated economic structures, yet the Czech Republic has managed to maintain an unemployment rate of 4 percent or lower, while in Hungary and Poland about 25 percent of all jobs were lost and the unemployment rate peaked around 15 percent. This indicates that the Czech transformation may have been more cautious than it appears. His Hungarian and Polish critics suggest that Václav Klaus, the former Czech prime minister, talks nineteenth-century liberalism and neoclassical economics but acts like a social democrat and a Keynesian. However, a more dynamic change in the Czech Republic did take place in the small private sector. The rate of self-employment was much lower there to begin with than in Hungary and Poland, but by 1993 it exceeded the Hungarian and Polish rates. As Eric Hanley (Hanley and Szelényi 1997) has found, there were many former cadres and many more former Communist Party members among the Czech self-employed than in the two other countries.

In other words, in these three countries, it seems that many former cadres always know where the sun is shining. If the high rewards stem from spontaneous privatization and the transformation of property rights in the corporate sector, former cadres will be there. If government policy is more favorable toward new small private business, which appears to be the case in the Czech Republic, former cadres will be found among the new smaller entrepreneurs.[4]

Can we conclude that in capitalist-oriented economies, markets become a major source of new inequalities and former cadres are the winners? For the first part of the proposition, the answer is yes. Inequality appears to be growing rapidly, and it is generated primarily by markets. Those still reliant on the redistributive mechanism are rapidly losing ground.

The answer to the second part of the proposition is more complex. First of all, it is simply untrue that *all* cadre elites converted their old privileges into new ones. A substantial fraction of the old elite are losers by any measure. Furthermore, when we consider who the winners are we need a more complex theory.

Hanley (Hanley and Szelényi 1997) pointed out that in capitalist-oriented economies there is evidence of the formation of not one but two new classes, one at the top and one in the middle of the social hierarchy: a new corporate bourgeoisie and a new petit bourgeoisie are in the making. Hanley also presents robust data to show that the recruitment processes into these two classes are quite different. Members of the new corporate bourgeoisie are likely to come primarily from the technocratic fraction of the old *nomenklatura*; the new petit bourgeoisie on the other hand is more likely to be recruited from the former middle and lower-middle classes.

Descendants of the precommunist era bourgeoisie seem, for the most part, to be doing quite well during the postcommunist era. Some of them had been living in self-imposed exile and, with the fall of communism, have returned home. Many have entered the business world using capital saved or accumulated in the West. Others have used their social and cultural capital to exploit newly available economic opportunities. Some countries—in this respect the Czech Republic was the most radical—restored precommunist property rights, thus offering members of old bourgeoisie a chance to regain their former socioeconomic status. While no such property restoration took place in Hungary, former bourgeois and even aristocratic families returned. Some used social capital they established with the first postcommunist (and politically conservative) regime; others used their business skills or financial capital they had acquired in the West. The descendants of the nonémigré former bourgeoisie are also likely to do well, benefiting from the cultural capital of a family tradition in entrepreneurship. Finally, even though many of the early participants of the second economy have been driven out as the paternalism of late state socialism is replaced by the fierce market competition of postcommunism, early entry into the private sector remains a major advantage. Social networks established during communist times, capital accumulated, and business skills acquired all can be very helpful in achieving postcommunist business success.

In sum, we assert that the big winners of market penetration in capitalist-oriented economies are members of the former technocratic elite. Descendants of the precommunist middle class also benefit, as do those who entered the second economy during late socialism. The big losers are the bureaucratic fraction of the cadre elite, the poor, and most workers.

Workers who were employed in those sectors of the economy most heavily subsidized by the redistributive mechanisms, that is, skilled workers in heavy industries, are the certain losers. One important consequence of the postcommunist transformation is the sharp reduction of jobs in heavy industry—mining, steel, metalworks, and the like. As the former bastions of socialism crumble, workers who were previously the most privileged and best-paid find themselves out of work and possessing unusable skills. However, workers with marketable skills can benefit from the increasing competitiveness of the labor market.

The adaptation of the labor force to postcommunism is a complex process, and it is very difficult to find a coherent explanation for unemployment. As Lim (1995) and Fodor and van der Lippe (1995) demonstrate, there does not seem to be a clear predictor of who is likely to be unemployed. Lim shows that large proportions of the population across social and demographic categories are not working, although the young and the more highly educated are not as strongly affected as others except in a few categories where there are too many people with high-level skills. Fodor quite unexpectedly finds that, at least in Hungary, women are less likely to be unemployed than men, while in Poland, gender is not related to unemployment rates. Her explanation for this surprising fact is that economic restructuring hit those sectors of the economy which, under state socialism, were the most privileged and therefore attracted more men than women. The new type of market penetration offers unique opportunities for women. While they were previously slotted into devalued sectors of the economy (in such tertiary sector jobs as finance), those sectors are now growing. Fodor argues that it is possible that women's advantages are only temporary and men will move back into the newly upgraded spheres of the economy. Still, at least in the short run, women may be benefiting from the transition. If women collectively play their cards well they may even create future positions and advantages for themselves.

The empirical evidence so far shows that in postcommunist Eastern Europe losers and winners are determined by the concrete institutional constellations, by the individual's skills and cultural capital, by the class capacities of actors who find themselves within these institutions, and last but not least by the historically contingent outcomes of their political struggles. It is not true, therefore, that the cadres are the winners: some of them, especially those who are older and lack proper educational credentials may be in real trouble in the postcommunist era. But it is also untrue that all cadres are losers: if they have the proper credentials, if they are properly networked, they may survive the challenges of transformation and come out on top again. Some from "below" made it; there are few postcommunist "self-made men," people who started small and grew big during the early postcommunist years. These are typically well-connected people with good credentials. The average second economy actor, however, is likely to be a loser since he or she cannot match the skills and connections of the former socialist managers. Thus, on the whole, the socialist entrepreneur has done worse than the socialist manager. It is important to note that this certainly would not have been the case had the old-line bureaucracy been successful in pursuing its agenda.

TOWARD A MACROINSTITUTIONALIST NEW ECONOMIC SOCIOLOGY

After distinguishing between the different types of market penetration we can again pose the question of whether the market or redistribution is the source of inequality, and who benefits from greater market penetration in late socialism or early postcommunism. The hypothesis concerning the equalizing impact of markets seems to be plausible so long as markets are local. However, as markets penetrate the economy more deeply and begin to allocate labor and capital as well, the market becomes a source, even the major source, of social inequality. Similarly, it is reasonable to assume that "direct producers," in particular ordinary people, benefit from market penetration under the conditions of local markets. When greater capital accumulation becomes possible in socialist mixed economies, cadres, former cadres, and members of precommunist elites begin to enter into and gain from market transactions. Thus a dual system of inequality emerges in which bureaucratic privileges and market advantages reinforce each other. Moreover, when the dynamics of social inequality changed once again during the postcommunist transformation in Eastern Europe after 1989, it is clear that the main beneficiary of this transformation was the technocratic fraction of the cadre elite. It has used privatization as a mechanism for the "primitive accumulation" of capital, converting public property into private wealth, even though the newly emergent forms of private property are not always unambiguously private. Even more important, the technocratic-managerial elite has been able to eliminate party and state control over its managerial activities, so that under postcommunist managerial capitalism it occupies the command positions of the economy without being controlled by either owners or state officials (Eyal, Szelényi, and Townsley 1997). Other players in the economic system—in particular those who invested in market transactions prior to 1989—have generally been pushed out of (or marginalized within) the newly emergent markets. This is important for our theory: after all, these actors acquired market experience and should have done well in the new economic system. Yet, as collective actors, they do not have much ability to act on their collective interests. While they are capable of running businesses, they are unable to influence government economic policies, particularly policies effecting privatization and government subsidies to new private ventures.

The interplay of institutions is clear in this history. Granovetter's claim about social change (1985, 506–7) is that one of the most important mechanisms of macro social change is actually at the micro level, namely in the networks of social relations in which economic life is embedded. In our argument, we have presented evidence that cuts across both the network and macro levels. It is our claim that attention must be paid to both levels if we are to fully grasp economic phenomena. Though we are more macro advocates than Granovetter is, we are nonetheless aware of the trap of the "over-socialized" individual criticized by Granovetter following Dennis Wrong. Such an individual has no agency, but only acts out social norms, economic and political forces in a completely predictable manner. Instead in our picture, an economic act is embedded within both micro and macro contexts. We have tried to demonstrate that individuals actively make use of resources in creative ways rather than simply following formal rules. When new institutions arise, the ways in which existing institutions can be used may change. For example, privatization transforms property rights but in rather unexpected ways. It does not necessarily create private firms as we know them under Western capitalism, but it changes the character of the previously state-owned companies. A new type of organization is in the making, which David Stark has called "recombinant property"—under what we have called "managerial capitalism"—a type of property that is not quite public and not quite private. Thus, changing socialist-era institutions serve as both limitations and resources. Throughout the political and economic shifts, the legitimate uses of those resources have been the subject of contention.

Our deepest claim is that the dominant integrative mechanism is the primary generator of inequality. Hence, inequality has a transsystemic character. What has varied has not been the existence of inequality but the extent and basis of inequality. Different class fractions have been fighting in different ways over how much of the pie they are entitled to. They have done so sometimes following individual strategies and sometimes group strategies, and certainly on the basis of different class capacities.

In the *socialist redistributive economy*, class struggle was latent, although political struggles did occur. While there were certainly conflicting class interests, people either worked within the system or were quite marginalized. There was no substantial alternative economy, so people might have worked slowly, but defection was not substantial.

In the *socialist mixed economy* a more active phase of class struggle began. People took advantage of new opportunities but for the most part did not structure their actions around a radically different future, and few defected from the socialist economy. In this era the so-called reforms undertaken by the state were actually quite reactive. While defections were still rare, people did begin to jockey for position. They struggled at the margins of the socialist economy, but they also struggled to build new types of economic opportunities.

In the current era, there is all-out class struggle (yet this is not the classical Marxist-Leninist picture of class struggle). Class struggle in this usage encompasses those conflicts that may give rise to new classes with new capacities and new venues in which to use existing resources. From this perspective, classes arise from *within* the context of class struggle. Tomorrow's classes are struggling to constitute themselves on shifting terrain without quite knowing what these classes will be. Hence the chaos of the current era. Nobody has a good fix on what the new economy will be at any level: What macro institutions will there be? What classes will exist? What networks of social relations will matter? There are new opportunities, it is clear, but which promise any measure of security? Uncertainty about the nature of macroeconomic structures and classes thus characterizes the current era. (The situation is somewhat similar in China, but China, unlike Eastern Europe, has managed to avoid large-scale disinvestment. In China, the struggle is also related to the formation of classes but under the belief that the socialist state will continue to play a major role in economic life.)

It follows from this analysis that changes in institutions are not at all exogenous, that they are the product of the complex interplay of economic strategies on many different levels. Therefore, we cannot look at purposive rational action alone, or social networks alone, or macro economic institutions alone, or state policy alone if we wish to understand the history of such change.

NOTES

1. The debate between the two perspectives has thus also been a debate across disciplinary boundaries. This volume is a conscious attempt to break out of the often unproductive competition between disciplines.

2. While Polanyi did not give a formal definition of the distinction between organizations and institutions, he clearly used the term "instituted" or "institution" in ways that were consistent with North's terminology. "Institutions are the rules of the game in a society . . . the humanly devised constraints" (North 1990, 3). Institutions are at a different level of abstraction than organizations. Organizations with well-defined boundaries and membership are directly observable empirically. Institutions are at a "deeper" layer of analysis: it can be demonstrated that such institutions exist not because they can be directly observed but because they shape the behavior of individuals and organizations.

3. Just one brief terminological point: Polanyi made a distinction between forms of economic integration (redistribution, exchange, and reciprocity) and the institutional structures that support them (states, markets, and kinship networks). Thus, proper Polanyian terminology distinguishes redistribution from market-exchange rather than simply the market.

4. A cynical view is that without such an awareness of where the sun is shining, these people would not have become cadres in the first place.

REFERENCES

Bian, Yanjie, and John R. Logan. 1996. "Market Transition and the Persistence of Power: The Changing Stratification System in Urban China." *American Sociological Review* 61: 739–58.

Eyal, Gil, Iván Szelényi, and Eleanor Townsley. 1997. "The Theory of Post-Communist Managerialism: Elites and Classes in Post-Communist Transformation." *New Left Review* 222 (March-April): 60–92.

Fodor, Éva, and Tanja van der Lippe. 1995. "Changes in Gender Inequality in East Central Europe." University of California, Los Angeles. Unpublished paper.

Granovetter, Mark. 1985. "Economic Action and Social Structure—The Problem of Embeddedness." *American Journal of Sociology* 91: 481–510.

Hankiss, Elemér. 1990. *East European Alternatives*. Oxford, England: Clarendon Press.

Hanley, Eric, and Iván Szelényi. 1997. "Changing Social Structure During Market Transition." Washington, D.C.: National Academy of Sciences.

Konrad, George, and Iván Szelényi. 1979. *The Intellectuals on the Road to Class Power*. New York: Harcourt, Brace and Jovanovich.

Lim, Nelson. 1995. "Income Inequality in Post-communist Eastern Europe." University of California, Los Angeles. Unpublished paper.

Lin, Nan. 1995. "Local Market Socialism: Local Corporatism in Action in Rural China." *Theory and Society* 24: 301–54.

Manchin, Robert, and Iván Szelényi. 1987. "Social Policy under State Socialism." In *Stagnation and Renewal in Social Policy*, edited by Martin Rein, Gosta Esping-Anderson, and Lee Rainwater. White Plains, N.Y.: M.E. Sharpe.

Nee, Victor. 1989. "The Theory of Market Transition: From Redistribution to Markets in State Socialism." *American Sociological Review* 54: 663–81.

———. 1991. "Social Inequality in Reforming State Socialism: Between Redistribution and Markets in China." *American Sociological Review* 56: 267–82.

———. 1996. "The Emergence of a Market Society: Changing Mechanisms of Stratification in China." *American Journal of Sociology* 101: 908–49.

Nee, Victor, and Peng Lian. 1994. "Sleeping with the Enemy: A Dynamic Model of Declining Political Commitment in State Socialism." *Theory and Society* 23: 253–96.

North, Douglass C. 1990. *Institutions, Institutional Change and Economic Performance*. Cambridge: Cambridge University Press.

Oi, Jean. 1992. "Fiscal Reform and the Economic Foundation of Local State Corporatism in China." *World Politics* 45: 99–126.

Polanyi, Karl. [1944] 1957. *The Great Transformation*. Boston: Beacon Press.

———. 1957. "The Economy as Instituted Process." In *Trade and Market in the Early Empires*, edited by Karl Polanyi, Conrad M. Arensberg, and Harry W. Pearson. New York: Free Press.

Róna-Tas, Ákos. 1994. "The First Shall Be Last? Entrepreneurship and Communist Cadres in the Transition from Socialism." *American Journal of Sociology* 100: 40–69.

Staniszkis, Jadwiga. 1991. *The Dynamics of the Breakthrough in Eastern Europe: The Polish Experience*. Berkeley: University of California Press.

Stark, David. 1996. "Recombinant Property in East European Capitalism." *American Journal of Sociology* 101: 993–1027.

Stark, David, and Victor Nee. 1989. "Toward an Institutional Analysis of State Socialism." In *Remaking the Economic Institutions of Socialism: China and Eastern Europe*, edited by Victor Nee and David Stark. Palo Alto: Stanford University Press.

Szelényi, Iván. 1978. "Social Inequalities in State Socialist Redistributive Economies." *International Journal of Comparative Sociology* 19: 63–87.

———. 1988. *Socialist Entrepreneurs: Embourgeoisement in Rural Hungary*. Madison, Wis.: University of Wisconsin Press.

———. 1991. "Karl Polanyi and the Theory of a Socialist Mixed Economy." In *Markets, State and*

Society at the End of the 20th Century, edited by Marguerite Mendell and David Salee. New York: St. Martins.

Szelényi, Iván, and George Konrad. 1969. *Az uj lakotelepek szociologiai problemai* (Sociological problems of the new housing development). Budapest: Akademiai Kiado.

Szelényi, Iván, and Szonja Szelényi. 1995. "Circulation and Reproduction of Elites During Post-Communist Transformation." *Theory and Society* 24: 615–38.

Walder, Andrew. 1992. "Property Rights and Stratification in Socialist Redistributive Economies." *American Sociological Review* 57: 524–39.

———. 1994. "Corporate Organization and Local Property Rights in China." In *Changing Political Economics: Privatization in Post-Communist and Reforming Communist States*, edited by Vedat Milor. Boulder, Colo.: Lynne Rienner.

———. 1995. "Career Mobility and Communist Political Order." *American Sociological Review* 60: 309–28.

Williamson, Oliver. 1975 *Markets and Hierarchies*. New York: Free Press.

———. 1985. *The Economic Institutions of Capitalism: Firms, Markets, Relational Contracting*. New York: Free Press.

Index

action; rational, 4, 7–8; self-reinforcing nature of system actions, 154; sociological foundation for economic (Granovetter), xvii–xviii, 127, 158; *See also* collective action
action models (Weber), 166–67
actors; in embeddedness concept, 159; in labor markets, 235–36; role in promotion of institutional change, 268–74
agency measures; of Maghribis and Genoese, 87
agency relations; effect of cultural beliefs on, 80–83; vertical and horizontal social patterns of, 86–88
agency theory; as institutional perspective, 155–56
agriculture, communal system; benefits, 287; byelaws in, 283, 285; costs of regulation, 286–87; restraints on use of land, 286–87
agriculture, noncommunal system; farm consolidation and enlargement, 289–90; irregular open and enclosed, 283–85; tenant farms, 290
authority; distinct from economic power (Weber), 165

bargaining; collective, 21, 231–32; for distributional advantage, 107–15
bargaining power; with asymmetries in resource ownership, 107–8; of bridewealth, 114; to change practice of female circumcision, 120; defined,

106; effect on norm creation and change, 107–8, 116–17, 120; ideology as supplement to, 116; in relation to Orma clan exogamy, 112–13
behavior; deviation from normal, 109; ideology and enforcement as decisions related to, 108–9; motivated by ideology, 117; neoclassical economics model of, 279; sources of social capital influencing, 129–31
belief systems; effects of, xviii; incentives in, 253; influence of community, xix
bounded rationality, 260
bounded solidarity; costs of, 140–45; determinants and consequences of, 132; example of, 132–33; in immigrant communities, 133–35, 137; as source of social capital, 130–31
bridewealth. *See* marriage payments (bridewealth).
business systems; defined, 170; factors in development of diverse, 170; role in economic organization, 170
buyers; influence on sellers (Walras), 161; in labor market, 226

calculability, 154
capital accounting system (Weber), 165–66
capitalism; capital accounting system, 165–66; global, 170; industrial relations of contemporary, 225; labor markets in,

226–27; postcommunist managerial, 323; price-responsive organizations of, 164–71
choice; in new institutionalism, 8; *See also* rational choice theory
circumcision, female; arguments for and against, 118–20; change in attitudes toward, 117–18, 121; decentralized enforcement of, 122
class; class-agency view, 306; class struggle, 308, 323–24; as rule for representation, 236–37
Coase, Ronald H.; Parable of the Farmer and the Rancher, 46–47, 54–56, 58–59; "The Nature of the Firm," 2–3, 20, 155; "The Problem of Social Cost," 2, 20, 46
Coase Theorem, 46–47
Coleman, James S., 8–9, 28, 30, 105, 128–29
collective action; among workers, 225; to change formal rules, 32–33; change of formal rules by, 33; coalitions in institutional change, 270–74; influenced by scope of representation, 236; influence of labor market actors on, 235–36; norms in and coordination of, 25–30; in organizational context, 258; to promote institutional change, 268–70; research in labor market, 239
collective bargaining; agreements in Germany, 232; effect on unemployment of national level, 231; Japan, 21